Economics

of

Planned Development

by

Nathaniel Lichfield
B.Sc. (Est. Man.), F.R.I.C.S., M.T.P.I., A.M.I.Mun.E.
Special Diploma in Town Planning of R.I.C.S.

THE ESTATES GAZETTE LIMITED
28 DENMARK STREET · LONDON · WC2

PRINTED IN GREAT BRITAIN BY
WALKER & CO. (PRINTERS) LTD.
NORCUTT ROAD, TWICKENHAM, MIDDX.

To the memory of F.L.

CONTENTS

APPENDICES

TABLES

ILLUSTRATIONS

FOREWORD

THE READERS and students to whom my share of this joint fore-
word is addressed are not so much the economic planners, active
or would-be, as the physical ones—the architects, engineers, landscape designers and others who are more concerned with how things
work and how they look than with their economic and monetary
value. It is for them, very particularly, that Mr. Lichfield has
prepared lectures and references, it is with them that he has argued
late into the evening, at University College and elsewhere, and it is
very much in their interest that he has now written this book.
I only hope that they—or perhaps I should say we, because I am
also one of the audience—will not find the title and the sheer weight
of information too forbidding. The subject is one of the most
important in the whole run of planning disciplines; and there is very
little else contained within a single pair of covers that attempts to
answer so many of the economic questions that perplex the town
planner. In terms of sheer usefulness, therefore, this book will be
a most welcome addition to the reading list of the student and to
the working libraries of those engaged in practice.

The material is original in many respects; not in terms of economic
theory but in the way it is applied to questions of land and building
development, to the analysis of private and social costs, and to the
planning process itself. It reminds designers and builders that there
is such a thing as legal preparation of a site as well as physical
preparation. It gives various examples of financial calculations for
development and then goes on to draw up what is described as "the
balance sheets of development and planning". These are, in effect,
the checks on the process by which individuals and authorities try
to balance their reason, their conscience, their prejudices and their
sentimental regard in coming to a decision as to whether development goes on or not. Mr. Lichfield performs a useful service in
pointing out what is calculable and what is not, and he does not
confuse the issue by suggesting either that the administrator can
arrive at the right balance by the exercise of ordinary common
sense, nor on the other hand that he can reduce expert advice of
many kinds to a comprehensive formula. Instead he makes a check-
list of private and social costs for such controversial subjects as the
preservation of agricultural land from development, road congestion
and traffic safety, the provision of parking facilities and the winning
of minerals. The book will thus be most useful as a reference on

those many occasions when the costs and gains of planning are disputed.

Lastly, there is a most interesting section on land values and land planning, which includes a description of the ways in which a knowledge of land values might be brought to bear on the preparation and implementation of a plan for an urban area. As one who is not a valuer, I am impressed by the humanity of this concluding chapter. It suggests to me that collaboration or team work between administrators, designers and land economists could be something more than a hopeful phrase. And it is because Mr. Lichfield has come forward from his section of the arena and offered his contribution in such a constructive, generous and undogmatic way that I feel confident in recommending it to the planners and the planned.

WILLIAM HOLFORD

Department of Town Planning,
University College London,
October, 1955.

FOREWORD

THIS COUNTRY now accepts the value of town and country planning. But it is increasingly apparent that if planning is to be effective those who practise and administer it must, above all else, have an understanding of the economic framework within which they operate. This understanding is too often sadly lacking with the result that wrong or impracticable proposals and decisions are made and consequently an unhealthy brake is put upon the process of land development and redevelopment. The Royal Institution of Chartered Surveyors recently added a Town and Country Planning Section to its examinations as its contribution towards meeting this unfortunate state of affairs. The syllabus of the new examinations gives particular emphasis to the importance of the administrative, economic and financial aspects of town planning; the examinee is expected to comprehend the part that the various private and public agencies play in the continual changes of land use. He must appreciate the economic and social forces which affect the development of land and which should not be ignored by the planner. He must know how those forces can be expressed in terms of land values. He must understand the developer's outlook and the various methods by which the developer is financed so that the planning advice which he is being trained to give will always be related to what is practicable. Many of these matters Mr. Lichfield deals with ably and most comprehensibly in this admirable book. Yet the book is not a text book in the normal sense for, as the author recognises in his treatment of the subject, no one is yet in a position to be authoritative about it. But the book is, as far as I know, the only one dealing comprehensively with the subject to which a student town planner can turn to prepare himself both for these examinations and for the world in which he will practise his art.

Mr. Lichfield is to be congratulated on his industry and his courage in pioneering in this field. I commend this book not only to town planners but also to all those who are actively concerned in land development.

HENRY W. WELLS

Royal Institution of Chartered Surveyors,
12 Great George Street, S.W.1
October, 1955.

PREFACE

THE SUBJECT of economics and town planning can be discussed around various main themes: the location and movement of industry, the economical design of public works, the capacity of communities to pay for realising their plans. The central theme of this book is one which comes more naturally than these to surveyors, their specialism lying in the handling and development of real property.

In all communities some change is continually taking place—whether it be in the domiciles of people, their size of families, means of transport, spending habits or choice of leisure pursuits. Some of these changes, but not all, give rise to pressure for new development by private or public agencies: for new uses of land and buildings in place of old, building on virgin land, public works or reconstruction of obsolete areas. It is upon these pressures that town planning has its immediate impact. The weight of the impact depends upon planning practice and legislation. In this country (and it is with Great Britain that we are primarily though not exclusively concerned) planning authorities must ratify all but the least significant of development projects, and they can and do exercise considerable influence. In doing so their aim is to secure planned development: so to guide, modify, suppress or stimulate projects that the form and sequence of development are more orderly and seemly, and better suited to the public interest, than might have occurred without planning. To this end the local planning authority adopts a plan as a guide to its decisions. In preparing and realising a plan for planned development many factors must be taken into account—social, aesthetic, geographical, economic. It is the description of the economic factors which is the central theme of this book. Other factors—and other themes— are touched upon as necessary in support.

Because this is an exploratory work in a subject which is not discrete there are numerous references in the text to show the paths which have been trodden, and also incursions into fields of economics in which the surveyor is no specialist. It is hoped that these ventures will encounter tolerance from specialists in these fields, and will encourage them to expand their contribution on this increasingly important aspect of town planning.

                                                        N. LICHFIELD.

London,
August, 1956.

ACKNOWLEDGMENTS

MY THANKS are given to those numerous friends, colleagues and others—in central and local government, academic life, institutions and private offices—who have been so generous with their time and knowledge. Because many of them must remain anonymous I am precluded from naming the others, as they will understand. I must however mention Ralph Turvey, B.Sc. (Econ.), who has helped me throughout from his insight into land economics.

I am indebted to those who have supplied me with information and allowed me to use their published material and illustrations. They are identified in the text. H.M. Stationery Office have given permission to reproduce pp. 208-9, 398-9 and Appendix 1 and the following to reproduce or adapt illustrations: West Hartlepool County Borough Council (Fig. 3), the Ordnance Survey Dept. (Figs. 3 and 4), Middlesex County Council (Fig. 9), University of Chicago Press (Figs. 11-14), United Committee for Taxation of Land Values (Fig. 15), Cuyahoga County Board of Commissioners (Fig. 16), Corporation of Bath (Fig. 17) and the Editor of *Planning Outlook* (Fig. 18).

I am grateful also to Miss Marilyn Marston, B.Arch., A.R.I.B.A., for many of the illustrations and to J. R. Jarmain, M.A., for undertaking the index.

N.L.

PART I

DEVELOPMENT AND THE DEVELOPMENT PLAN

INTRODUCTORY

Part I amplifies what is meant by planned development and brings out the economic and financial aspects of development, planning and planned development which are to be discussed in the remainder of the book.

Chapter 1 opens by describing development as a process in which many parties can co-operate, and which may last many years before it culminates in the execution of works and the new use of completed development. The process may be undertaken by both private and public developers; the practice of the two is distinguished. Since the process is complex and lengthy developers need to look ahead, perhaps three years or perhaps 20 or more. Their intentions, aims and aspirations as to development are called their " programmes of development." For a programme to have a reasonable chance of taking place a developer must, in preparing it, have regard to certain realities. The realities of an economic nature are the economic framework within which development takes place; the financial calculations which tell the developer what the money cost and values of a scheme will be, and the relation between the two; and the losses and benefits to other people which will arise from the development and which the developer may wish to take into account in deciding on his scheme.

Chapter 2 describes the nature of the development plan which is prepared under the Town and Country Planning Act, 1947, as a basis of a policy for guiding, controlling and initiating development. While this is only a summary of the other plans prepared in the planning office, it is taken as representative of them. The form and content of a development plan are described and the parties who participate in preparing it, and the reasons why in its preparation they have regard in the main only to development which is expected in the ensuing 20 years or so. The different aspects which a planning authority takes into account in preparing the plan are briefly described. One is picked out as particularly germane to the subject of the book: the development programmes that developers would like to undertake. These are the raw material of the changes proposed in the plan.

Chapter 3 discusses this aspect. In order to assemble this raw material the planning authority must, among other things, comprehend, as far as it is practicable, the programmes of development in its area. But in total these will not be sufficiently global or comprehensive, or for a sufficient period ahead, to provide all the raw material. The authority must therefore test and supplement them with its own forecasts of the development that will take place. An authority cannot always simply incorporate a development programme into a plan. Development and land planning objectives often diverge, and an authority may wish to guide, divert, influence, modify, alter, suppress or stimulate development. This leads to a discussion of land planning objectives and the need for the preparation of a planning balance sheet to assist an authority in reaching decisions on the more complex proposals of development, whether these are put forward as development programmes or as specific projects.

The plan is, in essence, a programme for planned development, using the term programme to cover aims, intentions and aspirations. There are advantages in its being as realistic as possible; co-operation between developers and planning authority at all stages is needed to make it so. In the planning office there is a need for familiarity with the considerations which make for realistic development proposals or programmes and for programmes of planned development. Parts II to IV of the book are intended to give a basis for this familiarity. They do so by elaborating on the realities of an economic nature (referred to under Chapter 1 above) which the developer has in mind in preparing a realistic development programme. The financial calculations are described most fully, in Part III, as they are of particular interest to surveyors.

CHAPTER 1

THE NATURE OF DEVELOPMENT

Meaning of Development—Variety of Uses Established by Development—The Development Process—Parties to the Development Process—Many Different Kinds of Developer—Private and Public Developers—Different Intentions Behind Private Development—Classification of Public Developers—Developers and Operators—Programmes of Development—The Economics, Financial Calculations and Balance Sheet of Development.

Meaning of Development

THE WORD " development " is used very widely in relation to land but, outside certain Acts of Parliament, it is rarely used with precision. Among architects, engineers and surveyors it generally means the process of carrying out the constructional works which are associated with a change in the use of land or of land with its buildings, or with a change in the intensity of the use of land, or with a re-establishment of an existing use. Such works would include the alteration, erection or re-erection of buildings and also the construction of roads and sewers, the building of a river wall or the laying out of playing fields. The word is used also to describe such land and works jointly when construction has been carried out.

Variety of Uses Established by Development

Many different kinds of use may become established through development, as can be seen from a perusal of any land use survey map. An indication of their diversity is given in the following list of groups of uses which was prepared to include, within one or other group, all those uses which involve the erection of buildings in a town. Uses such as car parks, open spaces and timber yards, which do not require buildings of any significance, were excluded.[1]

Group A Dwelling-houses.
Group B Residential buildings.
Group C Schools and residential colleges.
Group D Shops.
Group E Offices.
Group F Wholesale warehouses (i.e., buildings designed both for the storage of goods and transaction of business, other than retail trading).
Group G Storage warehouses (e.g., a builder's yard or furniture depository).
Group H Public buildings and places of assembly (e.g., cinema, police station, public library).

Group I   Special places of assembly (e.g., athletic ground, fun fair, greyhound track).

Group J   Light industrial buildings.

Group K   Industrial buildings.

Group L   Special industrial buildings (i.e., factories carrying on a noxious industry).

Group M   Other buildings (e.g., bus station, aerodrome, refuse destructor).

Within each of these groups there can be many different kinds of building. Shops, for example, include department stores, cafés, public houses; public buildings include cinemas, churches, schools; residential buildings include hotels, flats, hostels.[2]

Another indication of the diversity of uses established through development is given in Table 1 which shows, for the United Kingdom, the different uses established by all new constructional works in the years 1951, 1952 and 1953. The table also shows the proportion of the total works that went into each use; and incidentally how great a proportion of our building activity has gone into new housing.

TABLE 1

Money value of construction in New Building and Works in 1951, 1952 and 1953
Per cent in different kinds of use

	Type of Development	1951 %	1952 %	1953 %
1	Agriculture	2·7	2·1	1·9
2	Forestry	0·1	0·1	0·1
3	Fishing	—	—	—
4	Coal mining	1·4	1·7	1·8
5	Other mining and quarrying	0·1	0·1	0·1
6	Manufacturing industry	18·9	12·9	11·6
7	Ministry of Supply research and development	1·7	2·0	1·8
8	Building and contracting industry	0·5	0·5	0·4
9	Electricity	4·5	3·8	3·4
10	Gas	1·5	1·4	1·4
11	Water	3·0	3·2	3·0
12	Railways	1·0	1·0	1·0
13	Road passenger transport	0·5	0·4	0·4
14	Road goods transport	0·4	*	*
15	Roads and public lighting	0·7	0·7	0·7
16	Shipping	0·1	—	0·1
17	Harbours, docks, canals	0·1	0·7	0·6
18	Air transport	0·6	0·4	0·5
19	Postal, telephone and radio communications	0·5	0·5	0·5
20	British Broadcasting Corporation	0·1	0·1	0·1
21	Distribution and other services	4·8	3·9	3·3
23	New housing	46·1	51·7	54·8
24	Education	7·6	7·3	6·2
25	Child care	0·1	0·1	0·1

	Type of Development	1951	1952	1953
26	Health services	1·6	1·5	1·4
27	Police and prisons	0·1	0·1	0·1
28	Fire service	0·1	0·1	0·1
29	Sewerage	2·0	2·3	2·0
30	Arterial drainage and coast protection	0·4	0·4	1·1
31	Other central government services ...	1·6	0·7	0·5
32	Other local authority services	1·5	1·3	1·0
33	Total	100·0	100·0	100·0
	Total in money value	£807m.	£968m.	£1,152m.

* Note: Item 14 included in item 21.

Source: Central Office of Information, *National Income and Expenditure* 1946-53 (H.M.S.O.), adapted from Table 46.

The Development Process

The development of a particular piece of land is a process which involves much more than the mere carrying out of constructional works. It starts before, perhaps many years before, works and buildings are designed; and lasts, perhaps well beyond the time when the new works are completed, until the new accommodation is fully occupied and used. It may recommence on that land again after a short or long period. For development to take place this process must unfold itself, whether quickly or slowly, through the following stages, although on any one piece of land it does not necessarily follow this sequence of stages nor include all of them.

The preliminary stage lies in the general maturing of circumstances which will make realisable a change in the use of the land in the not too distant future: an increase in the number of people requiring accommodation, an improvement, through the building of a road, in the accessibility of the land, the extension of public utility services to it, the establishment of a factory nearby which makes the location convenient for the dwellings of the factory workers. The maturing of the circumstances may be stimulated or retarded by any owner of the land, but it may well be independent of action by him.

The process begins effectively when, against the background of these maturing circumstances, the idea takes shape that a change in use might one day be possible on a site which at the time is perhaps a field, or is covered with physically decaying property, or with property that is physically sound but approaching the end of its economic life. For the change to come about the site, or a leasehold interest in it, must be owned, or become capable of being owned, by persons who are prepared to develop; and before works are begun it may pass through the hands of several people, including land speculators: purchasers of land who do not intend to use or develop it but to make a profit on resale.

Before works can take place it will be necessary to remove any obstruction to their smooth execution. There may be subsidiary legal interests to be terminated or made terminable at short notice; rights of way to be diverted; rights of adjoining owners to be negotiated on; boundaries to be adjusted or additional land to be acquired to improve the shape of the holding.

One or more of the people who are interested in the development will prepare the development scheme: the surveys of the site, the designs and drawings, the estimates of cost and return. In its preparation there will be discussion of the possibilities of development with the bye-law, drainage, planning and licensing authorities, and perhaps with government departments. At some stage there will be the formal applications for the permissions and consents of all public authorities.

Before a contract for construction is let contract drawings, specifications and quantities must be ready, tenders invited, the possibilities explored of borrowing money both to finance the works and on long-term loan, and agreements made between parties who are to participate in the carrying out of the development.

When the time is judged right the works will be executed. Where the accommodation is not to be used by the developer, negotiations for its disposal will be initiated during the construction, or earlier negotiations will be pursued.

The process terminates when the works are completed, all accounts are settled, and the new accommodation is fully in occupation and use. It may start again when maturing circumstances make realisable a further change in the use of the land and buildings, or of the land only upon demolition of the buildings.

Parties to the Development Process

From this description it is seen that there might be many different parties involved in the process. There might be the original landowner or any subsequent purchaser of the land; the developer who undertakes the process; the building industry, including the professions connected with it; the legal profession; the public authorities; the persons lending money; the ultimate consumer who may be a tenant or owner of the finished development.

In a particular piece of development all or some of the parties may be represented by one individual or body. In another two or more parties may participate in carrying out the development as where, for example, a landowner leases land improved with roads, sewers and services to a builder who erects houses for sale. In another one party or more may carry out the process and yet another make some financial contribution towards it, as where a county council receives grants towards the cost of building schools from the Ministry of Education, or a local authority receives subsidies from the Ministry of Housing and Local Government towards the cost of providing dwellings.

Many Different Kinds of Developer

There are many different kinds of developer, and many different objectives in bringing about development. Perhaps an urban district council elects to use its Housing Act powers to build houses for people on its waiting list, or constructs a sewage works because of its duty to drain its area under the Public Health Acts; or a business man converts into offices a Georgian house in order to pursue his business; or an industrial estate company constructs roads and services on land which it hopes to sell off to industrialists for profit; or the British Electricity Authority builds a generating station so that it can carry out its statutory function of supplying electricity; or a trader pulls down a row of shops in order to build in its place a departmental store to expand his trade; or a local authority lays out a park in order to improve the residential qualities of its area; or the War Office builds barracks because it has the duty of training an army; or the Board of Trade builds factories in the development areas because it wishes to provide there opportunities for employment.

Private and Public Developers

The various developers can be broadly divided into two classes, those which are public and those which are private. Public developers include the central government departments, local authorities and *ad hoc* bodies which are set up and function under statute. Among the private developers are private individuals, insurance companies, colleges, private and joint stock companies, administrators of trust funds. Table 2 shows how much of the new works in Table 1 each class was responsible for, and the changes of recent years in the share of each class in the total.

TABLE 2

Percentage of Housing and Other New Work Carried Out by Private and Public Developers

	New Housing			Other New Building and Works		
	1951	1952	1953	1951	1952	1953
Persons	15·8	20·7	27·3	13·1	8·8	7·1
Companies...	—	—	—	28·2	25·8	25·0
Private	15·8	20·7	27·3	41·3	34·6	32·1
Public corporations ...	4·8	5·7	8·2	18·0	20·8	22·8
Central government ...	3·2	2·5	1·4	10·1	13·0	12·3
Local authorities	76·2	71·1	63·1	30·6	31·6	32·8
Public and semi-public...	84·2	79·3	72·7	58·7	65·4	67·9
Total of private and public	100·0	100·0	100·0	100·0	100·0	100·0

Source: *National Income and Expenditure* 1946-53, adapted from Table 43.

There are important differences in the practice of the two classes of developer. Firstly, private developers are regulated by law but are not directly responsible to central or local government; public developers are not quite so restricted by law, often receiving special privileges under statute, but are ultimately responsible to elected representatives. Secondly, private developers usually look for some financial reward for their development, and they will not usually undertake it without some prospect of this being present and adequate. Public developers on the whole, while not being indifferent to financial return, act primarily because some statutory duty is laid upon them or because they elect to carry out some statutory function. Thirdly, private developers generally build for their own or some other private use or occupation, although they occasionally build for public use as where property companies soon after the war built office blocks for occupation by government departments in the " lessor building scheme." Public developers usually carry out development for their own use and occupation, although they may occasionally do so for private occupation, as where the Board of Trade builds factories for industrialists in development areas. Fourthly, private developers almost invariably expect to cover their cost of development out of specific payments by users of the space or services provided. Public developers can sometimes expect to do this, either entirely or substantially, in what can be called their " remunerative " development (defined here as that for which they receive some substantial return): the comprehensive development of a business area, the building of municipal markets, car parks or bus garages, or of the offices of a water undertaking or the Post Office. But in what can be called their " non-remunerative " development (for example, traffic roads, open spaces, town halls, museums, schools, refuse disposal plants and sewage works) they know that they must cover all or a substantial part of the cost from rates, taxes or other public money. Fifthly, a private developer is usually one of many similar agencies providing the same kind of development in one area, and will usually consider a particular scheme in isolation. A public developer is often the one body responsible for a particular kind of development in an area and will often consider a particular scheme in relation to its other existing and intended activities. Sixthly, public developers often borrow from, and often receive some subvention from, public funds. Private developers do so very rarely, examples being where individual housebuilders receive loans on mortgage from local authorities or industrialists received grants from the Board of Trade when building factories in the Special Areas in the 1930's.

Different Intentions Behind Private Development

Private developers, whether big or small, whether individuals or bodies, usually develop with one or other of three different intentions.

They do so for their own occupation, as where an individual builds his house or an industrialist his factory; or for investment, as where a company builds a block of offices to retain and let; or for speculation, as where standard types of houses are built for sale.

Certain kinds of development may be carried out with any one of these intentions as, for example, are commercial buildings in a town's war-damaged central area. But other kinds are usually built with one or two intentions only. For example, private houses today are built by speculators for owner occupation, but rarely for investment, since it is thought that the high cost of building and relatively low rents that can be obtained are likely to result in an insufficient return on the capital invested.

Classification of Public Developers

Public developers fall into three classes: (a) the departments of state, (b) local authorities, and (c) *ad hoc* bodies set up by statute for the carrying out of special functions.

(a) *Departments of State.* Of the civil departments of state few carry out development themselves, although most of them spend money on development through the agency of *ad hoc* bodies or local authorities. The defence departments both build for themselves and have works carried out for them.

(b) *Local Authorities.* All local authorities undertake extensive development of many kinds, spending their own and central government money for purposes authorised by statute. The purposes for which an individual authority spends money depends upon whether it is an administrative county, county borough, county district or parish. Sometimes two or more authorities act jointly in spending money through a representative committee which is specially set up. An example is a joint sewerage or water body.

(c) Ad hoc *Bodies.* These are very varied in character, both as to the purpose for which they were set up and their form of organisation. This form has been steadily changing since one of the earliest, the Clyde Navigation Trust, was set up in 1809; and even the considerable number introduced since 1945 differ from each other in detail. Those *ad hoc* bodies undertaking development can be divided into:[3]

1. *Public Corporations.* These have a Board appointed either by the Crown or by a Minister. They can be either self-financing or dependent. It is intended that the former pay their way out of receipts but it is expected that the latter may need subsidies.[4]

2. *Representative Trusts.* These bodies were set up to manage local undertakings such as a dock or harbour, and were formed of representatives of the users of the services and of the appropriate local authorities. Many are still in operation. Examples are the Clyde Navigation Trust of 1809, Tyne Improvement Commission of 1850, Mersey Docks and Harbour Board of 1857, Metropolitan Water Board of 1902 and Port of London Authority of 1909.

3. *Public Utility Companies.* These were private bodies which were set up, mostly in the 19th century, to run public utilities such as gas, water, railways, canals, tramways and electricity. They had private stock and shareholders who appointed directors, and their dividends were controlled.

The gas, water, electricity, tramway and omnibus undertakings were more and more taken over by local authorities in the latter part of the 19th century; and in turn the gas and electricity undertakings have been taken over by public corporations. The railway and canal undertakings were gradually merged until they were mostly under the control of the Big Five Companies; and since 1948 these have been vested in the Transport Commission. Except for the water, tramway and omnibus companies, therefore, the public utility companies have largely disappeared.

Developers and Operators

Development takes place in order that land, or land and buildings, can be used for a new purpose, or that a former use can be carried on more intensively or efficiently. The use by an occupier starts, or is resumed, when the development process comes to an end.

Sometimes the occupation is for private enjoyment of the land, or land and buildings, as of a house or private tennis court. Very often, as in the occupation of a shop, factory or gas works, it is for the purpose of carrying on trade or production; or, as of a school or sports ground or railway station, for providing a service. Where the occupiers are operating for trade, production or service we will call them " operators." Sometimes the developer will carry out development for another to operate, as where a trading estate company erects factories for sale or letting. Sometimes the developer will also be the operator, as will be an education or electricity authority.

In most cases a distinction can be made between the processes of development and of operation, although in practice an operator will not consider them as distinct but his whole enterprise as one. We are in this book concerned primarily with the process of development and not with operation; but we shall also touch upon that of operation.

Programmes of Development

The process of development is complex and lengthy and, accordingly, developers need to look ahead. They must in effect prepare what we will here call " programmes of development," our general description for their statements of intentions, aims and aspirations of what they would like to do on particular sites, or somewhere within a particular area, when the conditions are ripe. Such programmes or parts of them will be made known to the local planning authority informally during their preparation, or formally when an application is made for planning permission.

The period ahead for which it is necessary to prepare a programme approximates at least to that of the expected duration of the development process. This period would depend on the duration of the different stages in the process, and these will vary with the times, the location of the scheme and with different kinds of development. A local authority which seeks to widen a road in the centre of a town needs, because of the multiplicity and intricacy of ownerships, to spend much more time on site acquisition than in buying farmland for a school. A local authority may need a few weeks for the design and construction of a surface car park, and perhaps three years for that of a school or housing estate, while the British Electricity Authority may need up to 10 years to build a large generating station, and the Coal Board up to 10 years to sink and equip a colliery or carry out the major reconstruction of a pit. Extension to a factory in an industrial area may require only a month to obtain planning permission; but where a project arouses controversy it may take the planning authority and Minister of Housing and Local Government some time to decide.

Some developers will look ahead only for the likely duration of the development process but others, particularly those who are also operators, may elect to look further ahead. An education authority, for example, may take account of trends in the growth and movement of child population over the coming two decades; a highway authority may consider road proposals which cannot be achieved for perhaps 25 years to see how they will link with more immediate projects; a sewerage authority, allowing for a population some 30 years ahead, may consider its land requirements for works which will not be built for 20 years; an industrialist might have a reserve programme for possible future expansion in the event of business prosperity; a cement manufacturer may look ahead 60 years and buy enough land to give some security for his initial expenditure on plant and other equipment; a speculative house builder may do so for 10 to 15 years in order to buy land to safeguard his future operations; and while public authorities have no need to buy land ahead for this reason where they have compulsory purchase powers, they may elect to earmark certain land five years ahead in future in order to avoid having to pay more than necessary for acquiring its development values.[5]

The period ahead for which programmes of intended development are prepared will accordingly vary among developers.

The Economics, Financial Calculations and Balance Sheet of Development

Developers' programmes of development are not prophecies that certain development will be carried out, but forecasts of intention to carry it out should future conditions be judged ripe. Innumerable circumstances may influence such judgment, and given circumstances will influence different kinds of developers in different ways. The outbreak of war in Asia might stimulate here the immediate extension of particular factories; an increase in unemployment might defer the building of shops and yet speed up a road-building programme. For programmes to be as realistic as possible, to have the maximum chance of coming about, those preparing them must have regard, as far as it is practicable at the time of their preparation, to the conditions which make for successful development. These conditions are not all of an economic character, but it is with those which are that we are here concerned.

For the development to take place at all there must be a developer, and also certain economic conditions which are favourable to him. Firstly, there must be some consumer demand for the development, the prospect that someone will be willing to pay money for its use when it is finished. Secondly, the developer must be able to carry out the development. For this he must be able to secure, out of the land which is available for development, sites which are suitable for his purpose; there must be a building industry with the capacity to carry out the development; he must have enough money at his command to enable him to invest in the development, that is to obtain the use of the land and to employ the building industry; and there must be no prohibition by public authority of his so doing. Thirdly, the different parties concerned in the development must be able to borrow money as necessary to supplement the amount they own; very little development would take place today if consumers, developers, landowners and builders were able to operate only with the money they actually possess. The economic framework which influences these conditions we will call here the " economics of development."

The developer must not only be able to carry out the development but must also be willing to do so. To reach a decision on this he will weigh up those implications of the development which he considers to be his concern. Some of these will be financial and some non-financial. The listing of the implications, both financial and non-financial, which concern developers we will call preparing the " development balance sheet." Methods by which developers appraise the financial implications of their proposals we will call the " financial calculations for development."

In preparing programmes of development which are to be realistic, that is to have some reasonable chance of taking place, a developer must have regard to the economics of development, prepare financial calculations for the development which is envisaged and draw up and consider his development balance sheet. Or, in general terms, developers in looking ahead must have regard to what we shall call the economics, financial calculations and balance sheet of development, and operators will need to consider what we can similarly call the economics, financial calculations and balance sheet of operation.

CHAPTER 2

THE NATURE OF THE DEVELOPMENT PLAN

The Purpose of a Development Plan—Development in the Town and Country Planning Act, 1947—Planning Authorities Under the 1947 Act—Planning and Development Agencies—What Constitutes a Development Plan—The Content of a Development Plan—The Period of the Development Plan—Significance of the Scale and Contents of a Plan—Flexibility of the Development Plan—Preparing a Development Plan—Design of a Plan—Reviewing an Approved Development Plan —Plans which are Not Part of the Development Plan.

The Purpose of a Development Plan

EVEN in the most static areas of the country, the remoter Welsh and Scottish counties, and much more so in other places, many different kinds of development take place. It is because of the ill-effects to the community's interest that flow from the absence of co-ordination of, and adequate public control over, this development that the need for land planning has arisen, and has been recognised on the statute book in this country since 1909. To meet the need in post-war Britain the duty was placed, in the Town and Country Planning Act, 1947, on local planning authorities, the county and county borough councils,[1] of controlling the development in their areas in the community's interest; and the requirement was accordingly imposed on developers of obtaining their permission when they propose to carry out development.[2] These powers of control are to be exercised having regard to the " provisions of a development plan so far as material thereto, and to any other material considerations."[3] The preparation of a development plan was, therefore, required of local planning authorities under the 1947 Act.[4] The plans were to be submitted to the Minister of Housing and Local Government for his approval by 1951. Many authorities were not, however, able to prepare and submit their plans within this time, but almost all did so by 1955.

The development plan is therefore a " framework or pattern of proposed land use, in the form of a coherent set of proposals for the use of land, against which day-to-day development can be considered."[5] It is made because it is a way of formulating a policy which can act as a basis for guiding, controlling or initiating development; for deciding, for example, whether development should take place at all on a particular piece of land, or which of two or more kinds of development should be preferred on it, or whether development should take the form proposed by a developer. It is expected that as a result of making the plan, and of steering development in accordance with it, the ill-effects of unco-ordinated development will be avoided, an area will be better to live and work in than it might have been without planning control, and some contribution will thereby be made to national wealth and well-being.

Development in the Town and Country Planning Act, 1947

The development over which local planning authorities have control, and for which they prepare their plans, is defined as " the carrying out of building, engineering, mining or other operations in, on, over or under land, or the making of any material change in the use of any building or other land." Building and engineering operations are interpreted in the Act, but not the other terms in this definition. Building operations includes " rebuilding operations, structural alterations of or additions to buildings, and other operations normally undertaken by a person carrying on business as a builder;" and engineering operations includes " the formation or layout of means of access to highways."[6] This corresponds to the popular meaning of the term which was described in Chapter 1, but is wider by the inclusion of mining operations, insofar as these are not constructional works, and of material changes in the use of land and buildings which are not associated with works.

It is not intended that planning control should concern itself with the minutiæ of development. Permission is not therefore required, for example, for minor building and engineering work, such as that to the interior of buildings and in maintenance of roads and services; or for minor changes of use such as those within the curtilage of dwelling-houses for purposes incidental to the enjoyment of the dwelling-houses, or from one use to another within certain groups of similar uses.[7] Further exemption from control is given to certain classes of development, such as temporary uses, camping, the coal mining activities of the National Coal Board, over which planning control would not be fruitful.[8]

Planning Authorities Under the 1947 Act

In addition to the local planning authorities, the county district councils also play an important part in planning since there has been delegated to them, to varying extents, a substantial part of the responsibilities of the county councils in relation to development control,[9] and they must be consulted in the preparation of development plans.[10]

The Minister of Housing and Local Government also has many responsibilities in land planning. For example, the local planning authority submit to him for approval not only their development plans, in the consideration of which he must take account of objections and representations from interested parties, but also applications to use many other planning powers in the Act, such as those for discontinuing authorised uses, or preserving trees or historic buildings;[11] and to him can appeal a developer who is aggrieved by a local planning authority's decision on a development application.[12] In the exercise of his planning functions the Minister may be considering purely local issues, such as whether a particular site should be used for a shop or not; or national and regional issues, such as whether the production in a particular factory is so important to the national economy that the factory should be allowed to expand even though it is badly sited. In carrying out his functions he is charged with the duty of " securing consistency in the framing and execution of a national policy with respect to the use and development of land throughout England and Wales."[13] He is not obliged to prepare a formal plan for the purpose, but in practice he does prepare plans, or have them prepared for him, as a guide to his decisions. In all this he has the co-operation of other departments; and to facilitate this co-operation there is in each administrative region of the country an inter-departmental Regional Physical Planning Committee.[14]

Other departments contribute to land planning apart from their work on this Committee. They may for example, like the Ministry of Agriculture or Ministry of Fuel and Power, present their views to the local planning authorities, as sponsors of particular land use interests, both during the preparation of a plan and in the control of development. The Board of Trade in particular must be mentioned. Application to the Board must be made whenever it is intended to erect an industrial building of more than 5,000 sq. ft., and no such building can be erected without the Board's Industrial Development Certificate that its erection would be consistent with its policy on the proper distribution of industry.[15]

The preparation and approval of a development plan and the controlling of development is thus not the work of an individual but of a local authority with its committees and officers, and in a county of two such authorities, committees and sets of officers, and of the Ministry of Housing and Local Government and other departments and their officials. On occasions, all these parties may be involved in considering a particular piece of development or part of a plan.

Planning and Development Agencies

The councils of county boroughs and administrative counties are both local planning authorities and developers. In consequence the processes of development and planning become intertwined as far as the development carried out by these authorities is concerned. They become very closely intertwined on those occasions when the development can be said to have a planning objective, as where a county borough council acquires and clears land of obsolete buildings and services and re-develops it comprehensively (see Chapter 15), or where a county council gives technical and financial assistance to county district councils in the attempt to stimulate development as visualised in the county plan (see Chapter 16), or provides places of refreshment, camping sites and parking places in or near a national park of which it is the local planning authority,[16] or acquires and reclaims derelict land in order to divert development from spreading onto agricultural land.[17]

In practice, however, the development and planning functions even of such authorities can be considered as distinct. The distinction is clear in the counties where there is almost always a separate county planning department and officer; but even in the county boroughs, where there are few separate planning departments, a considerable amount of development is carried out by departments, officers and committees who are not engaged in land planning. In practice, the distinction is more real than apparent, the spending committees standing in relation to the planning committees as developers, although specially favoured developers.[18]

The Ministry of Housing and Local Government does not carry out development itself, although it is the department principally concerned with the oversight of the development of local authorities, New Town Development Corporations and National Park Authorities. In this oversight the Ministry can be said to have development functions which are distinct from its planning functions.

What Constitutes a Development Plan

A development plan consists of the appropriate maps and written statements which describe the planning proposals. Its form has been defined by the Minister in order to indicate to authorities what they are required to submit to him for approval.[19]

Proposals in outline are shown on what are called basic maps. These indicate broadly the use of land in the area, as visualised and intended when the development which is expected during the period of the plan will have taken place. In the county boroughs, and the County of London and other urbanised county areas, the map is a 6-in. town map. In the remaining administrative counties it is a 1-in. county map. These basic maps must be accompanied by programme maps, to the same scale, indicating the stages during which the development is expected to be undertaken and substantially completed. The stages are normally three: the first five years from the approval of the plan, a further fifteen years or so, and anything beyond. But where it is not practicable to stage a proposal, such as the working of minerals, the programme map can indicate the period during which the proposal as a whole will be carried out, and the written statement the proportion, if any, of the proposal which can reasonably be expected to take place during the first five years. The basic and programme maps, and their written statements, are the minimum that can constitute a development plan; but a plan can also include any of the following maps and their written statements. These are intended, in general terms, to supplement the basic maps by showing proposals in more detail for certain parts of an authority's area.

For the towns which are not county boroughs a county council can prepare 6-in. town maps and their programme maps and written statements. For the first submission to the Minister it was not practicable for the counties to prepare plans for all their towns that needed plans, and it was left to them to decide how many and which they would cover.

Where an authority visualises development or re-development on any substantial scale in a part of its area covered by a town map it will find the map and its written statement inadequate for its work. This may arise, for example, where land is to be re-developed as a whole because it is war damaged or contains obsolete property, or where a housing neighbourhood is to be built on virgin land, or where a town is to be extended for the reception of immigrant population, or where there are a great number of projects in the central area of a town which should be related together. In these cases the authority can submit to the Minister larger scale maps (normally at 25-in. scale) showing its more detailed proposals. These maps may be of two kinds.

Where in the opinion of an authority an area of land, or land and buildings, whether in town or country, should be developed or re-developed as a whole within a reasonable period, because, for example, of conditions of war damage, bad layout or obsolescent property, or because it is required for relocating population or industry following re-development, or for other purposes, it can be defined as an area of comprehensive development. For such areas 25-in. comprehensive development area maps would be submitted, each with its 25-in. programme map and written statement describing the proposals. The programme map would show five-year stages of development or, with the Minister's approval, two five-year stages and a third stage of any length.

The definition by an authority of an area as one of comprehensive development is normally a preliminary to its request for powers of acquisition and grant for the purpose of re-development. Where the authority wishes to submit details for land outside areas of comprehensive development it cannot show them on a comprehensive development area map but must employ a supplementary town map; in contrast to the other maps which have been described the Minister's approval to its submission is required. A programme map may accompany a supplementary town map, but the authority is not compelled to submit one unless required by the Minister to do so. The stages for such a map would be similar to those for the basic map.

In the normal case an authority would submit one 25-in. map for an area which should be planned to the larger scale, the part covering any defined area being a comprehensive development area map and the part covering the remainder being a supplementary town map.[20]

We have so far considered larger scale maps only for areas covered by town maps. Where an authority wishes to submit a large scale map for development or re-development on a substantial scale in an area covered only by a county map (the re-development of a village slum, for example, or the building of a holiday camp on the coast) it can employ a comprehensive development area map but not a supplementary town map. In county map areas therefore an authority can submit large-scale proposals only for areas defined for comprehensive development.

While the map scales mentioned here are generally employed, the Minister may in a particular case agree to another scale for the whole or part of a map (for example, to parts of a county map at 2½-in. or 6-in. scale, to parts of a town map at 25-in. scale and to a comprehensive development area map at 1/1,250 scale) in cases where the complexity of uses or proposals make it desirable. The enlarged parts of the county and town maps are known respectively as county and town map insets.

The development plan can also designate land as subject to compulsory acquisition, provided it is to be acquired within ten years, or seven years if agricultural land, from the plan's approval. Such land may be that which is allocated by the plan for any of the functions of any Minister, local authority or statutory undertaker; or land in or adjacent to an area defined in the plan as an area of comprehensive development; or any other land which ought to be bought to secure its use in the manner proposed by the plan. For submission, the land is shown on 25-in. designation maps. When this designation is approved as part of the plan the appropriate developer can obtain powers of compulsory acquisition over it.[21]

As part of their initial development plans, those submitted by each authority for the first time after the passing of the 1947 Act, authorities submitted many comprehensive development area and designation maps, and county councils submitted many town maps. They will be adding to these and submitting supplementary town maps following the approval of their initial plans. These additions will, when approved, form part of the authority's development plan.

The Content of a Development Plan

Proposals Maps. The proposals maps show the existing land and buildings which are expected to remain and also proposals for future development. The kind of item which might be included on the maps, and the method of representation, have been standardised; those which might be contained on each kind of map are listed in Appendix I.

For town maps it will be seen that the proposals fall into three classes:

(a) Reservations of specific pieces of land for purposes which will involve their acquisition for development by a public developer.

Examples are reservations for schools, open space, railway extension whose sites are defined in the plan.

(b) Proposals which will usually involve the acquisition by a public developer of land for carrying out development, but which are indicated diagrammatically so that it cannot be seen precisely which land is affected. Examples are the indication on a town map by two parallel lines of constant width that certain roads are principal traffic roads, conveying the presumption that they may be widened or otherwise improved, without any specific indication that they will be; or the indication by a symbol that a school will be built in a particular area although the site has not yet been specifically defined.

(c) The indication by zoning that fairly large areas of land are allocated primarily for such uses as residential, industrial, business or shopping. An allocation for a primary use envisages that uses which are ancillary to the primary use will also take place on the land, such as shopping in a residential area or warehouses in a shopping area; and that uses other than the primary or ancillary one will also be permitted where no detriment will arise; and that the development and re-development within the allocated area will be either by public or private agencies.

The 25-in. comprehensive development area and supplementary town maps show proposals in a similar way, but more precisely than do the basic maps; they do not include any diagrammatic proposals but show only reservations or zoning. The 1-in. county maps are less precise; they show some of their proposals by way of a simple zoning and many by way of symbols.

Programme Maps. Programme maps pick out the development which is expected to be undertaken and substantially completed within the various stages shown on it; areas where no change is expected are left without notation. By and large, a programme map shows the substantial changes which are expected between the area as it exists and as it is visualised. But it does not show all the changes. It cannot show the small ones such as those which will be brought about by the sporadic erection or re-building of premises, or the adaptation of buildings to other uses. It does not show the relatively uncertain changes which may be brought about by the authority merely by control of private development. It does not show all the diagrammatic proposals on town and county maps; for example it shows a new section of a principal traffic road but not the intention to widen one.

For these reasons, while the programme map shows the difference between existing and proposed conditions it does not show the exact difference between a land use survey map and proposals map, even where these are drawn to the same scale. There is another reason for this; the maps do not give the same kind of information. The land use map shows the predominant use of individual buildings or group of buildings. The proposals map shows the primary use of zones, that is of areas allocated primarily to a particular use but within which are expected other kinds of uses.

The Period of the Development Plan

Since the plan is to steer development that is expected to take place regard must be had, if the plan is to be useful, to the likelihood of such development coming about. And since the different kinds of development envisaged must be related to each other in the plan, the new schools, for example, to the expected increase in child population, and the new sewerage works to the expected use of particular land for new housing, regard must be had to the dates when the development is expected to come about. In order to have regard to both these matters it is desirable, but not essential, to try and visualise all the development that will take place by a particular time ahead; it is not essential, and it is practicable for a plan to show roads and mineral operation, for example, which will be undertaken long after the housing and schools in the plan are completed. It is essential however to try and define the stages in which the different development will come about.

Since it is not possible or desirable to forecast development or its timing too far ahead, the initial set of plans were prepared to take account in the main only of development that was reasonably firm, which had a likelihood that is of being undertaken and substantially completed within about 20 years of the plan's preparation, that is by 1971. Regard was had also to any development of significance for which land should be reserved even if it could not be expected to come about within this period. Programme maps therefore did not show much development in the stage beyond 20 years from plan preparation.

While it is convenient to think of a plan being prepared as at a particular date, in fact this date cannot be defined. A plan is prepared and its proposals decided upon over a period of perhaps two to three years; it is formally completed by an authority when it is approved by them for submission to the Minister; it is legally completed and operative when the Minister's approval to it is advertised, perhaps one to two years after submission. The end of a plan period, or one of its stages, is equally difficult to date not only because of the difficulty of defining the plan's actual commencement but also because no one really knows how long the visualised development will actually take to bring about.

The length of time which must elapse between the initiation of the preparation of a plan and its coming into operation raises its

own difficulties in practice. Planning control decisions must be
given in relation to a plan which is not finalised; survey maps are
continuously becoming out of date; programme maps when approved
may show works which are completed; and the authority, landowners and developers are in many cases uncertain as to their
position.

Significance of the Scale and Contents of a Plan

The scale of the maps and kinds of items shown in a plan decide
broadly the nature and scale of the planning authority's interest
in preparing the plan, the kind of information it seeks and the
enquiries it makes. Since, for example, the town map deals only
with principal car parking places the authority need not concern
itself for the purpose of its preparation with small car parks; and
since on the comprehensive development area map there needs to
be shown the floor space index of business zones of different building
density, the authority may need to carry out surveys of existing
floor space to enable it to decide appropriate indices.[22] Generally
speaking the amount of work involved in defining a proposal on a
map is greater than would appear from its representation on the
map; proposals often need careful site investigation and the preparation of designs to larger scale before the smaller scale plans can
be drawn.

The scale of the maps and kind of items shown in a plan may
prevent the authority from showing its intentions in detail. For
example, an already developed area of mixed uses in a town may be
shown in a town map for business purposes and yet the authority
may not expect any substantial change in use nor intend initiating
such a change.

The authority's interest is not limited to the work it must do to
prepare plans for official submission (see page 26). Certain
proposals for a development plan need to be considered against the
background of others which will take more than 20 years to bring
about; and detailed studies of many parts of the area will be needed
to guide the authority in deciding on the proposals to be shown in
a basic map or its answer on a particular application for permission
to develop.

Flexibility of the Development Plan

Development plans are thus intended to be flexible instruments
for controlling, guiding and stimulating development. The basic
maps are drawn in broad terms and do not prescribe the exact
use of individual pieces of land, except sometimes where these are
specifically reserved for a purpose involving public acquisition, so
that the details of development can be decided when it is fairly
imminent.

The authority will continue to fill in details on the basic maps, when the time is ripe, by preparing and submitting for the Minister's approval designation, comprehensive development area or supplementary town maps, and town maps in county areas. Where new problems arise, unexpected development is proposed, development does not follow expected directions and opinions change, authorities may wish to alter their plans. They can submit proposals for alteration to the Minister, or can be required by him to do so at any time; and at least once in every five years from the Minister's approval of a plan, in practice about six to seven years from its submission to him, an authority must review its plan, or, more precisely, carry out a fresh survey of its area and submit to the Minister a report on that survey and any alterations or additions to the plan which appear to be required.[23] (See page 25.) When agreed to by the Minister these become part of the development plan.

While in granting permissions authorities must have regard to the " provisions of a plan so far as material thereto " (page 13) they must also have regard to other material considerations, and in practice have considerable freedom in giving permission for development which is not in accord with the plan. Where such development in their opinion " would neither involve a substantial departure from the plan, nor injuriously affect the amenity of adjoining land," authorities do not require the Minister's consent to grant permission; where it does, they do.[24]

This flexibility of plans and planning control is essential if development, and the life of an area, is not to be frustrated by decisions which are made before it is appropriate that they should be made. But it has its dangers. It can lead to vacillation in the control of development, to expediency, inconsistency and inequity between developers, and it can be invoked to protect a plan which is not founded upon a well-deliberated analysis of the area's problems and its development tendencies. Such a plan affords no useful guide to control and soon needs to be amended; and a plan which requires too frequent alteration would be frequently subject to opposition at public inquiry and to ministerial consideration, and also a burden rather than a help to developers who would continually need to be adjusting their programmes to it.

A middle course must be thus pursued between rigidity and vague uncertainty; and the successful pursuit of such a course is one of the most difficult tasks of planning authorities.

Preparing a Development Plan

To assist local planning authorities in the preparation of the initial set of development plans under the 1947 Act, government departments have issued advisory circulars and memoranda and their officers have given advice.[25] The authorities have, on the whole, followed the methods suggested by the departments and have all worked on similar lines, although there have been variations in detail. A generally accepted, but not completely standardised, method of preparing development plans can be said to exist.

The method will not be exactly followed in the preparation of additional town maps that will follow the approval of the initial plans.[26] There have been changes in ideas with the accumulation of experience since 1947 and the amendment of the financial provisions of the 1947 Act will have undoubted, if as yet unplumbed, consequences. (See Chapter 23.) Despite these changes, however, the process of preparing a development plan is likely to remain fundamentally the same as it has been; and this process will be briefly described.

The preparation of a development plan is a process whereby proposals are formulated in the light of an appreciation of the different aspects of the problem confronting the planning authority. These aspects can be divided into:

    (a) The existing conditions and trends in the area.

    (b) The problems in, and needs of, the area.

    (c) The development that development agencies would like to undertake.

    (d) Any central government decisions affecting the plan.

From an appreciation of these aspects a design can be completed, and maps and a written statement prepared, which will depict the plan. The word " completed " has been used advisedly and not " started " since there is no particular point at which the appreciation of one aspect starts and another stops, or at which the designing begins. A plan evolves to completion. It will probably start growing early on before the survey of all facts and opinions, and their analysis, has been completed. It will continue to grow, absorbing what can be learned from the survey, from consultations with developers and other interested parties, from an appreciation of the changes that are desirable to meet the town's problems and of the changes that are practicable, and from any views of central government on the planning policy to be adopted. All the aspects will influence each other. The plan evolves taking them all into account; and one of the tests of its soundness is the way in which this has been done. Some account will be given of these four different aspects.

    (a) *Existing Trends and Conditions.* The existing conditions and trends in an area are investigated by a survey whose purpose is to depict the character and working of an area so that these, and the problems of the area, can be fully appreciated. The investigation must delve sufficiently into the past for the current conditions to be seen against the background of history and geography.

The information so collected is represented in the form of maps, graphs, tables, charts and written matter. Such is the complexity of town and countryside that it is possible to collect unlimited information about their history, growth, population, economic activities and means of transportation. Since the object of the survey is the preparation of a plan and the control over development, it is necessary that the scope of the survey be related to the information which is needed for these purposes. Some guidance on this was given by the Minister for the initial set of plans and he required that summaries of certain survey material be submitted to him.[27] These are not part of the development plan.

By nature a survey is a static picture of various conditions in an area at a particular date. If the surveys are kept up to date, or repeated at intervals, it assists in the watching of movement or trends in conditions; and such trends are as important as the static picture in giving an understanding of the area.

(b) *The Problems and Needs of the Area.* There should emerge from an analysis of the survey and other information a picture of the problems, needs and defects of the area that need to be tackled by a plan; and of the assets that need to be protected from unharmonious development. Appendix II gives a list of typical problems that were revealed in a development plan survey. The clearer this analysis is made, and the more the needs and defects of the area are measured quantitatively, the easier will it be to design an effective plan.

The Minister requires that such a written analysis be submitted to him with a plan. He has suggested that it should assess the significance of the facts emerging from the survey of the area, discuss the problems to which the plan is intended to provide solutions, include an explanation of the grounds for adopting the proposals and examine the practicability of carrying them out and the effects they may be expected to produce.[28] This analysis is not part of the plan nor is it approved by the Minister. It forms, however, an indispensable background to a comprehension of the plan.

(c) *The Development that Developers Would Like to Undertake.* It does not take much consideration to see that all the changes that the planning authority is concerned and interested to see come about, in order that the area's problems may be solved and its needs satisfied, must come about by way of development or re-development. If the people are overcrowded in their dwellings, new dwellings must be built in order to relieve the congestion; if there is an obsolete area of buildings and streets which is no longer functioning properly, demolition and rebuilding must take place in order to improve it. In other words, the changes that developers would like to undertake, their development programmes, are the raw material which the planning authority must use in its plan to constitute the changes that it thinks desirable and would like to see. It cannot, however, normally accept all the programmes of all the developers just as they are formulated for incorporation into its plan, for its viewpoint and objective are not always the same as those of the developers. Of all aspects of a development plan this particular one is most germane to the subject of this book; and it will be amplified in Chapter 3.

(d) *Central Government Decisions Affecting the Plan.* The local planning authority must take into account the relevant decisions of central government as they affect the plan. These may be broadly of three kinds, each affecting the preparation of the plan in a different way.

Firstly, there are the activities of government departments as developers, as sponsors of development, in sanctioning spending by public bodies and in economic planning. These will affect the development that is likely to take place in an area and must be considered by the local planning authority as part of (c) above.

Secondly, there are the policies of departments as to the way in which development should be carried out. The Ministry of Education, for example, has prescribed the minimum size of sites for schools of different kinds and of their playing fields; the Ministry of Housing and Local Government has been pressing for higher densities in the provision of dwellings; the Ministry of Transport aims at securing that traffic roads should be as free as possible from development and from numerous intersections with streets.

Thirdly, there are government decisions relating to land planning policies which are capable of being reflected by an authority in a development plan; and which the authority is expected to reflect. Such decisions have flowed from the government's consideration of areas, such as Greater London, Greater Birmingham, Merseyside or South Wales, which should be planned as one unit although containing the areas of several local planning authorities. The decisions have related to such matters as the future grouping of population, lines for main roads, the preservation of agricultural land, the preservation of major open spaces, and amount of employment to be provided for.

Design of a Plan

Proposals will be formulated, leading to the design of the plan, which will take into account the factors described in (a) to (d). For its preparation there will need to be the necessary professional skills of the diverse kind now associated with planning, those of the architect, engineer, surveyor, economist, treasurer, sociologist, etc.; and also policy making by local planning authority and government departments on a great variety of issues, on whether, for example, industrial or civic buildings should be concentrated or dispersed, or whether a town should be restricted in growth. There will also need to be full consideration of the effect of draft planning proposals on the life and working of the area, and on property and other interests; and also consultations between the local planning authority and its officers and the interests concerned, both public and private, in order to build up the survey and analysis, to comprehend development intentions, to gauge public opinion, to test out draft plan proposals and to obtain reactions to development projects.[29]

It is difficult to describe briefly the process of making a plan out of all these different considerations, particularly as so much is the result of discussion and negotiation. It is possible, however, to review the reasons for a plan when it is completed, and to describe possible alternative proposals which have been rejected in deciding on those in the plan. The written analysis offers an opportunity for doing this.

Reviewing an Approved Development Plan

On the first review of development plans, to take place between 1955 and 1960, it is not expected that authorities will wish to make fundamental revisions of them; there has hardly been sufficient time to judge whether the plans need subs antial recasting and authorities are likely to be pre-occupied in filling in the detail of basic maps: the county councils in preparing further town maps and all councils in preparing comprehensive development area and supplementary town maps.

What is expected is that authorities will reconsider plans in the light of experience since their approval in order to decide in which respects, if any, they need amendment. For this purpose they will, among other things, take note of the development in the area since the initial plan was prepared, its amount, nature, location and trends; will compare this with the development they thought would take place in this period; will take account of development programmes formulated since the initial plan was prepared, such as those for slum clearance, and of changes in already formulated programmes; will review their experience in considering development applications and in contesting appeals to the Minister against their decisions; will consider to what extent the problems of the area have been met and its defects remedied, and the objects of the plan have been realised by the development that has taken place; will analyse any new conditions, problems and defects that have emerged; will take account of any other new factors of importance, such as changes in policy with regard to residential density or open space provision and greater knowledge of mineral deposits and workings; will consider whether changes are needed in their plans because of plans which have been approved by the Minister for surrounding areas, or of changes in such plans; will take account of departmental comment on their plan and criticism made by the objectors at public inquiries; and will take account of consultations with developers and other interested parties including other local planning and public authorities. To emphasise that it is this kind of review which is visualised, and not any major revision of the plans, authorities have been advised not to alter plans merely to take account of development that is expected to take place beyond the end date of the initial plans; alteration of the plans on this account will take place on the second review.[30]

Authorities are not generally expected, therefore, in their first review to go through the process just described for preparing a new plan, but to adapt it as necessary to meet their particular circumstances. They will not repeat the entire survey which was previously carried out but will probably bring it up to date and carry out any fresh survey only for particular problems which need to be tackled. They will not officially submit new maps but will submit, with their report of survey, any appropriate alterations to the plan and written statement. They will not submit a new formal programme map but will indicate in their report of survey the development in the plan that is expected to take place in its next ensuing five-year stage.

Plans which are Not Part of the Development Plan

It was indicated above that planning offices do not confine themselves to preparing plans for submission to the Minister, and that such submissions include a summary of many of the other plans that they prepare. They will, for example, prepare sketches of long term re-development proposals as a guide to those which should be included in the 20-year development plan; design road proposals to a large scale before summarising them on a basic map; make large scale studies of a particular area in order to contest an appeal to the Minister against a planning control decision; and plan some complex area in detail as a guide to officers and committee on development control decisions. It would not be simple for us in this book to consider all this background work to the development plan and our purpose will be served by referring in the main to the development plan itself. This is a summary of all the plans that are prepared, and it represents those proposals in which the authority have enough confidence for them to be put to the test of public criticism and of the Minister's scrutiny. What we have to say of development plans will apply in general to these other plans too.

CHAPTER 3

DEVELOPMENT AND THE DEVELOPMENT PLAN

Comprehending the Development Programmes in an Area—Possible Divergence Between Planning and Development Objectives—Some Land Planning Objectives—Positive Planning—The Planning Balance Sheet—Need for Co-operation in the Preparation of Development Programmes—The Planning Authority and Programmes of Development—Usefulness of Realistic Development Plans and Programmes.

Comprehending the Development Programmes in an Area

IT WAS seen in Chapter 2 that if changes are to come about in an area in accordance with a plan, they must arise from the development or re-development which is to be undertaken by developers. This leads the planning authority as part, but part only, of the preparation of its plan to try and comprehend what development would be likely to take place in the area if there were no planning control: in other words, what are the development programmes in the area. To comprehend these programmes it is desirable for the authority, as part of the general evolution of the plan, to consult with prospective developers, or with associations which represent them, as far as it is practicable, for information on their proposals and intentions, as far as these can be formulated. This approach to the problem of programming development in county boroughs was recommended by the Research Committee of the Town Planning Institute, when it said " The best approach to the problem is the direct one. Consultations with all interests, and a study of evidence of intention of and capacity to carry out developments, should greatly assist in allocating the potential output and forecasting the sequence of various works, thus creating the most probable and practicable programme."[1]

The form in which the information is sought must be related to the purpose of seeking it: its incorporation into plans which have the form and content we have described. For the town maps the information will normally be sought in terms of broad kinds of uses, their quantity, density and location, the time ahead when they are projected and the rate at which they will take place. For larger scale maps more particular information will be needed; and for county maps less particular. Sometimes, however, more detailed information will be required than will be shown on the maps, for some proposals need detailed examination before they can be translated into the form shown on a map. For example, where a road improvement is proposed in a built-up area the extent of property demolition will need to be considered, and therefore the precise alignment, in order to gauge the amount of consequent re-development that will be involved.

It is not practicable to approach and consult all the prospective developers in an area. It is simple, at one extreme, for a planning committee to approach other committees of its authority, or to approach a single body, such as the National Coal Board or Area Electricity Board, which is responsible for all development of a particular kind in the area, and which is centrally directed; but it is difficult, at the other extreme, for it to approach all the prospective shopping or industrial developers since they will be numerous, may not all be represented in associations such as the Chamber of Commerce, Federation of British Industries or Retailers' Federations, and will not all be persons who are established in the area.

Even where it is practicable to approach individual developers it is found that the total programme will not necessarily consist of the sum of the parts. This was experienced in connection with the rebuilding of shopping areas in bomb-damaged city centres where it was known that individual developers tended to be optimistic about the share of business that would come their way, and that their combined programme was likely to be more than the total that would be carried out by shopping developers as a whole. It is experienced too in connection with industrial development for it is known that an industrialist may make enquiries in many towns before deciding to go ahead with a new building. When dealing with numerous developers for a particular use, therefore, the planning authority must discount for probable over-estimate. This is done to some extent where one body co-ordinates individual programmes, whether it is a representative association, such as Chamber of Commerce or the Federation of British Industries, acting on behalf of many individual firms, or the Gas Council co-ordinating the programmes of its Area Boards.

It is not to be expected that the kind of information obtainable from the different developers will be of an even quality. Programmes for traffic roads or municipal housing are likely, in the nature of things, to be firmer and more certain of implementation than programmes for coal mining or office development; and programmes for gravel extraction or generating stations are likely to be prepared for a longer period ahead than those for factories or shopping.

In short, the information on programmes that can be expected, as a result of the fullest consultation with developers, is not likely to be sufficiently comprehensive, or for a sufficient period ahead, to provide all the raw material for the development plan. It will be necessary, therefore, for the planning office to form its own views as to the likely development of those developers whom it is not able to consult, and for the part of the plan period beyond which development programmes will not be formulated.

Possible Divergence Between Planning and Development Objectives

Even where a developer is able to formulate his programme with some success, it will not necessarily be acceptable to the planning authority as it stands for incorporation into the plan, since the viewpoints and objectives of developers and planning authorities are not always identical. In considering why they diverge, why planning decisions do not always reflect the wishes and interests of developers, we are led to consider the nature of land planning objectives.

In contrast to the position under the Town and Country Planning Act, 1932, where the objectives of planning schemes were defined,[2] land planning objectives under the Town and Country Planning Act, 1947, while generally well understood, are rarely described with precision. The 1947 Act merely states that the development plan shall indicate the manner in which the local planning authority " propose that land in their area shall be used (whether by the carrying out of development or otherwise) . . ."[3] We are not taken much further by the statutory description of the functions of the responsible Minister, which is very general (see page 14), or by official statements that have been made on the objects of planning, such as that they are " to secure that all the land in the country is put to the use which is best from the point of view of the community,"[4] or " to secure a proper balance between the competing demands for land, so that all the land of the country is used to the best interests of the whole people."[5]

It will be necessary, therefore, for us to try and formulate some at least of the planning objectives behind the making of planning decisions: to consider how in fact decisions are made as to what is the best use of land. Such decisions may be made by a planning authority not only when consulting with developers in preparing a plan but also when considering whether or not to give permission when a formal or informal application is made to them on a particular proposal. They can also be made by the Minister when considering appeals against development control decisions of a local planning authority. While an application for permission to develop is normally considered in greater detail than are programmes when a plan is being prepared, the objectives behind planning decisions are similar in all such cases and can be considered together.[6]

Before analysing the planning objective two general reasons can be given for divergence between the planning and development viewpoints. The planning authority is always concerned with looking as far ahead as it can into the future, but developers are sometimes concerned only with the immediate future; and the planning authority's horizon of interest is always at least its whole planning area, whereas the developer's is normally restricted to one site, or perhaps to a few sites which might be in the same locality or in different parts of the country. In considering a particular proposal, therefore, the authority would consider, as far into the future as it could, the implications for other land within its area. This is the sense in which town planning has been called estate management on a large scale, for this also would be the horizon of the owner and manager of an estate covering the whole area. This aspect of town planning is increasing in importance with the continuing break-up of large urban and rural estates.

Since a local planning authority is a county council or county borough council its planning horizon is often limited to its administrative area, and its plans are necessarily stamped with its policy and viewpoint. One authority, for example, which is short of open land within its boundaries might encourage high housing densities to minimise the export of rateable value and the number of people to be housed over the boundary. Another authority in a similar position might plan for a considerable overspill of population with a view to attracting boundary extension.

The authority's horizon is wider than its own area, however, when it writes into its plan government policy and proposals which have been considered on a regional or national scale, such as those relating to population grouping, volume of employment, major open spaces and roads. An example of this is seen in the attitude of the London County Council to the expansion of industry in its area. It is government policy that industry be diverted from following its tendency to expand in Greater London and the Midlands at the expense of the rest of the country, particularly of the Development Areas.[7] It is in sympathy with this policy, and not entirely because of conditions in the County of London, that the Council intend to preserve land in industrial zones in its plan for the re-organisation of existing industry which must remain in London, and to exclude from it new industries or those coming from outside London.[8]

Where planning decisions are made by the Minister his horizon is clearly that of the whole country even though local issues are involved.

Some Land Planning Objectives

It may be necessary to resist development in pursuance of land planning objectives such as the following. These are not exhaustive.

(a) *Regard for Interests of the National and Local Economy*. It is a land planning objective that regard should be had to the interest of the national and local economy. It is in this interest for example that capital expenditure on roads and utility services should be kept to a minimum for a given amount of development; that such services should not be constructed before existing ones are fully used; that good farmland should be conserved; that good farmland should not be used uneconomically in small holdings;

that a scarce mineral deposit should be protected from being sterilised by surface development.

(b) *Regard for the Objectives of All Public Authorities.* Since land planning is carried out by central and local government, its objectives absorb those of all public authorities. If only because of this land planning aims to secure, and resists development which threatens, an accident-free road system, good sanitary conditions, good housing conditions and unpolluted atmosphere, rivers and water supplies.

Certain objectives of this kind have become absorbed by planning merely because they cannot be pursued by any public authority under its current powers. In such circumstances planning, in cricket terms, acts as a long-stop for balls which cannot be fielded by other public authorities. For example, the Ministry of Works, while having statutory duties with regard to ancient monuments, has but limited obligations in respect of architectural treasures which are not ancient, such as the period country house, and the protection of these has fallen to planning. The Forestry Commission could conceivably take under its wing the protection of woodlands and trees but, since it does not, this falls to planning. The building bye-laws are not suitable for securing enough space about buildings to ensure adequate daylighting to them, and the protection of daylighting has accordingly fallen to planning.

While planning authorities aim to supplement the powers of other public authorities they do not aim to duplicate them. In a circular giving advice on the drafting of planning permissions the Minister has pointed out that the Planning Act powers are for " regulating the development and use of land; and the powers which it confers are only available for these purposes. Conditions which have no relevance to planning have no place in a planning permission: planning ought not to be used as a sort of universal long-stop when other powers are not available."[9] For example, in deciding an appeal the Minister thought that it was for the Post Office to take action should physiotherapy apparatus threaten to interfere with wireless and television reception, and that the imposition of the necessary conditions to minimise interference was not appropriate to planning.[10] And where the local planning authority refused permission for development because it would injure public health by polluting water supplies, the Minister thought that the necessary control to avoid pollution should be exercised by the public health and not planning authorities.[11] But it is not always clear whether an objective should be pursued under planning or other powers. The circular just quoted says that " Exceptionally there may be circumstances which make it desirable to supplement a specific control (e.g., where relevant legislation is out of date or where preventive action is preferable to reliance on the statutory remedy). But, in general, the powers of the Planning Act ought not to be used to duplicate or alter the impact of more specific legislation, particularly if the result would be to deprive the developer of compensation to which he would otherwise have been entitled." And where the Coal Board proposed working some 7,000 acres under a river valley and was refused permission, the Minister on appeal decided that since underground mining is development, planning powers could be used to secure the support of the surface land after mining, despite the existence of other statutory powers whereby this could be secured.[12] And where a local Act gives an authority more powers than it possesses under a general Act to for example control mineral workings, then in that locality planning powers will probably be less used to control mineral workings than in others.

(c) *Preservation, Protection and Creation of Amenity.* Land planning embraces, and has done since its earliest days, the preservation, protection and creation of amenity in the widest sense. Included in this are the preservation of buildings of special architectural or historic interest; the control of advertisements; the concern with architectural appearance; the preservation of trees and woodlands; the protection of established living or working conditions. The threat to amenities in part comes from the manner in which development is carried out, and control over the appearance of buildings becomes a planning objective precisely because the building industry, in its widest sense, cannot achieve a high standard in the execution of works. In part it comes in certain places from any change by development however well it is carried out: the holiday camp on the unspoilt coast, the electricity pylon in Snowdonia, the new office block to replace a Georgian house and the underground car park which would require the destruction, and prevent the replanting, of forest trees in central London squares.

In its regard for amenity, planning will often impose conditions on development, or stop it altogether, in order to prevent nuisance being caused to adjoining residents, whether such a nuisance would be actionable at law or not. It will aim, for example, at suppressing noisy machinery or the disturbance by night working in a factory, and at avoiding the loss of privacy caused to house dwellers when they are overshadowed by a block of flats. In all this planning displaces, to some extent, the need of people to resort to law in order to abate private nuisances.

(d) *The Protection of Assets.* An objective which is similar to that of protecting amenity is that of protecting assets which are threatened by development. A principal aim, for example, in an advisory plan for the City of Cambridge was the restriction of the growth of the city so that its university functions would not be swamped as have those of Oxford by the growth there of industry.[13]

(e) *Resistance to the Aggravation of Problems of the Area.* Sometimes development will be resisted because, if carried out, it will aggravate known problems and defects in the area. For example, where there is a dangerous traffic junction the building there of a large cinema would be undesirable in that it would attract yet more people and traffic to it. Where there is an insufficiency of playing fields in an area, and little prospect of early additions to them, the building over of a private sports ground, used by an industrial firm for its employees, would aggravate the shortage. Where in an industrial city there is already shortage of labour and housing, new factories which offer additional employment would increase the competition for them.

(f) *Securing Co-ordinated Development.* It is an important function of the planning authority to facilitate and secure co-ordinated development, to influence developers towards greater co-ordination of their works. The need for this arises where a traffic road is not projected until well after the factories that will need it are built; or houses are projected in the flightway of a proposed aerodrome; or one of a group of villages is selected for the site of a new school although expansion in population is proposed for another of the group; or housing is projected in a location which will not enable economical expansion of a sewerage system to take place; or similar kinds of development which are proposed on adjoining sites are not integrated with each other. It is sometimes also possible to achieve better co-ordination of development on one piece of land. For example, by staging development in mining areas which are liable to subsidence, surface development and the extraction of coal can take place on and under the same piece of land; or by arranging the tipping of waste, land which has been excavated for surface minerals can be later on used for open space.

(g) *Raising Standards of Development.* The planning movement has since its early days been associated with the attempt to raise the standards of development, since it has been appreciated that the realisation of a good plan depends, fundamentally, on good development. For example, the movement has played a great part in the attempt to secure that housing layout after the second war should be an improvement over inter-war housing in having its complement of properly sited schools, adequate open space, convenient shops and appropriate public buildings. It has left its mark in the more rational layout and improved siting of factories which are associated with industrial development today. Development might be inacceptable therefore where its standards are below what is thought appropriate and what can be achieved in the circumstances.

(h) *Keeping Available for Development Sites which will be Required for Specific Purposes*.   Before planning powers existed it was possible to earmark a site for a specific purpose only by purchase and not, as today, by having it reserved for that purpose in a plan in advance of purchase.   One result of this was that development took place on land which, for example, a highway authority wished to see reserved for their road but for which they had not yet received powers of purchase, or a university wished to use for extension but could not acquire.   This often led to the later acquisition by developers being much more expensive than it need have been; or perhaps to a complete frustration of the scheme for a new road or university extension.

(i) *Securing that Development is Well Situated in Relation to Other Existing or Proposed Development*.   It is a basic planning objective to secure that development is well situated in relation to other development which is either existing or intended: schools and local shops in relation to housing and factories and wholesale markets in relation to traffic routes.

Positive Planning

Not only will the planning authority attempt to influence development programmes that are put forward, but it can and should, where necessary, attempt to encourage and stimulate certain kinds of development; it should carry out what has been called " positive planning."   For example, if a planning committee thought that a city was lacking a well-laid out and suitably located entertainments centre, and should have one, it could consider suitable sites, prepare a possible layout and try to interest the cinema, theatre and restaurant interests; and perhaps attempt to persuade the local authority to buy the sites and make them available for private development.   Or where re-development was imminent in a town but its form was likely to suffer because of the multiplicity of ownerships or smallness and poor shape of plots, a planning authority could foster a scheme of pooling of ownerships, to be achieved either by private agreement or public purchase, and their redistribution on the basis of a new design.   Or where a coastline was being spoilt by sporadic caravan development a county council could foster a scheme whereby a local authority or private owner bought, serviced and maintained a well-ordered site for caravans so that permission for them could justifiably be refused on other parts of the coast.

In positive planning the planning authority will still need to rely on developers to carry out the development.   It follows that any proposal needs to take full account of their interests if they are to be encouraged to carry it out.

There is another way in which planning can actively stimulate or repress development. When a planning decision results, for example, in a retail market being located on site A rather than B, it will result, too, in uses ancillary to that market, such as retail shops and cafés, being attracted to site A; it will have stimulated the development of shops at site A and diverted them from site B. Many planning decisions set up chain reactions in this way.

The Planning Balance Sheet

In short, the planning authority may wish to guide, divert, influence, modify, alter, suppress or stimulate development. And it will wish to do so not so much to make the development conform to a plan but rather in order to pursue its land planning objectives; its attempt to secure planned development of high standard in the area, taking account of objectives such as we have described.

When a planning authority is weighing up the advantages and disadvantages of incorporating into its plan a particular development programme or proposal, or one in a particular form, or considering a development application, its outlook is not that of the developer. Its horizon of interest is wider and its objectives are different. It must hold the balance between all developers; and between them and the local and national interest. In other words, the implications of a particular proposal that weigh with the developer, and which he will list in preparing his development balance sheet, are not necessarily those which will weigh with the planning authority. There is, in other words, what we will call a " planning balance sheet." We will return to this in Part IV.

A difference in view between the planning authority and developers on the quality, appropriateness and location of proposed development can give rise to conflict in practice. Developers know their own job and can formulate their own programmes. They are usually prepared to accept comments on these which arise from considerations which are outside their horizon, but are naturally sensitive to comment on the manner in which they intend to do their job. The planning authority on the other hand feels that it is failing in its job unless it tries to improve standards of development, and knows that many developers, however expert, are as yet inexperienced in participating in planned development.

Need for Co-operation in the Preparation of Development Programmes

The reasons which have been given why development programmes may not be acceptable to the planning authority are also reasons for the greatest co-operation between them and developers in the preparation of programmes. Such co-operation will lead to more certain and more soundly based development programmes; to the planning authority being more fully aware of the wishes and interests of developers; to mutual confidence between developers and planning authority; and to a plan which is as soundly based and realistic as possible in representing how all developers will contribute towards its implementation.

There is also another reason for this co-operation. A planning office acquires through its normal activities a considerable knowledge of its area from all aspects, of its physical, social and economic history and conditions, its interrelationship with other areas, its people and their habits, the activities of its developers, the land which is suitable and can be obtained for development, and of its economic prospects and place in the regional and national economy. This knowledge will be equalled in any one or more of these aspects by that of other bodies or agencies; but it is often unique in being comprehensive of many aspects, and moreover in being found in one office. This knowledge is valuable to and convenient for any developer in preparing his programme. This is not to say, however, that a plan or planning office can give the developer all the information he would like, nor that he will necessarily allow the plan or planning authority's views and intentions to decide for him the nature of his development. There are many aspects of his development in which the authority will have no interest and which only he can investigate and decide for himself.

The Planning Authority and Programmes of Development

While the planning office will not be responsible as such for carrying out development it will thus nevertheless take part in the production of programmes of development. It will co-operate with the developers in their formulation, and negotiate with them upon development applications that it cannot accept. It may need to assess critically the soundness of developers' programmes and to foster modified ones as a result of its attempts to guide, divert, influence, modify and alter them. It will need to promote new ones as a result of attempts to stimulate or encourage development that would otherwise not have been undertaken and of visualising the programmes that are implicit in tentative planning proposals. It will need to gauge what development is intended by those developers whom it cannot consult; and what is likely to come about beyond the period for which developers find it useful to forecast.

If a plan, and the control or development under it, are to be realistic the planning office must, in its participation in the production of programmes, be at least as realistic as are the developers as to the development which is likely to come about. For, as the Schuster Committee said in 1950, " Now that the plan is no longer a series of broad restrictions, and has become a programme for development, every local planning authority must consider whether its proposals are feasible; within what period they can be carried out; whether, if carried out as planned, they will prove economically justifiable and how the burden of the cost is to be borne. Cost in fact must dominate positive planning, since there is no end to the improvements in environment which are ideally desirable. It is cost that sets the limit, and when cost is ignored—as indeed appears to have been the case in some of the contemporary planning proposals—then planning is just so much waste paper."[14] In the planning office, therefore, there is need for familiarity with the kind of programmes which developers prepare, and with the considerations which make for realistic development programmes: with what was called in Chapter 1 the economics, financial calculations and balance sheet of development.

It is intended here to give a basis for this familiarity. To this end we shall sketch in Part II the economics of development in this country today; in Part III we shall describe, fairly fully, as they are of particular interest to surveyors, the methods by which developers make a financial appraisal of their schemes before deciding on a programme; in Part IV as already mentioned we shall discuss balance sheets in development and planning; and in Part V we shall describe programmes prepared by developers in practice for their own purposes, the kind of programme it is reasonable to expect from them for development plan purposes, and the programming work carried out in planning offices. This includes one job which is quite distinct from that of any developer: that of relating, as far as it is practicable, and that is not very far, the sum of the development programmes in an area to the total amount of development that is likely to take place in that area. This comes about because developers formulate their programmes independently of each other, and there is no special body responsible for co-ordinating all development programmes in one area so that these take account of any likely limitation in the consumer demand and economic resources of that area. It falls to the planning office to do this in default of action by others, as part of the preparation of its plan.

Usefulness of Realistic Development Plans and Programmes

We have so far discussed the usefulness of realistic programmes as assisting in the formulation of realistic plans. While it is too early yet to write from considerable experience of development plans and programmes it is possible to indicate other ways in which, if realistic, they can be useful.

1. *Basis to which Developers can Work with Confidence.* The existence of a plan should help developers. In it they can see something of the intentions of other developers, and of the staging of their works, so that they can learn something of the background against which to prepare and pursue their programmes; and the existence of the plan and of the planning

authority gives some certainty that the development of the area
will follow, or fail to follow, certain lines. If the plan and programmes are realistic developers can use them as a basis with
some confidence; but they cannot do so if plans are not realistic,
and are, in consequence, unnecessarily liable to alteration and to
be departed from. In this event development will be hindered,
rather than helped, and perhaps hindered rather more than if no
plan existed.

2. *Basis for Securing Planned Development.* The development
plan is the basis for the important day-to-day work of the planning
office. It is used in co-operating with developers, in advising on
site selection, in advising bodies and organisations in the area as
to future developments, in making recommendations on policy
to the local and planning authorities and their different departments; in short in securing planned development. In all this the
work of the office will be assisted by a realistic plan.

3. *Basis for Decisions on Compensation for Loss of Development
Value.* It will be explained below (page 346) how, under the
Town and Country Planning Act, 1954, an authority can avoid a
claim for compensation on loss of development value, where
permission for development is refused on the ground that it would
be premature, and that in giving such a decision it may rely, in
part, on the order of priorities, if any, indicated in the development
plan. It will be apparent that for use for such a purpose a realistic
programme map is desirable if decisions are to be sound.

4. *Basis for Co-ordination of Local Authority Development
Programmes.* Complete co-ordination in general administration
and the exercise of functions cannot be said to exist among local
authorities today. There has been immense improvement in this
since the end of the 19th century when the local authorities took
over from a multitude of independent bodies, in conditions where
there was " a chaos as regards authorities, a chaos as regards
rates, and a worse chaos as regards areas."[15] But despite the
improvement Mr. Gwilym Gibbon could still in 1931 find " In a
number of local authorities, at any rate, there is room for more
co-ordination between the different departments. Each department, each principal committee, tends to go its own way, almost as
an independent authority; this is the nature of circumstances. If
there is virtue in consolidating services—and if there is not, then
much of the development of the last fifty years has been mistaken—
it fails if the several branches of the local authority each goes its
separate way." To overcome this he suggested, *inter alia*, the
setting up of a " committee of carefully selected members of the
council, with the particular duty of formulating, so far as that was
necessary, long-term programmes for the decision of the council
and still more . . . of seeing that such programmes are prepared by

the various committees and of co-ordinating the plans."[16] The
recognition of the need for more co-ordination today was
indicated by the proposal by the City of Coventry to set up a
special committee for, among other purposes, greater co-ordination
of the council's work. They did this following an investigation
into their administration by the Organisation and Methods
Division of the Treasury which found, *inter alia*, that " the
outstanding feature of the corporation's organisation structure,
and indeed that of local authorities generally, . . . is the large
number of virtually self-contained departments each responsible
through its controlling committee to the council."[17]

The growth of town and country planning has facilitated and been
part of the growth of local authority co-ordination. In his study of
the need for, and methods of, achieving co-ordination in the work
of a local authority, H. R. Page recognised, in 1936, that while planning was not particularly significant in relation to co-ordination in
the organisation sense, " there is every reason to believe that co-
ordination of policy in the widest sense is inseparably bound up
with planning, and more importantly, with financial planning."[18]
By planning Mr. Page had in mind not merely the preparation of
schemes for the control of development under the 1932 Act but also
the formulation of programmes for individual municipal services
and the co-ordination of programmes for all services. To assist in
this there would need to be financial forecasting of capital expenditure to show the combined effect of individual programmes on
local authority finances. This kind of planning would assist in the
co-ordination of local authority policy by, for example, presenting a
picture of future commitments in the light of which individual
committees and the council could take decisions. As Mr. Page said
". . . it is only by the definite statement of policy and lines of
development in advance that co-ordination can be attained in any
but the minor and purely operative functions. Planning alone
makes possible co-ordinated progress."[19]

These possibilities which were visualised under the 1932 Act are
much nearer realisation today, and development plans are becoming
recognised as a means whereby local authorities can co-ordinate all
the proposed long-term capital expenditure of their different
committees, and county councils can co-ordinate that of the county
districts. In the process of making the plan authorities can prepare
their programmes of municipal expenditure, integrate their works
for the development of the town, and carry out long-term capital
budgeting and financial planning. This attitude was indicated by
the chairman of the London County Council Town Planning Committee when he stated with reference to their development plan,
envisaging an expenditure over 20 years of £27 million per annum
on municipal development, that " . . . the plan fully justified itself

if it did nothing else more than bring all the council's own proposals together and fit them into a programme instead of allowing each service to compete for any physical or technical resources that might be available."[20]

PART II

THE ECONOMICS OF DEVELOPMENT

INTRODUCTORY

We have referred above (page 10) to the economics of development as the economic framework within which development takes place. We shall describe this framework by discussing in turn the significance for development of each of the factors listed above—consumer demand, sites for development, the building industry, investment of resources and financing. Since these are all influenced by government intervention in economic life, by what we have come to call economic planning, we shall first describe the significance of this for development and land planning.

While government intervention in economic life has been going on for centuries, and economic planning took place in both world wars, peace-time economic planning on any scale was introduced only in 1947. The system then envisaged was never completely put into practice, and changes in the system that was introduced have been and are continuously taking place. It is not possible, therefore, to describe the system simply. What is attempted in Chapter 4 is an outline of the main elements in the process and machinery of economic planning since 1947 and a note of changes since then. Particular reference is made to planning for investment since this vitally affects the carrying out of development. The chapter ends by contrasting economic and land planning.

Consumer demand regulates the carrying out of development and it must be forecast at some stage in the development process. Chapter 5 introduces the nature of consumer demand, and contrasts direct and derived demand, and individual and collective demand. In connection with collective demand we discuss how the views of the final consumer are reflected in its expression, how that of different local authorities varies and how government grant influences that of local authorities. The forecasting of individual demand is touched upon. The forecasting of collective demand is closely tied up with the machinery by which decisions are taken to spend public money. This machinery is described.

To carry out works of construction a developer must have a suitable site and must employ the building and civil engineering industry, using the term in its widest sense. Chapter 6 opens with a description of the seven kinds of requirement which will affect a developer's choice of site. It is the last of these, that the price will be appropriate, which is of particular interest. The explanation of how a private developer knows what price will be appropriate leads to an explanation of economic rent in land, both rural and urban. For him to secure the site the private developer's appropriate price must be higher than what others are prepared to bid. The successful bidder secures the site, and on development will effect a change in use. A public developer finds difficulty in knowing what its appropriate price should be. When using compulsory powers of acquisition it need not bid in the market to secure the site. But on securing the site it effects a change in use. This explanation of how uses change is of significance in planning. It is taken further in Chapter 18. Chapter 7 opens by describing the four different sections of the building and civil engineering industry in its widest sense. This is a preliminary to posing the question " What limitations are likely to exist in the industry which will restrict its capacity to carry out a given programme of works? " The answer is suggested, in relation to each of the four sections of the industry, firstly, if the question is raised by the government for the country as a whole, secondly, by a local planning authority and thirdly, by an individual developer. The local planning authority would find that the availability of labour in the locality is, in general, the limiting factor. This suggests that the capacity of the industry to carry out a programme in a locality can be tested by estimating what labour is likely to be locally available. The technique of such a test is discussed.

In carrying out works on land the developer is creating capital goods, or investing. Very little investment in development would take place if the parties to the development process could not borrow money. Chapter 8 opens by describing the nature of investment, distinguishing between various kinds. The place of investment in economic life is shown, and the proportion that goes into development. The factors which influence the decision to invest are discussed, including the effect of economic planning of investment and control over it. The need for, and methods of, providing for depreciation in capital goods are introduced. Chapter 9 discusses the practice of borrowing, or obtaining finance. The common sources for borrowing money are first described and then the particular sources used by the parties to the development process, both private and public, and the periods for which they normally borrow. The factors which influence the rate of interest on loans are described and the methods of repaying long-term loans. Government control over borrowing and the rate of interest is introduced. Comparisons are made of the amount of interest paid for loans of different duration.

CHAPTER 4

ECONOMIC PLANNING AND DEVELOPMENT

Growth of Government Intervention in Economic Life—Government Economic Activity and Development—Introduction of Peace-time Economic Planning—System of Economic Planning in Britain—Publication of Economic Plans—Economic Planning and Land Planning.

Growth of Government Intervention in Economic Life

IN RETROSPECT the inter-war years seem a time of free and individual enterprise in comparison with the period during and since the recent war. In comparison they were; but there was in fact a great deal of government intervention in economic life between the wars, just as there has been in this country for centuries. In the 17th and 18th centuries, for example, when nations were struggling for international trade, governments introduced laws controlling all kinds of economic activities, in accordance with what are now called mercantile theories. In his " Wealth of Nations," published in 1776, Adam Smith, while not opposing various forms of State intervention, was attacking these theories and making a plea for free enterprise or *laisser faire* in order to increase wealth. In the middle of the 19th century, perhaps the golden age of *laisser faire* in this country, there was control over working conditions in factories and mines, State trading in the Post Office, municipal trading in gas, water and port undertakings, and restriction on building in the interest of public health. Since about then there has been a steady growth in the amount of government intervention, a growth which has been stimulated sharply by each of the two world wars and the economic crises of the inter-war years. Since the recent war the government has participated very actively in economic life, and it is not possible to discuss the economics of development without taking full account of its participation.

Government Economic Activity and Development

In its economic activity the government greatly influences in many ways, both directly and indirectly, the amount, kind and location of development which takes place. Some of these ways are in the spending of money, directly or via local authorities, on development; in affecting by taxation and the payment of subsidies the spending and saving of money by individuals and companies; in controlling the kind of development which is permitted to absorb investment resources where these are in great demand. These activities are not conceived, nor are the influences exercised, independently of each other but within the framework of a policy for the economic life of the country as a whole; in other words, within what we have come to call an economic plan. It will assist in understanding how these government activites and influences are brought to bear if the practice of economic planning in this country is first comprehended. In this chapter, therefore, we will briefly describe the process and machinery of economic planning as it has been carried out in Great Britain of recent years. This will also enable us to see to what extent the process of economic planning is related to the process of land planning.

Introduction of Peace-time Economic Planning

The object of economic planning is to " use the national resources in the best interests of the nation as a whole."[1]   It is undertaken by governments when they consider it necessary to co-ordinate the economic activities for which they are responsible, and to regulate, by deliberate policy, matters which should no longer be left solely to the interplay of economic forces. Different governments will pursue different kinds of economic planning, according to their general complexion; each will be influenced by the " economic circumstances of the country, its stage of political development, its social structure and its methods of government."[2]

In this country, a continuation of war-time economic planning after the second world war was considered by government to be necessary for a variety of reasons. The war-time Coalition Government accepted as a primary aim and responsibility the maintenance of a high and stable level of employment after the war and this, it was thought, could not be achieved without some measure of economic planning[3]; the government was deeply engaged in economic activity such as state purchasing; our economy had to be re-adapted for peace; and as the war receded our economic condition remained acute because of the problems created by the impoverishment of our capital equipment, the continuing need for armaments, the adverse balance of payments and the tendency towards inflation.

There was also after the war some growth in international economic planning. The United Kingdom, for example, is one of the sixteen West European countries which set up the Committee of European Economic Co-operation (O.E.E.C.) in June, 1947, at the request of the United States, soon after Marshall Aid was offered them. The Committee prepared the European Recovery Programme (E.R.P.) and have continued to co-operate in its implementation. There is the co-operation too in economic affairs between all the European countries who belong to U.N.O., in the European Economic Commission (E.E.C.), between the Commonwealth countries in the Colombo Plan, and between various important trading countries in the General Agreement on Tariffs and Trade (G.A.T.T.).

System of Economic Planning in Britain

While the Coalition Government in 1944 set out the general lines on which the economy of the country was to be planned after the war, it was to the Labour Government of 1945 that the task fell of preparing the plans and of attempting to carry them into effect. It was the first such administration that had ever succeeded to office in this country with a clear majority. Its policies and practices not only embraced the views of the Coalition Government, in which it had been a partner, but also the principles which the labour Party had been preparing and maturing for half a century as against the day when it would obtain power. For example, it was for full employment and the avoidance of cyclical slumps in the country's economy, of which there had been seven since the great depression of 1870; it intended to achieve a more equitable distribution of the income of the country between social classes, both by taxation and the increase of social services; it intended that there should be public and semi-public ownership of important enterprises. All these matters affected its methods of dealing with the economic conditions of the country.

In 1947 this Government described the chief elements in the system of economic planning which they were seeking to develop.[4] These were:

" (i) An organisation with enough knowledge and reliable information to assess our national resources and to formulate the national needs.

(ii) A set of economic " budgets " which relate these needs to our resources, and which enable the Government to say what is the best use for the resources in the national interest.

(iii) A number of methods, the combined effect of which will enable the Government to influence the use of resources in the desired direction, without interfering with democratic freedoms."

The system as envisaged in 1947 was never completely put into practice. With the growth of experience since then, and changes in economic conditions and in political climate, many changes have been introduced in the system that was in fact established, and changes are continuously taking place. Nonetheless in 1955 the Economic Secretary to the Treasury in the Conservative Government was still able to say that " planning " in the broad sense of the word is constantly needed by governments in order to follow the objectives of maintaining a high and stable level of investment and of keeping a close watch on the balance of payments and the international strength of our currency. He contrasted the then current economic planning with that undertaken in the country in the late 1940's by saying that the latter was " a rather more detailed planning of the activities and development of industry than we on this side of the House consider to be proper for the government to try to undertake."[5]

Because of these changes it is difficult to describe simply our system of economic planning. But our purpose will be served by describing briefly the chief elements listed above, which have continued to be its basis, and by drawing attention to the particular aspects in practice which are of importance to land planning.[6]

As the system of economic planning in this country has evolved so has the organisation for it. This is an integral part of the government machine. It was grafted on to that machine for the planning that was necessary during the recent war; and, without fundamental alteration, it has been incorporated into the Treasury in order to carry out peace-time economic planning.

(i) *A Picture of Resources and Needs.* A preliminary to the making of a plan is the collection of information and statistics which will give a comprehensive picture of the past and current economy in all its aspects: the total population, the working population and the employment it follows, the output of different industries, the pattern of national expenditure. This is done in practice by the Central Statistical Office, a part of the Treasury, which processes statistics collected from a variety of sources such as the decennial census, the censuses of production and distribution, the returns received by government departments from industrialists, local authorities and taxpayers.[7] Parallel with this picture of resources another can be drawn of the requirements and needs of each important sector of the economy. This can be derived in practice from what are called the " production " or " economic " or " sponsoring " departments of the state. Between them these departments cover all our economic life, although boundaries are not clearly drawn. Their responsibilities extend to both the private and public sectors of the economy: to the undertakings depending on private enterprise as well as on the activities of public bodies. For example, the Board of Trade has been responsible for the consumer goods and Ministry of Supply for the capital goods industries, the Ministry of Transport for roads and railways, the Ministry of Fuel and Power for coal, gas, electricity and oil, the Ministry of Works for building and civil engineering, the Ministry of Education for schools, the Ministry of Housing and Local Government for houses, local government and town planning activities, and the Ministry of Agriculture for farming, forestry and fishing.[8]

(ii) *Making the Plan.* In addition to the annual budget of government income and expenditure, statements of resources and needs, or " economic budgets," can be prepared for the different important sectors of the economy. Such budgets, for example, can relate the future working population to the number of workers required industry by industry; the estimated product in goods and services of the working population to the requirements of the total population; our prospective exports, visible and invisible, to the imports we require for consumption and production; the prospective output of the industries which produce and maintain capital goods, such as the building and civil engineering industry, to what is required and to the amount of savings that is likely to be available for investment; the prospective output in fuel and power to the domestic and industrial requirements for them. The budgets can be prepared for any period, but are usually prepared for the forthcoming year against the background of any longer term budgets, such as those for the forthcoming four years which are prepared for O.E.E.C.

These economic budgets when compared will reveal inconsistencies which make intervention by the government necessary or desirable. A prospective demand on the building and civil engineering industry which is beyond expected resources will require a decision as to which classes of building shall be permitted in preference to others; or a prospective demand for certain consumption goods, which would leave no balance of goods for export, would need to be curtailed by, for example, the imposition of a purchase tax. The striking of a balance in the budgets, and the formulation of a policy as to how it is desirable that scarce resources should be used, are the essence of making the economic plan.

As conditions have changed since 1947 there have been changes too in the matters for which economic budgets have been prepared, as a study of successive Economic Surveys will reveal. Manpower budgets, for example, were abandoned when manpower became no longer, as it was during the war, the most common factor in short supply. The financial budget of government revenue and expenditure has increased in relative importance since the government has of recent years increasingly exercised its intervention in economic affairs by financial rather than by physical means; the national income and expenditure budgets have been retained as an appropriate background to such intervention.

The work of making the plan is done in discussion and negotiation between government bodies: the Treasury, various production departments, cabinet committees of Ministers or officials and interdepartmental committees of officials.[9] Assistance is obtained in the work from numerous bodies and working parties representing consumers, trade unions, employers, industry and other interests. In particular there is the Economic Planning Board, with representatives from the Treasury, employers, Trade Unions and the government departments chiefly concerned. The Board's terms of reference were " to advise H.M. Government on the best use of our economic resources, both for the realisation of a long term plan and for remedial measures against our immediate difficulties."[10]

The key department in all this is the Treasury. Its economic staff, in co-operation with the section of the Treasury responsible for budgetary and financial affairs, helps to co-ordinate the work of the production departments by considering the various aspects of the economy as a whole, various special economic problems, the interrelationship of the different departmental programmes, the contributions of the country to the work of O.E.E.C., and N.A.T.O. The economic staff is also generally responsible for forward thinking on economic problems.

As a result of the discussions the plan is formulated. If agreement cannot be reached, if, for example, the Ministry of Transport is asking for more capital investment resources than can be allowed it, the issue goes to official or ministerial committees or perhaps to the Cabinet. The Cabinet finally agree the plan.

Our particular interest in the making of economic plans is the preparation of that part of the plan which deals with capital investment. Investment programmes were prepared for several years after the war for the country as a whole; but of recent years, as the need to restrict capital investment has lessened, programmes have been prepared more particularly for the public sector, to tie in with government plans for the spending of public money. In their preparation regard has been paid to what is happening in the private sector.

The preparation of an investment programme is approached from two directions. On the one hand an investment budget is prepared. Each of the production departments gives a statement for its sector of the economy showing past and current formation of capital investment, and also what investment its sector would like to see come about in the following two years. There is also estimated, using departmental or other expert sources, the investment output of different kinds that is likely with current resources. This is based on past performance with any adjustments that are considered necessary in the light of known events and trends. For investment by the building and civil engineering industry, for example, the capacity of the labour force that is likely to exist is estimated, and also any limitation that will be imposed by any estimated scarcity of critical building materials such as steel, softwood, cement or bricks. On the other hand there is also estimated the amount of savings that is likely to be available for investment, an amount which is very sensitive to the taxation policy of the government and which can be supplemented by the government from budget surpluses.

With such a picture of requirements, trends in investment output, capacity of the industries concerned and the amount of savings that will be available, a programme can be formulated in the light of economic conditions, needs and policy.

In addition to preparing the annual investment programme those concerned have also taken a continuing interest in the working out of programmes by different industries for their development. These programmes may look forward for several years. (See Chapter 20).

(iii) *Implementation of Economic Plans.* The techniques of preparing economic plans are fairly common in different countries; it is in the methods of implementing their plans that governments of different countries and times will vary most.[11] In Great Britain the current government's attitude seems much the same as that of 1947 which stated:

" Under democracy the execution of the economic plan must be much more a matter for co-operation between the Government, industry and the people, than of rigid application by the State of controls and compulsions. The Government must lay down the economic tasks for the nation; it must say which things are the most important and what the objectives of policy should be, and should give as much information as possible to guide the nation's economic activity; it must use its powers of economic control to influence the course of development in the desired direction. When the working pattern has thus been set, it is only by the combined effort of the whole people that the nation can move towards its objective of carrying out the first things first, and so make the best use of its economic resources.[12]

Following this policy a variety of methods have been used by post-war governments to influence economic activities in the directions indicated by the plan. For example, in addition to regulating their own expenditure they have limited the capital expenditure of all *ad hoc* bodies and local authorities, and a large part of the revenue expenditure of local authorities, and have influenced the general policy and expenditure of the public corporations. By taxation and subsidies they have influenced private spending on consumption goods and services, and the amount of saving that has been possible out of personal incomes. They have raised enough taxes to provide budget surpluses which have been used to finance capital investment for which there would otherwise have been insufficient savings.

Through the production departments the government have also influenced the various sectors of the economy by acquainting trades unions, industrialists and others of the general objectives of the plan as regards their industry.

They have used controls under which sanction is needed for certain economic activities, a sanction which has been given with regard to government policy and planning. The controls were a continuation, under regulation or statute, of those introduced during the last war. Of these some, but not many, were abandoned in 1945, and there has been a steady relaxation since of others. With the relaxation of these physical controls there has been an increasing reliance by the present government on the use of the Bank Rate and restriction of credit.

Publication of Economic Plans

It is not possible in this country to find a detailed account of any central economic plan. There is, however, some broad guide given annually in the Economic Surveys published by the government in March or April of each year; and in the Budget speech of the Chancellor of the Exchequer each April and at other times.

The Economic Survey does not take a standard form, but attempts each year to do much the same thing. It reviews progress in economic affairs since the previous survey, discusses the major economic problems that have emerged, discusses the prospects of the coming year and problems of production, exports, imports, investment, consumption, financial policy and defence, and outlines the particular changes and trends that are required to promote the aims of economic policy, defining general objectives. It outlines the government's own proposed action, other than in fiscal matters, to achieve the objectives, insofar as it has control over economic affairs. It also suggests the general action required of people in the large sector of private enterprise which exists in the economy.

In his Budget speech, which is made primarily to obtain Parliament's approval to proposed government expenditure and taxation, the Chancellor takes the opportunity of reviewing the economic situation and prospects for the whole of the economy. In this there is a great difference from pre-war days when the Chancellor would deal mainly with the problems of central government expenditure and revenue. This is an indication of the change in government responsibilities and of the Budget's character.

Throughout the year specific aspects of the plan, the raising of loans for public corporations, the amount of road building that is being permitted, the relaxing of particular controls, will come in for Parliamentary debate.

Economic Planning and Land Planning

Economic planning and land planning are distinct processes, as a description of some of the differences between them will emphasise. Economic plans are drawn up by central government on a broad national scale; land plans are prepared by local government and primarily on the local scale, although national considerations are incorporated in them. The objectives of economic plans are primarily economic and social; those of land plans include the economic but are wider. Economic plans are drawn up for the short term and are reviewed at short intervals; land plans are drawn up for a generation ahead and are reviewed at longer intervals. A government cannot ensure the complete implementation of economic plans; planning authorities have comparatively effective means of implementation. Economic plans are not incorporated in formal documents; land plans are summarised in maps and documents which follow lines laid down in statute and regulation. There is no formal machinery whereby an individual or public body can appeal to higher authority against any decisions made by central government in the interests of economic planning; there is formal machinery for appeal against a local authority's land planning decisions. There is no code of compensation for interests injuriously affected by economic planning decisions, although compensation is sometimes paid, but there is such a code for injury to property rights through land planning decisions. In short we have a comprehensive system of long term land planning within a very much looser system of short term economic planning.

It is possible for either economic or land planning to be carried out without the other in a particular country, but where they are both present the practice of the one will affect that of the other. Land planning machinery, for example, may facilitate the collection of statistics to be used in economic planning or the summation of local needs and requirements for capital investment resources in new development, and may help in securing that such investment is efficient and not wasteful. The decisions taken in economic planning will certainly affect the practice and technique of land planning. This can be illustrated by referring to some of the effects of changes in economic planning over the past few years on certain aspects of development plan preparation. In doing this it is not possible to divorce from the changes in economic planning the alterations in economic conditions which have led to these changes.

Firstly, as economic planning has been relaxed so has the collection of certain statistics, which were necessary for this planning, been abandoned by government. Local planning authorities, and others, are therefore less well informed about, for example, the current activities of the building industry, the distribution of the civilian population and of their shopping habits. Secondly, with the abandonment of licensing there also goes the selection of priorities among different kinds of development. Planning authorities may need therefore to plan in the short term for such development as cinemas, luxury flats, commercial buildings, private enterprise housing which, because of licensing policy, they had previously provided for in the later stage of their plans. Some of these kinds of newly released development present problems for the planning authorities which are different from those faced in the initial plans. In planning for private enterprise housing, for example, they cannot, as they could for local authority housing, obtain from the housing authorities a fairly complete picture of where the housing is likely to go, and of the total number of people for whom the housing is to be provided. They are in contrast faced with the need to consider many more housing developers and to budget for the fact that these developers will build dwellings as long as they can find and secure building land which they are permitted to use, and can obtain customers from wherever they may come. Thirdly, as economic controls have been relaxed so has, too, the degree of Board of Trade control over the location of new industrial buildings. Planning authorities are therefore no longer as assured as they were that the Board will operate its controls in the interests of proper location of industry and thereby retard the growth of certain towns or stimulate the growth of others.

CHAPTER 5

CONSUMER DEMAND

Needs, Wants, Desires and Consumer Demand—The Developer and Demand—Direct and Derived Demand—Nature of Individual Demand—Nature of Collective Demand—Collective Demand for Development and the Final Consumer—Varying Collective Demand of Local Authorities for their Services—Government Grants and Government Collective Demand for Local Authority Services—Forecasting Individual Demand—Forecasting Collective Demand—Central Government Spending—Local Authority Spending—Spending by ad hoc *Bodies.*

Needs, Wants, Desires and Consumer Demand

HUMAN beings have a great many needs, wants and desires. While people have much in common in this way, these needs, wants and desires will vary among individuals and, in any community, among the different sections and classes, depending, for example, on the economic and social development of the particular society or class, its education, traditions, opportunities, standards and culture.

Some of these needs, wants and desires are satisfied when individuals, or parents or guardians on behalf of families, elect to spend their money for the purpose. Others, a considerable and growing amount today, are satisfied on behalf of groups of individuals by some public or semi-public body which is nominated or elected for the purpose of *inter alia* spending the group's money collectively on its behalf. A father buying a house for his family is an example of the first of these; a local authority building a school, or traffic road or town hall, are examples of the second.

The satisfaction of all their wants, needs and desires, whether by individual or collective spending, is beyond the purse of most people. They must, therefore, select those on which to spend money. The quantity of goods and services that will be paid for at certain prices, in order to satisfy wants, needs and desires, economists call economic, effective or consumer demand. We will use the term consumer demand; and according to whether the spending will be individual or collective we will call it individual or collective consumer demand.

The Developer and Demand

Production in economic life is concerned only with consumer demand; that is with the goods and services for which people will pay either individually or collectively. In the words of Keynes, " Consumption—to repeat the obvious—is the sole end and object of economic activity."[1] More people than possess them would like to own television sets, motor cars and refrigerators, but industrialists are concerned to provide only the quantity that will be bought.

Consumer demand regulates in this way the carrying out of development. People need shelter and most families would like a home of their own; but developers can be relied on to provide only the dwellings that will be paid for. This is obviously so of private developers who build for profit. It is less obvious, but also true, when local authorities build houses. They will do so only if the costs will be covered jointly by the individual demand of the tenants and the collective demand of themselves and the state which are expressed in the payment of housing subsidies. It is least obvious but again true when the demand is entirely collective. No traffic road is built, for example, until the highway authority, Ministry of Transport and Treasury elect to spend money in satisfying the need for it.

Direct and Derived Demand

Either individual or collective consumer demand for development may come direct from the ultimate consumer or may be derived from his demand. Direct demand arises for consumption goods or, more precisely, for goods yielding consumption services, such as houses, swimming baths, cinemas, car parks, schools, churches and hospitals. The consumer demand for them is direct; the consumer will pay directly for the enjoyment of the services offered by the development, and the developer in estimating demand must directly consider the consumer. Derived consumer demand for development arises for producers' goods, such as factories, gas works, offices, shops or warehouses. In such cases the ultimate consumer is interested not in the space provided by the development but in the goods or services that can be produced with it. The gauging of this ultimate demand for consumption goods will be carried out by the industrialist, trader or business man, as the case might be; and from this a demand for development will be derived.

Nature of Individual Demand

The consumer demand of any individual or family depends in the first instance on the total money resources out of which their needs, wants and desires can be paid for; that is on their money income or capital resources after unavoidable outgoings such as taxation have been met. Secondly, it depends on the way in which they elect to spend their money. Just what decides how much of a given income will be spent on consumption rather than saved, where essential needs stop and non-essential desires and wants come in, and which goods and services will be bought, are subjective matters which are difficult to analyse. The pattern of spending by families earning the same total income can be very different. Tobacco may appear particularly important to one father, a car to another and his children's school fees to a third.

Nature of Collective Demand

Collective consumer demand depends also, in the first instance, on the amount of money resources available for spending by public bodies. These resources are not, however, always limited by a fixed income. While for individuals demand must flow from given resources, it is possible for public bodies to decide upon expenditure first and then levy taxes or rates to match. They must notwithstanding have regard to the amounts of taxes or rates that they can reasonably collect; and sometimes will determine expenditure after deciding upon the income that they will raise, as do local authorities when practising rate stabilisation whereby proposed expenditure is geared to an income which will flow from a predetermined rate in the £. Collective spending differs from individual spending also in the kind of goods and services on which it takes place. Collective spending has grown up in modern society, and is provided for in law, because it has been found necessary to satisfy certain wants, needs and desires in this way. The result is that although there is considerable overlap, the kind of wants, needs and desires that are satisfied by collective spending differ broadly from those which are satisfied by individual spending; and money collected in rates and taxes will be spent on different things than if it had been left in the pockets of ratepayers and taxpayers. It is possible to broadly classify the kind of development on which collective spending takes place under three heads:

(a) *Direct Governmental Functions.* The government of the country is responsible through certain departments of state for development connected with defence, the administration of government and enforcement of law. For example, the service departments will build naval docks, drill halls, aerodromes, service training grounds, the Ministry of Works the office buildings for all civil and revenue departments and the Home Office the prisons.

(b) *Public Monopoly Trading.* Under this head is included the development carried out for the purpose of monopoly trading by the government, by for example the Post Office; by local authorities, for example, for transport services, harbours, docks, piers and water supply; by public corporations (except regional hospital boards), representative trusts and public utility companies as described in Chapter 1.[2]

Whatever the differences in constitution of these bodies they have a common purpose: the provision of goods or services which are essential in order to maintain a certain standard of living in the country, and which it has been decided by Parliament are best carried on as a public or semi-public monopoly.

(c) *The Social Services.* In this third category are included the provision of all kinds of educational facilities, from nursery school to university, the health facilities of the regional hospital boards and the non-trading services of local authorities, including town and country planning itself. These can be described as part of the social services of the country: those services provided by public authorities for the purpose of improving the welfare, health or education of the population, either by improving the environment or by contributing directly to the needs of the individual.

Certain local and central government services do not sit very happily within this classification; housing, for example, is as much a trading as social service, and roads are used for industry and trade as well as leisure. But the classification will do for our purpose.

Collective Demand for Development and the Final Consumer

The collective demand for development which is expressed by the undertakings responsible for all kinds of public monopoly trading is an example of derived demand. The undertaking will gauge the final demand (that is of the ultimate consumers) for their goods or services and derive their own demand for development from this. The final demand will depend upon prices; and prices are usually fixed to cover average costs of production over a period.[3] If the final consumers cannot bear the total cost, or it is decided by Parliament that they should not, part will be spread on to taxpayers or ratepayers.

Since the final consumers in monopoly trading undertakings can indicate their views only in a limited way through their pockets, their interests are protected in other ways. Municipal trading undertakings are subject to the control of both the local electorate and of the government.[4] Public corporations have more autonomy, but they are subject to directions from the appropriate Minister, to the provisions in their statutes and to the scrutiny by Parliament of their annual reports and accounts.

Those corporations which receive their capital from, or are subsidised out of, Government funds have their affairs debated in Parliament when authority is sought to find money for them (see page 113 and page 284). With regard to those corporations " whose annual receipts are not wholly or mainly derived from moneys provided by Parliament or advanced from the Exchequer," the Government has set up a Select Committee of the House to keep Parliament better informed of their aims, policies, practices and problems.[5] The final consumer's point of view is also represented to the corporations in the machinery of the consumers' councils. For the coal industry there is an industrial and a domestic coal consumers' council; for each gas and electricity board there is a consultative council; for transportation there are transport consultative committees and also a transport tribunal. These councils consider matters connected with the industry which are referred to them by consumers, or such matters in connection with consumers which are referred to them by the boards. In effect, they act in liaison between the two sides, and act as watchdogs over the consumers' needs. For example, revisions in transport charges are suggested by the transport commission to the transport tribunal who hold inquiries into objections from interested persons and have power to confirm or reject the revision. It is not claimed that the views of consumers are completely represented in this way by consumers' councils, but their establishment is an indication of the problem that exists and is an attempt to solve it.

Where central or local government expresses a demand for development for the purposes of administration, law, defence or the social services, it is an example of direct demand. While these governments are democratically elected, they do not make their decisions as to spending in consultation with their electorate, or with those who are taxed to provide their income. Decisions as to central government development, for example, are made by the Cabinet and Parliament in the public interest with an eye to national administration and national budgeting; and these express direct consumer demand for the development. While governments are politically sensitive to the views and wishes of the people, they do not ask them directly whether they are willing to purchase out of their incomes, at certain prices, government offices, aerodromes, parks, bridges or prisons;[6] nor do they normally take into account in levying rates and taxes the benefit that particular individuals will derive from particular spending. Rural district councils do take this into account, however, when making assessments for special rates. These are levied over parts of the rural area to meet certain classes of expenditure, as for example on drainage or coast protection which render local benefits.

Varying Collective Demand of Local Authorities for their Services

There is great variation in the collective demand of different local authorities for their services and facilities. Firstly, authorities are not compelled to provide all the social services that they do, since some of their powers are permissive and they can elect to use them or not. Secondly, even where the provision of services is mandatory the amount of expenditure in practice is very much a matter of local initiative. Within the legal and financial framework set up by government, expenditure by a local authority for different services will depend upon many things, such as the amount of its potential income, the debt it has incurred in the past, the burdens it has inherited from the past, the political complexions of the elected members, the authority's quality and tradition in municipal affairs, its efficiency and that of its officers, the pressing needs of its people. The question of why the level of expenditure of different county borough councils varies so much from place to place was investigated by J. R. and U. K. Hicks in 1943.[7] They found that spending (measured as rates per head of population) was related not only to the local authority's policy on spending but also to its wealth (measured as the yield of a 1d. rate per head of population). It was possible to classify most of the county boroughs in the following way:

(1) Seaside resorts and big spenders who had high rate yields and high expenditure.

(2) Cathedral towns and other towns (called middling stinters) which had large rate yields and low expenditure.

(3) Poor towns, with low rate yields, some of which spent highly (poor spenders) and others who did not spend much (poor stinters).

Government Grants and Government Collective Demand for Local Authority Services

Government departments share the cost of certain local services with the local authorities by way of a specific grant, one paid towards the cost of particular services. In Part III below are examples of such grants which are made towards the cost of carrying out development. In consequence the department in question is a party to the demand for these services. It is a very important party since few authorities could afford to build traffic roads, or re-develop for housing or build schools, if Government participation by grant were not forthcoming.

Departments do not merely participate in expressing the demand; they may influence it drastically by making the payment of grants subject to conditions which prescribe a minimum standard in the quality of the service which is to be provided. These conditions may be laid down in an Act, as in the Housing Act, etc., 1923, which stipulated the minimum sizes for local authority houses if they were to attract subsidy; or in regulations under statute, as in the Ministry of Education regulations on school requirements which prescribe the minimum size for sites of schools of different kinds, and of their playgrounds and playing fields; or in advisory memoranda as in the post-war housing manuals and road construction memoranda which show the standard of designs to which Ministers will expect adherence if a project is to be accepted for grant.

In general, while authorities will have some regard to the total cost of a service, they are primarily interested in the amount that will fall on the rates after grant has been deducted (see Chapter 11). The more the grant the cheaper to the rates and, in general, the greater will be the authority's demand for the service in question. Because of this the Government is able, by providing generous grants, to stimulate the demand by authorities for certain services, or to create a demand by authorities which would otherwise not exist. Without the grants under the Town and Country Planning Act, 1947, for example, there would have been very little comprehensive re-development of war-damaged central areas.

Different kinds of specific grant will have different effects on local authority demand. Percentage grants, for example, such as those paid for roads, may encourage extravagant schemes since the government will bear a fixed proportion of the expense; and often a high proportion. But even such grants do not encourage the prolific spending which arose out of the short-lived scheme for housing subsidy under the Housing, Town Planning, etc., Act of 1919, where local authorities were responsible only for the loss up to an amount equal to the product of 1d. rate, the Exchequer bearing the remainder. Unit grants, on the other hand, stimulate output while encouraging economy since any excess cost over the assumed unit price must be found by the authority. An example is the standard subsidy for dwellings under the Housing Acts, 1946-52. A fixed amount is paid for each house or flat, irrespective of its size or cost, and any excess cost must be met either by the rates or the tenants.[8]

Grants policy can have a stimulating effect on the speed of development. In 1926 the Government announced that contributions towards the cost of houses built under the Housing, etc., Act, 1923, would fall from £6 to £4 for houses completed after the 30th September, 1927; and from £9 to £7 10s. for houses under the Housing (Financial Provisions) Act, 1924, which were not completed by this date. This had the effect of speeding up local authority demand for houses in the early part of 1927.[9]

The Housing Acts provide an example, it has been suggested, of government grant influencing the kind of dwelling provided by some housing authorities, since under the current housing subsidy scheme the flat subsidy makes the building of flats financially more attractive under certain circumstances to authorities than the building of houses [10] (see page 168).

One of the drawbacks of the specific grant is that it does not differentiate between the poorer and wealthier authorities. It is simpler for Bournemouth or Bristol, for example, to find 40 per cent of the cost of a new Class II road, or the rate contribution towards the cost of a house, than it is for Jarrow or Merthyr Tydfil. This is one of the reasons for the payment of exchequer equalisation grants, those made in aid of the general, not specific, expenditure of the poorer authorities, that is those county and county borough councils whose rateable value per head of " weighted " population is less than the average rateable value per head of " weighted " population in the country. In effect, the Government becomes a ratepayer of such an authority, paying its rate on the amount of rateable value necessary to bring its rateable value per head of " weighted " population of the authority up to the national average. The weighted population is obtained by adding to total population the number of children under 15 and, in those counties in which the population per mile of road is less than 70, one third of the additional population required to bring the figure up to 70.[11] By giving such special grants to the poorer authorities, the government has made it possible for them to spend more. They are able to spend the money on those services which they select, and many services which receive no specific grant may thus in effect be grant-aided by the exchequer equalisation grant.

Additional assistance to authorities in need, leading to an increase in their demand, is also given by special formula specific grants. An example was the grant offered, towards comprehensive re-development of areas of bad layout or obsolete development, under the Town and Country Planning Acts, 1947. This was calculated as a percentage of the loss involved; but the actual percentage was higher for the poorer authorities, and any authority, other than those entitled to the maximum percentage, was entitled to an additional grant if its re-development cost it more than a 6d. rate. (See Chapter 15.)

Forecasting Individual Demand

Since consumer demand regulates the carrying out of development, developers are faced with a need to forecast demand at some stage in the development process. Their problem differs according to whether the demand is individual or collective, direct or derived: and to whether they are building in speculation for unknown customers, or by contract for known customers.

The problems and techniques of forecasting individual demand for development, both direct and derived, are among the most complex in economics and can only be mentioned here. For the purpose economists might employ, *inter alia*, market research of consumers' tastes and preferences, business barometers, that is charts of indices, whose movements are considered to be indicative of impending economic changes in general business conditions on the basis that historical patterns reproduce themselves;[12] analyses of statistical trends in population growth, age, sex structure and migration; analyses of past patterns of spending; studies of the national and local economy and of trends in wages and salaries. For example, in estimating the amount of shopping required in the centre of new towns, economists might estimate the expected number of households; estimate from statistical data that these will have certain incomes and would spend a certain proportion of this in the new centre, in a manner which followed records of past consumption expenditure; and from this arrive at the number of different kinds of shops that would be needed to handle the estimated turnover in conditions where there was freedom of choice for customers and a reasonable living for shopkeepers.[13] For estimating the expected demand for housing in a locality at a future date American economists would compare (a) the estimated number of households that would be in existence at that date, classified by the rents or prices that they would be assumed to be able to afford or willing to pay, with (b) the estimated number of dwellings that will then exist, differentiated according to rental value. The number of households would be estimated by demographic means, and the rents or prices that they would pay by reference to the economy of the area and its employment and income potentialities. The estimated number of dwellings and their rental value would be derived from a survey of the existing stock of dwellings and its rental value, quality and occupancy, and expected changes in it through demolitions, conversions, rehabilitations, depreciation and obsolescence.[14]

This kind of estimate of housing demand differs in one important respect at least from the kind of estimates of housing need contained in the majority of development plans. In these plans there is estimated the total amount of new housing that would be needed over the period of the plan if dwellings were provided for the estimated increase of population (both by excess of births over deaths and by immigration) and for the accommodation of people to be displaced by a certain programme of re-development for slum clearance, new roads, etc. Thus the plan estimates are of need as opposed to demand, and little account is taken of the well-recognised likelihood that not all the families that will need dwellings in an area will be able to afford them. All will not be able to afford the increase above the current controlled level of rents which will result from charging rents based on current construction and land acquisition costs, even when these rents are subsidised by the government and local authorities; and fewer would be able to afford the rents were no subsidy payable.

Whereas economists for such estimates depend on consumer surveys and statistics, surveyors and others connected with the property market obtain a knowledge of demand for development more directly through their dealings with all aspects of the development process, and with the exchange and letting of property, and from their interpretation of observed changes in property values.

Their knowledge is essentially local rather than global, as is the economist's; and they are in touch with the derived demand of the developer as well as the final demand of the consumer.

Forecasting Collective Demand

The collective demand of a public body for development is usually satisfied by the body itself carrying out the development, so that its problem in forecasting is to gauge whether it, and any other public body which will participate in the development, will elect to spend money on the development at some time in the future. In gauging this it must, when its demand is derived from individual consumer demand for its products, as is the collective demand for gas works or collieries from the expected individual demand for gas or coal, also forecast individual demand.[15] We shall not discuss this here. But to understand how a public body forecasts its own demand it is necessary to know something of the machinery by which decisions are taken to spend public money.

Central Government Spending

Government spending is always made out of the Consolidated Fund, also called the Exchequer Account, the government's bank account at the Bank of England. Such spending may be of two kinds. It may be on the Consolidated Fund Services, when the payments are authorised by statute to be made periodically, and are not debated annually in Parliament: payments on the National Debt, to the Northern Ireland Exchequer, to the Queen's Civil List, to judges and other high officers of independent standing, to New Town Development Corporations for capital works, for compensation under Parts I and V of the Town and Country Planning Act, 1954. Of more importance to us is the spending on the Supply Services. This makes up the major part of government expenditure: £3,809 million in 1953-54 out of a total of £4,447 million, of which £1,497 million went on defence.[16] It has to be authorised annually by Parliament, and it is the machinery of so doing which will be described.

During each year each department of state prepares its estimates of expenditure for the forthcoming financial year, and also more tentative estimates for two years beyond then, and about November submits them to the Treasury. The estimates are subdivided into votes and the votes again into heads and subheads.

In the Treasury the individual sections of the estimates are examined critically. Changes without good reason from previous years may be queried, or the need for the expenditure at all, or its desirability if it does not conform to what the Treasury consider to be government policy.

The Treasury also have regard to the total amount of the estimates in the light of the revenue that will be asked for in the forthcoming budget. Cuts in estimates and postponement in expenditure may therefore be suggested. If the departments and the Treasury, or their Ministers, cannot agree on any points these are taken to the Cabinet and there settled.

The estimates are then published in the form shown by the following extract:

Class V, 1. *G*.1.—*Grants to Local Authorities under the Town and Country Planning Act,* 1947

	1952-53 £	1951-52 £
Grants in respect of:—		
(a) The acquisition and clearing of land for comprehensive re-development and of derelict land ...	260,000	240,000
(b) Compensation payable under Parts VII and VIII of the Act and loss incurred in the acquisition and clearing of land other than that referred to in (a) (Section 94 of the Act)	30,000	28,000
(c) Certain contributions and compensation payable by local authorities under the Town and Country Planning Acts, 1932 and 1943 (Section 96 of the Act of 1947)	10,000	10,000
Total ...	£300,000	£278,000

Source: *Civil Estimates and Estimates for Revenue Departments,* 1952-53 (H.M.S.O.), Class V, page 16.

At the end of February or early in March of the following year the estimates are presented to the House, by their respective Ministers for the defence services and by the Financial Secretary to the Treasury on behalf of other departments. The whole House goes into Committee of Supply to consider and vote the estimates; the need to vote each section of them is the reason for the sections being called votes.

Because of the size of the Committee and the detailed nature of the votes, it is not possible for them to be considered in detail. The debates are in fact on government policy. A motion to reduce a vote by a nominal sum is the Opposition's customary way of criticising the government. A small committee, the Select Committee on Estimates, therefore concurrently goes into certain of the estimates in more detail. They publish reports which include the Minutes of the Evidence that goes before them.

Before the close of the financial year the Committee of Ways and Means will agree certain of the expenditure in the estimates. The House will pass a Consolidated Fund Act authorising the expenditure, and the necessary money will be issued to the departments. The financial year is opened by the Chancellor's Budget speech wherein, among other things, his proposals for raising revenue to meet the estimates are announced. The Financial Statement which is issued at the same time compares these with the government's receipts and expenditure for the past year.

The Committee of Supply will consider all the estimates by the end of July and, when the votes are agreed, authority will be given for their spending in the Appropriation Act. Schedule B of this Act lists all the departmental votes that have been agreed, appropriating money to specific services. This follows the form of the published estimates but is not in quite as much detail.

Parliament thus appropriates expenditure to specific votes and a department cannot spend more on a particular matter than its vote without obtaining a supplementary vote. Civil departments cannot transfer money saved from one vote to meet excess expenditure on another, but Service departments can do so temporarily with Treasury sanction. All departments can transfer between subheads of votes, but only with Treasury sanction. This sanction is not needed only for such transfer. Despite the Appropriation Act, or statutory authority for spending on a Consolidated Fund Service, Treasury agreement may be needed during the financial year for any action requiring or affecting government expenditure for it is " now established constitutional practice that departments must seek Treasury approval, whenever in the year the necessity arises, for every new item of expenditure, for any new service, for any change in policy which involves increases in expenditure, or for any variations in the conditions on which expenditure may originally have been authorised."[17] For example, the Ministry of Housing and Local Government will obtain a vote for housing subsidies which it can pay without specific sanction since the liability is a clear one. But on its vote for grants towards re-development under the Town and Country Planning Act, 1947, it needs Treasury sanction in particular cases, where the expenditure is likely to be heavy, since the liability in the vote is not an apparent one; and the Ministry of Transport need specific sanction for expenditure above a certain amount on particular road schemes.

The Treasury's overriding control of the expenditure of spending departments, " the restriction of expenditure to no greater sum than is required for the purpose in view, and the ensuring that the fullest return is obtained for the money expended,"[18] makes for overlapping between their activities and those of other departments. Where Treasury control should stop short of curtailing the proper responsibilities of a department is, in practice, a delicate matter, in regard to which no clear statement of functions exists.

Local Authority Spending

The administrative counties outside London must each year prepare estimates of their expenditure in order to precept upon the county district councils.[19] The rating authorities are not, however, compelled by law to prepare such estimates. They must, however, levy a rate each year for the money they need to cover their estimated expenditure for the forthcoming year, or to meet contingencies, or to pay for past deficiencies, or to provide a working balance; and they cannot levy a rate in excess of these requirements for the year.[20] So that they may know just what rate to levy, the authorities are in practice annually compelled to prepare estimates of expected income from sources other than rates, and of expenditure in the forthcoming year for each particular service, taking into account the debt charges on past loans and also the prospective expenditure in running and maintaining their various services. In effect, therefore, they are compelled to prepare municipal budgets, which are the expression of their collective demand for services to be paid for out of rates in the coming year.

There is no standard form of budget in use. It would not normally deal with the large trading undertakings, although separate budgets might be prepared for them; but it might include items for those non-monopoly undertakings, such as cemeteries, which are subsidised out of the rates. Most authorities deal only with revenue and expenditure over the forthcoming year, but some prepare also a capital budget, that is a programme of capital expenditure for one or more years.

There is no uniform practice in preparing the necessary estimates. Spending departments might prepare them with or without the co-operation of the treasurer; or a special committee might do so, made up of representatives of the finance committee and of the chairmen and other members of spending committees.

There is also no uniform practice in the exercise of control by the finance committee, or treasurer, over the spending of departments. In some authorities there is control akin to that of the Treasury in central government spending while in others there is not.

Municipal budgets do not need central government approval, but much of the spending is subject to the very wide supervisory powers that central government has over local government. This in part comes from the need of authorities to obtain approval to grant earning expenditure, as described above; and also from their need to obtain central government sanction for the raising of loans required to finance capital expenditure (see page 108).

Spending by ad hoc *Bodies*

The machinery of spending by *ad hoc* bodies is very much simpler than that of central or local government. Public corporations, for example, on the whole carry on their business and make their decisions as to spending like any other large undertaking which is run by a board and has no shareholders; but they are subject to certain restrictions because of parliamentary and ministerial control. There is a limit to their capital expenditure since there is a statutory limit to the amount that they can incur in debt at any one time both on temporary and permanent loan; they must prepare capital expenditure programmes for approval of the appropriate Minister; and their programmes will perhaps be discussed in Parliament when the Minister presents a Board's annual report and accounts or a Bill seeking fresh powers or money for it. On the whole they are free to spend within their programme and debt limit as they wish, but the Coal Board and New Town Development Corporations are subject to additional departmental and parliamentary scrutiny since their borrowing is entirely from the government (Chapter 17).

The representative trusts and public utility companies are not uniform in their spending practice; but in general this is similar to that described for the public corporations.

CHAPTER 6

SELECTION AND SECURING OF SITES

Land in Economics—Selection of Sites for Development of Different Kinds—Economic Rent in Land—Rent in Agricultural Land—Rent in Urban Land—Rent, Change in Land Use and the Private Developer—Change of Use Without Constructional Works—Rent, Change in Land Use and the Public Developer—Public Developers and Market Price of Land—Rent as a Cost not a Surplus.

Land in Economics

IN ECONOMICS the land includes the " material and the forces which Nature gives freely for man's aid, in land and water, in air and light and heat."[1] Among these varied resources are the soil, seas, mines and rivers. In its broadest sense development might take place on any part of the *terra firma* on which people can live; and it is this part of the land with which we are here concerned, for it provides sites, that is land for development.

Selection of Sites for Development of Different Kinds

When a developer is faced with the need to consider what land is available for his particular development, and which of alternative sites he would prefer to use, there are at least seven different requirements which will affect his choice. These are briefly that the area of the site will be appropriate; that it will have the right kind of physical characteristics for the proposed development; that it will have the necessary utility services; that it will be suitably located in relation to environment, transportation services and existing and proposed development; that the right to use it for development can be obtained; that any restrictions imposed on its use by the rights and privileges of others, or by public authorities, will not prohibit its use for the desired purpose; and that the price will be appropriate. This applies whether the site is agricultural land, one covered with buildings which will need to be pulled down, or one which is derelict through, for example, gravel extraction.

From the land which is available the ideal site satisfying all requirements can rarely be found, particularly where, as in growing towns, there is limited land and many competing demands for it. In selecting sites, therefore, the developer must usually compromise on his requirements. Different developers will compromise on different requirements, since each will attach most importance to different things. The industrialist, for example, requires plenty of land and is prepared to sacrifice location in order to get it; the retail trader can rarely sacrifice on location but must have his site on the right spot.

Our main concern here is with price, and how it is judged whether this is appropriate or not. All the other requirements, however, have a direct bearing on the appropriateness of the price to the developer and it will first be necessary to consider them briefly.

(a) *Area.* The acreage required by different developers will vary enormously with the kind of development proposed. The units of different kinds of development require sites of differing sizes: the typical small house will take up perhaps one-tenth or one-fifteenth of an acre, a primary school might need four acres, a particular factory five acres and a hospital 20 acres. The number of units in different schemes of development will vary. Housing, for example, is composed of a large number of small units, and will require the greatest proportion of all developed land in any town; and hospitals, with a small number of large units, will have a small proportion. The acreage required for certain kinds of development, housing or offices for example, will depend not only on the size and number of units but also on the density of building.

(b) *Physical Characteristics.* The physical characteristics of sites required by different developers are not identical. Undulating fertile land with porous subsoil on the south side of a hill will attract the housing authority; flat land will attract the industrialist; rough, broken and well wooded land will attract the park authority. All developers prefer to avoid sites on which it is difficult to carry out works through, for example, their being in a derelict state or being covered with buildings which must be first demolished.

(c) *Public Utilities.* Most developers require that some or all of the public utility services are available, or can be made available, on their sites: gas, electricity, water and drainage. Some are more demanding than others. House builders in the country will proceed with only electricity and water and sometimes with neither; an industrialist may require thousands of gallons of water a day, with appropriate sewerage facilities, as well as gas and electricity.

(d) *Location in Relation to Environment, Transportation Services and Existing and Proposed Establishments.* Locations which suit one developer will not suit another. A site for housing, for example, would normally be preferred when it has a pleasant environment, is near other housing and is convenient for work, shopping, school and entertainment; it would be required that a primary school site be near the homes of the children who are to use it; a factory site would be preferred when it is near the dwellings of possible work-people, and is well served by transport services; a site for shops in a neighbourhood is preferred when it is easily and quickly accessible by foot to all the dwellings in the area which the shops are expected to serve; a site for shops in a central area is preferred when it is well situated in relation to bus stations, car parks and main streams of local traffic.

(e) *Legal Right to Develop.*   To carry out development it is first necessary to acquire the legal right to occupy and use the site for the purpose; that is to acquire a freehold or leasehold interest in it.[2] But the acquisition of such rights does not mean that the developer can carry out any development he chooses.

The freeholder of land can do what he likes with it, and all that is on, under and over it, subject to any restrictions imposed by public authorities and the rights and privileges of others. Examples of such rights and privileges which can restrict the use and development sites are: (1) Owners of adjoining land may have a right to the support of their land, and to the water which flows in natural and defined streams through their land not being interrupted, diverted, unreasonably reduced, dammed or polluted. (2) Owners of nearby land may have easements over the site, that is the right to use it, or to restrict the use of it, by way of a right of light, private right of way or right of support to buildings. (3) A site may be subject to a restrictive covenant which prohibits, for example, the erection of houses of less than a certain size or cost, or of certain kinds of buildings which might cause a nuisance. (4) The public may have the right to walk over the land, and do have the right to fly aircraft over it, a formidable right today. (5) Owners of underground minerals, both private and public, may have the right in their workings to endanger the stability of the surface, and may so inhibit development altogether.[3]

Where these rights and privileges would restrict the possibilities of development it may be possible to overcome them. Those under (1) and (2), for example, can often be suspended by payment of money to the person owning the right; restrictive covenants under (3) can be set aside where they are outmoded; public rights of way under (4) can often be extinguished on the offer of suitable alternative ways. Public developers have greater opportunities of overcoming the impediment to development of such rights and privileges than have private ones (see page 145).

Instead of a freehold the developer can acquire a leasehold interest in the land whereby on payment of an annual rent, or premium plus annual rent, he obtains exclusive possession of the land for a period and, by building lease, the right to carry out certain development. Only a lessee who has a lease of sufficient length will be prepared to undertake development; in this country he normally expects at least 75 to 99 years. The land would still be subject to the kind of rights and privileges just described; and also to any requirements of the lessor who might, for example, impose restrictive covenants to ensure that the development would not injure adjoining land and that buildings below a certain cost or size were not built.

(f) *Public Restrictions on Use.* Where a developer today wishes to use a particular site he must seek permission from various public authorities who may impose restrictions on its use. Firstly, there are the local authorities who administer Acts and bye-laws governing the construction of new buildings and new streets. Their requirements affect the form and cost of development. Secondly, there are the planning authorities who may prohibit development on particular land or permit only particular uses on it, or impose requirements as to the form, character and appearance of development. Thirdly, there are the highway authorities who may require land to be reserved for new roads, street widenings and improvements to junctions. Fourthly, there is the Board of Trade which may decide that a proposed new factory or extension of more than 5,000 sq. ft. does not accord with its policy on industrial location. Fifthly, between 1940 and 1954, there have been authorities for granting building licences. Their control resulted in many kinds of building, such as cinemas or luxury flats, not being erected at all during those years, and in others, such as offices and shops, being erected only rarely.

A developer must thus seek permission from various public authorities to develop land at all, and also to develop it in the form he wishes.

(g) *Price.* The price at which the developer can acquire the right to develop the sites in which he is interested is decided in the property market at the time he takes steps to acquire. The market is made up of the generality of owners who wish or are prepared to sell or lease property, and of purchasers who wish to acquire. The property market is distinct in character from other markets. Sales normally take a long time to mature and the mere transfer of ownership is a lengthy process. The market is a local one in that demand is satisfied on a particular spot, or in a particular area, and often cannot be satisfied elsewhere. There are relatively few transactions compared with the amount of property in existence. Details of transactions are not easy to come by. There is no readily available index of current or past prices. There is no central body which influences price levels. Many purchases are made for reasons of prestige or other non-commercial motives. Buyers have different preferences, some purchasing for investment, some for speculation, some for development and resale. Sites change hands in this market as a result of the demand for and supply of them; both demand and supply will be discussed.

The demand for sites by developers derives from the demand for completed development, as discussed in Chapter 5. The developers are interested in sites of differing sizes, having different qualities and in different locations, which they will be permitted to use for the purpose of satisfying this demand. These developers acting in competition constitute part of the demand side of the market for sites. They are part only of the demand since there are other would-be purchasers who are interested not in development but in speculation, that is in purchasing for resale to a developer or another speculator, or in occupation, as would be the owner of a house who wished to buy adjoining land to preserve his view. With these other potential purchasers, and among themselves, development agencies will compete for sites. They must consider what price they are willing to pay, bearing in mind the return they can expect; and which of alternative sites, at alternative prices, it will suit them best to acquire. The appropriate price in general will be that which is no higher than it need be considering the competition for land and is commensurate with the expected return (see page 77).

As to supply, the amount of land in the country is by and large fixed. We cannot substantially increase the supply to meet growing demand, as we can that of other goods and services, although we have been able to make some impact on this problem by, for example, reclaiming land covered by water or erecting tall buildings. The land in this country is owned by a great number of proprietors who put it, either themselves or by leasing to others, to a great variety of urban and rural uses according to the demand for such uses. There are usually a considerable number of owners willing to dispose of land where it is to their advantage to do so. As the demand for sites increases some of the large amount of land which was not formerly developed, or was underdeveloped, thus becomes available for purchase or lease as sites. Public authorities can do a great deal to influence which land will be chosen to satisfy the demand for sites by, for example, providing roads, sewers and railway lines.

Before we can see how the interaction of this supply and demand in the market will determine the price of sites we must digress and examine the phenomenon of economic rent in land.

Economic Rent in Land

The right to use land for development can be paid for annually by way of rent; or outright in a capital sum by purchase; or by both rent and a capital sum (a premium). For this chapter we shall consider the purchase price or premium merely as the simple capitalisation of annual rent at a given rate per cent. What we say about rent will, therefore, apply to both annual and capital payments for the right to use land.

The total rent that would be expected from the occupier of a newly completed building could be regarded as being made up of four parts: payment for the raw land representing nature's original gift; payment by way of return on the capital expenditure on building and works; an allowance for depreciation of the works; any continuing expense incurred in occupying and owning the land and buildings (see Chapter 10). The actual payment under a lease would be decided according to the circumstances as an individual transaction in the market. As for all markets, however, there is some economic theory which explains the general tendency of the various transactions.[4] The payment by way of return on capital will tend to follow the long-term rate in the market for the particular kind of investment; the allowance for depreciation will be related to the life and cost of the works; the continuing expenses will be related to those actually occasioned in occupying and owning the property. These payments will tend to be much the same for similar properties wherever located. On the other hand the first of the payments, for the raw land itself, will not. The explanation of why it should differ for differing pieces of land is attempted in theories relating to economic rent in land. By economic rent, therefore, economists have in mind something other than the actual payment under a lease for property, which is known as contract rent.

These economic theories were first worked out with regard to agricultural land and mines before the great urban spread began. Theories with regard to urban development are an adaptation of them. It will be simplest first to consider agricultural land.

Rent in Agricultural Land

In 1817 David Ricardo published his *Principles of Political Economy* giving his views on rent in agricultural land and mines. These were similar to, although not identical with, those of his contemporaries Richard West and Malthus. Ricardo has had his critics among the economists that followed, in, for example, James Mill, Marx, Jevons, von Thunen and Marshall, and economists of today differ from him in particular respects (see page 74). But the essentials of his theories form the basis of the generally accepted views today on rent in land; these are in fact often called Ricardian. A general account will be given, postulating a hypothetical farmer and landowner.

The farmer, wishing to rent a piece of land, will find that the landowner will normally expect as high a rent as he can reasonably obtain;[5] and that the landowner would have to be reasonable if he wished to let his land in competition with other owners. If he wishes to secure the land in competition with others, the farmer's offer of rent will have to be as much as he can afford to pay, since the highest offer would normally secure the farm. For rent to be offered at all by the farmer the estimated money value of the produce of the farm, the output, would have to exceed the estimated total cost to him of growing that produce, the imput. In this context cost includes a return to the farmer for his labour and enterprise, by way of an assumed salary or profit, but excludes anything for rent. The amount of rent that the farmer can afford to offer will depend upon the estimated excess of output over input.

In estimating this excess the farmer will compare the different possible combinations of capital goods and labour, in varying amounts and proportions and at certain costs, with the amounts of produce at certain values which will be produced by these combinations. In other words he will, in estimating, seek to visualise the most economical combination of capital goods and labour for the farm, one that will produce the maximum value for a given expenditure or a given result with least expenditure. In visualising this combination he would in fact be proportioning the factors of production in various combinations, so pursuing what economists call the principle of substitution.[6] Certain kinds of results which are found in following this principle are described in the law of increasing and decreasing returns, whereby from the application of successive units of capital or labour to land the amount added to the total product by each successive unit increases up to a certain point and then begins to diminish. The law is also described by the name of " variable proportions " and of " eventually diminishing marginal productivity."

The difference between what the farmer could expect to sell his produce for and its cost of production, under the conditions where this difference is at its maximum, is the biggest surplus that he could afford to pay the landlord for the right to cultivate; and if he were in competition with other farmers he would be forced to offer this amount. This surplus is the economic rent of the land; around this the level of actual rents for raw land will revolve. Since the price of the crops produced on any land would be about the same when sold in the market, it follows that the farmer could afford to pay more rent for the better farming land, as it would produce more and better crops with the same input of capital and labour; and more for the land near his market, since it would involve lower transport costs. There would be land, the marginal land, on which fertility was so poor, or distance from market so great, that the farmer could afford to pay no rent at all, or only a nominal rent. In other words, land with differential characteristics commands differential rents. Land is not homogeneous in quality but varies greatly as to fertility, topography, altitude and climate; and it is immobile and so varies greatly in location in relation to markets and centres of population. There are thus great differences in the characteristics of various pieces of land; they thus command different rents.

In considering the relation of input and output it is useful here to introduce another two words which are used about the productivity of land by American land economists: capacity and efficiency.

Capacity relates to the power of land to absorb units of labour and capital and continue to yield a product sufficiently valuable to compensate for the cost of the additional units; land capable of very intense farming has considerable capacity. Efficiency relates to the ratio of output compared to the input; efficiency is high when the ratio is high, as in very fertile land.[7]

Rent in Urban Land

The economic theory of rent in urban land has not received the same attention from economists as has that for rural land. There appear to be two main reasons for this. Firstly, the relative place of land in our economic framework is not so important today as it was before the great urban spread began; the problems of international trade, currency and business cycles have supplanted it. Secondly, many economists today, unlike their predecessors, think that rent is not peculiar to land. There is rent, they argue, in other things too which, while not being indefinitely durable, share the characteristics of land in taking a long time for their supply to adjust itself to changes in demand; in the skill of surgeons, for example, and in ships.[8] Some contemporary economists have gone further than this. Any factor of production, that is land, labour, capital goods or entrepreneurial skill, is capable, they say, of earning rent. Any of these factors, they argue, may be used in a variety of ways; and if its earnings when used one way are greater than can be obtained when used in another way or, if it is physically mobile, in another place, its rent is the excess of its actual earnings over these other (or transfer) earnings. It follows from this argument that a factor may have several rents. A piece of land may be capable of being used for a shop, factory or house. If used for a shop, the excess of the earnings over its transfer earnings as a factory would be more than over its transfer earnings as a house.

Where, however, the special characteristics of rent in urban land are recognised today, economic theory is based on the line of reasoning which has been outlined for rural land. A general statement will be given, illustrating the nature of urban rent by contrasting some of its essentials with those of agricultural rent, and by postulating a hypothetical private enterprise developer.

The rental value of agricultural land derives from the demand for agricultural produce and is realised in the sale of the output from annual agricultural production. In urban land it is use of space which is in demand, either of ground or of ground and buildings combined. The space is produced in the production of building and civil engineering works, a single and not a recurrent operation. The rent is realised in the use of the space. The use of the space, and its value, is capable of variation throughout the life of the works.

The farmer will visualise the most economical combination of capital and labour to assist him to estimate rental value, and may well vary the combination afterwards in accordance, for example, with fluctuations in price and government agricultural policy. The developer will need to make his decision as to the most economical development in the circumstances, and once he has implemented the decision he will not so easily be able to alter the combination. Buildings last a long time.

In making his decision the developer is faced with alternative possible uses which he can provide and alternative ways of providing for them and will employ the concepts of proportioning the factors of production, of substitution, capacity and efficiency. He will visualise the most economical scheme, one which will produce the maximum accommodation, for example, for a given cost; or the maximum yield with the lowest cost.[9] In seeking the most economical scheme the developer will find that the results of proportioning the factors of production operate in roughly the same way in building as in farming.   The cost of acquiring successive units of input of capital and labour of the same kind will be the same; but in erecting a building of several storeys, for example, the cost of creating successive units of floor space will not be the same.   Building, in this country at least, generally becomes more expensive per unit of floor space as height increases above the second floor.[10]

In farming, both the amount and the value of yield, per unit of input, will correspond with each other, because all of the same kind of agricultural produce off a given piece of land has the same market value. In erecting several storeys, however, the amount of floor space which is provided on each successive floor will diminish as more space is required for lifts, load-bearing structure, heating and ventilation plant, etc., and the value per unit of the floor space which is produced on each of the upper floors will not always be the same.   It follows from this that the most intense use of a site is not necessarily the most economical, in the sense of the term which is described above.   There is a point in any scheme of erecting buildings which are higher than two storeys where the returns to be obtained from the floor space in the top floor just about balances the additional cost of constructing it, without including in this cost anything for the land; and there is a point where it is cheaper to incur the cost of additional land for spreading this floor space horizontally rather than to include it in the upper floors of a building without incurring any additional land cost. Marshall refers to this marginal floor space as the margin of building: " that accommodation which it is only just worth while to get from a given site and which could not be got from it if land were less scarce."[11]

Agricultural rent is paid primarily because agricultural land is scarce in relation to the demand for agricultural produce; it varies from place to place according to fertility and location. Urban rent is primarily paid because urban space is scarce in relation to the demand for it; it varies from site to site because of location. But the influence of location is not the same in agricultural as in urban rent. In agriculture, location is significant in affecting transport costs between farm and market. In urban areas the location of a site is significant because of its degree of convenience and accessibility to people who might want to use it for a variety of purposes, including manufacture, buying and selling. American writers have used the apt word " situs " to describe the quality which attaches to urban land because of the attractiveness of its physical location to people. The situs of a site is decided by " physical location plus human choice "; by the consensus of human choice as to the convenience of a particular situation.[12]

Because location is so important in urban land there are many instances where there is heavy demand and comparatively few sites to satisfy the demand. This might arise in an expanding part of the town where a river or other physical feature limits the supply of well-situated sites, or where very heavy expenditure on services or a bridge is required to open up new land; or in a built-up part of the town where there are few sites which are vacant or ready for re-development. In such cases an owner may be led to demand, and might succeed in obtaining, a rent which is higher than if more sites were available. In the rent, in such cases, there will be an element of monopoly value.

Another distinction between rent in rural and urban land is that while, theoretically, there may be rural land which is so poor or inaccessible that no one will pay any rent for it, urban land is rarely valueless. If it is on the fringes of a town awaiting development it will have agricultural value, or accommodation value for its use as allotments or playing fields, and potential development value. An example of valueless urban land is that which is derelict after mineral extraction and requires considerable expense to restore it for use. This land would have money value if restored; but this would be less than the cost of reclaiming it for the use which will attract the value.

The range of agricultural rents is very modest: from perhaps 10s. an acre per year in the Scottish hills to £20 per acre for market garden land. The range in urban rents is enormous. Suburban housing land may fetch £50 per acre as ground rent while the central shopping area of a provincial city might command £15,000 per acre. This illustrates, too, the difference in the scale of agricultural and urban rents. Urban pursuits as a whole are capable of producing much bigger rents than agricultural ones because of the much greater intensities of use and capital investment in urban land.

Rent, Change in Land Use and the Private Developer

What has been said about rent will be summarised by returning to the private developer who is considering whether land, either already developed or undeveloped, would be available for his particular development and which of alternative sites he should use. One of his requirements is that the price for the site should be appropriate. If by price is meant the ground rent he should pay on building lease, or the capital sum which is its simple capitalisation at a given rate per cent, we can now see how he will know what price would be appropriate.

Let us assume that he is building dwellings for sale at profit. He is satisfied as to the demand for development, has surveyed the various alternative sites that are available, and has selected those which are suitable as regards acreage, physical qualities and location. He is satisfied that private rights and public restrictions would not obstruct the use of the site in the manner he intends. Armed with this knowledge the developer would be in much the same position as the hypothetical farmer mentioned above when faced with the question of deciding his offer of rent for a farm, or of rents for a number of alternative farms. He will know that the landowner will seek to obtain the highest rent, and that other prospective purchasers and lessees in the market will be considering the matter on parallel lines. He would, therefore, be forced to consider the maximum rent which he was prepared to pay; that is the maximum surplus he could afford to pay. This surplus he would arrive at by deducting, from the estimated market value of the space that would be created in the dwellings, the cost of providing them.

There would obviously be many ways of providing the dwellings (in alternative sizes, layouts and densities) and the principles of substitution, diminishing returns, capacity and efficiency would enter into the calculations. The maximum surplus would be based on a scheme which produced, for example, the greatest value for a given cost, or a certain value for the least cost.

The various private developers will compete for sites and think along similar lines. This bidding from a variety of private development agencies, all interested in particular sites, constitutes the demand side of the market. But they will not be motivated entirely in the same way. The bid of the developer who wants to build dwellings for profit will not be so high as to reduce the estimated profit below a certain level. The industrialist who wished to build a factory for himself would consider not merely the value of the building which he could produce, but also his potential profits from manufacturing in the factory; he would be in the same position as a brewer making a bid for farmland to grow hops for his brewery. Some developers will be able to offer higher rents or prices than others; the highest bid will secure the land to the particular developer who makes it, provided it is sufficient to induce the owner to sell or lease.[13] A new use of the land is accordingly decided; and since a transaction occurs a value for the potential use of the land is established in the market. The new use and new value are associated at this point in time.

Changes in land use do not always come about as simply and smoothly as we have described. Some imperfections in the process will be mentioned.

The parties are not always simply a number of developers for different uses on the one hand and the landowner on the other. Sometimes the developer will be prepared to carry out any kind of development and will make his bid on the most profitable one. Sometimes the developer will have to compete not only with other developers but also with speculators, or purchasers who do not intend to develop: a landowner, for example, who wants to buy to keep land open and retain his view, or an industrialist who wants to buy land for his employees' sports field. Sometimes the owner of the land might himself be interested in developing and not, therefore, in renting or selling.

When a site goes to the highest bidder he may not always be the developer who can extract most return from it. It may go to a special purchaser, the bank or chain store which, having the resources to outbid others and being determined to have a particular site for perhaps prestige purposes, makes a bid which exceeds the difference between estimated cost of works and estimated value of the finished accommodation. It may go to a purchaser who can put it to one of several alternative uses which will extract about the same return from it. This is most likely to occur where the site is, for example, on the edge of a town, or on the fringe of its central area, where there are several competing uses of about equal strength.

Accidents of ownership may obstruct the process. For instance, a site may not change hands, even though ripe for development, because it is owned by a special owner. An example is the lady who is determined to live out her days in the house of her parents even though it is engulfed in a spreading business centre, and who refuses a price far beyond that which would provide her with an alternative dwelling since the value of the house to her far exceeds its market value.

The process works least smoothly on re-development, for once buildings have been erected demolition and rebuilding is slow in coming about. An owner, for example, will not sell at the appropriate price for re-development if this is less than the value of the property for its current use, or where he is optimistically waiting for a higher bid for a more profitable re-development scheme. A freeholder cannot re-develop leasehold property, or sell for re-development, until he regains possession; and if he requires possession of several properties which have leases of different terms outstanding he may have to wait until all have expired before beginning his scheme. The leaseholders in such circumstances would not re-develop if their terms were too short. In a similar way, the most profitable re-development may be held up because a developer cannot acquire all the various parcels in different ownerships which are required for it.

A change in use might be obstructed, or fail to come about, through ignorance of the real value of the land in question. It has not been unknown for an owner to hold on to land in the over-optimistic expectation of realising a value which will never materialise; or for a purchaser to pay highly for a site in the over-optimistic expectation that he can realise development which he never in fact is able to carry out.

Change of Use Without Constructional Works

Where development takes place without any constructional works, as where a house is used as it stands for business purposes, the new use and new value will be decided precisely in the way described: as a result of bidding by would-be business users of the premises, or would-be investors who would let for business. But the calculations of the developers would not be complicated by the estimated cost of carrying out works, and their bidding would simply take into account the value in the market of the space for the visualised use.

Rent, Change in Land Use and the Public Developer

In the relatively few cases where a public developer proposes development similar to that which would be carried out by private enterprise, it can estimate the rent, or capital sum, it can afford for a site in the way we have described; in other cases it cannot. A public developer can certainly, in these other cases, estimate the cost of proposed development, and which of alternative schemes would be the most economical in giving, for example, the maximum amount of floor space for a given cost. It can certainly estimate the value to itself of a site; a school authority, for example, might not feel it worth-while to spend more than a certain rate in the £ per acre on land; or a transport undertaking might fix the maximum price it was prepared to pay for a bus station site by calculating the economies in operating costs which the use of the site as a bus station would bring it. But in the nature of things, a public developer cannot in such cases put a market value on its finished development, as can a private one, since there is no general market for it. It cannot estimate therefore what difference there will be between market value and cost, and from this what rent or price it can afford to offer in market competition.[14]

The difficulty of placing a value on property which is used for public purposes, and for which there is no general demand and therefore no market value, has been recognised in various statutes which prescribe the price to be paid by public bodies on its compulsory acquisition. For example, where land to be acquired is, and would continue to be, devoted to a purpose of such a nature that there is no general demand or market for it (e.g., a church) the basis for compensation is its reasonable cost of equivalent reinstatement elsewhere, if reinstatement is in fact intended by the owners;[15] and where land is held by a statutory undertaker for the purpose of its undertaking, one basis for compensation on its compulsory acquisition is the aggregate of the amount of expenditure reasonably incurred in making the necessary adjustment in the carrying on of the undertaking and the loss of net receipts directly attributable to the adjustment.[16]

Formula valuations such as these have become necessary for arriving at the development value of sites which are transferred, by new town development corporations or local authorities, to other public bodies for their development; or of sites which are bought by one service of a local authority and transferred to another service for development (see Chapters 9, 15 and 17). Similarly, formulae had to be devised by the Central Land Board when faced with the need to estimate, for development charge purposes, the consent value of land to be developed by local authorities. For example, land for housing or educational purposes, including school playing fields, was to be valued as for residential purposes; for public open space at a quarter of this value; for municipal offices and depots as the value of land for a comparable commercial use; and for public buildings and works at prevailing use value.[17]

These public bodies do not necessarily buy or sell at the values laid down by formulae. Where the buyer thinks that the formula price is more than the site is worth to it, it can refuse to buy and can seek another site at a more reasonable (formula) price. For corresponding reasons an owner can refuse to sell. But the negotiations revolve round the formula and not market price.

These bodies cannot, in general, pay what they choose, whether buying by agreement or compulsorily; they must pay no more than a price governed by law. But the law does not attempt to fix the price at a value related to what these bodies wish to do with the site, its value to them, but rather at a value related to what others in the market would do with it if it were available. Sometimes in legislation before 1939 this value was limited by the prescribing of hypothetical conditions which the market was considered to observe in arriving at its valuation, such as the condition that certain property in slum clearance areas was to be valued as a site cleared of buildings and available for development (see Chapter 12). Such limiting hypothetical conditions have more frequently been included in compulsory purchase legislation since the war (see Chapter 11).

In practice, therefore, public developers do not enter into competition with other developers and users in the market in quite the way we have described for private developers. Just as with private developers, to obtain land their bid must be at least the market one, that which could be obtained from the highest bid of other would-be purchasers, that which the land is worth to these others; but it is not, as it must be with private developers, necessarily also that which it is worth to them. In other words, public developers can decide the new use of a site, but not the new market value for such a new use, as do private developers.

Public Developers and Market Price of Land

This is not to say that public developers in their search for sites have no effect on the market price of land. They do. For example, where public developers wish to carry out development that would not be undertaken by private developers the demand for land increases, and land which otherwise would not be built on acquires a building value. Or where the supply of land for all development is limited, the requirements of public developers will result in a smaller amount of land being available for private developers and an increase in the price that they will have to pay for such land. Or where the supply of land suitable for particular kinds of development is limited, for example for high-value dwellings, and public bodies take over some of this land, the effect will be to increase the price of the remainder. On the other hand, however the earmarking by public developers of particular sites for their future development, by, for example, designation in a development plan, will usually result in a lessening of their market price because of the compensation code for public acquisition, and of the unwillingness of purchasers to buy such sites from the current owners (see Chapter 24).

Rent as a Cost not a Surplus

We have seen how rent is a surplus remaining after the cost of production has been met and is not part of this cost. From the individual's point of view, however, the payment which is made for the use of property must be regarded as a cost to be covered by the value of the goods or services produced from it. As such it has its effect in deciding the use of land. For example, if an industrialist wishes to build a factory in a business street he must pay for the site, and cover as part of his costs, at least the higher bid that would be paid by a developer for business purposes; or if there are builders bidding for a farm, the highest bid is also a cost to the farmer which he must cover in the value of his output if he wishes to stay, for by retaining the land in its current use he is forgoing the differences between the current and potential use values; or if a landowner wishes to develop his own land he must count as a cost the highest bid that others would offer him for the opportunity of developing it. And we can summarise from this aspect what we have said about public developers and rent by saying that if a public developer wishes to buy a site it must count as a cost the price which private owners are prepared to pay for it.

These examples illustrate what is meant in economics by "opportunity costs." The cost of the land in question to the industrialist, farmer, landowner or public developer is its value if put to that alternative use which is foregone which would earn the maximum yield.

CHAPTER 7

CAPACITY OF THE BUILDING INDUSTRY

Importance of the Industry for Development—Sections of the Industry —Control of the Industry by Government—Development Programmes and the Capacity of the Industry—Relating Programmes to the Capacity of the Industry.

Importance of the Industry for Development

THE BUILDING and civil engineering industry is one of the constructional trades of the country (see page 102), and is concerned with the production, renewal and maintenance of building and civil engineering works of great variety. It is fundamental to development for two reasons. Firstly, because there are few instances where development does not call to some extent upon the resources of the industry; and, secondly, because it is the only industry, using the term in its broadest sense, which is called upon in the carrying out of development, although other industries, such as those producing furniture, plant and machinery, are called upon by occupiers of the finished works.

Sections of the Industry

For the purpose of carrying out its work the building industry, as we shall call it, is organised into four sections: the employees, firms, manufacturers and distributors of materials, and professions. All these sections do not contribute to every job; speculative housebuilding, for example, is often carried out without professional collaboration. Furthermore, on any particular job where all the sections do contribute, they may not be clearly distinguishable; for example, architects, engineers and surveyors are often employed directly by the building firm. For the industry as a whole, however, the sections are fairly distinct. They will each be described briefly.

1. *Employees.* Employees in the industry include the operatives, the men working on the site, and administrative, technical and clerical staff who mostly work in the firm's offices. Building operatives are broadly divided into those having a skilled trade, the tradesmen, who normally serve an apprenticeship; and the remainder, the labourers, who have had no particular craft training but may nevertheless be very knowledgeable in the practices of the industry. Table 3 shows how the total number of operatives employed in July, 1948, were divided between tradesmen and labourers, and also between building and civil engineering work.

TABLE 3

Building and Civil Engineering Industry—Numbers of Insured Males in Various Crafts, July, 1948

	Number	Percentage
Carpenters	142,560	15·0
Bricklayers	110,370	11·6
Masons	9,020	1·0
Slaters and tilers	11,210	1·1
Plasterers	33,890	3·5
Painters	149,460	15·7
Plumbers and glaziers	60,430	6·3
All other occupations (mainly labourers)... ...	437,100	45·8
Total building industry	954,040	100·0
Total civil engineering industry	173,980	18·0
Total building and civil engineering	1,128,020	118·0
Total working population	20,265,000	—

Source: *Building*, Table VIII, and *Ministry of Labour Gazette*.

It will be seen that the tradesmen made up just over half the total number, and that of these about four-fifths were carpenters, bricklayers or painters; and that the total number of men in civil engineering was about one-fifth of those in building.

A census is made by the Ministry of Works each May of the number of men employed in the industry, and of the different kinds of work on which they are engaged. While comprehensive licensing of work was in operation the Ministry also knew, from the monthly returns made by firms for each licensed job, just how the industry was currently engaged (see page 299).[2]

2. *The Firms.* The firms are responsible for organising and carrying out the work. The biggest employers of building labour in the country as a whole are the general builders, who carry out all kinds of building and civil engineering work, and employ sub-contractors and labour of all kinds. They have been classified in the following way:

(a) A few large firms of building and civil engineering contractors capable of dealing with the biggest jobs and with any type of work, in any part of the country and, in some cases, abroad;

(b) a greater number of medium-sized firms (some of them also engaged in civil engineering) capable of most forms of building and civil engineering except the very biggest jobs, and confining their operations usually to their own localities;

(c) a yet greater number of general-purpose builders whose work consists mainly of alterations, additions, repairs and maintenance, but who often erect small groups of houses or single houses;

(d) a number of speculative building firms, some of considerable size, who develop housing estates to their own designs and specifications;

(e) a very large number of jobbing builders, many employing only a few operatives, who are occupied almost exclusively with repair and maintenance work.

In addition to the general builders there are firms which engage in one or more trades only, and mainly employ specialist labour. In England these firms generally act as sub-contractors to the general builders; but sometimes, as in Scotland, they may be engaged directly by the developer, who will arrange for their co-ordination and do without a general builder.

The general builders and the specialist trades which are pre-dominantly concerned with the industry are grouped into the " Thirteen Main Trades " in the statistics compiled by the Ministry of Works; the specialist trades which are not so commonly engaged in construction are grouped into the " Seven Trades."

The number of firms engaged in the " Thirteen Trades," and their site employees, in 1948 and 1953 are shown in Table 4. This excludes those firms made up of working builders who employ no operatives at all, and are probably engaged for the most part on repairs and maintenance. The number of firms in the " Seven Trades " are shown in Table 5.

TABLE 4

Building and Civil Engineering Industry—Number of Firms of Different Kinds in the " Thirteen Main Trades " and Their Site Employees, February, 1948, and May, 1953

Thirteen Main Trades	1948 Firms	1948 Employees	1953 Firms	1953 Employees
General builders	41,411	474,407	37,856	454,577
Building and civil engineering con-tractors	1,963	265,359	2,017	294,872
Civil engineering contractors ...	861	43,370	998	55,259
Plumbing contractors	7,400	37,533	7,080	34,728
Joinery and carpentry firms ...	4,674	25,638	4,767	24,821
Painting contractors...	10,268	49,916	4,291	46,356
Roofing contractors	1,500	14,812	1,459	14,504
Plastering contractors	2,525	21,141	2,440	22,365
Glazing contractors	515	5,813	450	4,487
Demolition contractors `... ...	230	2,675	174	2,326
Scaffolding specialists	25	1,775	28	3,359
Shopfitters	—	—	160	4,721
Miscellaneous	385	4,613	489	7,008
Total	71,757	947,052	67,209	969,383

Source: *A Review of Productivity in the Building Industry* (British Productivity Council, 1954), Table 11.

TABLE 5

Building and Civil Engineering Industry—Number of Firms of Different Kinds in the " Seven Trades," May, 1949

Seven Trades	Firms
Construction engineers	580
Reinforced concrete specialists	121
Heating and ventilating engineers	746
Electrical contractors	5,004
Asphalt and tar-spraying contractors	190
Plant hiring contractors	118
Flooring contractors	195
Total	6,954

Source: *Building*, Table VI.

Table 4 shows how large is the number of general builders and how small the number of firms engaged only on civil engineering work; and also how large are the numbers of firms engaged solely on plumbing, painting and electrical work.

Work is also carried out directly without the assistance of contractors, that is by direct labour, by the Ministry of Works and other government departments, certain of the local authorities, nationalised industries and public utility undertakings, and a number of industrial and commercial firms. Most direct labour is engaged on maintenance and repair, and perhaps on new work of a minor character; only a small proportion carries out new large works. No comprehensive figures are available for the men employed by direct labour for comparison with those working for the firms. In May, 1949, the local authorities, the largest employers of direct labour, had 144,000 operatives on building and civil engineering repair, maintenance and similar works, and 27,000 on new construction, of which 17,000 to 18,000 were on housing. Government departments at this date employed about 20,000 men on maintenance work. Such labour is not of great moment, therefore, for work on development in the country as a whole, but it may be of significance in a particular locality.

As described above, the size of the firms which are included in Table 4 varies enormously. The kind of work which these firms of different sizes carry out also varies. The position in 1949, with which no doubt that today broadly corresponds, is seen in Tables 6 and 7; these relate only to the " Thirteen Trades," and thus exclude firms employing no operatives.

TABLE 6

Percentage Distribution of Operatives Amongst Different Types of Work According to Size of Firm, May, 1949

Size of Firm by Operatives Employed	All Types of New Construc- tional Works	Ordinary Repairs and Maintenance	War Damage and Conversion of Houses	Total
1-5	13·5	71·9	14·6	100·0
6-19	28·5	51·5	20·0	100·0
20-99	46·2	37·9	15·9	100·0
100-499	62·4	28·9	8·7	100·0
500-999	72·8	21·2	6·0	100·0
1,000-4,999	78·2	17·5	4·3	100·0
5,000 and over	88·1	10·4	1·5	100·0
All firms	48·0	38·9	13·1	100·0

Source: *Building*, Table IV.

TABLE 7

Percentage Distribution of Operatives Amongst Firms of Various Sizes According to Type of Work, May, 1949

Size of Firm by Operatives Employed	All Types of New Construc- tional Work	Ordinary Repairs and Maintenance	War Damage and Conversion of Houses	All Types of Work
1-5	3·1	20·3	12·2	11·0
6-19	11·5	25·7	29·7	19·4
20-99	30·4	30·8	38·4	31·6
100-499	27·6	15·8	14·1	21·3
500-999	7·6	2·7	2·3	5·0
1,000-4,999	14·2	3·9	2·9	8·7
5,000 and over	5·6	0·8	0·4	3·0
All firms	100·0	100·0	100·0	100·0

Source: *Building*, Table V.

Table 6 shows that the operatives in the Thirteen Trades throughout the country were about evenly divided between new work on the one hand and conversion, repairs and maintenance on the other; and that the larger the firm the greater proportion of its total work was new construction. From Table 7 it can be seen that the bulk of all work, including the new work which was carried out by the firms, was done by those with less than 500 operatives.

While the number of tradesmen and labourers are about equal in the industry as a whole (Table 3) they are not so evenly divided in firms of different sizes. Table 8 shows the distribution.

TABLE 8

Percentage Distribution of Craftsmen and Labourers Amongst Firms of Different Sizes, May, 1949

Size Group	Craftsmen	Other Occupations (mainly Labourers)	Total
1-5	13·9	6·1	11·0
6-19	23·6	12·3	19·4
20-99	34·1	27·3	31·6
100-499	18·4	26·2	21·3
500-999	3·5	7·5	5·0
1,000-4,999	5·2	14·5	8·7
5,000 and over	1·3	6·1	3·0
Total	100·0	100·0	100·0

Source: *Building*, Table VIII.

As the firms increase in size the proportion of tradesmen to labourers decreases. It is about two to one in the smallest firms and one to five in the largest.

3. *Manufacturers and Distributors of Materials and Components.* The materials which are incorporated into the finished works are very mixed and varied in character. A distinction can be drawn between those, such as sand, ballast, cement and timber, which are obtained from natural sources, and are usually used as raw materials and appear in the finished building other than in the raw state; and building components, such as lavatory basins and door furniture, which are manufactured and built into the structure in the form in which they arrive on the job. Many of the materials and components are used by other industries.

Materials reach the building site, whether from abroad or other parts of the country, through a variety of channels. The greater part is distributed through builder's merchants who buy from manufacturers and producers. Such merchants may be wholesalers distributing over a wide area, or wholesalers and retailers distributing within about 30 miles' radius, or the local ironmongers. The function of these merchants is to stock the material, assemble it as necessary, deliver it, provide credit facilities to builders and also technical advice and trade information. Other materials may be delivered by manufacturers direct to the firms either at their depots or on site. Just how the materials travel, and through what hands, depends very much on their nature, whether they are heavy or light, can or cannot be stored, are standardised or not, and also on trade practices. The cost of transport is particularly heavy for certain raw materials such as granite or sand, which are heavy and bulky and found only in certain localities.

4. *The Professions.* An integral part of the industry is the large number of architects, engineers and surveyors whose work

lies in the design of works and buildings, the preparation of drawings and specifications of materials and methods of construction, the preparation of bills of quantities, the inviting of tenders, the supervision of work to see that it is well carried out and in accordance with the design, and finally in the settlement of the account of the contractor. These professional men and women work either independently of the firms on the one hand and of the persons or bodies paying for the work on the other; or directly for the building and civil engineering firms; or directly for the developers.

Control of the Industry by Government

The control of the building industry became essential with the outbreak of war in 1939. Whereas the gross output of the industry had been £421 million in 1937, £455 million in 1938 and £442 million in 1939, government expenditure on new defence construction alone in 1940-41 was to be over £300 million; and this was to be carried out with a labour force that was to be reduced, and so drastically that in 1944 it was to be less than 40 per cent of its pre-war strength.[3] The purpose of the war-time controls was to ensure that only work of importance to the war effort would receive the necessary materials and be carried out; and that labour was available for this work wherever it was to be carried out.

As will be explained in Chapter 8, the capital investment policy of post-war governments required continued control over the industry, to ensure that it was engaged only on work which the government considered to be of most importance. But the direction of building labour to particular jobs, to ensure that the important work could be carried out, was soon dropped after the war. Another piece of machinery, that of the Inter-departmental Building Committees, was introduced into each administrative region to award priorities, and to avoid the overburdening of the industry in a particular locality where it was already fully engaged and able to cope only with its current commitments.[4]

Development Programmes and the Capacity of the Industry

Since development is so completely dependent on the industry the question arises, in considering programmes of development, whether, given the demand for the development and the willingness of developers to carry it out, the industry will be able to cope with it; that is, whether there will be any limitations on its capacity for carrying out the programmes. The answer to the question will not be the same for each of the four sections of the industry which we have described; and the considerations which govern the answer will differ if the question is raised by the government for the country as a whole, or by a local planning authority for the particular locality covered by its plan, or by an individual developer.

For development in the country as a whole no enduring limitation arises from the number of firms, since this would readily adjust itself; or from the supply of materials, since shortages of a particular kind can usually be overcome by employing substitutes, or by importing materials from abroad if there is currency to do so. But a more enduring limitation arises where there is a limited quantity at any particular time of labour and professional workers. This arose with regard to labour both during and since the war, and also immediately before when the government was embarking on an armaments programme.[5] With a given quantity of labour and professional workers in the country, the output of the industry can be gradually increased by more mechanisation, improved organisation and greater efficiency, but only gradually. Where there is too little labour its numbers can be increased by training, but only gradually. Such training was initiated soon after the recent war when the industry was at a low ebb and the government visualised a large post-war construction programme over the following 12 years.[6]

Before considering the possible limitations on the carrying out of the combined programmes of all developers in a particular locality two points must be mentioned. Firstly, all constructional works must be provided on certain sites which are selected by the developers: the carrying out of the works is not concentrated in a few particular areas, as are the other constructional trades, but is distributed throughout the country. Secondly, the distribution of the firms and professions roughly follows the opportunities for employment; they have become settled among existing concentrations of people in large and small towns, particularly among the wealthier concentrations. In each locality there is thus a pool of firms, men and professional workers who naturally would elect, given the opportunity, to work near their homes. The question arises, therefore, whether the carrying out of works in any locality is limited by this; whether, in other words, a developer can, where necessary, attract the sections of the industry to a particular locality from outside it. We will consider the position in relation to each of the sections described above.

1. *Employees.* On the whole employees will obtain work, if it is available near their homes, within a distance which is limited by the amount of daily travel to and from work which they are prepared to face. This was recognised by the Ministry of Works when, for the purposes of their statistics, they subdivided the administrative regions of the country into zones, some 100 to 150 in all. These were areas around a town or group of towns, the boundaries of which were normally defined as the limit of the daily journey to work from the principal centre of the area. Where zones can be suitably defined men will therefore, on the whole, work within a particular zone and not in different zones,

so that the amount of resident labour employed in such a zone will remain fairly constant. For geographical and other reasons it is not possible to define zones accurately, so that the amount of labour in them will in fact vary.

Some employees, however, such as the key men of the large general or specialist firms, will work wherever their employers undertake contracts. Not all the employees of such firms need to do this however since it is the firms' practice, in order to keep costs down, to employ as many men as they can, both tradesmen and labourers, from the vicinity of the works.

That building and civil engineering labour does not in total move to any great extent around the country in search of work is indicated, in some measure, by Table 9. This shows the distribution of the employees in the industry throughout the various regions of Great Britain in 1949 (columns 2 and 3) and how the number of employees in the industry in most regions remained fairly constant throughout the years 1950 to 1954.

2. *Firms.* Of the general builders, the larger firms are available for work outside their localities, but the medium-sized firms, the general-purpose and jobbing builders, will normally operate only locally. Of the specialist firms in the Thirteen Trades a higher proportion will work outside their own locality, and a higher proportion still of the seven trades.

3. *Materials and Components.* These find their way to sites from all parts of the country and also from abroad. In consequence the carrying out of development in a locality is rarely limited by there being no local production of building materials or components; it is becoming even less limited with the growth of the practice of processing and prefabricating of materials in factories.

4. *Professions.* The professions are normally concerned with the bigger schemes, and will undertake work wherever it is to be done.

In general, therefore, the combined programme of all developers in a particular locality is hardly likely to be limited by the availability of local building materials and components or professional skill; it is more likely to be limited by the availability of local firms; and most likely to be limited by the availability of labour. It was the small amount of building labour that could be found only some 20 to 30 miles from Central London that delayed, in part, the progress of the London New Towns in their early days.

TABLE 9

Distribution of Employees in Building and Civil Engineering Industry Throughout Administrative Regions of Great Britain Between 1949 and 1954.

Region	1949		1950	1951	1952	1953	1954
	No. of Employees in Industry	Col. 2 as % of Total Civilian Employee Population	No. of Employees in the Industry Based on 1949 (Col. 2) as 100				
1	2	3	4	5	6	7	8
London and South Eastern	336·570	6·6	98	94	94	92	92
Eastern	77·520	7·4	106	106	106	109	111
Southern	70·170	7·6	105	110	106	108	110
South Western	81·740	7·8	99	95	98	100	97
Midland	88·180	4·5	100	101	100	103	112
North Midland	75·360	5·5	102	103	106	106	111
East and West Ridings	82·620	4·7	102	103	100	101	102
North Western	136·370	4·7	102	106	105	107	103
Northern	74·440	6·1	104	97	96	100	102
Scotland	141·650	6·8	100	97	99	102	100
Wales	61·370	6·7	100	100	97	97	90
Great Britain	1,225·990	6·0	100	99	99	100	101

Source: Total civilian employee population—*Ministry of Labour Gazette.*
Employees in building and civil engineering trades,—figures supplied by Ministry of Labour and National Service.

Where the supply of labour in a particular locality is likely to limit a programme the government has no powers of remedying the position by direction of labour comparable with those it had during the war.

The individual developer is rarely concerned with the capacity of the industry since he assumes that he can obtain a share of the local capacity even if others cannot; or if there is insufficient local capacity, as where the Scottish Hydro Electric Board builds in a remote valley, he relies on importation of men and firms. But importation may be expensive; and where cost is a critical factor the absence of local labour may be a deciding factor against the carrying out of a scheme.

Relating Programmes to the Capacity of the Industry

In order to be able to relate a programme to the expected capacity of the industry, the output that it should be capable of producing over a given period, it is necessary to find some means of equating the two in similar terms. It is simplest to do so in terms of the amount of labour, that required for the programme and that which is expected to be available; and it is most useful to do so in these terms since, as we have seen, the supply of labour is the most critical limitation on the capacity of the industry to carry out a programme in a particular locality and in the country as a whole.

We must first consider how the output of the industry can be measured in terms of labour power.

The output of work on any building or civil engineering job can be measured in money terms from the basic costs of labour, materials and plant, professional fees, a variety of overhead costs, which are roughly proportional to the size of the job, and the contractor's profit. The proportion of the total cost which goes into these items will vary from contract to contract, and for different sections of a contract, for different parts of the country, and on different sites, according to such things as the weather, the time of year, transport problems, the efficiency of the firms, the class of work and the efficiency of the operatives. But if a sufficiently large number of jobs for a particular class of work in a particular locality over a relatively short period can be considered, such as local authority houses, single-storey factories, primary schools or offices, it is found that the proportions become fairly standardised. For example, in 1954 it was stated that the proportions for commercial buildings was approximately labour, 40 per cent; materials, 50 per cent; overheads, etc., 10 per cent;[7] and the proportions of the total cost of the average local authority three-bedroom house built since the war was found to be as follows:

TABLE 10

Proportions of Total Cost of Average Local Authority Three-bedroom House Attributable to Different Elements in Industry, 1947-51

	1947 House of 1,029 ft. sup. %	1949 House of 1,050 ft. sup. %	1951 House of 1,050 ft. sup. %
Labour	33·5	30·8	29·6
Materials	56·3	59·4	60·5
Plant	1·8	1·7	1·6
Overheads and profit	8·4	8·1	8·3
	100·0	100·0	100·0
Architects' and Surveyors' fees ...	3·0	3·0	3·0

Source: *First, Second and Third Reports of the Committee on the Cost of House Building (Girdwood Committee)* (H.M.S.O.), 1948, 1950, 1952.

Since, in the circumstances described, the cost of labour for particular classes of work is a fairly constant proportion of the total cost of work, it follows that for particular classes of work in particular localities, over a reasonably short period of time, the output, in money terms, of the industry over a period can be expressed in terms of the cost of labour that has been employed. Since the cost of labour is roughly proportional to the number of operatives employed and their working time, and since the number of tradesmen and labourers for any particular class of work are present in some fairly standardised proportion, it follows again that output can be expressed in terms of the amount of working time that a particular number of operatives have spent at work. Since working time is roughlv proportional to calendar time, it finally follows that output in money terms can be equated to the amount of operative man-days, man-weeks, man-months, or man-years in calendar time which have been spent. In other words, the output of the industry for particular classes of work for different localities can be expressed as £x of total work per man-month or man-year.

Analyses of the output of the industry in these terms have been made by the Ministry of Works for the country as a whole and for the different administrative regions, and figures were made available by the Ministry to local planning authorities for use in connection with the preparation of their initial development plans.[9] Many authorities have quoted them in their written analyses. Table 11, for example, shows figures quoted in the *City of Plymouth Development Plan*, 1952, for the value of the industry's output in 1950-51, in £ per man-month, for England and Wales and for the South Western administrative region. Variations from the national average are seen in this as in all other regions.

TABLE 11

Productivity of Building Labour on New Work, 1st April, 1950 to 31st March, 1951

Type of Work	England and Wales		South West Region	
	Average Number engaged per month	Productivity Figure (value of work done per man-month) £	Average Number engaged per month	Productivity Figure (value of work done per man-month) £
Factories, works and industrial premisès ...	63,765	103·1	1,871	101·1
Storage warehouses and depots...	7,131	89·4	413	85·6
Schools and universities	32,540	86·8	2,170	81·9
Water, sewerage and sewage disposal ...	16,802	82·7	1,639	72·5
Highways	1,363	100·5	53	*
Electricity	15,236	103·5	745	92·9
Gas	6,072	108·5	572	*
Hospitals	3,956	82·2	419	79·2
Offices (except government)	8,573	92·0	249	*
Government buildings (central and local) ...	4,574	85·6	298	*
New permanent housing	202,838	85·8	18,312	82·2
Miscellaneous	102,072	90·2	7,222	88·0
All types	464,924	90·2	33,964	85·4

Note: * Productivity figure not quoted because it is unrepresentative.
Source: *City of Plymouth Development Plan*, 1952, *Report of Survey*, page 100.

Such figures must be adjusted if used for later years for the money value of output of work has increased drastically over past years, if only because of rises in cost of materials and labour and falls in money values. In illustration Graph 1 shows the proportionate increase in money terms of cost of building, for the normal local authority house, and of materials and wages between 1946 and 1955. The rise in the money value of output has not been uniform for all the classes of work shown in Table 11, but the Graph shows the degree of change since 1950-51. As money figures tend to change rapidly a more stable factor for relating programmes to the capacity of the industry is useful. This can be obtained by equating the output per man in the industry to physical units. Table 12 gives examples which were used in preparing the 1951 Development Plan for the County of Middlesex.

These output figures do not remain the same year by year but change if, for example, there are improvements in the efficiency of the men, greater mechanisation, more efficient organisation on the site, or more prefabrication. Table 13, for example, shows how expected changes in productivity were allowed for in the County of Hertfordshire Development Plan, 1951.

We can now come to the problem of considering whether the building industry would be able to cope, in terms of manpower, with a particular building and civil engineering programme. The size of the programme could be expressed either in physical or money terms.

In physical terms it can be expressed with varying degrees of precision. For example, a housing programme might be given as dwellings for 3,500 persons; or as 800 houses and 200 flats; or 1,000 dwellings subdivided into groups of different sizes in terms of rooms, floor space or cubic content. The degree of precision with which the programme is formulated will depend on its purpose and the period ahead for which it is prepared. For relating the programme in a development plan to the capacity of the industry over 20 years or so the kind of precision given in Tables 12 and 13 is appropriate. In money terms the programme can be expressed as the amount of money for which, at the current or some other level of prices, building or civil engineering contractors could be expected to carry out the work.

In either case, it could be translated into the number of man-months or man-years that the industry would need to carry out the programme at its current rate of output.[10] This could then be compared with the number of men who are currently engaged in the locality. If it is assumed that this number will remain fairly constant, or will increase or decrease by a certain amount, it can be calculated how long the programme will take; or if a certain period is assumed it can be calculated how many men will be required to carry the programme out. The application of this method to development plan programmes is considered in Chapter 21.

GRAPH 1

*Cost of Building Labour and Materials, and of Local Authority
House-Building, 1946 to 1955*

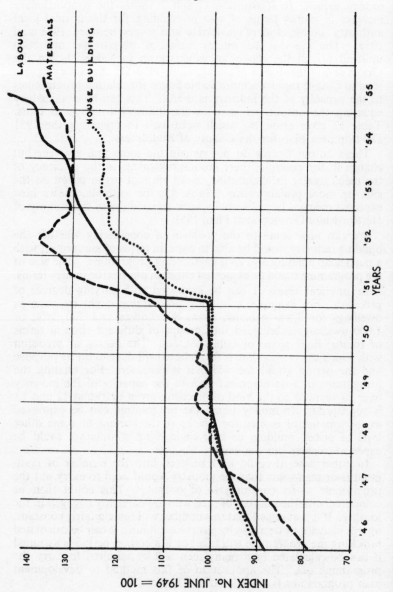

GRAPH 1

Source :

1. The cost of labour is the combined wages of one tradesman and one labourer (London rate) with no allowance for holidays with pay, etc. Taken from Ministry of Labour Gazette.

2. The cost of materials is the wholesale price of materials used in the building and civil engineering industry. Index No. taken from Monthly Digest of Statistics.

3. The cost of local authority housebuilding is the average per foot square in tenders approved for 3-bedroom local authority houses in traditional construction. Taken from the Third Girdwood Report (see note to Table 6) and Report of the Ministry of Housing and Local Government 1950/1-1954 (Appendix 1, Table E).

TABLE 12

Man-Years Per Unit Quantity of Building County of Middlesex Development Plan 1951

Category of Work	Man-years 1947	Man-years Corrected to March 1950
(1) Houses—Man-years per house of 900 ft. super	1·31	1·31
(2) Shops—Man-years per 1,000 ft. super of shop space	3·05	2·68
(3) Churches—Man-years per church of average size of 500 seats	28·16	24·70
(4) Licensed Premises—Man-years per licensed premises of average size of 12,000 ft. super ...	43·68	38·32
(5) Cinemas—Man-years per 1,000 seat cinema ...	38·45	33·73
(6) Health Centres—Man-years per health centre of average size of 2,000 ft. super	9·72	8·53
(7) Offices—Man-years per 1,000 ft. super of office space	3·36	2·95
(8) Factories and Warehouses—25s. per foot super, £1,200 per man per annum	—	—
(9) Schools—		
Nursery—Man-years per school of average size of 40 pupils	3·54	3·11
Infants—Man-years per school of average size of 200 pupils	24·20	21·23
Juniors—Man-years per school of average size of 320 pupils	38·71	33·96
Secondary—Man-years per school of average size of 470 pupils	78·17	68·57
Special—Man-years per school of average size of 200 pupils	36·20	31·75
County College—Man-years per college of average size of 400 students	87·40	76·67
(10) Roads and Services—		
(a) Water Supply and sewerage, including works and mains—£35 per head of population in new towns and £25 per head of population in other towns. 1·38 man-years per £1,000	1·38	—
(b) Roads, sewers and gas and electricity services to houses. £100 per house, 1·60 man-years per £1,000	1·60	—

Table 12—*cont.*

Category of Work	Man-years 1947	Man-years Corrected to March 1950
(11) Main Roads—		
(a) New Towns : £50 per head of population	—	—
(b) Expanded towns (over 40% expansion on 1938 population). £45 per head of population	—	—
(c) Expanded towns (under 40% expansion on 1938 population). £30 per head of population. 1.72 man-years per £1,000 ...	1·72	—
(12) Hospitals—Man-years per 500 bed hospital ...	721·00	632·46

Notes.—
The 1947 figure is supplied by the Ministry of Works.
The 1954 figure is adjusted to take into account any increase in productivity between 1947 and 1950.

Source : *Report of Survey of Middlesex C.C.—Development Plan 1951. Table 62.*

TABLE 13

Expected Changes in Man-years per Unit Quantity of Building Allowed for in County of Hertfordshire Development Plan, 1951—Productivity Factors

Item and Unit	Man-years		
	First Period	Second Period	Third Period
	Prior to approval of Plan	First Five Years after approval of Plan	Remainder of period of Plan
House—average size	1·2	1·1	1·0
Shop—1,000 sq. ft. shop space ...	2·7	2·5	2·3
Add house unit for flats above.			
Add office unit for offices above.			
Licensed premises—average size 12,000 sq. ft.	39·0	36·0	33·0
Office—1,000 sq. ft. office space ...	3·0	2·8	2·5
Church—500 seats	25·0	23·0	21·0
Cinema—1,000 seats	35·0	32·0	29·0
Hospital—500 beds	650·0	595·0	540·0
Health centre—2,000 sq. ft.	9·0	8·0	7·0
Industry—1 acre completely covered by buildings	75·0	70·0	63·0
Civic buildings—per £1,000 of work...	1·7	1·5	1·4
Housing roads with services—per £1,000 of work based on cost at £110 per house	1·3	1·2	1·1
Schools—per £2,500 of work (varies slightly with type, details available)	1·0	1·0	1·0
Other buildings in traditional construction—per £1,000 work	1·0	1·0	0·9
Other small civil engineering work—per £600 work	1·0	1·0	0·9
Other large civil engineering work—per £1,500	1·0	1·0	0·9

Source: *County of Hertfordshire Development Plan, 1951, Survey Report and Analysis,* Appendix 18.

CHAPTER 8

INVESTMENT

Development is the Production of Certain Kinds of Capital Goods—Raw Land is Not a Capital Good—For Development there Must be an Investment of Savings—The Amount and Source of Savings for Investment, 1948-53—Not All Savings are Used for the Creation of Fixed Capital Goods—The Decision to Create Capital Goods—Depreciation of Capital Goods—Investment in Post-war Economic Planning—The Controls Over Investment.

Development is the Production of Certain Kinds of Capital Goods

ECONOMIC life has been described as " an organisation of producers to satisfy the wants of consumers."[1] These wants are satisfied by the exchange of the goods and services which are produced for money which is obtained out of production. Economic life, therefore, does not reckon with the invaluable work done by housewives or social workers who do not sell their services for money.

During any particular period producers will provide goods and services either for consumption or for use in production. Those for consumption will be for direct enjoyment by consumers. Of these, some will be for a single use which does not last, such as food or entertainment; and others for a durable use, which lasts a long time, such as houses or furniture. Goods and services for use in production again might be for single use, such as oil, flour or electricity; or for durable use, such as factories or machinery which are used in industry. The new goods and services which are produced might in turn be either for production or consumption.

In economic life, therefore, the constructional works associated with development consist of the production on land of certain kinds of durable use goods, either for production or consumption. These and all other durable use goods are also called " capital goods " or " fixed capital goods." This adjective " capital " is different in meaning from the noun " capital " which popularly describes assets of different kinds including money, shares, capital goods, land, etc.

Raw Land is Not a Capital Good

The constructional works associated with development are clearly produced, just as are machines, clothes or furniture. Raw land which has been improved by roads, drainage or services, or reclaimed from the sea, can also be said to have been partly man-made or produced; in many cases the production has been taking place over centuries. The raw land itself, however, is a gift of nature and cannot be said to have been produced. In other words, it is not a capital good, although it may have capital goods such as buildings fused with it for a few years or perhaps for centuries.

For Development there Must be an Investment of Savings

In carrying out development, a developer spends money at all stages in the development process pending its completion: on buying or renting land, paying fees, paying the builder. This money will be mostly used forthwith by its various recipients in buying goods and services; but the goods and services which are to be provided by the development will become available only gradually over its life. The heavy initial expense of building a factory, for example, is repaid in the yield of perhaps 20 years of production; and of a house in the benefit of some 60 years of occupation. In other words, money, as purchasing power, is set aside to be tied up in the finished development, and it is reimbursed only gradually out of the yield or benefit from the finished development. The setting aside of money in this way in the purchase of land and employment of the building industry is called investment.

Investment in development is thus of two kinds. It is in part the acquisition of land which, like the acquisition of any existing property such as securities, blocks of flats or ground rents, is merely the transfer of ownership of assets between individuals or bodies, and results in no addition to the national stock of capital goods; and in part it is the creation of new capital goods. Either of these kinds can be carried out with borrowed money. The lender of this money is also investing; but we shall describe his activities as financing (Chapter 9). In this chapter we are primarily concerned with the investment of the second kind which leads to the production of new capital goods; we shall call this " Investment," using the word " investment " for the first kind. In later chapters we shall not distinguish between the two.

For Investment to take place the money to be set aside must be saved out of income arising from production, for example by individuals after paying taxes and satisfying consumption needs. The saving may be made by a developer for development; but more commonly it is made by others and borrowed by developers for the purpose of Investment.

Savings Equals Investment for the Country as a Whole

Savings arise out of that part of the income of individuals, government and companies which is not spent on consumption. But not all savings will be Invested. An individual, for example, might prefer to keep his money in liquid form at the bank in case of need, or because he is saving to buy a car; a joint stock company may prefer to build up a reserve fund instead of spending part of its profits on new machinery.

For any individual or body the amount of saving thus may not equal the amount of Investment. For a country as a whole, however, during any given period, savings and Investment do balance; or to be more precise the savings that are made by persons or companies, after spending on taxation and consumption, added to any savings by government out of taxation, are equal to Investment at home or abroad; or

Savings plus imports plus tax revenue = Investment plus exports plus government spending.

This equation is accepted by government economists in making the official estimates of national income and expenditure.[2]

The Amount and Source of Savings for Investment, 1948-53

The amount of savings in the country as a whole in the years 1948 to 1953 are shown in Table 14 as a roughly consistent 16·5 per cent of the national income from 1948 to 1951 and as slightly more since then; that is, as a fairly constant proportion of the value of the goods and services which are produced during each year out of economic activity and become available for consumption, the creation of capital goods and the replacing of worn-out capital goods.[3]

TABLE 14

Gross Savings and Gross National Product, 1948-53

	1948 £	1949 £	1950 £	1951 £	1952 £	1953 £
1 Gross national product	10,250	10,970	11,545	12,715	13,738	14,796
2 Gross savings ...	1,688	1,764	1,906	2,124	2,371	2,759
3 2 as percentage of 1	16·5	16·1	16·5	16·7	17·3	18·7

Source: *National Income and Expenditure*, 1946-53, adapted from Tables 1 and 6.

This saving comes from a variety of sources in the economy as shown in Table 15.

TABLE 15

Source of Savings for Investment, 1948-53

Savings, including provision for depreciation of capital goods by:—	1948	1949	1950	1951	1952	1953
Persons*	−99	−93	−54	−1	614	762
Companies	753	823	822	783	1,048	1,282
Public corporations ...	21	126	92	67	155	178
Central government ...	723	784	741	647	467	296
Local authorities ...	100	121	97	82	93	137
Tax dividend and interest reserves ...	181	28	184	521	6	48
Residual error† ...	9	−25	24	25	−12	59
Gross savings	1,688	1,764	1,906	2,124	2,371	2,759

Notes: * Persons include non-profit making bodies and un-incorporated businesses (e.g., sole traders and partnerships).

† The item of residual error is included to balance independent estimates which do not agree.

Source: *National Income and Expenditure*, 1946-53, Table 42.

The table shows that except for 1952 personal savings, as defined, were negative in amount. This was because taxes on private capital, mostly as death duties, were larger than the amounts saved by private persons as a whole out of their incomes.[4] The table also shows, when the savings of public companies are added to their additions to dividend and tax reserves, how large a proportion of the saving came from this source. Central government saving was very substantial, too, largely through budget surpluses. Public corporations and local authorities did not save much.

Not All Savings are Used for the Creation of Fixed Capital Goods

Not all the savings shown in Table 15 were used for the creation of new capital goods inside the country. Some was accounted for in the physical increase in stocks and works in progress at the end of the year over that in existence at the beginning, and some in investment abroad. Table 16 shows that about 80-90 per cent was left for the formation of new capital goods at home, including for the replacement of worn-out capital goods.

TABLE 16

Savings and Investment, 1948-53

	1948 £	1949 £	1950 £	1951 £	1952 £	1953 £
1. Gross savings ...	1,688	1,764	1,906	2,124	2,371	2,759
2. Amount of fixed capital formation	1,396	1,554	1,682	1,866	2,066	2,333
3. Value of physical increase in stocks and work in progress	153	35	−216	600	50	201
4. Net investment abroad	139	185	440	−342	255	225
5. Item 2 as percentage of 1	83%	88%	88%	88%	87%	84%

Source: *National Income and Expenditure*, 1946-53, adapted from Table 6.

Proportion of Capital Goods which are in New Constructional Works

Of the fixed capital goods which have been created only a proportion has been in new constructional works. Table 17 compares this proportion, about 50 per cent of the total, which is divided between new housing and other new buildings and works, with that for other types of fixed capital goods.

The way in which the non-housing works were divided among the various kinds of uses is shown in Table 1 (page 2).

TABLE 17

Different Kinds of New Capital Goods, 1948-53

	1948 %	1949 %	1950 %	1951 %	1952 %	1953 %
1. Vehicles, ships and aircraft	16·8	17·2	15·8	14·4	12·9	13·8
2. Plant and machinery	35·5	35·8	37·6	39·5	38·2	35·1
3. New housing ...	24·5	21·5	19·7	19·9	23·6	27·1
4. Other building and works	23·3	25·5	26·9	26·2	25·3	24·0
Total %	100·0	100·0	100·0	100·0	100·0	100·0
Total £000	1,396	1,544	1,682	1,866	2,066	2,333

Source: *National Income and Expenditure*, 1946-53, adapted from Table 43.

The Decision to Create Capital Goods

While there is a certain volume of savings available for Investment during a given period, whether or not Investment takes place in any particular project depends on the decision of individual producers. Before deciding to Invest the producer would consider whether it would be worth his while to do so. A shopkeeper or industrialist, for example, before extending buildings, would attempt to estimate the cost, and the net return in increased business, that he could expect from the extension. By net return is meant the gross return after allowing for the cost of producing it and for the depreciation of the capital good. This estimated (or actual) return can be expressed as a rate per cent of the estimated (or actual) capital cost.

If the creation of all capital goods were undertaken out of the savings of the actual entrepreneurs or developers who were carrying it out, the decision to Invest might be decided solely by the relationship between the prospective return and estimated cost. In fact, it is normally undertaken with savings borrowed from others; and these savings would be hoarded, and not loaned to be tied up in capital goods, if there were no payment to the lenders. The necessary annual payment for the privilege of using borrowed money, the interest on loans, is also expressed as a rate per cent. The way in which this rate is decided is described in Chapter 9.

Since money as a rule is borrowed for investment, the decision to create capital goods is influenced by the relation between the rate of net return and the rate of interest. Investment will be encouraged where the prospective net return is more than the interest on the money to be borrowed. If it is less, entrepreneurs or developers will not undertake the creation of capital goods with loans, since they would lose money; and where a developer or entrepreneur owns money which he can use for Investment he might prefer to lend the money rather than Invest it. This explains how it was that the particularly low rate of interest on long-term loans in the years following the war, that is particularly cheap money, tended to increase the demand for capital Investment, and why the particularly dear money of 1955-6 tends to restrict it.

Because the rates thus influence each other the rate of return on investment and the rate of interest on loans, although decided in different ways, tend to equal each other in the market for enterprises which are comparable in such things as the safety and liquidity of capital and in the safety and regularity of income.

Depreciation of Capital Goods

All capital goods depreciate and eventually become unusable either through natural decay, as with the fabric of a building, or through wear and tear, as with machinery and plant, or through obsolescence, as when factories are no longer suited to modern production. All or any of these kinds of depreciation will appear in any particular capital good. This depreciation must be made good out of current production if the stock of capital goods in the country is not to decrease; and Investment and savings are required for this as described earlier.

In the accounting system of any public undertaking, or private firm or the country as a whole, some provision should be made for making good depreciation to the capital goods used by the undertaking. This provision takes the form of setting aside money to accumulate so as to enable the capital good or its value to be replaced at the end of its life. For production goods the setting aside will be out of the proceeds of current production, and for consumption goods out of income. If nothing is set aside it means that the undertaking is consuming its capital.

Just what provision to make is not an easy matter to decide. Firstly, what is the total amount that should be set aside? The actual, or " historical," cost is known; but when replacement of the good is necessary its cost may have risen above this through money inflation, or fallen below through that type of good having becomes cheaper.[5] Secondly, what is the ultimate value of the capital good going to be when it is finished with? This will affect the actual amount to be written off. In some cases it will be negligible, as when old houses are demolished; in others it may be negative in quantity as when basements of old houses need to be filled in; in others it may be more than the historical cost as where houses are converted to other uses. Thirdly, what is the life of the good, the period over which depreciation should be written off? Will it be able to endure for its potential physical life or will changes in fashion or the technique of production make it obsolete before this?[6]

The last question is considered by central government when local authorities receive sanction to borrow money for the purpose of

carrying out capital works. They require this sanction for all but
the smallest of projects, for they can rarely raise enough income, nor
are they permitted to accumulate enough funds, for large ones. It
is the practice of some authorities to pay for capital works out of
revenue, but only up to say a 6d. rate in any year or £1,000 in
cost; and while all are permitted, to create reserve funds to be
spent on capital works, wherein are accumulated the proceeds of say
a 2d. rate each year, this can grow only to a specified maximum
amount. It is a general principle of local authority borrowing that
a loan, if possible, should be repaid before the capital asset which it
has created has outlived its usefulness, either through decay or by
becoming obsolete. If it is not, it means that new borrowing may
have to be undertaken for new capital goods before the old loan
has been paid off, and future ratepayers will have two debts for one
asset. When local authorities receive loan sanction, therefore, the
maximum period for repayment is specified for each loan. The
period is fixed having regard to the kind of works being undertaken,
to the expected life of typical works of this kind, and risks of
obsolescence.[7] Where one project includes works of different kinds,
for example the provision of sewers, erection of brick buildings and
tree planting, different periods may be fixed for them and for
the acquisition of land. In practice, particular works may last a
longer or shorter time than the period of the loan. If they need to be
renewed while the loan for them is still being paid off, the authority
will be paying off two loans for the same service. If on the other
hand, use is still being made of a sewer, or rent is still received for a
house, on which the loan has been discharged, then the authority
is in a fortunate position of possessing a capital asset which it has
paid for out of revenue.

When the total amount to be provided for is decided, and the
period over which this is to be done, there is a choice of three
methods of making provision.

1. *Straight Line.* For each year of expected use there is taken
an equal proportion of the total amount.

2. *Reducing Balance.* In each year there is taken a fixed
percentage, this being calculated each time on the value remaining
after the total of previous annual provisions are deducted.

3. *Sinking Fund.* As with the straight-line method equal
provision is made each year. But the amounts taken are those
which if invested each year would accumulate at compound
interest to the total sum to be provided for.

In practice depreciation to buildings and works is not as often
provided for as depreciation to plant and machinery. There are at
least four reasons for this. Firstly, since buildings and works have a
long life provision for their depreciation is much smaller in relation
to return on investment than for, say, short-life machinery, and does

not, therefore, seem so important. Secondly, they often change hands during their life and there is then no single owner who would benefit from making a depreciation allowance. Thirdly, while buildings may waste away physically, falls in value on this account have often been compensated for by falls in the value of money, or rises in land values following increase in population and wealth. The hope of this encourages owners to ignore the need for depreciation allowances. Fourthly, an allowance for depreciation of buildings is not recognised by the Inland Revenue for income tax purposes, except for factories which are considered to be used up in production as would be industrial plant and machinery.[8]

Where property is bought during its life, the purchaser takes past depreciation into account in considering his price. In making his provision, if any, for future depreciation he will consider not the historical cost of development but the actual price he has paid. Depreciation is written off in this way between vendor and purchaser.

Investment in Post-war Economic Planning

In reviewing the position of the country immediately after the war, the government found that there was a huge demand for the use of resources for the creation of capital goods. This was due, firstly, to the depredations of the war. Not only was there loss through destruction, but also excessive depreciation arising from the under-maintenance of existing capital equipment. Secondly, it was due to the increase in population and families for whom houses and other capital goods had not been provided during the war, and also to the general expectation that we were all going to live at a much higher standard than before, a higher standard for which an increase in capital goods per head was necessary. For example, when local authorities were asked in November, 1945, to send to the Minister of Health a statement on the programme of capital expenditure and maintenance on capital works that they would like to undertake in the years 1946-49, the money totals were found to amount for the three years to £550 million, £770 million and £810 million respectively. This was optimistic for during these years the total new fixed capital to be created for the whole country was only £1,259 million, £1,393 million, and £1,491 million at 1948 prices.[9] Thirdly, there was a considerable amount of money available for Investment, as, for example, in depreciation allowances which had accumulated during the war since they could not be spent.

The physical resources available for the production of capital goods were less than those demanded. Thus any government would have found it necessary to devise a policy for control of investment if severe inflation, and perhaps more serious trouble, were to be avoided. The Labour Government adopted such a policy, tinged with its party's political philosophy. In brief the policy amounted to encouraging rather than discouraging the demand for investment

by making money cheap to borrow; to limiting the total amount of
the country's resources that would be devoted to producing capital
goods; to exercising this limitation selectively, permitting for
example, only those projects considered to be of assistance in our
economic recovery (e.g., factories producing for export), or to be
socially desirable (e.g., housing and schools); to controlling directly
the expenditure on investment by public agencies and extending
this control through the nationalisation of major undertakings; to
creating budget surpluses so that the supply of savings for investment
was increased to meet the demand for them envisaged in the investment programme.

This kind of policy has been pursued, by and large, ever since,
except that the Conservative Government has made money dearer
to borrow; has sought to rely more on the supply of savings in the
market than on savings out of budget surpluses; and with the
falling off in demand for capital goods has more and more found
it unnecessary to restrict their creation, in the private sector of the
economy at least.

The Controls Over Investment

For the implementation of an investment policy controls were
necessary. Adaptation was possible of those existing during the war
and it was not found necessary to introduce new kinds. They were
used with varying severity as the circumstances demanded, and have
been gradually relaxed. We will describe briefly the machinery
whereby capital investment in development has been controlled in
order to reflect the economic planning policy of the government.

Arising from the investment programmes section of the economic
plan (see page 48) each government department has had allocated
to it a certain volume of capital investment to be used for development. Some was allocated for the departments themselves and some
for the *ad hoc* bodies, local authorities and private investors whom
they sponsored. Each department was given the responsibility of
distributing its allocation. They used various methods according
to which of the different agencies referred to was going to carry out
the work. The methods will be briefly described.

The amount of investment to be permitted to each of the *ad hoc*
bodies was agreed by the government in general terms; the manner
of spending was worked out by the particular body in conjunction
with the appropriate department. For example, it was perhaps
agreed that the British Electricity Authority should provide new
generating power to the extent of a certain quantity of megawatts.
The authority would agree details with the Ministry of Fuel and
Power and the area boards would work out a detailed programme
of works. In doing this they would have regard to the views of the
consultative councils and also to the proposals of other departments

as to, for example, the building of the new towns or the expansion of industry in the development areas.

Until licensing was abandoned in November, 1954, private developers had to apply for a building licence and out of their applications were selected priorities to take up the investment allocated to the private sector. Responsibility for licensing rested with the Ministry of Works. They did not, however, consider all the applications for licences themselves but delegated to others the authority to issue them; to local authorities, for example, for housing and to the Board of Trade for factories and warehouses. The licensing authorities took account of the advice of sponsoring departments.

In obtaining an allocation for local authority expenditure on development, the departments would have obtained approval for certain specific important projects. For selecting priorities among the generality of local authority development, however, the departments used licensing machinery and also the traditional means of loan sanctioning to which we have referred. Licensing has been abandoned but loan sanctioning is still in existence. Unless it has local Act powers to raise a loan, an authority applies to the appropriate department for permission to do so, for example to the Ministry of Education for schools and Ministry of Transport for roads. The department will decide whether to sponsor the application. If it does agree it cannot normally sanction the loan itself but must pass the application to the Ministry of Housing and Local Government. This department will authorise the loan unless there is some particular financial reason for not doing so, as, for example, the excessive indebtedness of the authority. There was at one time a statutory limit to the total possible indebtedness of authorities but this restriction was abolished in the Local Government Act, 1929, Section 74. The central loan sanctioning department, however, still had to ensure that authorities do not borrow too heavily. " For this purpose the Minister, in deciding on loan applications, takes into account in addition to questions of the necessity, cost and planning of the works, general considerations of the financial resources of the applicant authority, their existing loan commitments, and the additional burden on the ratepayers involved by any new loan."[10] It is seldom that an authority is in fact refused a loan sanction today on these grounds.

CHAPTER 9

FINANCING

*Parties in the Development Process Work on Borrowed Money—
Sources for Borrowing Money, and Periods of Loans—Sources of
Borrowing and Period of Loan for the Finance of Development—
Factors Controlling the Rate of Interest on Borrowing—Government
Control of Borrowing—Methods of Repaying Long-term Loans—
Period of Loans and the Interest which is Paid—Allowance for
Depreciation—Repayment of Loans and Terminable Annuities.*

Parties in the Development Process Work on Borrowed Money

IN CHAPTER 8 we saw that developers will commonly borrow
money for obtaining command over the resources which are
necessary for carrying out development. Other parties in the
development process will also borrow to play their part: the builder,
for example, to buy materials and pay men in advance of receiving
payment. All these parties will resort to the market where are
brought together those who have money to lend and those who
wish to borrow. They will not all borrow from the same sources,
nor for the same length of time, nor pay the same rate of interest,
nor repay the loan in the same way. Before considering the arrangements for financing development in particular we will look at the
general market in this country of which these form part, the market
for lending and borrowing money for the purpose of investment,
purchase, trading and consumption.

Common Sources for Borrowing Money, and Periods of Loans

It is useful to consider the common sources for borrowing money
in this country under the following heads, which indicate the
comparative length of time for which the money is borrowed.

(a) Short period, varying from day to day to a few months.

(b) Intermediate period, varying from a few days to a few
years.

(c) Long period, of more than a few years.

(a) *Short Period.* The simplest kind of short-term borrowing,
other than from the banks, is by the promissory note, a commercial
form of I.O.U. This is not often employed and more frequently
such borrowing is by a commercial bill, such as a bill of
exchange, whereby, for example, the buyer of goods promises
to pay the seller in, say, three months, and the seller's security
is not only in the standing of the buyer but also in the right to

the goods on default. The commercial bill becomes a bank bill if its security is increased by the endorsement of a bank or accepting house who, for a commission, guarantee to meet the claim on maturity.

Where the Treasury needs to bridge the gap temporarily between expenditure and revenue it will offer Treasury bills, to tender in the market, or "through the tap" to the Bank of England or government departments who have accumulated funds. This bill is a kind of promissory note, first introduced about 1875, whereby the Treasury promises to pay the holder the face value in a period of, say, two to three months for the immediate loan of the discounted value of this sum at a stated rate of interest.[1]

(b) *Intermediate Period.* Loans for periods of a few days to perhaps a few years, and up to 10 years for buying owner-occupied houses, are generally obtained by direct loan or overdraft from the commercial banks. Such loans are frequently raised while arrangements are being made for long-term loans. The banks are free to lend to whom they choose; but in practice they follow the lending policy suggested by the Treasury, as laid down, for example, in the Chancellor's instructions to the Capital Issues Committee (see page 118). Loans are repaid in a lump sum or by arrangement; and are subject to recall by the bank at any time.

(c) *Long-period Loans.* Loans which are redeemable after a stated number of years, and permanent loans, are raised by both private and public bodies from investors in the new issue market. The work preliminary to raising the money is normally undertaken by promoters, who may be individuals, or specially formed companies or specialist financial institutions called issuing houses. The issue is advertised in a form required by law, in which full information must be supplied about the proposed undertaking; and the Council of the Stock Exchange must be asked for permission to deal. For this purpose officials of the Exchange investigate the proposed undertaking. In this way savings from different sources, from individuals, banks, insurance companies, trust funds, are made available for large and long-term investments. For their loans, the lenders receive interest-bearing bonds or debentures, or stocks and shares, which are secured in the assets and prospective assets of the borrowers.

In addition to the new issue market there are other sources for long-term loans to special kinds of borrowers. We will consider four sources from which loans are obtained for development.

1. The Treasury can borrow from the Bank of England, or from sources, such as the Post Office or Trustee Savings Banks

or social insurance funds, which are controlled by the National Debt Commissioners.

2.   Some industrial concerns are too small to float new issues, and they cannot obtain long-term loans from the commercial or private banks; these do not, in this country, give long-term finance to industry. To meet their needs the Bankers' Industrial Development Company, a subsidiary of the Bank of England, was set up in 1930. In 1945 it was replaced by two new corporations which obtain their funds from the banks, and from insurance and trust companies. The Finance Corporation for Industry is intended to assist in the long-term reconstruction of industry; for example, it supplied a great deal of the finance for the Margam steel works. Its minimum loan is £200,000. The Industrial and Commercial Finance Corporation is intended to enable new and growing concerns to get on their feet. It lends between £5,000 and £200,000 at a time to small and medium-sized businesses.

3.   Those who wish to borrow on the security of land and buildings and to repay over a period up to 25 years and, exceptionally, up to 35 years, can do so from building societies. The modern building society originated in the terminating societies, first formed at the close of the 18th century; they were so called since they terminated their activities when all members had acquired houses out of their combined subscriptions. Today there is no such link between the subscribers of capital and borrowers. Subscribers do not buy shares on the Stock Exchange but direct from the society, and can withdraw their money after a period of notice. Those who wish to borrow for buying or constructing dwellings for owner-occupation can, if these are below a certain value, do so from local authorities.

4.   Loans for development are sometimes obtainable from a miscellaneous group of lenders who are in charge of funds held in trust for others. Examples are the insurance companies, trade unions, the administrators of trust, pension and super-annuation funds, and the Ecclesiastical Commissioners.

5.   Industrialists who go to the Development Areas can apply to the Treasury for loans for the building of factories. The Treasury is advised by a Development Areas Treasury Advisory Committee. Loans are not usually granted unless the applicant has been unable to obtain finance from other sources.

Sources of Borrowing and Period of Loan for the Finance of Development

The sources to which the different parties in the development process will go for their loans will depend upon the part they play. The builder is interested only in relatively short-term finance for he merely has to bridge the period between advances to his men and merchants and payments by the developer; the others are interested in long-term loans where they wish to tie up the money in development, or in shorter term loans where they visualise the fairly rapid transfer of their interest or wish to make temporary arrangements while works are under construction. The sources to which the parties will go will also depend upon whether they are individuals, public companies, local authorities, etc., for there are differences in the ways in which these borrow money.

(a) *The Builders.* A firm will usually rely for short-term finance on the commercial banks. Where it is a big public company, it may prefer to borrow through an issuing house. Finance which is required for the direct labour departments of a public body will be raised by that body by the methods described below.

Both firms and direct labour organisations can take advantage of one form of short-term borrowing we have not mentioned, which is open to many purchasers of goods and services: trade credit. Builders' merchants and building material suppliers do not normally demand payment on receipt of goods, but within, say, a month. For this period they are in effect contributing towards the finance of the works.

(b) *The Remaining Parties.*

1. *Individuals, Firms and Private Companies.* For short-term loans these will resort to the commercial banks or to private lenders. For the longer term they will rely on building societies and the miscellaneous investment funds. Industrialists may go to the Industrial Finance Corporations.

2. *Public Companies.* These will have the same sources as the borrowers just mentioned; and in addition they can go to the new issue market for long-term loans.

3. *Central Government.* Since all government expenditure is made out of the Consolidated Fund, any government development may be financed indiscriminately out of short- or long-term loans or out of taxation.[2] Short-term loans are borrowed by short-term bills as already described. They constitute the government's floating debt, one which is continually changing. Long-term loans are raised from the public and financial institutions through the new issue market. Most government stocks are redeemable. Usually they must be redeemed by a particular time, perhaps in 60 years, and may, at the government's option, be redeemed earlier. Some, however, such as Old Consols, are irredeemable, constituting a permanent loan. The effective day-to-day business of floating and liquidating government loans is, under Treasury control, in the hands of the Comptroller General of the National Debt Office. There is also a government broker who assists in the buying and selling of stock.

4. Ad hoc *Bodies*. In almost all cases the public corporations and other *ad hoc* bodies raise their money from the banks for short-term loans, and from the new issue market or their own accumulated funds for long-term loans. They issue stock in the same way as public companies except that they are subject to departmental control in so doing. In certain cases, for example, in the borrowing by the British Electricity Authority, the Gas Council, Transport Commission and Civil Aviation Corporations, the Treasury guarantees the redemption of the stock and the payment of interest, so enabling the corporations to borrow almost at gilt-edged prices. The Coal Board and New Towns Development Corporations are financed by advances from the government, exclusively in the latter case and all but for small temporary loans in the former.

Treasury guarantee is not available for representative trusts or utility companies, but their issues are subject to Treasury requirements as to form and amount.

5. *Local Authorities*. Local authorities have no general powers to borrow in the short-term market although some have such powers in local Acts. They have general powers to borrow temporarily from banks or otherwise for any purposes for which they have been authorised to raise a loan, pending the raising of the loan.[3] For long-term loans, the principal sources for borrowing are:

(1) *Public Works Loan Board*. The Board had its origins in 1817 but was set up in 1875 in its modern form as a means of supervision by the Local Government Board over the finances of the smaller local authorities. Its finance as a rule was extended to authorities with a rateable value of less than £200,000 who could not easily raise money by any other methods.   While before the recent war the Board was thus relatively unimportant as a source of local authority borrowing, between 1945 and 1952 it was, with a few exceptions, the sole source.[4] Since 1952, authorities have been able to borrow from it or any of the sources mentioned below, but the Board is still being used extensively. Before the war the Board was financed out of a Local Loans Fund which was supplied by the National Debt Office, but since 1945 it has been financed direct from the Consolidated Fund. The Board fixes the rate of interest to correspond with the rate at which the government currently is able to borrow; this continues throughout the period irrespective of what happens in the money market subsequently. The authority cannot repay on maturity but must repay gradually over the loan period.

(2) *Mortgages*.[5] This was the most popular method before the war for all but the largest authorities. Mortgages

are sought, for example, from private investors, banks, insurance companies, or the Public Works Loans Board, the security being the rates and revenues of the authority. The periods for repayment can vary from a few to 60 years; and where land is acquired for certain purposes, including housing, the period can extend up to 80 years.

(3) *Issue of Stock*.[6] Loans can be raised in the money market by the issue of redeemable stock, either with the consent of the Minister of Housing and Local Government under general powers or under local Act. Stock has to be redeemed by a specified date, usually within 20-30 years, but sometimes at the option of the authority it can be redeemed earlier. This method is more suitable for larger authorities than smaller, since their credit is better in the market. Before the war it ranked second in importance to the mortgage method.

(4) *Housing Bonds*.[7] With the consent of the Minister of Housing and Local Government, authorities can raise money for a minimum of five years by housing, or local, bonds for the finance of housing only.

(5) *Corporation Bonds*. Powers are given in certain local Acts to raise money by the issue of corporation bonds for any authorised capital expenditure purpose of the authority.

(6) *Internal Sources*. Authorities can borrow from funds they have accumulated for certain purposes.[8] Such funds are those which have accumulated out of the sale of property; or are set aside by all authorities for the superannuation of employees, or the repair of local authority houses or as sinking funds for the repayment of loans; or by some authorities under local Acts for insurance purposes or capital reserves.

Factors Controlling the Rate of Interest on Borrowing

From the borrower's point of view, interest is the necessary payment to owners of money for the opportunity of using their money. From the money owner's point of view it is the reward for giving up, for a short or long period, command over the use of the money and of the freedom to switch it from one use to another; in other words for not hoarding. In general, rates of interest will depend upon the pressure to borrow on the one hand, and on the other the readiness or otherwise of owners of money to give up their command over it. In Chapter 8 we saw that the pressure by developers to borrow will depend upon the relation of the rate of interest on the loan to the rate of yield that can be expected from the use of the loan. We will consider here the relation of the rate of interest to the readiness or otherwise of money-owners to lend.

A given rate of interest will influence the way in which owners of money will employ it. If the rate offered is too low or falls then money will be hoarded and not offered to borrowers until it rises again sufficiently. If with a given supply of money there is a strong wish by the holders of the supply to keep their assets liquid, then a high rate of interest will be necessary if they are to lend.

The owner of money does not require the same rate of interest from all kinds of prospective borrowers. He would be influenced to accept a particular rate by various factors, such as the loan period, generally requiring higher rates for the longer period as Graph 2 shows in relation to rates required by the Public Works Loan Board; the arrangements for repayment; the possibility of the loan not being repaid because of failure of the borrower; the degree to which his money will be readily realisable, either through repayment from the borrower or through the sale of the asset which is obtained as security; his money being realisable at least at the amount of the loan; and the income being certain, regular and trouble-free in its collection. All kinds of lender will not, therefore, be attracted by the same kind of borrower. Trustees and mortgagees look for security of their loan; banks in addition look for realisability; lenders in the new issue market often look for the prospects of capital appreciation.

In other words the rates that would attract savings will not be the same for the gilt-edged security offered in a British Government Consol, for debentures of an industrial company, for ordinary shares in the same company, for mortgage advances to the developer of an industrial trading estate. Gilt-edged stock is the one in respect of which least interest would be required, or, in other words, most money would be paid for the same income; and the interest required from other kinds of borrowers will be higher than this depending upon the security, etc., offered by the borrowers.

What has been described is the general interplay of market forces; but the government and Bank of England also have a part to play in deciding the level of interest rates. They may have various objectives in doing so. They may wish to have a low rate in the long-term market in order to minimise the interest that needs to be paid on long-term government borrowing; or a high rate in the short-term market as part of a general policy directed to combating inflation or to encouraging the inflow of foreign funds; or a high rate in the intermediate market to discourage domestic borrowing from the banks; or a low rate in all markets to encourage the creation of capital goods in times of economic depression; or a low rate in the long-term market to keep cheap the provision of local authority housing. It is not always possible for a government by a financial policy to achieve all its objectives, for some may call for a low rate of interest and some a high. But once a policy is decided the government will accordingly influence certain rates of interest. In particular it fixes the Bank Rate, that at which the Bank of England agrees to discount bills and lend money, so affecting the rates in the short-term market and those at which banks will lend in the intermediate market. It also influences the short- and long-term rate by its borrowing and funding operations in the discount and new issues market.

Since all loan markets are inter-connected, movements in one will produce sympathetic movements in another and would-be long-term lenders will be influenced, for example, by the rates at which the commercial banks will lend. Graph 2 shows the general inter-relationship between 1946 and 1956 of the Bank Rate, the gilt-edged rate, that charged by the P.W.L.B. and building societies. But the short-term and long-term rates do not move precisely in step because, for one thing, lenders and borrowers in the long-term market are naturally much more influenced by long-term expectations than are those in the short-term. For example when the Bank Rate was violently changed from $2\frac{1}{2}$ per cent to 4 per cent in March, 1952, some building societies, but not all, increased their rates for lending on mortgage by $\frac{1}{2}$ per cent.

To summarise, in the long-term market there are series of different rates which borrowers need to pay, according to the attraction that their undertakings offer to lenders; and these are subject to the general influence of government and Bank of England financial policy.

Government Control of Borrowing

The governments' concern with lending and borrowing since the war has taken three important forms. Firstly, it has needed to ensure that the amount of savings in the country was adequate to match the amount of investment in capital goods that it wished to see undertaken; secondly, that the rate of interest was assisting economic policy; thirdly, that only approved projects should receive a share in the supply of savings. We have already touched upon the first two; we will now consider the third.

Since 1946 the Treasury has continued to exercise powers it operated under Defence Regulations throughout the war; its consent has been needed by all borrowers, including *ad hoc* bodies and local authorities, who wish to raise new loans of over £50,000 within a period of 12 months, except for temporary purposes or in the ordinary course of business or, if local authorities, from internal sources.[9]

GRAPH 2

Source:

1. The Building Society rate for house purchase is that recommended by the Council of the Building Societies Association to its members for loans to house purchasers for owner occupation.

2. The yield taken for $2\frac{1}{2}$ per cent Consols is that shown in the *Monthly Digest of Statistics* as the monthly average for working days in each month.

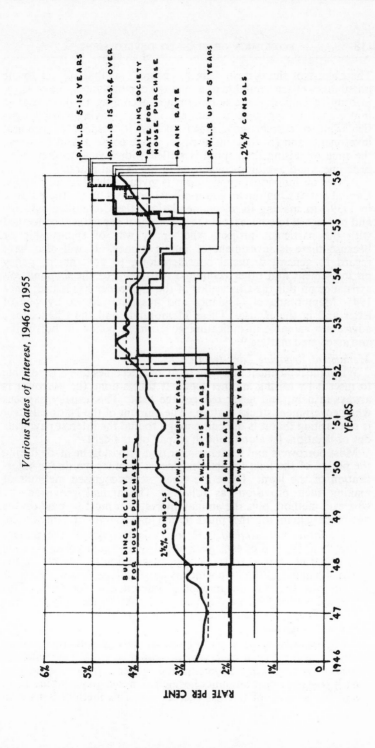

Various Rates of Interest, 1946 to 1955

The objects of the control were to ensure " (a) that subject to the possibilities of the capital market and the circumstances, the order of priority of capital issues is determined according to their relative importance in the general national interest, having regard, particularly, to current government policy in respect of physical investment; and (b) that, in all cases, where consent is to be given, the time of raising the capital is settled with a view to preserving orderliness and avoiding congestion in the capital market."[10]

Advice on individual applications is given to the Treasury by the Capital Issues Committee, a non-official body set up for the purpose in 1939. In making its recommendations the Committee asks for and has regard to advice from the government department concerned with the particular project, whether by way of sponsorship or because there is investment of public money. It will also have regard to general financial considerations, to government policy on investment and other economic matters. For the Committee's assistance on this the Chancellor of the Exchequer has issued, since 1945, Memoranda of Guidance and has given advice by way of letter and in the House. These Memoranda and the Chancellor's advice are valuable in indicating government policy on borrowing and associated matters.[11]

Methods of Repaying Long-term Loans

When the repayment of a long-term loan becomes due it is possible to meet it by raising another loan. If this is done the borrower is always in debt, and never reduces the debt. This usually happens when government stocks mature. The amount of the National Debt is so crushing that it is difficult enough to find the interest payments out of taxation, let alone enough to pay off the debt.

Most borrowers and lenders prefer that provision be made during the period of the loan for its repayment; in other words for amortisation of the loan. There are three well recognised methods of making such provision, as follows. The annual provision, by whatever method, plus the annual interest that must be paid on the outstanding loan, together make up the loan charges or debt service.

(1) *Instalment Method.* At intervals throughout the period, usually at the end of each year or half-year, equal portions of the principal are repaid to the lender, in addition to interest on the actual balance of the loan which is outstanding. As this decreases from year to year the amount of interest also decreases. This method is used for repaying loans to banks, to the Public Works Loans Board, to insurance companies, trusts or private lenders and to mortgagees.

(2) *Annuity Method.* At intervals throughout the period, usually at the end of each year or half-year, equal payments are made covering both repayments and interest. In consequence as each year passes the amount of principal in each payment increases and the amount of interest decreases.[12] This method is used in

repaying loans to building societies, insurance or trust funds, and mortgagees; to the Public Works Loan Board; to the government by the New Town Development Corporations.

(3) *Sinking Fund.* Payments are made, periodically, not to the lender but into a sinking fund. The payments are such that they will accumulate to the amount of the loan at the end of the period when the loan can be discharged in a lump sum. Since there are no payments to the lender, the debt is not reduced year-by-year and interest each year is paid on the full amount of the loan. If the borrower in turn lends the money accumulating in the fund, for example to a bank on deposit or by the purchase of securities, he will receive interest, usually at a lower rate than that at which he borrows, which can be used to supplement the fund. In effect the interest he receives, less the income tax payable on it, enables him to reduce the payments paid into the fund.[13] This method is used wherever repayment by instalment or annuity is not being resorted to, and provision is required against the need to repay a lump sum in the future. It could be used, for example, where a mortgage is to be repaid in a lump sum after a certain number of years, or where stock is to be redeemed at a certain date.

The government uses a sinking fund, known as the National Sinking Fund, for the repayment of its mature stock. This has been in existence about 150 years, having been formed to pay off the national debt after the Napoleonic Wars. This debt, which is largely the result of intensive government borrowing during past wars, stood in March, 1954, at £26,580 million, involving the country in £580 million of annual interest and management expenses.[14] Into the fund, it was intended, should be paid each year monies which would eventually redeem this debt. There is no regular sum allocated but the receipts from certain sources are paid in including, since the recent war, substantial budget surpluses.

Where he could choose his method of amortising a loan a borrower would be influenced by the relative advantages or disadvantages to him of the methods. These will be outlined.

Firstly, the amount of interest which is paid for a given loan under the three methods is not the same. Table 18 illustrates this by showing the total amount of interest that would be paid under each for a loan of £100 at 4 per cent over a period of 10 to 80 years.[15]

The table shows that least interest is paid by the instalment method; that the same amount is paid by the annuity and sinking fund method when the sinking fund earns the same rate of interest as is paid on the loan; that if the sinking fund earns less than this, which is usual, most interest is paid by this method.

TABLE 18

Total Amount Paid in Interest at 4 per cent for Different Loan Periods Under Different Methods of Repaying Loans

| Period for Repayment | Total Amount Paid in Interest on £100 Loan at 4 per cent | | | |
| | Instalment Method | Annuity Method | Sinking Fund Method with Compound Interest at: | |
			2 per cent	4 per cent
10	22·0	23·3	31·3	23·3
20	42·0	47·2	62·4	47·2
30	62·0	73·5	93·8	73·5
40	82·0	102·1	126·4	102·1
50	102·0	132·7	159·0	132·7
60	122·0	165·2	192·8	165·2
70	142·0	198·9	226·7	198·9
80	162·0	234·4	261·3	234·4

Notes: Instalment.   Interest on the outstanding balance paid at the end of each year.

Annuity.   Annual payments at the end of each year.

Sinking fund.   Sinking fund set apart at end of each year. Compound interest at 2 per cent or at 4 per cent on the fund payments is deducted from the actual interest on the loan.

Secondly, in the repayment of a given loan the annual payments of principal and interest by the annuity or sinking fund method are equal throughout the period, but under the instalment system the payments are heaviest in the early years when the interest runs high. For example, in the repayment of a £100 loan at 4 per cent over 20 years, the annuity and sinking fund method, with reinvestment at 2 per cent, would require 20 equal payments of £7 7s. and £8 2s. respectively; but the instalment method payments would fall from £9 in the first year to £5 4s. in the last. It follows that where the maintenance costs of works are expected to be light in the early years and to become increasingly heavy, it will be an advantage to use the instalment method. And an authority who, in raising a loan, knew that other heavy capital expenditure could be expected in a few years, might prefer the instalment system since it would be in their interest to clear off as much of the loan as possible before the future expenditure was upon them. Conversely, if a golf course, for example, is not to be fully used for many years, so that initial income will be low, it will be a disadvantage to use the instalment system for raising the loan and so have to meet heavy repayments in early years.

Thirdly, the sinking fund method provides most trouble, since the payments must be invested if interest is to be earned. On the other hand it offers the borrower control over the repayments until the loan matures, and he can use them temporarily as he wishes including for another scheme of development.

Period of Loans and the Interest which is Paid

Table 18 shows one feature that is common to all methods of repayment, a sharp increase in the total amount of interest that is paid for a given loan as the period for repayment increases from 10 to 80 years. Table 19 and Graph 3 show for one of the methods, the annuity, the effect on this total amount of interest of varying the rate from 3 per cent to 5 per cent. In this table the payment of the annuity is assumed to take place half-yearly instead of yearly as assumed in Table 18. By comparing the tables it will be seen that half-yearly payment results in slightly less interest being paid.

TABLE 19

Total Amount Paid in Interest for Different Loan Periods and at Different Rates Per Cent, Repayment by Annuity (Half-yearly)

Period of Loan	Interest at 3 per cent	Interest at 4 per cent	Interest at 5 per cent
10	16·5	22·3	28·2
20	33·7	46·2	59·2
30	52·4	72·6	94·4
40	72·4	101·3	132·0
50	93·7	132·0	173·0
60	116·2	164·6	216·0
70	139·8	198·7	261·2
80	164·4	234·1	308·0

It will be seen that the extra interest paid for the longer periods is larger for the higher rates. For all periods the proportionate increase in the total amount of interest paid on the higher rates is about the same, although it is slightly larger as the period increases; over a period of 10 years 71 per cent more interest is paid at 5 per cent than at 3 per cent, but 87 per cent more is paid over 80 years.

Sometimes when repaying a loan, as, for example, when there is only a limited income available, it is the average annual amount of interest and repayment that is of moment rather than the total amount. Table 20 and Graph 4 show the position.

TABLE 20

Average Annual Repayment of Principal and Interest Combined for Different Loan Periods at Different Rates per cent, Repayment by Annuity (Half-yearly)

Period of Loan	Average Annual Repayment of Principal	Interest at 3 per cent — Interest	Interest + Repayment	Interest at 4 per cent — Interest	Interest + Repayment	Interest at 5 per cent — Interest	Interest + Repayment
10	10·0	1·6	11·6	2·2	12·2	2·8	12·8
20	5·0	1·7	6·7	2·3	7·3	3·0	8·0
30	3·3	1·8	5·1	2·4	5·7	3·1	6·4
40	2·5	1·8	4·3	2·5	5·0	3·3	5·9
50	2·0	1·9	3·9	2·6	4·6	3·5	5·5
60	1·7	1·9	3·6	2·7	4·4	3·6	5·3
70	1·4	2·0	3·4	2·8	4·2	3·7	5·1
80	1·2	2·0	3·2	2·9	4·1	3·8	5·0

3 *Total Amount Paid in Interest for Different Loan Periods and at Different Rates per cent (Annuity System)*

4 *Average Annual Repayment of Principal, Interest and Principal plus Interest for Different Loan Periods at Different Rates per cent (Annuity System)*

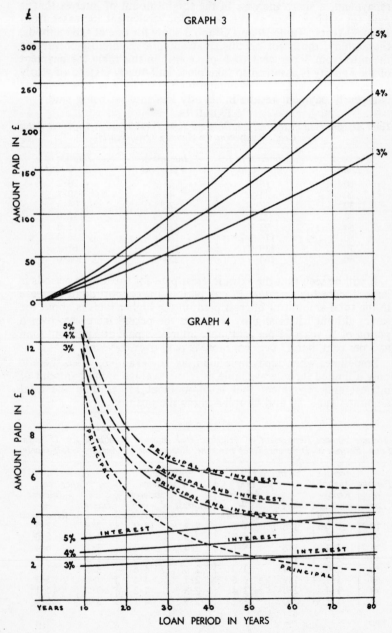

The average annual amount of interest increases as the period of the loan increases; at 3 per cent the amount is 25 per cent more over 80 years than over 10 years, and at 5 per cent it is 33 per cent more. But the average amount of capital repayment falls, very sharply as the period of loan is increased from 10 to about 30 years and much more slowly thereafter. When capital repayment and interest are considered together these tendencies neutralise each other to some extent; but as the graph shows the fall is much sharper over the early 30 years than thereafter.

In deciding upon a particular period for repaying a loan both the average annual repayment and the total should be considered. As the period is shortened the average annual amount of interest increases but there is a decrease in the total amount which is to be paid. Where borrowers wish to keep the total amount to a minimum they will prefer a short period; but too short a period may mean too heavy an annual burden.

In considering different loan periods it must also be kept in mind that loans over the shorter period will probably attract lower rates of interest.

Allowance for Depreciation, Repayment of Loans and Terminable Annuities

There is similarity in making provision for depreciation of a capital asset and for the repayment of a loan. The two are distinct, however. We shall return to the point in Chapters 10 and 11 There is also similarity between sinking funds for the repayment of loans and for the recoupment of money which has been paid for an asset, such as a leasehold property, the income from which is terminable after a specific period. In these cases what is bought is an income for the particular period. On expiry of the period, although the property will still exist the money sunk in its acquisition will be lost as well as the income, unless some provision is made. Such provision is usually by a sinking fund to accumulate at compound interest over the period to the original purchase price.

PART III

FINANCIAL CALCULATIONS FOR DEVELOPMENT

INTRODUCTORY

In Part III we will consider what we have called the financial calculations for development: the calculations which developers make in appraisal of the financial implications of their schemes. Such calculations will be made with various objects and at various stages in the development process. They will be made, for example, to assist a private developer when considering his bid to make for a site. or the current value of a site which he already owns, or which of alternative schemes would show a better return on cost, or whether it is financially practicable or worthwhile to undertake development at all, or what rents will have to be charged to cover the estimated cost of a particular scheme, or what he could afford to spend knowing that certain rents will be obtainable; and to assist a local authority in estimating the prospective rate burden of a road scheme, or which of alternative road schemes would result in a lower rate burden, or their capital cost for grant and loan sanction purposes. The object and method of calculation will be similar at all stages of the process. But there will at varying stages be a varying degree of preciseness: calculations will generally be approximate when the execution of work is long deferred and increase in precision as this approaches. And at all stages the element of time must be allowed for; if it is thought, for example, that works could begin on a site in 1960, a bid in 1955 for the site will be its 1960 value discounted for 1955.

While the calculations of all developers are similar, there are important differences between those made by private and by public developers. This is because their objectives in development differ, as do their kinds of development and methods of financing; and also because public bodies have special powers, privileges and obligations under statute and perhaps receive financial assistance from the government. There are differences, too, between the financial calculations of different public developers, since each works under different statutes and receives different kinds of government financial assistance. We must introduce, therefore, the legal and financial framework within which developers work, for these affect their calculations.

We shall describe the financial calculations of the different developers in a comparative way so that their similarities and

differences can be noted. We will begin with an account of those
made by private developers. They were formulated before public
development was practised on the scale we know it today; and
they form the foundation on which methods of calculations for
public development have become based. We shall then consider
public development calculations in general (Chapter 11), and then,
in more detail, calculations for six kinds of public development,
which are commonly associated with the work of land planning.
These are the construction of subsidised housing by local authorities,
housing associations and New Town Development Corporations;
the construction of roads and streets by highway authorities; the
construction of car parks, the re-development of war-damaged
and obsolete areas and the extension of existing towns by local
authorities; and the building of new towns by New Town Development Corporations. In considering car parks and town extension
we shall also touch upon the financial calculations for operation
where the developers are also operators.

It is not possible to describe all the forms of calculation which
will give the answer to all the questions of a financial character which
a developer will pose. So much depends on the test to which he is
seeking to put the scheme; and these vary as indicated by the above
examples of objects of calculations. In practice the test must be
decided first and the form of calculation devised afterwards to suit.
For this reason we suggest a variety of possible tests and devise a
standard statement from which all the tests can be made.

It will be appreciated that in considering how financial calculations
for different schemes are made, how their costs are built up from
different items, where their yield comes from, and how the two are
related, we shall not be merely learning how to make the necessary
calculations. We shall also be seeing how to influence the design
of schemes in order to make them financially successful; or in order
to produce the most economical scheme to achieve a given objective;
or how to estimate the difference in cost for alternative design
solutions to a given problem, and how to select that which would give
the best value for its estimated cost. This can be illustrated by a
simple example from the field of architectural design, where the
problem was to provide a unit of 24 hospital beds either in four
six-bed rooms, or six four-bed rooms. The architects estimated
that the six four-bed rooms would require slightly larger outer
walls, more windows and more sanitary and electrical fittings. The
extra cost in annual loan charges, maintenance and heating on this
would be £86 per year, and it would involve extra walking distance for
staff and more daily cleaning at an extra annual wages cost of £84
per year. They could thus see which was the cheaper scheme, and
know what extra cost the design with smaller rooms would involve,
and consider whether its advantages were worth the extra cost.[1]
In a similar way draft schemes for private or public development

can be costed and valued and their economics compared, and designs can be influenced in the draft stage. But the process is often more difficult in the design of development schemes than in architecture because it is necessary to deal with land costs and future values as well as construction costs. Furthermore, it is often more difficult in a public than in a private development scheme. The test for economy in the latter is usually the simple one of profitability of the particular scheme. The test for economy in a public scheme is not straightforward profitability where both remunerative and non-remunerative uses are provided, or where different schemes are interdependent. A variety of tests for public development are therefore considered throughout Chapters 11-17.

CHAPTER 10

PRIVATE ENTERPRISE DEVELOPMENT

The Financial Calculations of Private Developers—Capital Cost— Annual Costs—Money Yield from Development—Exercise 1: A Neighbourhood Business Centre—Methods of Financial Appraisal of Schemes—Time and Development.

The Financial Calculations of Private Developers

WHILE all private developers are concerned to estimate whether the net money yield that they can expect from development will show them some gain over the costs that they will have to bear, they do not all have the same criteria or tests in considering the relation between estimated yield and cost. Where a developer is improving land to let on ground rents, or erecting buildings to let, as in factory estates, the amount of capital value created will not interest him so much as the return on the investment that the rents can be expected to show throughout the years. House builders who are only interested in selling would, however, consider the new capital values to be created, since the profit over capital cost that they could realise on sale would be their test of gain. Were such builders working in a fading market they might also consider the prospective return on investment in case they were forced to retain and let the houses. A property company which operates with borrowed money would be primarily interested in the return on its own capital rather than cost; and if it had only a small amount of capital of its own might have as its main aim a very substantial margin between capital costs and capital value, because the greater this margin the greater the proportion of capital cost that it could borrow.

The kind of calculation made by all these developers would be much the same; but the individual developers would vary them according to the objects of the calculations, as earlier described, to whether or not they intended to dispose of the development, to whether this would be by sale or letting or a combination of both, and to their intended methods and scale of financing. We shall not here consider the differences in approach of various kinds of private developers but shall describe all the items which might appear in all their calculations, although not all in any particular calculation. This will be done under the following four heads, which we shall retain for the discussion of different kinds of public development so that comparisons can be made.

I. The capital cost of carrying out the development.

II. The continuing or annual costs of the development after
it is completed.

III. The money yield from the development, the payments to
be made by its final users.

IV. The methods of appraising the financial implications of the
development, that is, of *testing the relation between estimated cost
and yield.*

Private developers will not necessarily make a calculation in this
order since much will depend on its object. They will often start
with *III*, the yield that they can expect, and design a scheme at a cost
which will be covered by the yield.

For simplicity we shall assume that only one developer is involved although, as described above, a particular scheme might have
more than one (Chapter 1); and we shall assume that the developer
is considering his scheme in isolation and not in relation to other
schemes or undertakings.

I. Capital Cost. The total estimated cost of the scheme would
be made up of various items, as follows:

(*a*) *Acquisition of Land.* In addition to the purchase price, the
cost of acquisition will include expenses such as those of obtaining
possession, solicitors' charges, stamp duties on the conveyance
deed or lease, and any professional fees paid for advice from an
architect, engineer or surveyor prior to the purchase.[2] If the
land is already owned, and was bought at a price substantially
different from its current value (the amount which it would
currently cost to acquire) this value should be taken as cost. By
this means any profit or loss on land holding is separated out in the
calculation. In calculating such profit or loss account must be
taken of the interest which the capital invested in the land would
have earned if otherwise employed.

(*b*) *Legal Preparation of the Site.* Before the new works can
begin some preparatory legal work may be called for. It may be
necessary to close rights of way;[3] to discharge restrictive covenants;[4] to buy out easements or perhaps acquire them over other
land; to redeem tithe redemption annuities or land tax; to adjust
boundaries with adjoining owners.

(*c*) *Physical Preparation of the Site.* Where an area is to be
re-developed, demolition and clearance may be required; and on
a virgin site it may be necessary to clear scrub, hedges or trees.

(*d*) *Construction of Roads, Sewers and Services, and Planting.*
The contract would normally include works in (*c*) above. In
addition to the contractor's price there would be fees for the
architect, landscape architect, engineer or surveyor for preparing
the scheme and supervising the works. In estimating the cost
of the works the law relating to them must be reckoned with.

Streets are considered in Chapter 13. Gas or electricity under-takers can demand payment for laying service mains beyond a certain distance from existing mains; a water authority can demand a contribution over and above the water rate where this will be low in relation to the cost of carrying out the necessary works; local authorities may ask for contributions when laying new sewers to drain an area to be developed.[5]

(e) *Construction of Buildings.* In addition to the contractor's price there would be the fees of the architect, engineer and surveyor for preparing the scheme and supervising works. In practice, on the smaller jobs one contract would be let for both civil engineering and building work.

(f) *Interest on Capital Used During the Construction of Works.* There is a considerable amount of money tied up in the con-struction of works pending their completion. If this money is borrowed by the developer interest will need to be paid on it during this time. If it is not borrowed it could be earning interest if otherwise employed. The total amount that would need to be paid in interest, for the period between the time when the money is borrowed and the date when a yield is expected, is included in the cost. The total capital cost is not borrowed immediately works are begun. For calculation purposes it is often assumed that interest will be paid on the total capital for half the total period referred to.

(g) *Profit on Enterprise.* The profit that the developer counts on if he is to undertake the entrepreneurial work of developing can be considered as a cost to be covered by yield. The amount of profit that would be expected will vary from scheme to scheme according to the risk, length of time that the development will take and nature of development. There is no one accepted method of allowing for this in calculations. A common allowance is between 5 per cent and 20 per cent of the total cost of works excluding land, or of the values to be created.

(h) *Disposal Expenses.* Expense is incurred in arranging the tenancies, leases or sales which are necessary to dispose of the land or buildings; that is in estate agency fees, solicitors' charges and stamp duty on contracts and conveyances for sale, or leases and agreements for tenancy.

(i) *Total Capital Costs.* Of the total, the costs under (c), (d) and (e) are the measure of the demand on the building and civil engineering industry, and also of the new investment required in capital goods. The costs under (a), (b) and (f) are transfer payments from one person or body to another.

II. *Annual Costs.* During the period of development there will be a variety of continuing charges or expenses (which we will call

annual costs) as follows. All of these except (k) and (l), the interest
on and repayment of any loan, the developer will normally expect
to be paid for by the final users of the development.

(j) *Return on Investment.* Whether it is owned by the developer
or not, the capital which is sunk in the development should
earn an appropriate return at a rate equal to what it would
have earned if invested elsewhere in an enterprise of corresponding nature and risk. The smallest return normally expected
in development is on land which is improved with roads and
services and leased at ground rents. On this, to attract developers
the prospective return needs to be generally about $1\frac{1}{2}$ per cent to
2 per cent above that currently received on government securities.
The amount of capital on which the return is to be earned is the
total invested, that is, capital cost (i) less profit (g).

(k) *Interest on Any Loan.* Where part or all of the capital cost
is borrowed, interest must be paid on the loan until it is repaid.
The rate is usually decided at the time of borrowing, but sometimes provision is made for changes throughout the period in
response to changes in market rate. The rate of interest is normally
lower than the rate of return on investment, particularly where the
loan is well secured, as where only a portion of the total capital
cost is borrowed by way of mortgage. The difference in rates leads
to a margin which results purely from borrowing at one rate
and investing at another. Where the developer borrows part of
the cost he will, while the loan is outstanding, receive the yield
on the investment on that portion which he himself owns, his
equity; and a profit margin on the amount which he has borrowed.
Where he borrows the entire cost at a rate of interest lower than
the rate of yield, as where a joint stock company with a good
trading record borrows for future expansion, there would be a
profit margin on the whole cost.

(l) *Repayment of Any Loan.* Where part or all of the capital
cost is borrowed it must be normally repaid by a fixed date, and
provision for repayment must be made.

(m) *Depreciation.* Some provision should be made against
the day when the development needs to be reproduced, on the
basis that capital should be maintained, even if it is known that
the owner or occupier of the completed property will not in fact
make any such provision in his accounting, and will be content
to consume capital. For making such provision one of the three
methods described in Chapter 8 will be used; in the reducing
balance method the annual average of the total provision over the
selected period should be taken. In development calculations the
amount to be written off is usually taken as initial (that is,
historical) capital cost of the works which will require renewal.
This might be taken as the total capital cost (i), less the cost of
acquiring and preparing the land (a), (b), (c) and the profit (g)

and perhaps any part of the cost of site works which will not require renewal (d).

(n) *Annual Occupation Expenses.* These are the annual expenses which are incidental to the occupation of the property. For example, it must be kept in good repair so that it can serve its purpose satisfactorily for as long as possible; the general, special and water rates levied by the local and water authorities must be paid, and premiums for insurance of the property against unexpected damage or destruction; the cost of services to tenants, for which rents are paid, must be met.

(o) *Annual Ownership Expenses.* These are the annual expenses which are incidental to ownership of property. For example, there is work involved in its management: the collection of rents, the arrangement of new tenancies, the initiation and supervision of repairs and maintenance. In certain properties, such as blocks of service flats, these may be very heavy. An owner may also be liable for certain taxes, such as land tax or tithe redemption annuity, which he must pay whether or not the property is occupied.

(p) *Total Annual Cost.* If the development is to be financially attractive, the annual costs (j), (m), (n) and (o) must be met by the ultimate occupiers of the development, so that the developer is left with (j), his yield, after the occupation and ownership expenses have been met and depreciation provided for. If the developer intends to borrow in order to earn the return, then the interest on and repayment of loan (k) and (l) should, for development calculations on the scheme in question. be considered as charges on this return, and not as costs to be covered by yield, even though the developer, in practice, will not consider them so. Should he, for example, intend to meet the interest on loan but make no provision for its repayment, in the expectation that he will reborrow when the loan is due, that is his idea for disposing of the return; he prefers to consume his loan rather than save to repay it. The enumeration of annual costs should be unaffected.

Income Tax. A property owner is always liable for income tax on income he actually receives or is deemed to receive if in occupation. Since the liability is personal to him, the actual rate of tax varying with his other income and the amount of his assessment depending upon whether or not he is in occupation, it is in a different category from other ownership expenses and not normally taken into account in development calculations when considering income from property. It must be taken into account, however, when considering payments to be made out of the income, such as interest on and repayment of loan, for such payments can only be made out of the residue of yield after paying tax.

III. Money Yield from Development. Money yield from development can be realised in alternative ways. The developer could

FIGURE 1.—*Plan of Section of Neighbourhood Shopping Centre—*
Exercise 1

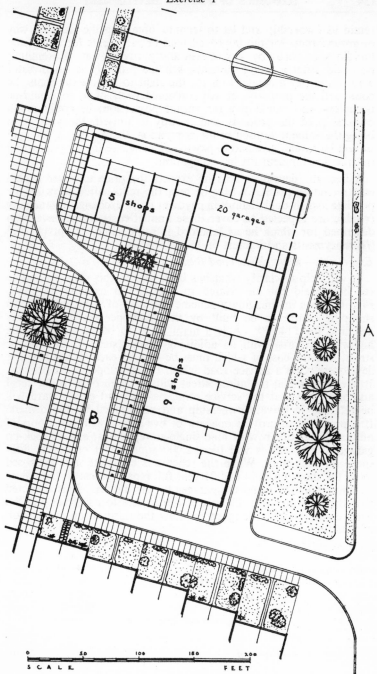

C

5 shops

20 garages

C

A

9 shops

B

0   50   100   150   200
SCALE   FEET

retain its ownership and let to tenants, obtaining the yield by way of ground rents for the improved land or rack rents for completed buildings, or partly by way of rent and partly by way of premium; he could, after letting to tenants, sell the property to an investor who would pay a capital sum for the right to receive the rents; he could sell the property, or self-contained parts of it, to would-be occupiers who would pay for vacant possession; he could retain ownership of the property and occupy it himself, the yield then being the value to himself of the occupation, that is, the capital sum or rent he would have had to pay to someone else for having carried out the development for his occupation.

Where the developer sells he expects the price to cover capital cost including profit. Where he lets, the rents, after allowing for possible loss through default in payment or on exchange of tenancies (voids), are expected to cover those annual costs which have been described for which he as landlord is responsible, except (*k*) and (*l*), repayments and interest on loan.

Exercise 1.—*A Neighbourhood Business Centre.*

It will help to clarify what has been said in this chapter, and to see how yield can be related to cost, if an example is given. Fig. 1 shows an imaginary scheme for part of a neighbourhood shopping centre to be built by the developer on land he has acquired for £14,000. A is a main street to be provided by the highway authority with its adjoining open space. B is a minor street, half the cost of which must be met by each of the fronting developers. C is a service road which the developer must provide. It is expected that the minor street will be taken over by the local authority, but that the service road, paving, and garage yard will be retained in private ownership and maintained by the owners. It is proposed to provide one row of five shops, with two floors of offices above; one row of nine single-storey shops; and 20 lock-up garages. The offices will have 2,000 square feet of usable floor space on each floor. When the scheme is complete it is proposed to let the shops on 7, 14 and 21-year full repairing leases; the offices on shorter lettings; and the garages by the month. It is expected that the buildings will take about three years to construct and let. The calculations are designed to show the position on completion of building.

I. Capital Cost

		£	£
(*a*) Acquisition of land		14,000	
Legal and other professional expenses		500	
			14,500
(*b*) Legal preparation of site			200
(*c*) Physical preparation			400
(*d*) Roads, paving, sewers, services and planting, including fees			10,000
Carried forward			25,100

		£	£
Brought forward			25,100
(e) Buildings, including fees 5 shops		10,000	
9 shops		20,000	
Offices		12,000	
20 garages		5,000	
			47,000
(f) Interest during construction and letting: 1½ years at 6 per cent of (c) to (e), i.e., £57,400			5,200
(g) Profit on development: 10 per cent of (a) to (f), i.e., £77,300			7,700
(h) Disposal expenses: 10 per cent of annual rents ...			600
(i) Total capital cost			£85,600
Total capital invested, (i) less (g)			£77,900
Total cost for depreciation, (i) less ((a) + (b) + (c) + (g))			£63,200

Of the investment it is assumed that £60,000 will be borrowed by way of mortgage at 5 per cent, to be repaid as a lump sum at the end of 20 years. Provision for repayment will be made by sinking fund, to be invested to earn 2½ per cent free of income tax.

II. *Annual Costs to be Met*

(*j*) *Return on the Interest.* A scheme of this kind might be expected to earn about 7 per cent on the investment of £77,900 throughout its life: that is, £5,500.

(*k*) *Interest on Loan.* At 5 per cent the interest on the loan would be £3,000 per annum. As repayment is by lump sum this would have to be paid throughout the 20 years.

(*l*) *Repayment of Loan.* To repay £60,000 in 20 years, by a sinking fund accumulating at 2½ per cent free of income tax, £2,350 per annum would be required.

(*m*) *Depreciation.* The garages would have a shorter life than the remainder; but ignoring this and assuming a life of 60 years, an annual sinking fund to replace the total capital cost minus the cost of land and profit (that is £63,200) in 60 years at 2½ per cent free of income tax would require £480 per annum.

(*n*) *Occupation Expenses.* These would consist of general rates at say 20s. in the £ on the rateable values of £150 per annum for each of the smaller group or shops, £175 for each of the larger group and £300 for the double shop; at £200 for the first floor offices and £150 for the second; at £8 each for the garages. Annual water rate would be levied at 8 per cent to 10 per cent on the rateable values. Repairs to the buildings and maintenance of the roads, planting, paving, etc., and cleansing and lighting of the common parts of the office and garage premises, might average £600 per annum. Fire insurance would come to about 2s. per cent on the cost of the buildings, or £50. The total occupation expenses would be about £4,000.

(*o*) *Ownership Expenses.* There would be little expense in the management of shops, but more in the management of the offices and garages. In total it might amount to about 5 per cent of the gross rents, or £300 per annum.

(*p*) *Total Amount of Costs* to be covered by rents:

		£
(*j*) Return on investment of £77,900		5,550
(*m*) Depreciation on works of £63,200, say		500
(*n*) Occupation expenses...		4,000
(*o*) Ownership expenses		300
(*p*) Total		£10,350

III. Money Yield

It is assumed that the property is let at inclusive rents. Following are the net rents that could be expected over the years: that is, the inclusive rents after deducting the amounts (totalling £4,800) necessary to cover allowance for depreciation, occupation and ownership expenses.

	£	£
Shop rents: 5 at £300 per annum	1,500	
8 at £350 per annum	2,800	
1 at £600 per annum	600	
		4,900
Office rents: 1st floor — 2,000 ft. at 5s. 0d. per annum ...	500	
2nd floor—2,000 ft. at 4s. 0d. per annum ...	400	
		900
Garages £20 per annum		400
Total net rents		6,200
Less voids		200
Net income		£6,000

IV. Methods of Financial Appraisal of Schemes

The financial estimates which are made under *I* to *III* are a preliminary to the financial appraisal of the scheme: that is, the relating of estimated cost and yield. There are at least three tests for doing this, each of which is applicable whether the developer intends using his own capital or obtaining partial or complete financing. Not all these tests will necessarily be used in any particular scheme; the developer might have one or two particular criteria as to the relation of cost and yield, as already described, and might only concern himself with tests appropriate to them.

Tests Without Financing (items (*k*) and (*l*) in *II* are ignored)

Method (*A*). The total capital cost of the scheme (*i*) is compared with the total price which the finished development will sell for in the market; or, in other words, the new market values which will be created. Since an amount for profit is included in (*i*), if the new values equal the cost then this amount of profit will be realised. If the estimated new values are more or less than the estimated capital cost, the profit will be more or less accordingly.

In the example above the scheme when completed might sell for about £87,500, calculated as follows:

Blocks of:	£		£
Shops and offices	2,325 net rents per ann. at 7% - 14·2 years' purchase		33,000
Shops alone	3,300 net rents per ann. at 6½%-15·4 years' purchase		50,750
Lock up garages	375 net rents per ann. at 10% - 10 years' purchase		3,750
	6,000		87,500

This is about £1,900 more than the estimated capital cost including profit of £7,700, so that the developer would in fact receive a profit of £9,600 for his work. This additional £1,900 can be considered as profit on the land transaction, for the developer could have paid about £16,000, instead of £14,000, for the land and still made his appropriate developer's profit.

Method (B). The net yield by way of rents is calculated as a percentage of the total capital invested in order to test whether this would earn its expected market rate of return. In the example, the rents of £6,000, after allowing for voids, would be 7·6 per cent of £77,900, the total capital invested. This is better than the expected market rate of 7 per cent.

If the developer were to sell at £87,500 after holding for a while he would be getting 6·85 per cent of the £6,000 (14·6 years purchase) and not 7·6 per cent (13 years purchase). The difference, 1·6 years purchase or £9,600, would equal the capital profit of method (A).

Method (C). The estimated net yield in rents is compared with the estimated annual return required on the investment (j). In our example, the rents are £6,000 and the expected return £5,500. This is another way of expressing what was said under method (B), that the estimated return would be more than 7 per cent.

Tests with Financing

We will consider how the three tests which have been described are adapted when money is borrowed.

Method (D). As in (A) the total capital cost (i) is compared with the total of the new values which will be created; but from each is deducted the amount of the loan. This will give the proportion of capital cost put up by the developer, his equity, and the proportion of the capital values which will remain with him should he repay the loan after selling the completed development. The developer's profit can then be considered in relation to his equity. In our example, £25,600 of the developer's money will have been spent (£85,600—£60,000) and about £27,500 of new value will remain with him should he sell (£87,500—£60,000). He would thus be making a profit of £9,600 on his own capital of £25,600: a profit of 38 per cent.

Method (E). As in (*B*) the net yield is related to capital cost; but from the rents is deducted the interest on loan (*k*) and from the capital cost is deducted the amount of the loan. The difference between rents and interest can be expressed as a percentage of the developer's equity. In our example the difference is £3,000 and the equity is £17,900. The return on equity is 16·8 per cent. The £3,000 is made up of £1,380, which is the return of 7·7 per cent on the equity (see method (*B*)), and of £1,620, which is the profit margin of 2·7 per cent on the loan of £60,000.

Method (F). As in (*C*) the estimated net rents are compared with the estimated return which is required on the investment, but from the rents is deducted the interest on the loan, and the estimated return is taken only on the equity. In our example the rents less the interest on loans amount to £3,000 and the expected return on equity is £1,250 (7 per cent of £17,900).

Summary of Tests. If financing is not taken into account the scheme will show a capital profit and return on investment greater than that required to justify it; and the profit and return will be even greater if financing is taken into account, because the rate at which money is borrowed is less than that at which it is earned.

If the developer did not have enough capital of his own, however, he might not proceed with the scheme for quite another financial reason: he would be unable to repay loans out of taxed income. Out of his net rent of £6,000 he would, over the period of the loan, have to pay income tax of, say, £1,200.[6] After deducting interest on his loan he would have a net income of £1,800, which would be insufficient to meet his loan repayment of £2,350 per annum. He would not be able to proceed unless he could make some arrangement to bridge the gap. For example, he could temporarily draw on other funds during the 20 years; or, on the assumption that he could borrow a new loan of, say, £30,000 at the end of the loan period, set aside only £1,175 per annum to repay £30,000 only at the end of the 20 years.

Testing of Alternative Schemes

When testing individual aspects of a scheme, or a scheme as a whole, it is often necessary to consider the effect of alternative possibilities: the using of one site rather than another, a combination of blocks of flats of varying heights to produce a given density, the building of a five-storey office building rather than a four or six-storey, the provision or not of upper parts over shops. These alternatives can be compared by costing out each scheme in the way described and comparing the totals of each. Another approach is to start with figures which are common to the various alternative schemes and to gauge the effect only of the possible variations, or marginal differences: to test the marginal cost against marginal yield.

To give an example, in the design of the scheme described it would probably have been necessary to consider the possibility of building offices over the row of nine shops. This would have added 4,000 sq. ft. of usable space on each floor which could be let at 4s. per foot on the first and 3s. per foot on the second floor, a total net rent of £1,400, or £1,350 after allowing for voids. The additional cost of construction, including fees, would be £24,000.

The total additional capital cost would be:

		£
(e) Buildings, including fees		24,000
(f) Interest during construction and letting: 1½ years at 6 per cent of £24,000		2,160
(g) Profit: 10 per cent of (e) and (f)		2,620
(h) Disposal expenses: 10 per cent of annual rents		140
(i) Total capital cost		£28,920
Total capital invested (i) less (g)		£26,300
Total cost for depreciation (i) less (g)		£26,300

Of the investment, £20,000 would be borrowed by mortgage. At 5 per cent the interest would be £1,000.

The tests would be as follows:

Method (A). For an additional capital cost of £28,920 new capital values would be added of £18,100 (£1,350 at, say, 7½ per cent, or 13·4 years purchase).

Method (B). On the investment of £26,300 there would be a return of £1,350, or 5·1 per cent.

Method (C). The net yield of £1,350 would be lower than the required return of £1,840 (7 per cent of £26,300).

Method (D). The cost of £8,920 to the developer, including profit, would produce a capital value which would be less than the amount of the loan.

Method (E). On the equity of £6,300 the yield less interest would be £350 (£1,350 — £1,000) to show a return of 5·5 per cent.

Method (F). The rents less interest (£350) would be less than the 7 per cent return required on equity (£440).

The result of these tests is clearly that on any of the methods (A), (B), (C), and even taking into account in methods (D), (E), (F) the profit margin on financing, the yield would bear a relation to cost which is much less favourable than in the main scheme itself. The larger scheme would therefore be unattractive.

This method of comparing the marginal costs and yields of alternative schemes should be much less laborious in many cases than comparing total costs and yields; and it has the advantage that the differences in the schemes are picked out clearly for examination. But there is one point to be watched: the significance of the results of the test must be considered not merely in relation to the part of the scheme that is tested, but to the whole scheme. In our illustration, the new value is about £11,000 less than the total cost including profit. This is significant on a scheme which is going to cost about £90,000; it would not be so significant on one costing, say, £250,000.

Time and Development Calculations

As mentioned in Chapter 1, development is a lengthy process. Time can therefore have a great effect on the financial outcome of a scheme. In buying his land the developer must discount for the period which will elapse before works begin. If he discounts for too short a period he will have paid more than its value; and this will reduce his realisable profit. When works start money must be sunk and the yield should cover the interest on it; any time wasted during construction will therefore add to the total capital cost which ought to be covered by yield. If the works are completed and are not immediately disposed of to produce a return, the delay results in annual costs being incurred with no income to balance them over a longer period than necessary.

In each of these three ways, therefore, time is important for development. Bad timing can clearly ruin an otherwise financially sound scheme, and development calculations which do not take full account of the effect of time upon cost and yield will not be accurate. In our example above the calculations were designed to show the position when development would be completed, and interest was therefore allowed on capital sunk prior to this. If they had been made to show the position when works would begin, this interest would have been ignored but allowance would have been made for the fact that the receipt of rents or capital value would be deferred for three years. Their discounted value would have been taken at a rate of interest of, say, 6 per cent.[7]

We have seen, too, that time is important in another sense, that over which the developer is budgeting to obtain his return. A speculator may be interested only in selling in the immediate future, an investor in a continuing return over the life of the property, a freeholder, who creates leases, in the period of the lease and also in the ultimate reversion. The time over which a developer is budgeting will influence the way in which he seeks to relate yield to cost.

CHAPTER 11

PUBLIC DEVELOPMENT

Capital Cost—Annual Costs—Money Yield—Financial Appraisal of Public Development Schemes—Testing Cost and Yield of Several Sites Together—Profit Margins—The Annual Cost of Local Authority Development and its Relation to Rate Resources—The Incidence of Rates.

IN CHAPTERS 12 to 17 we shall consider the financial calculations carried out for six kinds of public development which are commonly associated with the work of land planning. These calculations are not the same for each kind, but they have a great deal in common. In this chapter we shall discuss the common ground.

I. Capital Cost

(*a*) *Acquisition of Land.*[1] Public bodies can buy land by agreement for any of their functions. If they want it immediately, local authorities do not need ministerial approval to the purchase, but if in advance of requirements they do.[2] If public bodies cannot buy by agreement for their functions they can usually compel an owner to sell. The relevant statutes enable them to acquire the land after due legal process, and sometimes to enter into possession in advance of this.

Except in times of national emergency, authority for compulsory purchase must derive from private or public Acts of Parliament. Private Acts usually contain specific authorisation to acquire. Under public Acts it is generally necessary to obtain ministerial confirmation of an order giving the powers. This is sometimes asked for after preliminary ministerial agreement in principle has been obtained that the land in question can be bought, compulsorily if necessary, for a specific purpose. This is done, for example, in the designation of the site of a new town under the New Towns Act, 1946, section 1; and the definition of an area of comprehensive development under the Town and Country Planning Act, 1947, section 5.

When buying land by agreement with its own funds a local authority can pay what it chooses. But if it requires government approval in any way to the purchase (in order to obtain loan sanction, for example, or to obtain grant) this approval will not normally be given for purchase at a price above that certified by the District Valuer. This certificate will relate to the compensation payable were compulsory powers used where these are available, and to market value where they are not. Should a price above that certified be paid, the authority would probably not receive sanction to borrow or grant. We are primarily interested therefore in the compulsory purchase price.

To know the price to be paid on compulsory purchase it is necessary to have regard not only to the particular Act giving powers of purchase but also to the Lands Clauses Acts, 1845, etc., and the Acquisition of Land (Assessment of Compensation) Act, 1919, in so far as they are incorporated into the particular Act. The general basis for compensation by public bodies was laid down in the Lands Clauses Act, 1845, at a time when statutory undertakers were buying extensively, as the value of the land to the owner at the time, with all additional loss that would be suffered by him in consequence of the acquisition. This additional loss might be due to disturbance of occupation, or to damage to other lands of the same owner because of severance or injurious affection (see p. 143). Furthermore, compensation is also payable for injurious affection to lands which are not held with the lands which are to be taken, but only in certain restricted circumstances (see page 144).[3] Subject to the amendments brought about by the Town and Country Planning Acts, the Lands Clauses Acts still govern the assessment of compensation for disturbance, severance and injurious affection, but the 1919 Act governs the price to be paid for the land itself. We will consider the two separately.

As to the land, the 1919 Act gave six rules, the most important for our purpose being Rule 2 which states that, in general, the value of the land shall be " the amount which the land, if sold in the open market by a willing seller, might be expected to realise."[4] This value includes development value. The Town and Country Planning Act, 1944, amended this by stating that market value was to be ascertained not by reference to prices in the current market but to those ruling in 1939, with additions for owner-occupiers.[5] Current market prices were reverted to under the Town and Country Planning Act, 1947, but the acquiring authority was to pay only for the value of the existing use rights at the time of purchase, with some discounting for the scarcity values of owner-occupied properties; the development rights in all land were to be bought by the Central Land Board, whether the land was to be acquired by a public body or not. Payment was to be made following the lodging of claims by owners for loss of such rights, as they existed in 1948, and agreement on their value. The total payment for them in England and Wales was to be £300 million.[6] Now, under the Town and Country Planning Act, 1954, in addition to the existing use value of land public bodies also pay, in general, the amount of the unexpended balance of the established claim for the value of the1948 development rights in that land. This is the agreed claim less that part of it which has been deducted (on account of compensation for refusal of permission having been paid or permission for development having been granted subsequent to 1948) plus one seventh of the balance remaining (which represents interest on it at $3\frac{1}{2}$ per cent less income tax at normal rates).[7] But where land belonging to government departments, statutory undertakers or local authorities is acquired the value continues to be, on the whole, existing use or prevailing use value, but having regard to cost of acquisition in certain circumstances.[8]

In this price nothing is included because the purchase is compulsory or because the land has a special suitability or adaptability which only a public body or particular purchaser could use, or value is increased by illegal or unhealthy use.[9] As stated earlier, where there is no general demand or market for the property to be acquired, and therefore no market value, the basis is the reasonable cost of equivalent reinstatement elsewhere, if reinstatement is in fact intended by the owners.

As to compensation for disturbance, severance or injurious affection, Rule 2 of the 1919 Act on its own might have excluded any at all, for the value was to be that in the open market and not that to an owner whose continued occupation had been disturbed. This compensation was however retained by Rule 6 as an addition to the price for the land taken. But its level was also affected by the Town and Country Planning Acts. The 1944 Act restricted the level to 1939 prices. The 1947 Act limited the compensation to damage to the existing use value. The 1954 Act provides that compensation for severance and injurious affection will no longer be confined to damage to the existing use value of the land affected but will, broadly, also be payable for damage to the development value up to the amount of the unexpended balance, while compensation for disturbance will be assessed as though the land being acquired were being bought at market value.[10]

The compensation for disturbance includes, for example, the cost of removal of the owner's furniture and goods; the cost of the owner's fixtures or an allowance for their depreciation or removal; depreciation in stock; diminution in value of goodwill; and loss in profits owing to dispossession. The amount of disturbance payable will in some cases be very heavy, amounting to as much again as the cost of the property or even more. The disturbance to a business might be less, and the compensation accordingly less, if the acquiring authority were to make available land for it to be sited elsewhere, and to permit of removal at the convenience of the displaced trader or industrialist.

Where only part of an owner's land is acquired he is also entitled to compensation for severance or injurious affection to his lands which have not been taken. The lands need not necessarily be contiguous but must be " so near together and so situated that the possession and control of each gives an enhanced value to all of them."[11] Loss by severance occurs where a house is separated from part of a garden to the detriment of its remaining privacy, or where a road cuts across a farm or the curtilage of a factory and causes increased cost of working; and loss by injurious affection occurs where part of a garden is taken for a road and the residential amenity of the house suffers from the dust, noise and loss of privacy that will arise from the new road, or the prospective value of building land suffers because of a proposed sewage farm on part of it.

Where only part of a " house building or manufactory " is required by an undertaker working under the Lands Clauses Act, 1845, the owner can require the undertaker to take the whole if he is able to sell it. But it is common today for the Act under which public bodies acquire to incorporate a " material detriment clause." Under this the owner cannot compel the acquiring authority to buy the whole if the tribunal by whom the compensation is to be assessed determines that part of the house, building or manufactory can be taken without material detriment to it, or part of a park or garden of a house without seriously affecting the amenity or convenience of the house.[12]

Injurious affection may also be caused to lands owned by a person from whom land has not been acquired, by, for example, physical interference with property and trade arising from the execution of works or subsequent use of the works.[13] But the courts have decided that compensation is payable for this only in fairly restricted circumstances, where in fact the injury:

(1) results from some act made lawful by the acquiring body's statutory powers and which would have been actionable but for such powers; and

(2) arises from the execution of works and not their subsequent user; and

(3) affects land, and is not merely a personal injury or an injury to trade.

It is the construction of works in this case which must give rise to the claim. There is no claim merely because the acquisition and use of land by a public authority depreciates the value of adjoining land, as where a new sewage farm destroys existing or potential residential amenity, or a new local authority housing estate depreciates the value of existing high-value dwellings. But the Housing Act, 1936, section 44, contains a provision enabling local authorities to depart from this principle. They may, but are not compelled to, contribute towards removal expenses and loss of trade of any person, carrying on a retail shop in the locality of a clearance or improvement area, whose property had not been affected by works but who would sustain personal hardship through a material decrease in the local population. (See page 171).

Public bodies may also be put to expense in securing sites just because they have public responsibilities. For example, where a local authority displaces people living on land acquired by it for re-development under the Town Planning Acts it must provide residential accommodation for such persons in advance of their displacement where there is not otherwise accommodation available on reasonable terms; and there is a general obligation on any authority, company or person who is acquiring land under a local or general Act, and who is displacing more than 30 persons, to satisfy the Minister that adequate provision is being made for the rehousing of the people concerned.[14]

In many cases public bodies pay less on acquisition than would a private purchaser, as where land is bought having development value which has risen since 1947 and for which they therefore pay less than current market value. But they often pay more than a private purchaser would do, as where the site of a building destroyed in the war and attracting a cost of works payment is bought as though the building were restored, the authority receiving only the value payment from the War Damage Commission.[15] The expenses to be met by a public body in compensation for disturbance, rehousing, severance and injurious affection will in some cases be more and in some cases less than a private purchaser would have to pay in securing the same land. Their legal and professional expenses are usually more than those of a private purchaser, for in addition to their own they generally have to pay those of vendors too.

(b) *Legal Preparation of the Site.* Public bodies have been given powers of liquidating, in a much simpler way than can private developers, the kind of legal encumbrances on ownership which, if they were not liquidated, would restrict development. For example, both private and public development can take place on land acquired by a local authority under the 1947 Act notwithstanding interference with any easement or restrictive covenant, or with private rights of way and the rights of laying down, erecting, continuing or maintaining any apparatus in the land.[16] Also under that Act, after following certain procedures, local authorities can extinguish public rights of way; can, in face of restrictions, carry out development on consecrated land, burial grounds and open spaces;[17] and can obtain possession of rent-controlled houses on land which they acquire for development.[18] Compensation is payable for any damage to property rights.

(c), (d), (e) *Cost of Site Works and Buildings.* There is little difference in practice between the way in which public and private developers carry out their construction works, or the cost of these works to them.

(f) *Interest on Capital During Construction.* Public bodies must find the interest on capital which is laid out during the construction of works but the argument for adding it to capital cost is not so clear with them as it is with private developers. We will defer consideration of the argument until later in this chapter (page 149).

(g) *Profit.* Public bodies do not normally sell completed development, nor do they normally require a profit to induce them to undertake development, since they have the other motives which we have discussed. And since on the whole their development does not pay for itself they are normally interested in seeing merely that yield will cover expenditure actually incurred. There is rarely need therefore for them to include profit as a cost to be covered by capital values.

(h) *Disposal Expenses.* When they are not building for their own occupation, public bodies will incur the same kind of expenses in disposing of development as do private bodies.

Staff. The legal and professional work required in connection with development by a public body is generally carried out by its salaried staff. Their salaries and establishment must therefore be charged to the cost of the works.

II. Annual Costs.

(j), (k), (l), (m) *Return on the Investment, Interest on and Repayment of Loans, Depreciation.* A great difference between the financial calculations for private and public development arises from the differences in their practice of financing. Whereas private development calculations start with the assumption that the developer owns the capital, and the effect of financing is considered as a secondary even if important one, public development calculations start with the assumption that all capital will be borrowed, and that provision must be made for its repayment and for interest pending repayment. It follows, therefore, that public developers are in general not primarily concerned with earning the market rate of return on their capital (since they have put none up, and there is often no market rate for their kind of investment), but rather with earning the rate of interest that the lender requires on the loan. The actual rate taken will depend upon the circumstances. A local authority which borrows from an internal loans pool (into which are paid all loans, all internal funds available for investment, all repayments for past maturity loans, and out of which are paid all interest and repayments on loans) might take the rate currently required to balance the interest charges on the pool, or that which will be required over the next few years. Where it does not have a loans pool, but has loans earmarked to specific projects, it would take the rate at which it raised the particular loan. A public corporation might take the rate to be paid on the issue of stock out of which the particular project is being financed, or perhaps the average rate which it is thought will be necessary to meet all loans during the next few years. It also follows that where the public development is remunerative there is likely to be a profit margin (see page 152) on the whole and not part of the capital cost.

This profit margin is normally greater than would be earned by a private developer: public developers pay a lower rate of interest than do private developers, usually about gilt-edged rate, since their loans are secured not on the particular projects for which they are raised but on all the resources of the public body in question, and sometimes on those of the Treasury.

With regard to the provision for depreciation (*m*) and repayment of loan (*l*) there is no uniform practice adopted by public developers in their development calculations. *Ad hoc* bodies, on the one hand, write down their assets in their accounts,[19] and may accordingly follow good private enterprise practice and provide for depreciation in their calculations. They will not also count the repayment of their loan as an annual cost, but will, as do private developers, regard the repayment as a matter of disposing of income, or perhaps of past income which has accumulated in, say, depreciation reserves. Local authorities, on the other hand, do not provide for depreciation in their accounts; they argue that by the time the renewal of the asset is necessary the loan should have been paid off, and they will be in the same position as when they started and raise another. They accordingly do not charge for depreciation but for repayment of loan in their development calculations. This and the interest on loan are their " loan charges " or " debt service."

The methods of calculating for annual depreciation or repayment provision are much the same, as we saw in Chapters 8 and 9, but the actual figure obtained by each of these two approaches may be different. For one thing, depreciation is not provided on the cost of acquisition and legal and physical preparation of land, since the land is a permanent asset, whereas repayment must be; this can be significant where expensive land is acquired. For another, the provision for depreciation may need to be increased where money prices are rising but the provision for repaying a loan need never be. For another, the period for depreciation is related to the estimated life of buildings and works, whereas the period for loan may be shorter. This last source of difference is removed, however, if local authority practice is followed of calculating loan repayments over the expected life of the works irrespective of whether the loan will in fact be repaid earlier.

In providing either for depreciation or for repayment in their calculations, and no more, public development practice differs from that of private enterprise developers. These expect the return on investment, after allowance for depreciation, to show a profit margin over the rate of interest on loan, a margin which could be employed to repay the loan. They would not develop where the expected rate of return on investment of a 100 per cent loan was equal to the rate of interest on loan. It could be argued that public developers should also earn a return on investment which is above their rate of interest on loans, and should similarly provide for both. There is no difficulty in their doing so when the development will be as profitable as that undertaken by private enterprise, particularly as their rate of interest on loans is lower that that of private enterprise. But when, as in most of their remunerative development, there is difficulty in obtaining a yield which will cover costs, and when, as in their non-remunerative development, the costs must be met out of rates and taxes, it is reckoned too great a burden on current consumers, ratepayers or taxpayers if yield is expected to cover both. The debt or replacement of asset, as the case might be, is not to be borne by the generations that will be alive during the life of the asset but by their successors.

(*n*) (*o*) *Annual Occupation and Ownership Costs.* These will not differ for comparable kinds of development from the costs to be met by private developers; even local authority rates must be paid, with very few exceptions, in cases where the development is occupied by the public body itself. The annual costs of the authority's staff concerned with the repairs and maintenance of the property, and its supervision and management, will need to be included.

Where a public body is occupying the development itself it will also be faced with the annual costs of operation. These will, for our purposes, be considered as distinct from those of occupying the development; in practice they cannot be.

(*p*) *Total Annual Costs.* For public development the yield must therefore cover, in addition to the occupation and ownership expenses (*n*) and (*o*), the interest on a loan equal to the whole cost (*k*) and either the repayment of the loan (*l*) or provision for depreciation (*n*).

Income Tax. Local authorities are liable for income tax on property in much the same way as private persons: under Schedule A for income from property in lands and buildings, under Schedule D for any rent income from property which is in excess of the Schedule A assessment, and under Schedule D for any profits on trading undertakings. But they are not liable to tax on their rate and grant income. In common with private persons they deduct from any annual payment they make by way of interest on loans, etc., income tax at the standard rate in the £, and are accountable for this to the Inland Revenue; and where they can show that such payments have been made out of income which is liable to tax they are entitled to retain the amount they have deducted. This amount is offset against their total tax liability; and since, with the considerable indebtedness of local authorities, it is generally more than the tax for which they are liable on all their taxable income they generally do not in fact pay income tax.[20]

III. Money Yield. As stated in Chapter 1 (page 6) the yield from particular public development will come, substantially or entirely, either from the payments of specific consumers for the space or services provided (remunerative development); or from ratepayers and taxpayers as a whole (non-remunerative development).

Sometimes public bodies obtain a yield from the disposal of surplus land, that land which they have acquired and do not need for the purpose of the scheme. But this is relatively insignificant since, in general, their acquisition has been confined to just the land which has been needed for their statutory requirements. The Lands Clauses Acts in fact restricted promoters from taking compulsorily more land than actually required for their undertaking. Local authorities have not therefore often been able when carrying out a public improvement to buy land for recoupment, that is land adjoining that taken for the purpose of the improvement " with the object of securing to the authority (by subsequent sale, lease, etc.), the benefit of any increase in value of that adjoining land brought about by the execution of the improvement."[21] (See page 336.)

Where they dispose, public bodies are not so free as private persons, and this influences their money yield on disposal. Local authorities, for example, need specific ministerial consent to use land for a purpose other than that for which it was acquired, that is, to appropriate it to another service of the authority, or to lease land for a term of more than seven years, or to sell it when no longer required for the purpose for which it was acquired or is being used.[22] The figure at which authorities can transfer land is also subject to this consent, and the District Valuers are asked to certify what it should be. Before the passing of the Town and Country Planning Act, 1944, they had to obtain open-market value. But when the Town and Country Planning Act, 1947, was introduced, formula values for disposal became necessary for land on which development charge would not be payable. With the abandonment of development charge, in the Town and Country Planning Act, 1953, land is sold to private persons at current market value for the use that would be permitted. Land continues to be leased to private developers at full market rents, and transferred between public authorities at existing use and prevailing use values, but having regard to cost of the original acquisition in certain circumstances.[23]

Interest on Capital During Construction

We can now discuss whether or not this item should be included in the capital cost of public developers. A public body certainly incurs, just as a private developer, the cost of interest on capital during construction, for it must then begin to borrow money, whether as part of its long term loan for the works or on short term pending the long term loan. But it does not raise in its loan, and a local authority does not include in its loan sanction application, an amount over and above the cost of land and works to cover interest during construction; it is merely under obligation to start paying back the loan before the works are completed.

Such interest does not therefore inflate capital expenditure. But, the question remains: should the public body aim to recoup itself for this expenditure during the life of the works, or should it not? If it wishes to recoup itself, then the item must be included as part of the cost to be covered by yield. If it does not, then it should not. For remunerative development it is likely that the body will wish, and be able, to recoup itself during the life of the works. For the non-remunerative development of a local authority there is little point in the authority doing so, unless it wished to avoid levying the necessary rates during the construction period. It would merely mean, if it did, that instead of levying rates to cover the actual loan charges during the period of the loan, it would levy higher rates to cover the loan charges spread out over the residue of the loan period which remained when the works were completed.

A local authority can in fact refrain from making annual provision for the repayment of a loan for works forming part of an undertaking of a revenue producing character, during the period that the works are unremunerative up to a maximum period of five years; and it can arrange with the Public Works Loans Board to suspend repayment of capital and interest in the early years of their loans. In either case the total loan is repaid during the remaining years of the loan sanction period.[24] Authorities have not often used these facilities.

IV. Financial Appraisal of Public Development Schemes

It follows from the distinctions that have been drawn that the financial appraisal of a public development scheme must differ from that outlined for private development schemes in Chapter 10. We will consider first to what extent the methods (A) to (F) there outlined are applicable to remunerative schemes; and it will be found that even here they have but a limited application.

There may be cases where it is possible to compare the new capital values which have been created with capital cost, (A), but where the new use is not one which would be normally provided by private enterprise, there can be no market value for it and therefore no comparison.

The comparison of annual yield with capital cost, (B), can always be made; but the difficulty here is to know whether the calculated rate per cent is any guide at all as to the viability of the scheme. If a private enterprise factory development scheme shows an estimated return on capital cost of 8 per cent the market will indicate whether this is reasonable. But the market is not interested in municipal housing or city car parks and cannot, for such schemes, therefore give any such guidance. Even where the market has some interest, as for example in the re-development of business areas, it is not possible strictly to compare the calculated rate per cent with a market rate. For one thing the capital costs would not be comparable in both cases; in public development the acquisition costs may be well above or below the cost which private developers would have to pay because of the compensation code; and interest during construction is often not included in the capital cost of public development, and never in that of local authorities' schemes. This apart, private enterprise rarely tackles, and the market therefore rarely quotes, for the scale of development that local authorities undertake in developing business areas. Private enterprise would deal with an odd site or group of sites in an otherwise relatively static area; a local authority in re-developing may buy and unload on the market large areas at the same time, and amid conditions of uncertainty. What return should it earn under these conditions?

For these reasons, too, it is difficult to see the application to public development of (C), the relating of estimated net yield with the return which the investment should show. It is difficult to know what the rate of return should be.

With regard to the tests which take financing into account, (D), (E) and (F), none is applicable to public remunerative development; as stated above, public bodies generally carry out development entirely on borrowed money and in consequence rarely have an equity.

None of the tests (A) to (F) is therefore generally applicable. It is necessary to devise another one, (G), which is similar to (C). In it the estimated net annual yield is compared with the loan charges, or with the interest on the loan plus depreciation on works.

Turning now to the non-remunerative schemes, it can be readily seen that none of the methods (A) to (G) can be used for relating yield to cost. As to (A) no market value can be put on the new use; as to (B), (C) and (G) there is no money yield since the annual costs are met out of rates, taxes or other public funds, and no guide to what the return from the investment should be. For these reasons, and because there is no equity, tests (D), (E) and (F) are also not applicable. It is necessary, therefore, to devise another test, (H). In this the annual subventions from rates or taxes which are necessary to meet the total annual costs are compared with the annual financial resources of those meeting the cost. This is a well-tried test for local authority schemes, whereby the loan charges on a highway, school or housing scheme are related to the yield of a 1d. rate. We return to this below (see page 153).

Testing Cost and Yield of Several Sites Together

Private developers will usually test their schemes only in relation to the particular site which is being developed, but they may on occasions, particularly as operators, also test them in relation to other schemes, or to their existing businesses or undertakings. Public bodies usually carry on development of the same kind in many different places, perhaps in different parts of the same town or county, or in different parts of the country as a whole. They will, in consequence, much more than private developers, consider their schemes in a wider context than the individual site. In fact in many cases unless they do so they cannot obtain a true accounting. This might arise either because the schemes on different sites are parts of a whole, as, for example, are sections of a town's principal traffic road; or because while different schemes are not interdependent, they should be considered together since they are all in one ownership. Examples are the provision of housing or car parks by a local authority.

Profit Margins

We have seen that where an authority spends money which it has borrowed at a gilt-edged rate of interest, and earns on it a higher rate of return, it receives a profit margin on the whole loan. This may arise, for example, where it purchases a standing property and lets it at a market rent, as when purchasing in advance of re-development; or when it builds factories for letting at market rents. If it has bought in order to demolish for re-development, and does not demolish for some years, the profit margin can be used towards paying off the loan. Table 21 shows, in illustration of such a case, and for varying rates of profit margin, the number of years which it would take to pay off a given loan if the profit margin were allowed to accumulate in a sinking fund at $2\frac{1}{2}$ per cent free of tax. Income tax liability on the profit margin is ignored.

TABLE 21
Profit Margin at Varying Rates of Return with Interest on Loan at 3 per cent and 4 per cent

Average net rent throughout period as percentage of purchase price	5%		6%		7%		8%		9%		10%	
Rate per cent at which authority borrows ...	3%	4%	3%	4%	3%	4%	3%	4%	3%	4%	3%	4%
Profit margin	2%	1%	3%	2%	4%	3%	5%	4%	6%	5%	7%	6%
Period in years over which loan will be repaid if profit margin allowed to accumulate as sinking fund at 2½ per cent free of tax ...	32	51	25	32	20	25	16	20	14	16	12	14

The Annual Cost of Local Authority Development and its Relation to Rate Resources

Where a local authority wishes to appraise the finances of a scheme of non-remunerative development it will, as we have seen, compare annual costs with its expected rate resources (H); and it will also do this when it wishes to subsidise out of the rates a remunerative scheme, such as the provision of car parks or a swimming bath. This test requires amplification as we are discussing local authority development extensively in later chapters.

Where an authority does not occupy its development but lets to tenants, its annual costs will be those we have described above. But where it occupies itself it will also have operating costs. In running a school, for example, there is furniture and equipment to be bought by an outlay of capital on which loan charges are paid, meals to be provided, and salaries to be met, and also the expenses of cooking, lighting and heating. And in running a police station there are not only the annual costs properly associated with development, but also wages and salaries of the police force and other staff, and the expense of clothing, equipment and the maintenance and running of vehicles.[25]

Once the total capital cost of the development is estimated, and the loan period established, it is a simple matter to estimate future liability for loan charges at assumed rates of interest. But it is not so simple to forecast the authority's operating costs since, as

in any business enterprise, these must be influenced by future
money values, wage levels, efficiency of organisation and cost of
materials. In forecasting these operating costs it is necessary
to be as precise, at least, as in forecasting loan charges, for an
authority's operating costs are normally a greater proportion of its
total annual expenditure than are its annual loan charges, although
the proportion varies from service to service.[26] The best guide,
and usually the only one, is the record of the authority's actual costs
analysed in a suitable way. Analyses of such costs, under the name
of unit cost statistics, are prepared by most local authorities for
the purpose of cost accounting of services, the checking of waste
and extravagance, the securing and maintaining of greater economy
in services and of assisting in financial control over them. The
units are selected as suitable for this purpose, and are not always
suitable for guidance as to the operating costs of development.
Analyses of unit cost statistics are published.[27] For example,
there is available for each county borough and county council the
amount spent, per pupil in primary or secondary schools, on salaries,
furniture, etc., books, stationery and materials, rent, rates and
taxes, upkeep of buildings and grounds, fuel, light and cleaning.
In 1951-52 the county boroughs spent on these services an average
of £41·3 per secondary pupil and £22·4 per primary pupil; and the
counties an average of £44·0 and £24·9 respectively. But spending
by individual authorities varied considerably from the average;
Brecon County spent £59·99 per secondary pupil and £33·13 per
primary pupil, while Barnsley County Borough spent £30·22 per
secondary pupil and £21·72 per primary pupil.[28]

The total annual cost of any project is not met entirely from
rate income each year for, as Table 22 shows, authorities have
other sources of income.

TABLE 22

The Sources of Income to Local Authorities in England and Wales,
1951-52

	£ million	%
Income from:		
1. Rates, or payments in lieu...	331·9	40
2. Specific government grants	293·6	35
3. Non-specific (mostly exchequer equalisation) grants ...	55·9	6
4. Rents, fees, tolls, licenses, fines, etc.	155·9	19
5. Transfer from profits of trading services...	1·5	—
	838·9	100

Source: *Local Government Financial Statistics, England and Wales*, 1951-52
(H.M.S.O.).

The prospective cost of a project to the rates, the incidence on
the ratepayers of its estimated annual cost, must be obtained,
therefore, by deducting from the total estimated annual expenditure all possible contributions from other sources. Firstly, there

is the income which does not come from either rates or grants (lines 4 and 5 of the table). Where an authority has such an income it can usually spend it on whatever it wishes among the purposes for which it has power to spend money; it could devote it to financing a particular kind of development which would thus be no charge on the rates. In line 4 there are included the rents from corporate properties, including those owned after acquisition for re-development; fees for the registration of births, deaths and marriages; charges on toll bridges or for facilities such as swimming baths and games in parks, and receipts for licences for dogs, guns, theatres and moneylenders. In line 5 are the profits from trading services. For the purpose of the annual Ministry of Housing and Local Government summary of Local Government Financial Statistics these are housing, water supply, passenger transport, harbours, docks and piers, burial grounds and cemeteries, civic restaurants, provision of entertainments, other trading services and corporation estates. While the total amount of profit in such services is comparatively small, the profit or loss on the services of different authorities varies considerably.   For example it was estimated that Great Yarmouth C.B. in 1954-55 would be able to draw the equivalent of a 2s. 5d. rate (19s. 2d. per head of population) from its trading undertakings; while Northampton C.B. on the other hand would find it necessary to contribute towards its undertakings, to water supply in particular, a 3s. 5d. rate (27s. 9d. per head of population).[29]

The second source of income which does not come from rates is the specific grants from government towards rate expenditure (line 2). These were discussed in Chapter 5.

Thirdly, there are the non-specific exchequer equalisation grants (line 3), which are certainly the most complicated to budget for (see page 59). There is a direct contribution from government to most of the county boroughs, to 56 out of 83 in 1954-55. Those that receive the grant benefit to a varying extent. In 1954-55, for example, Portsmouth received a rate of 5d. (3s. 4d. per head) and Bradford a rate of 8d. (5s. 1d. per head); but Barnsley a rate of 10s. 6d. (59s. 6d. per head) and Merthyr Tydfil the most, a 36s. 2d. rate (147s. 11d. per head). The income of a county district will generally be influenced by equalisation grant in two ways. Firstly, any exchequer grant to the county council is passed on to the county district by way of a deduction from the county precept on that district. In other words each county district in a county will offset from its gross requirements the same rate in the £ on account of the county's equalisation grant, so that each will take its share in the proportion that its rateable value bears to the total county rateable value. In 1954-55 some 121 county district councils received nothing at all in this way, whereas Jarrow, for example, received an 18s. 7d. rate (97s. 2d. per head). Secondly, all county districts must receive a capitation grant from their county councils, a grant per head of population, whether or not the county receives the equalisation grant.[30] This grant is calculated by dividing the total amount of equalisation grant for all counties in England and Wales outside London by the total population of those counties. Half this amount is paid per head of population to boroughs and urban district councils and one quarter to rural district councils. In 1954-55 the grant amounted to 20s. 7d. and 10s. 3½d. per head for the urban and rural areas respectively.

Since counties can obtain their money for capitation grants only by way of precept, the total amount of capitation grant is contributed to by county districts in proportion to their rateable values; and the same total amount is redistributed among them according to their population, urban authorities receiving twice the amount per head as rural authorities. In 1954-55, for example, the county districts in Hertfordshire were precepted with a rate of 2s. 2d. to pay for capitation grants whereas Hoddesdon U.D. received a capitation grant amounting to a rate of 2s. 11d., Cheshunt U.D. of 3s. 3d., and Hatfield R.D. of 1s. 3d.

Fortunately, it is not necessary for any authority to attempt to calculate afresh for each project the proportion of its estimated expenditure which will fall on the rates. It has available its records of expenditure and income, and those of other authorities, and can see the proportion that has been contributed in the past from other than rate sources to similar projects. It can assume that this, or some other proportion, will continue. (See pages 217 and 297).

It will be aware that its position relative to other authorities may change in such a way as to affect income from equalisation grant; a fall in population through emigration, for example, which was proportionately greater than a fall in rateable value, might increase an authority's rateable value per head of weighted population and deprive it of some of this grant.[31] It is impossible, however, for an authority to foresee what the relative changes of this kind are going to be. Assumptions must therefore be made such as, for example, that the equalisation grant, expressed as a rate in the £ or per head, or as a proportion of rate expenditure, will remain at the same level.

Having estimated what proportion of the total annual costs in a particular scheme of development will fall on the rates this will then be related to the likely rate resources. There are two common methods. Firstly, the prospective rate expenditure can be translated to the rate in the £ that would have to be levied on the rateable value in the local authority area to meet it. This rate in pence is calculated by dividing the estimated costs by the estimated product of a 1d. rate; the amount that would be collected by a rate of 1d. in the £ on the authority's rateable value, after allowing for costs of collection of rates and bad debts.[32] Secondly, the prospective expenditure can be related to the total rate expenditure that will have to be borne per head of population in the area. This can be calculated by dividing the estimated cost by the total population of the authority's area; or by multiplying the rate in the pound arrived at as above by the rateable value per head of the authority area. Since both rateable value and population will change year by year, and also possibly through the influence of the very development which is being considered, it will be necessary in either method to take these prospective changes into account where they are at all significant.

The Incidence of Rates

It does not follow that each person in the area will pay the calculated rate expenditure per head. Since the rates are levied on occupiers, and they pay according to rateable value, a large family living in a house with a low assessment will pay comparatively little, while a shopkeeper in a good shopping street will pay not only on his house but also, and heavily, on his business premises too. A more precise method of defining the actual rate burden per head of population comes from recognising that the rates levied in an area fall on to two broad classes of people: on the occupiers of dwellings and on the occupiers of the other premises, which are mostly used for business, manufacturing or trade. Rates on the former come out of the pockets of the area's inhabitants and are part of the price that people have to pay for shelter and services. Those on the latter are not paid for directly by the inhabitants, nor are they in the ultimate borne by the people carrying on business or trade; they are part of their cost of trading or production and may be paid for indirectly out of purchases by the consumers, perhaps the local inhabitants, or visitors to a seaside town, or customers spread over the world. It is apparent that the greater the proportion of residential rateable value in an area the greater the proportion of rate expenditure which will come directly from its inhabitants. The position of any area in this respect can be seen from an analysis of its rateable value by kinds of property. Table 23 shows such an analysis for all county boroughs, urban and rural county districts. It is based on a standard form of classification of properties which is used by authorities throughout the country. Figures for all authorities were first published for the position in April, 1952. It is to be expected that the proportions in each use will differ from this when the new assessments made under the Local Government Act, 1948, are available.

TABLE 23

Analysis of Rateable Value as at 1st April, 1952

	County boroughs Per cent	Urban areas in counties Per cent	Rural areas in counties Per cent
Domestic	56·6	67·2	65·8
Commercial	23·2	14·7	6·0
Licensed premises ...	3·2	2·6	2·7
Entertainment and recreational	2·0	1·7	1·1
Public utility	3·3	3·1	6·2
Educational and cultural	2·4	2·2	1·9
Industrial	4·3	4·2	4·6
Miscellaneous	5·0	4·3	11·7
	100·0	100·0	100·0

Source: **I.M.T.A. and S.C.T.,** *Analysis of Rateable Value of England and Wales as at 1st April, 1952.*

The proportions for individual authorities differ considerably from these averages. Among county boroughs, for example, in April, 1952, Newcastle-on-Tyne had the lowest proportion of rateable value in domestic properties (50·3 per cent), and Wallasey the highest (74·6 per cent). While, therefore, the nominal rate expenditure per head of population for 1952-53 in Newcastle was £8 1s. 3d. and in Wallasey £9 0s. 9d., the burden per head falling more directly on the residents was £4 1s. in Newcastle and £6 15s. in Wallasey.

In either of these two methods of measuring rate burden per head of population, care must be exercised in preparing figures for towns such as seaside resorts, where there is a seasonal influx of people who pay no rates in the town, or garrison towns, where there is always a large number of people who pay no rates at all.

CHAPTER 12

SUBSIDISED HOUSING

(A) *Local Authorities: Housing Authorities—Acquisition of Land—Kinds of Development—Powers of Disposal—The Subsidy Scheme—Housing Revenue Account—Fixing of Rents—Financial Statement for Subsidised Housing—Exercise 2: A Given Housing Programme and Re-development at Four Alternative Densities—Conclusion on the Four Schemes. (B) Housing Associations. (C) New Town Development Corporations.*

WHERE dwellings are provided by private enterprise without subsidy the financial calculations will be those described in Chapter 10. Where subsidy is paid some modification is necessary. In this chapter we will discuss the kind of calculation made by those housing agencies concerned solely or primarily with the provision of new subsidised housing: the local authorities, housing associations and new town development corporations. Local authorities will be discussed first and then the other two more briefly.

(A) *LOCAL AUTHORITIES*

Housing Authorities

Housing authorities outside London are the county and non-county boroughs, urban and rural districts; and within London the London County Council, metropolitan boroughs and City Corporation.[1] Their general duty with regard to new housing is to consider the needs of their districts for housing accommodation for all members of the community, and to frame and submit proposals, to the Minister of Housing and Local Government, for the provision of new housing for them. Before 1949 this duty was to be exercised with regard to members of the working classes only, but this limitation now no longer applies.[2]

The administrative counties outside London are, therefore, not housing authorities. They may, however, agree with any rural district council to exercise all or any of the powers of that council in the provision of new housing accommodation; they have rarely done so. They must make specific contributions towards the cost of certain houses provided by county district councils and can make further contributions, with the consent of the Minister, to the housing expenditure of these councils.[3]

Acquisition of Land

Authorities can obtain land for new dwellings in a variety of ways. They can acquire, for the purpose, developed or undeveloped land inside or outside their boundary.[4] They can purchase land in a clearance area, together with land surrounding or adjoining such an area, in order to secure satisfactory re-development; or land in a clearance area which has been cleared of buildings by the owner under a clearance order but upon which re-development has not been initiated by him within eighteen months of the order becoming operative; or land in a re-development area in order to secure its re-development; or land outside a re-development area for the purpose of providing accommodation for the persons displaced from it. They can appropriate for housing any land which is currently vested in them.[5] For all these Ministerial consent is required except, outside re-development areas, for purchase by agreement. A clearance area is one in which the houses are by reason of disrepair or sanitary defects unfit for human habitation, or are by reason of their bad arrangement, or the narrowness or bad arrangement of the streets, dangerous or injurious to the health of the inhabitants of the area, and where the other buildings, if any, in the area are for a like reason dangerous or injurious to the health of the said inhabitants.[6] A re-development area is one where there are fifty or more working-class houses; at least one-third of the working-class houses in the area are overcrowded, or unfit for human habitation and not capable at a reasonable expense of being rendered so fit, or so arranged as to be congested; the industrial and social conditions of their districts are such that the area should be used to a substantial extent for housing the working classes; it is expedient in connection with the provision of housing accommodation for the working classes that the area should be re-developed as a whole.[7]

Since the recent war most new dwellings have been built on virgin land, some on land in, surrounding or adjoining pre-war clearance areas, and some on land cleared by bombs. Little was built in new clearance areas, since the shortage of housing accommodation made it possible to demolish only a few thousand of the worst houses. The Housing Repairs and Rents Act, 1954, section 1, initiated an increase in the land to be made available through slum clearance.

The Town and Country Planning Act, 1947, provides a means of re-developing obsolete and outworn areas which is an alternative to the re-development area procedure in Part III of the Housing Act, 1936 (see Chapter 15). This procedure was not used to any great extent before the war and will no doubt lapse in favour of that in the 1947 Act when demolition for re-development of such areas becomes practicable.

Kinds of Development

An authority is not confined to providing dwellings under the Housing Acts. It can also provide and maintain, either for new schemes or those already completed, alone or jointly with any other person, " any building adapted for use as a shop, any recreation ground, or other buildings or land which in the opinion of the Minister will serve a beneficial purpose in connection with the requirements of the persons for whom the housing accommodation is provided." Included in this would be facilities for obtaining meals and refreshments and for doing laundry.[8] In practice these powers are wide enough to do more than build housing estates. They are used for building complete neighbourhoods; and the London County Council has used them to build their satellite towns around London. They were not thought by the Reith Committee wide enough to build complete new towns.[9]

Powers of Disposal

Where authorities have bought land in, surrounded by or adjoining a clearance area, or for providing dwellings, they may sell, lease or exchange it for other land; and must obtain the best price or rent that can be reasonably obtained.[10] Where they have acquired land for providing dwellings, they can sell or lease it to another who will erect and maintain dwellings in accordance with plans approved by the authority, or use the land for other purposes which are associated with the scheme, such as factories, workshops, places of worship or places of recreation. The authority can contribute towards the cost of site works for this development.[11]

Authorities can also sell a completed house.[12] In doing so they are not compelled to obtain the best price, which might require them to take advantage of the scarcity of houses, but they cannot sell below a minimum price. For houses completed before May, 1945, this is 20 years purchase of the net annual (economic) rent, and for houses completed after this date the all-in cost to the local authority.[13]

The Subsidy Scheme in the Housing Acts, 1946-52

Local authorities were given powers to provide working-class dwellings as far back as 1851 but, until given government subsidy in 1919, they made little use of the powers. Of the 200,000 additional houses built between 1909 and 1915 local authorities provided only 11,000.[14]

The Housing, Town Planning, etc., Act of 1919 saw the introduction of government and local authority contributions towards the cost of new working-class housing. Their purpose was to enable the dwellings to be let or sold at rents and prices within reach of working-class incomes. These contributions were continued under various Housing Acts until 1934, each Act introducing its own scale of contribution according to the policy of the current government and level of building costs. Subsidies were paid between 1930 and 1939 for slum clearance and the abatement of overcrowding. Between the wars some 4,193,000 dwellings were built in all in Great Britain of which about 1,513,000 were subsidised.[15]

After the recent war building costs were so high that a renewal of subsidies for new housing was recognised as necessary in order that rents could be kept within the reach of tenants. Of the 2.24m. new permanent dwellings built in Great Britain between April, 1945 and December, 1955, some 1.7m. have been subsidised by the government and local authorities.[16]

The post-war subsidy scheme for new dwellings was introduced in 1946 and amended by Acts in 1949 and 1952.[17] A further amendment, operative in April, 1955, was introduced by order in 1954.[18] (A revised scheme was announced in October, 1955; see Appendix III). Whatever the purpose for which new dwellings are provided, whether for population increase, or relief of overcrowding, or to replace dwellings cleared in the re-development of war-damaged areas or of areas formerly covered with slums or obsolete property, the subsidies are the same. Contributions are payable annually, for each dwelling which is erected, for 60 years from its completion, by the exchequer (annual exchequer contribution) and local authority (annual rate fund contribution). For most purposes the latter is one-third of the former. The exchequer pays its contribution for each dwelling erected under housing powers; and an authority cannot refuse the exchequer contribution for any of its dwellings so provided, nor avoid paying its rate fund contribution.

Graph 5 illustrates the 1952 Act scheme, and Graph 6 the 1955 scheme, for new standard type housing. They show how the sum of the combined exchequer and rate fund contributions varies with the capital cost of land as developed. (For definition see page 165). Both schemes will be described by reference to the graphs. The figures for the 1955 scheme are in brackets.

For most of the housing in the country the same contributions (A) are paid for any kind and size of dwelling, whether house, flat, bungalow or maisonnette. These are all included in the term "house" for subsidy purposes, a house being any part of a building " which is occupied or intended to be occupied as a separate dwelling."[19] The contributions are £26 14s. (£22 1s.) per annum by the exchequer (general standard amount) and £8 18s. (£7 7s.) out of rates (normal rate fund contribution).

Where land is expensive higher subsidies may be paid on this account, whether houses or flats are built on it. And where " blocks of flats " are provided on this land (that is a " building which contains two or more flats, and which consists of three or more storeys exclusive of any storey constructed for use for purposes other than those of a dwelling ")[20] higher subsidies may also be paid because such flats are more expensive to build and maintain than houses. The intention is to offset the additional cost of land, or of building and maintenance, so that dwellings provided on expensive land and in flats can be let at rents which are about the same as those of dwellings

GRAPH 5

House and Flat Subsidy Scheme for New Dwellings under Housing Acts,
1946-52

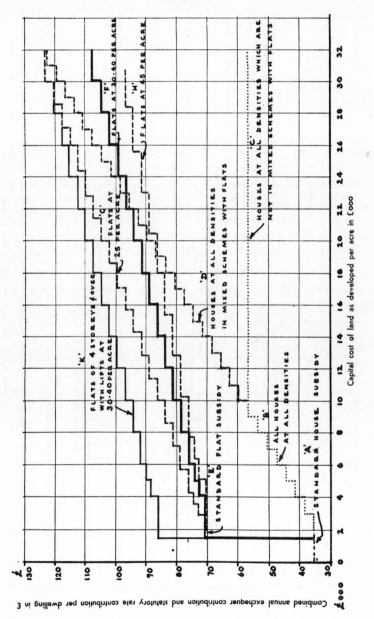

GRAPH 6

House and Flat Subsidy Scheme for New Dwellings under the Housing (Review of Contributions) Order, 1954

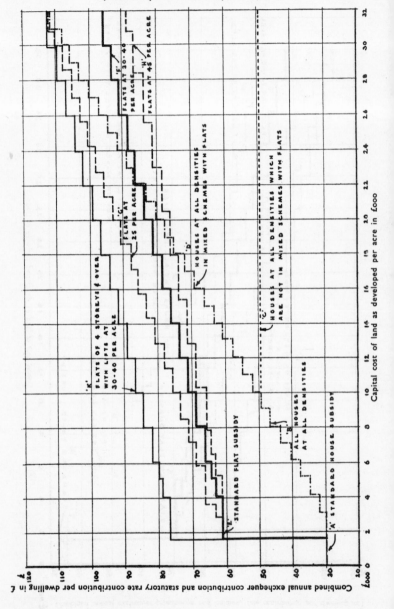

on cheaper land. These provisions, which echo those made in the Housing Act, 1936, are primarily intended for the cities where there is re-development of expensive land, and where high density requires that a substantial number of flats be built. Flats which are built on non-expensive land, such as those in the new towns, do not attract the higher subsidy.

Expensive sites are those which, when accommodating blocks of flats of over three storeys, exceed £1,500 per acre in " cost as developed "; and £3,000 per acre when accommodating lower dwellings. The cost as developed of a site which has been purchased under the Housing Acts is its purchase price or, if the site has not been so purchased, its value before site works have been incurred, plus in either case the expenses " properly incurred for making the site suitable for the purpose of providing the houses [or flats] to be provided thereon."[21] The expenses referred to include those in the construction or widening of streets; the construction of sewers; the erection of any special works rendered necessary by the physical characteristics of the land, such as the demolition and clearing of existing buildings; the provision of access to the site by road and sewer; the provision of extra deep sewers and foundations to buildings. Not all expenses on such works are in practice chargeable as expenses " properly incurred " for the purpose of providing dwellings, and therefore to be added to the cost of site works for calculating the cost of site as developed.

Where houses alone are provided on an expensive site, that is one costing as developed over £3,000 per acre, the combined contributions rise at the rate of £3 (£2 16s.) per £1,000 of site value (B) to offset the rising cost of land. Where the density equals about 15 dwellings per acre the contributions completely offset this rising cost.[22] This increase goes on until a site cost as developed of £10,000 per acre is reached; the subsidy remains constant for all sites costing more than this (C). But where houses are provided with flats in a mixed scheme, the house subsidy continues to increase as site cost rises beyond this (D).

Where flats in blocks of three storeys or over are built on an expensive site, that is one costing over £1,500 per acre as developed, whether alone or in mixed schemes, the additional subsidy to offset the higher cost of building is £26 2s. (£23 17s.) from the exchequer and £8 14s. (£7 19s.) from the rates. The combined contributions for flats are thus £70 8s. (£61 4s.). This is paid up to a site cost as developed of £4,000 per acre. Where the site cost is over £4,000 per acre the contributions rise to offset the rising cost of land; but in this case the increase is not uniform at all densities. Where this is between 30 and 40 flats to the acre the combined rate of rise is £2 12s. (£2 8s.) per £2,000 (F); this exactly offsets the rising cost of site where the density is 35 dwellings per acre.[23] Where the density is lower than 30 flats per acre the contributions are increased, and where above 40 they are reduced, the purpose being to ensure that, by and large, whatever the density of flats, none of the cost of site over £4,000 per acre need be passed on to the tenant. The actual contributions where the density is below 30 or above 40 are calculated by multiplying the actual cost of the land by $\frac{35}{D}$, where D is the density in flats per acre, so arriving at a notional site cost.[24] The contributions are then made as though this were the actual site cost. The graph illustrates the manner in which the scale rises where the density is 25 (G) and 45 flats to the acre (H).

Where flats of at least four storeys have lifts, an additional contribution is paid, the same for all densities and cost of land, of £10 10s. (£10 10s.) from the exchequer and £5 5s. (£5 5s.) from the rates. For lifts the rate fund contribution is one-half of the exchequer's, although in all the other cases it is one-third.

It is to be noted that only one contribution is made by the exchequer or out of the rates for each dwelling, and this includes any additional subsidy on account of expensive land, expensive construction and maintenance and lifts.

These contributions are for standard type housing; there are special contributions for others. For example, where county district councils provide houses for their agricultural population the exchequer contribute £35 14s. (£31 1s.) and the county district and county councils pay £2 10s. (£2 10s.) each.[25] There are additional contributions from the exchequer to authorities with heavy rate burden, with corresponding reduction in rate contributions;[26] and increased exchequer contributions for houses on which extra cost has been incurred by, for example, their being constructed in stone in order to preserve the character of the surroundings.[27]

Calculations on which Subsidy is Based

The kind of calculation which is made to arrive at the subsidy is of interest in considering the financial calculations for subsidised housing. As explained above, where land is not " expensive " the same contributions are paid for each dwelling: for dwellings that vary in kind, area, number of rooms, costs of construction or in rents that are likely to be received. Urban authorities receive and pay the same contributions as do rural authorities except, as noted above, where county district councils provide for their agricultural population. To arrive at this standard contribution a typical dwelling is selected, a normal three-bedroom house, at a typical cost and for which a typical rent will be received. It is assumed that if contributions based on this are deficient for certain dwellings they will be generous for others; and that the higher or lower levels of building costs in different parts of the country will be met by higher or lower rents.

The official calculations for subsidies in the 1946 and 1952 Acts and in the 1955 scheme are set out below;[28] it is possible to compare in this way the effect on the subsidy in these years of differences in cost of building, or management and maintenance, interest rates and rent levels.

	1946 £ s. d.	1952 £ s. d.	1955 £ s. d.
Loan charges for 60 years at current rate of interest:			
1946—3⅛ per cent on £1,100 ...	40 14 0		
1952—4¼ per cent on £1,525 ...		70 5 0	
1955—3¾ per cent on £1,583 ...			66 10 0
Add			
Repairs, maintenance and management	7 8 0	12 0 0	12 0 0
	48 2 0	82 5 0	78 10 0
Less			
Fair net rent that could be expected: 10s. in 1946, 18s. in 1952 and 19s. in 1955	26 0 0	46 16 0	49 8 0
Total subsidy required...	£22 0 0	£35 12 0	£29 2 0
Rate contribution	£5 10 0	£8 18 0	£7 7 0
Exchequer contribution	£16 10 0	£26 14 0	£22 1 0

For the 1946 subsidy a three-bedroom house of 950 sq. ft. was taken at a capital cost of land and buildings of £1,100; the interest rate was taken at 3⅛ per cent, that charged by the Public Works Loan Board for loans of 60 years; it was estimated that tenants could reasonably be expected to pay 10s. per week exclusive of rates. The principal reason for raising the subsidy in 1952 was the increase in Public Works Loan Board interest rates to 4¼ per cent in March, 1951. In the calculations there was taken a capital cost of £1,525, to reflect the substantial increase in cost of building since 1946, although smaller houses were being built; and a higher figure for repairs, maintenance and management to reflect increased costs; and an increased rent, 18s. per week exclusive of rates, which it was thought reasonable that tenants could pay out of their increased money wages. The decrease in the 1955 subsidy reflected the decrease in Public Works Loan Board rate of interest to 3¾ per cent and also took account of increased costs of building, economies which had been introduced in house construction and lay-out, and an increase in average earnings.

The calculations on which the flat subsidies have been based have not been made public. A sub-committee of the Association of Municipal Corporations in 1949 reported that the calculation for the 1946 Act flat subsidy was as follows, based on a flat of 800 sq. ft. and a capital cost of land and buildings of £1,464.[29]

								1946 *Act*		
								£	s.	d.
Loan charges for 60 years at current rate of interest (3⅛ per cent) on £1,464								54	3	0
Add Repairs, maintenance and management								15	1	0
								69	4	0
Less Fair net rent that could be expected of 12s. per week								31	4	0
Total subsidy required...								£38	0	0
Rate contribution								£9	10	0
Exchequer contribution								£28	10	0

In the 1952 Act the flat subsidies were increased, and in the 1954 revision reduced, to the figures mentioned earlier (page 165), for the same reasons that alterations were introduced in the house subsidies. The rent assumed in the official 1952 Act calculations was 21s. 6d. per week.[30] The total annual cost of providing, maintaining and managing the typical flat of three storeys and over without a lift was thus taken at £126 6s. (rent of £55 10s. per year plus combined rate and exchequer contributions of £70 8s.); and of one with a lift at £142 1s.

In Chapter 5 reference was made to the suggestion that the subsidy scheme makes the building of flats financially more attractive to authorities, under certain circumstances, than the building of houses. The above figures throw light on the reasons behind this suggestion.

Two-storey houses, of which most housing programmes are made up, do not vary much in size or in costs of construction, repair, maintenance and management. A two-bedroom house of 780 sq. ft. might cost to build (in 1954 in the Provinces) about £1,300 and a four-bedroom house of 1,120 sq. ft. about £1,700. A particular house subsidy for all houses does not, therefore, require the levying of widely varying rents for the costs of individual schemes to be balanced.

Flats on the other hand do vary in cost, and a particular subsidy for all flats may, therefore, require varying rents if schemes are to be individually balanced. If flats are small and in low buildings they cost about the same as, or less than, houses. One-bedroom flats, for example, in two-storey buildings might cost £1,000 each to build (in 1954), requiring loan charges (at 4 per cent) of £44 each and perhaps £8 per year to maintain and manage. Two-bedroom flats in three-storey buildings might cost £1,800 each to build (in 1954) requiring loan charges (at 4 per cent) of £79 and perhaps £16 per year to maintain and manage. If the flat is large and in a tall building, say a four-bedroom flat in a five-storey block, it might cost some £3,000 in building (in 1954), requiring loan charges (at 4 per cent) of £132 and perhaps £30 to maintain and manage. On comparing these figures with those in the subsidy calculations above it is seen that it is possible to let the smaller flats in low buildings at reasonable rents with the help only of the standard subsidy, particularly as a small flat can command a rent which is high in proportion to its size and cost when compared with houses and larger flats.[31] Small flats thus become financially attractive to the authority which is concerned with keeping down rents when the additional subsidy is paid for them, that is when in blocks of three storeys and over on expensive land. The figures also show that the larger and more expensive flats are not financially attractive in the same way, even where the higher flat subsidy is paid; and that where this subsidy is not paid, as on the " non-expensive land " in new towns, such flats need to be let at very high rents to balance the cost.

Housing Revenue Account

Also of interest in the financial calculations for local authority housing is the Housing Revenue Account which an authority must keep, and balance, each year.[32] It includes in the account, with minor exceptions, its income and expenditure with regard to all the new dwellings which it has provided since February, 1919, not only on virgin land but also in clearance and re-development areas. The principal items which are to be debited and credited in each financial year are.[33]

Debit

(1) The loan charges on capital sums borrowed for housing since February, 1919.

(2) Rents, taxes and other charges (except rates and water charges).

(3) Actual expenditure on supervision and management.

(4) Allowance for repairs, being the amount, and at least a stipulated minimum, that the authority think proper for the repair and maintenance of the dwellings. The minimum is £8 for each " house, building or dwelling," having been increased from the £4 stipulated in the 1946 Act.[34]

Credit

(1) The rents of all the dwellings covered by the account, excluding payments for rates or water charges.

(2) The income from the investment or other use of any capital money received from the sale or other disposal of any of the dwellings covered by the account.

(3) The exchequer contributions payable to the authority during the year.

(4) In the case of rural district councils any contributions received from county councils.

(5) The authority's own contributions out of the general rate fund. This will be not only the statutory contribution described above but also any additional contribution which the authority must make out of the rates to balance any deficit in the account in any year.[35] In 1952-53 the county boroughs as a whole paid in additional rate contribution some 22 per cent of their statutory contribution, although nearly half of them had a surplus in the account.[36] Should there be a surplus it must be disposed of in a stipulated manner.[37]

Fixing of Rents

Although the calculations for subsidy assume a rent which is related to cost, authorities do not, in fixing rents for a particular scheme, necessarily base them on its cost. They can view all their dwellings, both pre-war and post-war, as a whole, and can if they wish charge some rents below cost and some above; and since the Rent Restrictions Acts do not apply to local authority dwellings they can, and do, raise rents of even pre-war houses and so let post-war dwellings at rents which do not balance costs. In addition authorities may " grant to any tenant such rebates from rent subject to such terms and conditions as they may think fit,"[38] and many authorities have for many years been operating rent rebate schemes by which the financial circumstances of the tenants are taken into account in fixing rents. Conversely, many authorities charge market rents for certain dwellings, for which they receive subsidies, to the benefit of the rents that must be found by the remaining tenants. In short, authorities can adopt a rent policy, for all their dwellings, which pools all costs and yields. The only requirement is that any annual deficit in the Housing Revenue Account is balanced out of the rates.

Financial Statement for Subsidised Housing

We will consider for our statement only that development which would appear in the Housing Revenue Account: dwellings, a few local shops, a tenants' hall. Where part of the land is used for other uses such as major open space, traffic roads or schools, it will have been appropriated at formula value to the particular service of the authority.

Capital Cost

(a) Acquisition. The normal compensation code applies, but there are in addition the following rules: (1) in clearance areas, the compensation for land, including any buildings thereon, shall be its value as a cleared site available for development within its existing use, except for the site of those buildings which are included in the area only because of their bad arrangement in relation to other buildings or the narrowness and bad arrangement of the streets;[39] (2) when unfit houses have been well maintained the Minister may require payment additional to site value to be made on this account;[40] (3) where premises are acquired otherwise than at site value and their rental is enhanced by their being used for illegal purposes or being overcrowded any resulting enhancement of value is to be discounted;[41] (4) in clearance areas the authority will have the additional cost of providing accommodation for the persons to be displaced, and can incur the expense of contributing towards removal expenses and the loss of trade of a retail shop, whether this is due to the displacement of the trader or a material reduction in the number of his customers.[42]

(b) *Legal Preparation of Site.* A local authority has, when buying in clearance areas, powers of extinguishing public rights of way by order; and private rights of way, easements, rights of laying down, etc., of apparatus on completion of purchase, on payment of compensation to any person suffering loss.[43]

(c) (d) *Physical Preparation of Site and Works.* The total cost of works must be included in the calculation and no regard paid to the rules which are used for determining the cost of " site as developed " for subsidy purposes.

(e) *Construction of Buildings.* As with (c) and (d) no regard is paid to the rules of calculation for subsidy purposes (for example in relation to deep foundations) in getting at the cost of buildings.

(f) *Interest on Capital During Construction.* This is not included in capital cost. It is not included in the Housing Revenue Account, subsidy calculations or in the amount of the loan which is raised for housing. On the other hand its burden on authorities is partly relieved in that they receive subsidies for a dwelling for the whole year in which it is completed.

(g) *Profit.* This is not allowed for.

(h) *Disposal Expenses.* These rarely amount to much.

II. Annual Costs

(j) *Return on Investment.* This does not arise.

(k), (l) *Interest on and Repayment of Loan.* Capital is usually found by 100 per cent loan so that annual loan charges are taken. Authorities can for housing schemes borrow over a period of 80 years for the land, 60 for the buildings, 30 for sewers and 20 for roads; or over 60 years for the whole loan.

(m) *Depreciation.* This is not allowed for.

(n) *Annual Occupation Expenses.* These are similar to those described in Chapter 10. The Housing Revenue Account, it should be noted, includes the actual costs of repairs, which will fluctuate from year to year, while the house subsidy calculations assume the statutory minimum. General and water rate do not appear in the Housing Revenue Account or subsidy calculations.

(*o*) *Ownership Expenses.* These are similar to those described in Chapter 10. The Housing Revenue Account includes the actual cost of supervision and management, while the subsidy calculation assumes a particular figure which is not, however, a statutory one.

III. Money Yield

The yield from subsidised housing is almost always by way of a weekly rent which is " gross," that is including for rates, repairs, management and all other expenses. In housing, this gross rent, less the amount of general and water rates, is called the " economic rent." From this is deducted the annual exchequer and rate contribution to arrive at the subsidised rent.

Money yields will also sometimes arise from sales of both land and houses, and appropriations of land to non-housing services.

IV. Financial Appraisal of Scheme

For the purpose of testing cost and yield subsidised housing shares the characteristics of both remunerative and non-remunerative development. Insofar as it is remunerative, it is not possible to apply method (*A*) as a market value cannot be estimated for sites which are to be used for municipal housing, or the houses themselves; by definition, private enterprise is not interested in building, without subsidy, houses which can only be let if there is subsidy, 100 per cent loan at low interest rates, and no allowance for interest during construction or for profit. For similar reasons, methods (*B*) and (*C*) are not applicable since there is no market rate per cent for subsidised housing. Method (*G*) would appear to be usable, the comparison of annual loan charges with annual yields; and this is the criterion used in the Housing Revenue Account and subsidy calculations.

Insofar as housing is unremunerative, an authority is also interested in the rate burden which will arise from its normal rate contributions, subventions from the rates to the Housing Revenue Account and possibly other subventions to the wages and salaries of staff which are employed on, but whose cost is not charged to, housing. Method (*H*) is, therefore, also usable: the relation of this expenditure to rate resources.

Although it is necessary to test individual schemes for cost and yield, it is also desirable for an authority to consider together all its housing development. For example, a particular scheme of tall flats on an expensive site may not be pursued on account of its cost when considered in isolation; but were it considered as part of the cost of all housing in the area, it might make so little difference to the average cost per dwelling or person, that it might be financially acceptable. The existence of the Housing Revenue Account offers opportunity for this wider kind of consideration; in it are pooled all costs and yields, the cheap land with the expensive, the high costs and rents with the low.

This approach is included in the following example which has been worked out in full to illustrate many of the matters encountered in practice in financial calculations for local authority housing.

EXERCISE 2: *A Given Housing Programme and Re-development at Four Alternative Densities*

A county borough council with a population of 300,000 is formulating its programme for providing new local authority housing for 56,000 people during the period of its development plan. For simplicity it is assumed that this will be provided on its own without private enterprise housing. There will be available for residential use, after it has been cleared, some 250 acres of land in the centre of the town which will cost an average of £6,650 per acre. The authority is considering the alternatives of developing this inner land at net densities of 200, 140, 80 and of 60 habitable rooms to the acre, any balance of the 56,000 people to go on to agricultural land on the outskirts costing £200 per acre. Whatever the number of people accommodated on the inner land it is assumed that the range of dwelling sizes to be provided will be the same and that all dwellings will be occupied at the same average occupancy rate of one person per habitable room.[44] For simplicity it is assumed that whatever the plan in all these dwellings the living quarters consist of one habitable room. The range of dwelling sizes per 1,000 habitable rooms would therefore be:

	Size of Dwellings					
	1 h.r. Bed-sitting	2 h.r. (1B)	3 h.r. (2B)	4 h.r. (3B)	5 h.r. (4B)	Total
Number of habitable rooms ...	16	30	513	396	45	1,000
Number of dwellings	16	15	171	99	9	310
Average size of dwelling ...						3·23 h.r.

The inner land is distributed in several parcels so that the people living on it could use the existing shopping, business and entertainment facilities, thus requiring only new playing fields (at 3·5 acres per 1,000 people at the 200 density, 4·0 acres at the

140 density and 4·5 acres at the 60 and 80 density) and primary schools (1·5 acres per 1,000 people) to be provided for them out of this land. Further playing fields for the people on the inner land (2·5 acres per 1,000 people) would be provided on the outskirts. All their secondary schools will be on inner land other than the 250 acres.

At the alternative net densities, the average number of people per acre on all the 250 acres of inner land would be 100 at the 200 habitable room density, 79 at the 140 habitable room, 59 at the 80 habitable room and 44 at the 60 habitable rooms densities.[45] On the outskirts the dwellings would be provided in residential neighbourhoods with all facilities, such as shops, open spaces, schools and public buildings. These dwellings would be built at an average net density of 60 habitable rooms per acre. There would be 12 acres per 1,000 persons for neighbourhood facilities, so that the average gross density would be 35 persons per acre.[46]

The alternative schemes are depicted diagramatically in Fig. 2 and can be summarised as follows:

Density on inner land ...	Scheme A 200 h.r./acre		Scheme B 140 h.r./acre		Scheme C 80 h.r./acre		Scheme D 60 h.r./acre	
	acres	h.r./ persons	acres	h.r./ persons	acres	h.r./ persons	acres	h.r./ persons
Inner land: Dwellings ...	125	25,000	143	20,000	169	13,500	184	11,000
Open spaces and schools	125		107		81		66	
Outer land: Dwellings ...	520	31,000	600	36,000	710	42,500	755	45,000
Neighbourhood facilities	372		432		510		540	
Playing fields for inner people ...	62		50		34		27	
Total inner and outer land ...	1,204	56,000	1,332	56,000	1,504	56,000	1,572	56,000

In this exercise we shall consider only the provision of dwellings, and will compare the costs and yields for each of the schemes. It will be simplest to prepare the calculations in terms of the average cost and yield per habitable room. Loan charges in all cases are taken as an annuity over 60 years at 4 per cent; that is, at 4.4 per cent per annum.

I, II. Capital and Annual Costs of Providing Dwellings

(a) (b) *Acquisition of Land and Legal Preparation of Site.* The cost of the inner and outer land used for dwellings is taken as the average cost of £6,650 and £200 per acre respectively.

(c) *Physical Preparation of Sites.* It is assumed that the average cost of demolition and clearance of the inner land is £1,000 per acre; and that of physical preparation of the outer land is £50 per acre.

(*d*) *Site Works*. It is assumed that the cost per acre of site works on the inner land in all schemes is £5,000 per acre; and on the outer land £3,000 per acre. In practice the cost on the inner land would vary with the density; and on the outer land the larger spread might mean higher average costs because of additional trunk sewers, etc.

(*a*)-(*d*) *Acquisition and Preparation of Site and Site Works*. The totals of these works per acre would be for all schemes:

	Inner Land £	Outer Land £
Acquisition and legal preparation ...	6,650	200
Physical preparation of site ...	1,000	50
Site works	5,000	3,000
	12,650 per acre	3,250 per acre

The average cost per habitable room would be:

	Capital £	Annual £
Outer Land		
All Schemes, £3,250 per acre at 60 h.r. per acre ...	54	2·4
Inner Land		
Scheme A, £12,650 per acre at 200 h.r. per acre ...	63	2·8
Scheme B, £12,650 per acre at 140 h.r. per acre ...	90	4·0
Scheme C. £12,650 per acre at 80 h.r. per acre ...	108	7·0
Scheme D, £12,650 per acre at 60 h.r. per acre ...	211	9·3

(*e*) (*k*) (*l*) *Cost of Building Dwellings: Capital Cost and Annual Loan Charges*. The proportion of houses and flats, and the heights of the flats, will vary at the different densities.[47] This will affect the costs of construction at different densities for in typical local authority dwellings, with fairly standard size of rooms, the average cost per habitable room increases with the height of buildings above two storeys but decreases with the size of dwelling. The costs per habitable room quoted below reflect both these factors.[48] It has been assumed that where flats are to be provided the larger dwellings are in the lower buildings.

Outer Land

All Schemes. At 60 habitable rooms to the acre it is possible to accommodate all the population in two-storey dwellings. It is proposed to provide 20 per cent of the rooms in flats.

800 h.r.	228 dwgs.	in two-storey houses at £450 per h.r. ...	£360,000
100 h.r.	41 dwgs.	in two-storey flats at £675 per h.r. ...	£67,500
100 h.r.	41 dwgs.	in three-storey flats at £725 per h.r. ...	£72,500
1,000 h.r.	310 dwgs.	Total	£500,000
		Average capital cost per h.r.	£500
		Average annual cost ...	£22

Inner Land

Scheme D. At 60 habitable rooms to the acre—all as for outer land.

Scheme C. At 80 habitable rooms to the acre it is not possible to provide all the dwellings in two-storey houses since a reasonable average density for such

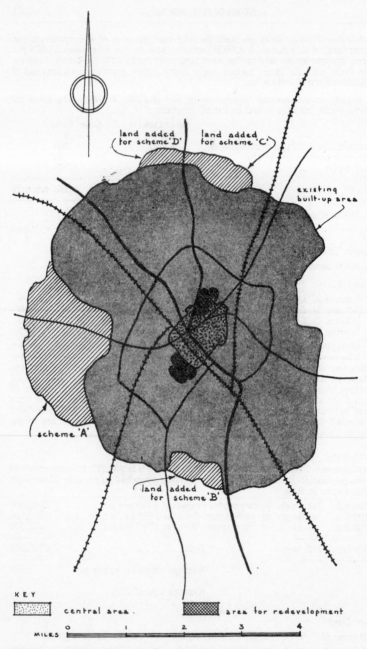

land added
for scheme 'D'

land added
for scheme 'C'

existing
built-up area

scheme 'A'

land added
for scheme 'B'

KEY

central area.

area for redevelopment

MILES 0   1   2   3   4

FIGURE 2.—*Sketch Plan Showing Location of Overspill in Alternative Schemes A. B. C. D.—Exercise* 2

houses is 60 habitable rooms to the acre. It is proposed to provide five-storey flats, which will have an average density of approximately 140 habitable rooms per acre, and the maximum number of dwellings in two-storey houses.

558 h.r.	147 dwgs.	in two-storey houses at £450 per h.r.	...	£252,000
442 h.r.	163 dwgs.	in five-storey flats at £775 per h.r.	...	£342,000
1,000 h.r.	310 dwgs.	Total		£594,000
		Average capital cost per h.r.		£600
		Average annual cost ...		£26·4

Scheme B. At 140 habitable rooms per acre even less dwellings can be provided in houses. It is proposed to provide 10-storey flats, which will have an average density of approximately 200 habitable rooms per acre, the maximum number of dwellings in two-storey houses at an average density of 60 habitable rooms per acre and three-storey flats at an average of 80 habitable rooms per acre.

110 h.r.	25 dwgs.	in two-storey houses at £450 per room	...	£491,500
110 h.r.	27 dwgs.	in three-storey flats at £600 per room	...	£66,000
780 h.r.	258 dwgs.	in 10-storey flats at £775 per room	...	£605,000
1,000 h.r.	310 dwgs.	Total cost		£720,500
		Average capital cost per h.r.		£720
		Average annual cost ...		£31·7

Scheme A. At 200 habitable rooms per acre all rooms will be in 10-storey flats at an average capital cost of £750 and annual of £33.

(*f*) (*g*) (*h*) *Interest on Construction Cost, Profit and Disposal Expenses.* These are not allowed for.

(*h*) (*i*) *Occupation and Ownership Expenses.* These are assumed as follows per dwelling:

	Houses	Two-storey and three-storey flats No lifts	Five-storey and 10-storey flats With lifts
Occupation — repairs and maintenance (rates excluded) ... £	8	12	18
Ownership — supervision and management ... ... £	4	8	10
Total ... ... £	12	20	28

The cost of each scheme per habitable room would be:

Outer Land

All Schemes.

	£	£
200 h.r. in 82 flats (two-storey and three-storey) at £20 ...	1,640	
800 h.r. in 228 houses at £12	2,736	
		4,376
1,000 h.r. 310 dwgs.		
Average per h.r. ...		£4·4

Inner Land

Scheme A.

		£	£
1,000 h.r. in 310 flats (10-storey) at £28			8,680
	Average per h.r. ...		£8·7

Scheme B.

		£	£
110 h.r. in 25 houses at £12		300	
110 h.r. in 27 flats (three-storey) at £20		540	
780 h.r. in 258 flats (10-storey) at £28		9,224	
			8,064
1,000 h.r. 310 dwgs.			
	Average per h.r. ...		£8·1

Scheme C.

		£	£
558 h.r. in 147 houses at £12		1,764	
442 h.r. in 163 flats (five-storey) at £28		4,564	
			6,318
1,000 h.r. 310 dwgs.			
	Average per h.r. ...		£6·3

Scheme D. As for outer land.

			£
	Average per h.r. ...		£4·4

III. *Annual Yield*

If from the total annual costs are deducted the annual subsidies from both exchequer and rates there will be left the rents that will need to be found for each scheme if annual costs are to be covered by annual yield.

Subsidies

Outer Land. All the dwellings, whether houses or flats, would attract the standard subsidy, since the land would not be considered as expensive.

Inner Land. For calculation purposes the cost of site as developed will be averaged over the whole land; that is, £12,650 per acre. (In practice the subsidies would be calculated on individual areas as they were developed. The cost of these would differ from the average subsidies for individual areas would also vary). So that:

Scheme A. The actual density is $\frac{200}{3 \cdot 23} = 62$ dwgs. to the acre.

The notional cost of site is $£12,650 \times \frac{35}{62} =$ £7,150

The subsidy for each flat is—exchequer £67 10s.
rate contribution £24 5s.

Scheme B. This is a mixed scheme of houses and flats.

Houses. Subsidy for houses in mixed schemes on expensive sites—
exchequer £49 4s.
rate contribution £16 8s.

Flats. Total net acreage = 143

The notional flats acreage is $\frac{890}{1,000} \times 143 =$ 127

The number of flats is $285 \times 20 \cdot 2 =$ 5,750

The notional density is $\frac{5,750}{128}$ flats =   45

The notional cost of site is £12,650 $\times \frac{35}{45}$ = £9,820

Subsidy for three-storey flats—exchequer		£58 19s.
	rates	£19 13s.
Subsidy for 10-storey flats—exchequer		£69 9s.
	rates	£24 18s.

Scheme C. A mixed scheme of houses and flats.

Houses. As in Scheme B— exchequer   £49 4s.
                                        rates   £16 8s.

Flats. The total net acreage =   169

The notional flat acreage is $\frac{442}{1,000} \times 169 =$ 75

The number of flats is $163 \times 13\cdot7 =$ 2,230

The notional density is $\frac{2,230}{75}$ flats =   30

(Therefore no adjustment to land cost for density required.)

Subsidy for five-storey flats — exchequer   £73 7s.
                                        rates   £26 4s.

Scheme D. A mixed scheme of houses and flats.

Houses and two-storey flats.

As in Scheme B— exchequer   £49 4s.
                                        rates   £16 8s.

Three-storey flats.

The total net acreage =   184

The notional flat acreage is $\frac{100}{1,000} \times 184 =$ 18·4

The number of flats is $41 \times 10\cdot9 =$ 446

The notional density is $\frac{446}{18\cdot4} =$ 24·2

The notional cost of site is £12,600 $\times \frac{35}{24\cdot2} =$
                                        £18,400

Subsidy for three-storey flats—exchequer   £68 14s.
                                        rates   £22 18s.

Subsidies per Habitable Room	AEC	SRC	AEC	SRC
Outer Land.	per dwelling		Total	
All Schemes.	£	£	£	£
1,000 h.r. in 310 dwgs. (two-storey houses, two- and three-storey flats)	26·14—	8·18—	8,270	2,760
		Total subsidy ...	11,030	
		Per h.r.	11·0	
Inner Land.				
Scheme A.	£	£	£	£
1,000 h.r. in 310 dwgs. (10-storey flats)	67·10—	24·5—	20,950	7,600
		Total subsidy ...	28,550	
		Per h.r.	28·5	

	per dwelling		Total	
Scheme B.	£	£	£	£
110 h.r. in 25 dwgs. (two-storey houses)	49· 4—	16· 8—	1,230	410
110 h.r. in 27 dwgs. (three-storey flats)	58·19—	19·13—	1,600	530
780 h.r. in 258 dwgs. (10-storey flats)	69· 9—	24·18—	17,900	6,430
		Total subsidy ...		28,100
		Per h.r.		28·1

	per dwelling		Total	
Scheme C.	£	£	£	£
558 h.r. in 147 dwgs. (two-storey houses)	49·4—	16·8—	7,230	2,410
442 h.r. in 163 dwgs. (five-storey flats)	73·7—	26·4—	12,000	4,300
		Total subsidy ...		25,940
		Per h.r.		25·9

	per dwelling		Total	
Scheme D.	£	£	£	£
800 h.r. in 228 dwgs. (two-storey houses)	49· 4—	16· 8	11,200	3,740
100 h.r. in 41 dwgs. (two-storey flats)	49· 4	16· 8	2,030	680
100 h.r. in 41 dwgs. (three-storey flats)	68·14	22·18	2,820	940
		Total subsidy ...		21,436
		Per h.r.		21·4

Summary of Annual Costs and Yields per Habitable Room

	Outer Land	Inner Land			
	All schemes	A	B	C	D
Loan charges on capital cost:					
Land and site works	2·4	2·7	4·0	7·0	9·3
Building	22·0	33·0	31·6	26·4	22·0
Total	24·4	35·7	35·6	33·4	31·3
Add Annual costs of repairs, maintenance and management... ...	4·4	8·7	8·1	6·3	4·4
Total annual cost	28·8	44·4	43·7	39·7	35·7
Less Annual exchequer and rate contribution	11·0	28·5	28·1	25·9	21·4
Annual amount to be found out of rents and rates	17·8	15·9	15·6	13·8	14·3

SUMMARY OF ANNUAL COST AND YIELDS FOR SCHEMES A, B, C, D for 56,000 PEOPLE

	Scheme A			Scheme B			Scheme C			Scheme D		
	Inner land	Outer land	Total	Inner land	Outer land	Total	Inner land	Outer land	Total	Inner land	Outer land	Total
Habitable rooms ...	25,000	31,000	56,000	20,000	36,000	56,000	13,000	42,000	56,000	11,000	45,000	56,000
Loan charges on capital cost:	£	£	£	£	£	£	£	£	£	£	£	£
Land and site works...	67,000	70,000	142,000	81,000	86,000	167,000	92,000	102,000	194,000	101,000	109,000	210,000
Buildings	825,000	686,000	1,511,000	637,000	791,000	1,428,000	348,000	936,000	1,284,000	240,000	1,000,000	1,240,000
Total annual loan charges	892,000	761,000	1,653,000	718,000	877,000	1,595,000	440,000	1,038,000	1,478,000	341,000	1,109,000	1,450,000
Total capital cost* ...	20,300,000	17,300,000	37,600,000	16,300,000	20,000,000	36,300,000	10,000,000	23,400,000	33,400,000	7,750,000	25,250,000	33,000,000
Add Annual costs of repairs, maintenance and management ...	218,000	137,000	355,000	164,000	158,000	322,000	83,000	187,000	270,000	48,000	199,000	247,000
Total annual cost ...	1,110,000	898,000	2,008,000	882,000	1,035,000	1,917,000	523,000	1,225,000	1,748,000	389,000	1,308,000	1,697,000
Less Annual exchequer and rate contribution	712,000	343,000	1,050,000	567,000	395,000	962,000	341,000	468,000	809,000	233,000	498,000	731,000
Annual amount to be found from rates and rents	398,000	555,000	953,000	315,000	640,000	955,000	182,000	757,000	939,000	156,000	810,000	966,000

* Loan charges divided by 4·4 per cent.

Conclusions on the Four Schemes

The authority with 250 acres for housing in the centre of its town and 56,000 people to house would thus find, on the assumptions here given:

1.   That the total cost of providing land and dwellings would decrease as density on the inner land decreases; at 200 h.r. to the acre it would be £1,653,000 per annum (capital £37·6 million) and at 60 h.r. per acre £1,450,000 per annum (capital £33·8 million). The 200 h.r. per acre scheme would thus cost £203,000 more per annum than the 60 h.r. per acre scheme (capital £4·6 million) and proportionately for the intermediate schemes. This £203,000 is made up of an additional cost of building of £271,000 (£6·2 million) against which is offset a saving in cost of land and site works of £68,000 (£1·6 million).

2.   The annual cost of repairs, supervision and maintenance in the 200 h.r. scheme would be about £108,000 more per annum that at the 60 h.r. scheme.

3.   The 200 h.r. scheme would cost about £82 more in capital cost to house each person; and about £5 10s. more in annual cost over 60 years to house and maintain each person. The annual costs of repair, maintenance and management are a small proportion of the annual costs of construction: 21 per cent in Scheme A falling to 17 per cent in Scheme D.

4.   Although the 200 h.r. to the acre scheme would cost about £200,000 more per annum than the 60 h.r. scheme, the subsidies paid are such that in all schemes much the same total rent would need to be collected to balance the housing revenue account. This demonstrates that the subsidy arrangements perform their intended function of keeping rents fairly even in different kinds of schemes, when the same range of dwellings is provided in them. About £324,000 more subsidy would be payable in the 200 h.r. to the acre scheme than in the 60 scheme. Just over one-quarter of this would fall on the rates.

5.   The extra cost of providing dwellings in the higher density schemes can be taken as a measure of the cost of saving the land for agriculture by adopting such schemes. For example, the highest density scheme would save for agriculture some 368 acres of land which would be developed in the lowest density scheme. This figure is made up of some 235 acres which would be covered by dwellings, plus 168 acres by neighbourhood facilities and open space, less 35 acres which would not be needed for playing fields for the inner people. The 235 acres would be kept open at an extra capital cost of £4·6 million, or £19,500 per acre; or at an extra annual cost over 60 years of £1,320 per acre in providing and maintaining dwellings (equivalent to a capital cost of £30,000 per acre).

These conclusions are not necessarily typical for all towns: a variation in the amount of inner land, occupancy rates, cost of land and cost of building may lead to different conclusions. But the example shows the kind of analysis that is necessary before deciding that particular densities are appropriate; and also that because an authority can pool costs, rents and subsidies in the housing revenue account, and can look at its programme as a whole, it can reach different conclusions than by merely considering individual schemes.

Only the cost of dwellings has been considered here. For an authority to reach its decision on density it would need to consider not only this but the cost of all other residential facilities (schools, open spaces, etc.), local authority services, public utilities, transportation of goods and people. These facilities and services would on the whole be more economically provided and used as people are housed more compactly; their cost would thus in general decrease per person as density increased.

(B) HOUSING ASSOCIATIONS

Housing associations originated over 100 years ago when housing conditions were very poor, and local authorities had insufficient powers or money to make much contribution. Voluntary associations of persons were formed to provide dwellings for the working classes at rents which they could afford to pay. They number about 350 today, and have been set up by would-be occupiers, industrialists, local authorities, co-operative societies, colleges, rotary clubs, churches, chambers of trade.

The object of an association is the " constructing, improving, managing or facilitating or encouraging the construction or improvement of houses for the working classes."[49] The dwellings so provided are usually let, not sold.

Societies obtain their equity capital from share and stockholders and borrow from building societies, the Public Works Loans Board or local authorities.[50] The loan is by way of mortgage on the security of the dwellings they build. They do not trade for profit, and cannot pay interest on capital at a rate exceeding that for the time being prescribed by the Treasury.

Where an association makes arrangements with an authority to carry out housing which would otherwise be done by the authority, it receives housing subsidies, the rate contribution coming from the local authority and the exchequer contribution from the Minister via the authority.[51] The arrangements cover such matters as rents to be charged, and where it does, the association will calculate these rents as will a local authority. In other cases it might adopt a kind of financial calculation which is midway between that of private enterprise and a local authority. In this it would include interest on capital during construction; it would need to earn on its equity at least the rate which it pays to its shareholders, and loan charges on its loans: and where the loans were from building societies the repayment would be over less than 60 years.[52]

As to testing cost and yield, the methods it will use will be nearer to those of private enterprise than of public agencies; and no question will arise of supplementing yield out of the rates.

(C) NEW TOWN DEVELOPMENT CORPORATIONS

A new town development corporation may receive its housing subsidy in different ways. It is deemed to be a housing association and, as such, may act by arrangement with any authority, including that of a congested area which seeks to house its people in the new town, when it would receive the exchequer subsidy via the authority as well as the rate contribution from it.[53] Alternatively, if a corporation provides a house for a tenant nominated by an authority of a congested area, the Minister would pay the exchequer contribution and the authority may pay the rate contribution by agreement for a period of at least 10 years.[54] Or the Minister may pay the exchequer contribution direct to the corporation for the dwellings it builds for its population, and the rate contribution too.[55]

The rent policy of a corporation must be different from that of a local authority. It has no reserve of pre-war houses at low rents which can be raised to make possible reduced rents for post-war nouses; and it has no rates out of which to subsidise rents. In consequence, the corporation must, in order to pay its way on housing, which it has been instructed by the Minister to do, charge rents on dwellings which are based on cost after allowing for subsidy. Since costs have been steadily rising, and have fluctuated from scheme to scheme, there are differing rents for similar dwellings throughout each of the new towns. These fluctuations may be evened out in future for dwellings in new towns were freed from rent control in 1954,[56] and corporations will therefore be able to have regard to the cost and yield of dwellings as a whole.

CHAPTER 13

ROADS AND STREETS

The Highway System—Highway Authorities—Powers in Relation to the Construction and Improvement of Roads and Streets—Disposal of Land—Exchequer Grants to Highway Authorities—Financial Statement.

The Highway System

THE TERMS " roads " and " streets " have various meanings in various statutes. We are here adopting their popular meaning. The former relates to routes which are primarily used for carrying traffic, and the latter to those which are developed with adjoining buildings and are primarily used for giving access to these buildings.

For development plan purposes roads and streets are grouped into trunk roads, other principal traffic roads, main and minor streets, according to their traffic functions. In considering the calculations for roads and streets two other ways of grouping them are of interest. They are grouped into public and private roads and streets, in order to indicate whether highway authorities are or are not primarily responsible for their construction, improvement and maintenance; and public roads are also grouped into trunk roads, classified roads (I, II, and III) and unclassified roads, by the Minister of Transport and Civil Aviation, to indicate the proportion of their cost in new construction, maintenance and improvement that he is prepared to contribute by way of grant. This last grouping aims, broadly, at defining the degree to which roads are or will be of importance for through as opposed to local traffic. Trunk roads form the principal routes for through traffic in the country; Class I roads connect large centres of population and other roads of outstanding importance for through traffic; Class II roads form important links between Class I roads and smaller centres of population; Class III roads are of more than local traffic value; and unclassified roads are of purely local importance.

Highway Authorities

The Minister of Transport and Civil Aviation is the highway authority for all trunk roads in Great Britain. As such he pays the full cost of all work to them, but he delegates responsibility for their maintenance and day-to-day administration, normally to the highway authorities of the areas through which they pass. These authorities carry out work as agents for the Minister, being recouped with the cost of the work and a percentage in addition to cover administrative expenses. On large new schemes the Ministry will sometimes carry out the works itself.

13

The remainder of the public roads and streets in the country are in the care of one or other of the local highway authorities; that is, the counties, county boroughs, non-county boroughs and urban districts.[1] In the County of London the metropolitan borough councils and City Corporation carry out minor improvements and maintain the roads, while the London County Council carries out major improvements and maintains certain of the Thames bridges, tunnels and embankments. In the area of a county borough, the council is the authority for all except trunk roads. In administrative counties, the county councils are the highway authorities for all classified roads, excluding trunk roads in non-county boroughs and urban districts, and for all public roads, again excluding trunk roads, in rural districts. The councils of boroughs and urban districts are responsible for the unclassified roads within their boundaries; and if they have a population of over 20,000 they may claim the right to take care of classified roads, in which event they become statutorily responsible although the county council reimburses their expenditure. County district councils, including a few rural districts, also have certain responsibilities delegated to them on county roads, acting as agents of the county.

Powers in Relation to the Construction and Improvement of Roads and Streets

The law relating to the powers and duties of highway authorities as to the construction and improvement of roads and streets is complex. It has evolved mainly over the last century.

(a) *The Construction of New Roads and the Improvement of Existing Ones.* With the coming of railways, which were largely constructed between 1830 and 1850, travel on the roads and canals diminished disastrously and both fell into disuse. The Turnpike Trusts, which had built and maintained arterial roads in the eighteenth century, became insolvent and lost their powers. No machinery survived them for improving roads or building new ones, since there was no responsibility for this at common law, and no statutory powers until the passing of the Development and Roads Improvement Fund Act, 1909. A Road Board was then set up with power to construct and maintain any new road required to facilitate motor traffic, and to authorise any highway authority to do so and to make advances to it. The Board or highway authorities could acquire land for the proposed road, and the Board, in its schemes, could also buy for recoupment on either side, within two hundred and twenty yards from the middle. Because of the 1914 war, and reasons of policy and personnel, no new roads were built by the Board or by highway authorities under its influence. In 1919 the Ministry of Transport was set up and took over the Board's functions.

Apart from emergency Acts which were passed in 1920 and 1930,[2] to facilitate the acquisition of land for road construction and general municipal works respectively, in order to relieve unemployment, the next major road building Act was the Restriction of Ribbon Development Act, 1935. Under it any highway authority can buy land, compulsorily or by agreement, within 220 yards from the middle of any road " for the purpose of its construction or improvement or of preventing the erection of buildings detrimental to the view from the road." It can also by agreement acquire any land in the neighbourhood of any road, in order to preserve the amenities of the locality in which it is situated; this includes preventing the erection of buildings detrimental to the view from the road.[3] It is under this Act that land for the construction of new roads is now generally acquired where a local Act is not used. The Minister of Transport and Civil Aviation can, as a highway authority, acquire land under it for the construction or improvement of a trunk road, and any additional land for preserving amenity; and also for the provision of buildings or facilities to be used in connection with the construction and maintenance of a trunk road.[4] Where motorways, and other roads for special classes of traffic are to be built, the special road authority will also be able to acquire under it for these purposes.[5]

Highway authorities can also acquire for road building and improvement under the Town and Country Planning Act, 1947, where land is designated in an approved development plan for the purpose of their highway functions, or where it is within or contiguous or adjacent to an area of comprehensive development.[6] Furthermore, any land acquired or appropriated by a local authority under this Act can be appropriated or transferred to a highway authority for building or improving a road.[7]

(b) *The Widening and Improvement of Public Roads and Streets.*
At common law the parishes were responsible for the repair and maintenance of public roads and streets. Over the past century there has been a gradual centralisation of authority, a widening of the area administered by highway authorities and the introduction of statutory powers to improve existing roads and streets.[8] These powers still exist in the main, and have been added to in this century, although the use of highway powers for protecting road and street lines has been largely superseded by the use of planning powers.[9] Under highway powers, an authority can seek to improve a street which is narrow, inconvenient, or without any sufficiently regular boundary line, or is in need of widening, by prescribing an improvement line to which the street is sooner or later to be widened. It can then prohibit new buildings, erections or excavations between the improvement lines; and can buy any land not covered by buildings between such line and the boundary of the street.[10] And highway authorities have general powers of purchasing any land for the purpose of widening, opening, enlarging or otherwise improving

any street, or for the purpose of making any new one, including the improvement and development of frontages or of the lands abutting on or adjacent to any streets.[11]

(c) *The Construction of New Streets.*   New streets which are not required for public development are almost always constructed at private expense, when their level, width and construction are subject to bye-laws.[12] The erection of buildings along an existing highway, or the continuation of an existing street, may amount in practice to the forming of a new street; and, the authority may declare the new section to be a street in order to have it constructed according to its bye-laws.[13]

The widths required under bye-laws have not changed since these were first formulated under the Public Health Act, 1875. These widths are not always appropriate for good layout today since they do not allow for enough variety in type of street, and so can result in some streets being too narrow and some too wide for their functions. The Minister has advised authorities to agree to more suitable widths, where appropriate. Where the bye-law width is too great for the street's function, some relaxation of the bye-law is necessary.[14] Where the bye-law width is not sufficient, authorities can ask for a greater width to be laid out. Compensation is payable only for land devoted to the street in excess of 20 feet more than the maximum width in a bye-law or enactment and where compensation is payable it is possible to set off against it the benefit of the widening to the land owner.[15]

Sometimes, too, the location of a street, while suiting the layout of the particular developer, will not accord with the general layout of the area. In such cases the authority can vary the intended position, direction, termination or level of the new street in order to secure more direct, easy or convenient means of communication with any other street or intended street.[16]

With regard to construction, few bye-laws include any actual specification which must be observed. To obtain a suitable standard of construction the authority relies on street works procedure. Under this it can insist on the street being made up to a certain specification before it will assume responsibility for its maintenance; or it can make up the street to this specification, and charge the frontagers who benefit their due proportion of the cost.[17] The effect of this is that if new streets are to be taken over by the highway authority the cost of constructing them to a certain standard must be found by the developers or the purchasers of the finished development. When building plans are submitted under the building bye-laws, the authority must, except in certain cases, ask for the deposit of the estimated cost of street works.[18]

Street works procedure could not, until the 1947 Act, be initiated for widening a public street or before a street existed. Under this

Act new machinery is devised for applying the procedure in such cases. Land for the construction of a new street, or the widening of an existing public street up to bye-law width, can be defined in a Street Authorisation Map in a development plan and designated as land to which private street works procedure can be applied.[19]

Disposal of Land

The disposal of land acquired for highway purposes can only arise in relation to surplus land, that which has been acquired but is not needed for the actual road or its ancillary works. In practice, there is not very much surplus land. Although, as mentioned above, powers of acquiring recoupment land have been given in various general Acts, they have not in fact been much used;[20] and such powers are not given in the 1935 Act. The general policy of the Ministry of Transport has been to limit the payment of grant, and in consequence the acquisition, to land required just for highway purposes. A highway authority must specify to the Minister of Transport and Civil Aviation the purpose for which it intends to use the land which it wishes to acquire under the Restriction of Ribbon Development Act, 1935, and must use it for that purpose; and must not let, sell or exchange any of the additional land it has acquired for amenity purposes without an order of the Minister of Housing and Local Government.[21] As a result of this policy any increase in land value, consequential on the improved access afforded, has gone into private instead of public pockets; and until the passing of the Restriction of Ribbon Development Act, 1935, highway authorities had no direct control over development adjoining the road and could not prevent its interference with the efficient and safe use of the new road. Furthermore, in built-up areas the execution of a road scheme has frequently resulted in relatively small areas of surplus land being left with the authority. Authorities are free to sell such land should they wish, but small pieces are not readily saleable and there has usually been difficulty in securing a proper re-development of the new frontages.

Recoupment is possible where roads are built as part of a housing or other development scheme. In these cases only the site of the road would be transferred or appropriated to the highway authority so that any benefit of recoupment would accrue to the developing authority, which would not always be the highway authority.

There have been many attempts under private Acts to recover betterment by recoupment in the construction and widening of roads and streets in urban areas, as, for example, in the private Acts under which were built Charing Cross Road, Shaftesbury Avenue, Northumberland Avenue, and Kingsway, London; The Headrow, Leeds; Inner Ring Road, Leicester; Lower Parliament Street, Nottingham. A recent analysis of various such schemes carried out by the Metropolitan Board of Works, the predecessor of the London

County Council, shows that the recoupment purchases increased rather than diminished the net cost of building Gray's Inn Road, Charing Cross Road, Shaftesbury Avenue and Marshalsea Road in London. The loss on the land in the actual road works (that is capital cost of land less value remaining upon completion) was less than that on the total scheme which included recoupment.[22]

The reason for this was, largely, the generosity to property owners of the compensation rules on acquisition before the passing of the Acquisition of Land (Compensation for Compulsory Purchase) Act, 1919. But even with the less generous rules that prevail today, an obstacle to financial success of recoupment is the weight of loan charges that must be paid during the long time that elapses before all properties are disposed of in a big scheme. In the Kingsway scheme, London, for example, it took about 16 years from completion of work in 1905 to sell the $14\frac{1}{2}$ acres of surplus land. In 1920 the value and sales of surplus land amounted to £4,431,000, about £600,000 less than the cost of acquisition, and ground rents (about £135,000) were equalling annual interest charges. But the interest on loan and provision for redemption of capital had accumulated over the previous 30 years, since property began to be bought, to £2,500,000.[23]

Exchequer Grants to Highway Authorities

Between 1921 and 1955 grants to highway authorities came from the Road Fund. This was established in 1920, taking over the assets of the Road Board's Road Improvement Fund, and into it have been made such payments as the net proceeds of taxes on mechanically propelled vehicles, of fees received by the Traffic Commissioners and fines and penalties imposed for motoring offences. From 1926 the Fund was not used entirely for roads but also by governments to supplement revenue. This position was recognised in 1937 since when these proceeds have been paid into the Exchequer and, until 1955, the estimated amount to be spent on grants voted annually by Parliament into what was still called the Road Fund. In 1955 the Fund was abolished and the Minister of Transport and Civil Aviation pays money for roads out of votes. Out of these he pays for practically all the expenditure on trunk roads and a proportion of the cost of new construction, improvement, and maintenance of all classified roads: at present 75 per cent for Class I, 60 per cent for Class II and 50 per cent for Class III. No grant is made for unclassified roads nor towards the maintenance and minor improvement of roads in London.[24]

For the purpose of paying, grant road works are divided into those of (a) maintenance and minor improvement and (b) major improvement and new construction. Maintenance is defined very widely. It includes normal repair work to the road, fencing and surface-water drains; sweeping and cleansing; maintenance of traffic signs. Minor improvements include improvements in the construction of the road, its surface, superelevation and foundations.[25] From this it is seen that a road improvement of any substance is a major improvement, including all those which require the acquisition of any land at all. It is on the execution of these major improvements and new construction that there has been, in particular, considerable restriction since the war.

Table 24 shows the total amount of money spent on roads in 1951-52 and 1952-53, and the proportions on maintenance, etc.; major construction; new construction; cleansing, watering and snow clearing; and local authority administration. It furthermore shows how this total was divided between the Road Fund and other expenditure: primarily that of local highway authorities from loans and rates supplemented by exchequer equalisation grants.

TABLE 24

Road Expenditure of Different Kinds on All Public Roads—Proportion of Rate Fund Contribution

	1951-52		1952-53	
	Total	From Road Fund	Total	From Road Fund
Total expenditure...	£80·670	£28·070	£85·170	£30·600
	Per cent	Per cent	Per cent	Per cent
Maintenance, repair and minor improvement	70·7	84·4	71·0	84·1
Major improvement	5·2	7·3	4·7	7·1
New construction...	1·6	1·6	1·7	2·1
Cleansing, watering and snow clearing	11·0	3·2	11·7	3·4
Administration expenses of local authorities	11·5	3·5	10·9	3·3

Source: *Report on the Administration of the Road Fund*, 1952-53, Appendix VI.

The Ministry grants are paid each year for maintenance and minor improvements after the estimates of such expenditure for all roads in each class has been approved. For major improvements and new construction estimated to cost over £5,000, lump sum grants are paid after each individual scheme has been approved. These latter grants are towards the " net cost of the scheme falling on the highway authority, after deducting costs which should properly be borne by transport or other undertakings and allowing credit for contributions from frontagers, statutory undertakings or other sources and after deducting the cost attributable to any elements of the scheme that may be of the nature of a ' town improvement,' i.e., a feature which is required primarily in the interests of the locality and is not essential to the scheme from the point of view of traffic requirements."[26]

The effect of paying grants in lump sums is that for improvements and new construction a highway authority raises a loan for less than the full capital cost. Thus in contrast to exchequer contributions which are made annually, such as education grants, the exchequer grant for roads is not available to finance loans. This paying for capital works out of revenue by the government has often been criticised in that it unnecessarily limits the amount of money that can be spent on roads in the near future; and, it is urged, that just as large programmes of other works are financed out of loans and repaid gradually out of revenue, so could a programme of badly needed roads be built quickly if the income spent on roads were used in this way.[27] In considering such a road loan the potential burden of interest on it should be taken into account. If such a loan were financed at £15 million per annum, which the Minister of Transport envisaged in 1953 would be the annual expenditure from the exchequer for a period of years on major improvements and the construction of new roads,[28] some £260 million could be borrowed immediatley at 4 per cent for 30 years and spent as fast as the resources and commitments of the civil engineering industry would allow. But this same expenditure per annum out of revenue would amount to a programme of £450 million over the same 30 years.

Financial Statement for New Road

For our statement we will consider a major road scheme where land is acquired under one of the Highway Acts, or under another Act and transferred to the highway authority. There are small parcels of surplus land but no acquisition for recoupment. Were there recoupment, the estimates for the road construction and recoupment could be kept separate; ' and the appraisal for the latter might follow that for housing or comprehensive development (Chapters 12 and 15).

I. Capital Cost

(a) (b) Acquisition of Land and Legal Preparation of Site. The powers of acquiring land under the various Acts have been referred to. In general the compensation codes for acquiring and transfer are those described in Chapter 11. In some Acts there is a provision for set off: the taking into account, in assessing compensation for compulsory acquisition, of the extent to which remaining and contiguous lands belonging to the same owner may be benefited by the proposed work for which the land is acquired.[29]

Because of the shape of land required, many properties are liable to be affected by a scheme for constructing or improving a road or street, particularly by a street widening scheme in a central area. This gives rise to claims for injurious affection as well as for land acquisition. For example, in rural areas compensation may be attracted through splitting a farm and making the portion detached from the farmbuildings difficult to work. And in urban areas it may be attracted where a street widening takes so much off the depth of fronting properties that the remaining plots are virtually useless. In such cases it may be cheaper for the authority to pay for acquiring the whole of the property affected, and to use or dispose of the surplus land, rather than to pay for the required part and for injurious affection to the remainder. In such cases, in fact, the owner of the lands may insist upon the acquiring authority taking the whole, often with success (page 144). Both in aiming at economy in designing the road line and in estimating the likely compensation for land taken these factors must be taken into account.

(c) (d) (e) *Cost of Works.* The construction of roads involves mostly civil engineering and little building work. There is the forming of embankments, cuttings and retaining walls; the laying of sewers, surface-water drains, water mains and other services; the provision of foundations, surfacing and kerbing to carriageway, footpaths, cycle tracks; the planting and landscaping of verges, refuges and roundabouts; the provision of street lighting and boundary fences, walls, etc.

(f) *Interest on Capital During Construction.* This is not normally included in the capital cost for the purpose of obtaining loan sanction.

(g) *Profit.* No allowance for profit is made since there is no question of disposal of the development.

(h) *Disposal expenses.* The works always remain the property of the highway authority, even if another acts as agent for construction. No disposal expenses arise therefore except where there is surplus land.

II. Annual Costs

(j) *Return on Investment.* This does not arise.

(k) (l) *Repayment of Loan and Interest.* Loan charges would be taken on that part of the capital cost which the authority raises by loan.

(m) *Depreciation.* This is not provided for.

(n) *Occupation Expenses.* These include all the expenses incurred in the repair, maintenance, cleansing and keeping in condition of the road. In 1952-53 the average per mile in Great Britain was £950 on trunk roads, £830 on Class I, £430 on Class II, £240 on Class III and £180 on unclassified roads.[30]

(*o*) *Ownership Expenses*.   These hardly arise.

III.   Money Yield

Roads in general are non-remunerative, and highway authorities receive no specific income for them.   Apart from paying general rates and taxes vehicle owners contribute via motor taxation, and passengers in taxis and public service vehicles via their fares, but pedestrians and cyclists make no contribution at all.

Where additional land is acquired there will be yields from selling or appropriation.   This apart, there are two other occasional sources of income.   Firstly, in some local Acts under which road or street schemes have been carried out there are powers for levying improvement charges.   The City of Coventry, for example, when building a by-pass under the Coventry Corporation Act, 1936, was able to levy from owners of land within a defined improvement area a charge of 30s. 0d. per foot frontage of their lands to the by-pass.   Secondly, it may be practicable to levy a toll for the use of the road.   There are about 100 toll roads in this country today, and it is being urged that we build roads with turnpikes again in order to finance their construction.   The Minister of Transport, when introducing the four-year road programme in February, 1955 (see page 284), stated that the government had in mind the introduction of tolls which would contribute towards the cost of certain of the major projects of national importance in the programme.   Toll roads are being built again in the United States, where the initial 160-mile section of the first 20th century turnpike, the Pennsylvania Turnpike, was opened in 1940, and also in Europe.

IV.   Relation of Cost to Yield

The annual costs to the highway authority of a road scheme can be tested only in relation to its financial resources in rates or taxes.   Method (*H*) provides the only suitable test.

CHAPTER 14

CAR PARKS

Car Park Authorities and Powers—Financial Statement for Car Parks—Alternative Forms of Parking in Large Towns—Pooling Costs and Yields.

Car Park Authorities and Powers

THE POWERS of providing car parks rest not with highway but with local authorities. They may provide suitable parking places for vehicles where it appears to them to be necessary, for the purpose of relieving or preventing traffic congestion.[1] They may, *inter alia*, acquire or appropriate land for the parking place, or for a means of ingress or egress to it; authorise for use as a parking place any part of a street within their district; provide and maintain buildings and underground parking places and any necessary cloakrooms and other conveniences; and appoint staff, to supervise the parking places.

Financial Statement for Car Parks

It is thus possible to provide parking places in several forms: on streets, on sites which are cleared and surfaced for the purpose, in buildings of one or more storeys, in basements under buildings, or underground below some public property such as a road or open space. The financial calculations for all forms will be considered together. Development by a local authority is assumed, and the operation of the parking place by the authority. In this chapter, therefore, the finance of operation will be considered as well as that of development.

I. Capital Cost

(a) (b) *Acquisition of Land and Legal Preparation of the Site.* The powers for acquiring land have been quoted. The cost of acquiring land for car parks varies considerably. It will cost nothing where a street surface or other public space is used, unless it is necessary to replace the space elsewhere, at perhaps substantial cost; perhaps 3d. a square foot adjoining a new suburban railway station which is being built on agricultural land; perhaps £1 per square foot in a provincial business centre; or £1 to £5 per foot in the West End of London.

(c) (d) (e) *Cost of Works.* This will also vary enormously. The surface car park will need just a concrete or tarmac apron, planting and a simple office; the multi-storey car park is a very substantial structure with either closed or open sides between floors; the basement car park requires normal basement construction with drive-in ramps; a multi-storey underground park requires deep excavation and complicated drainage, ventilation and access arrangements. There are no generally accepted comparable figures of cost, but the following table illustrates the order of the difference:

TABLE 25

Comparative Capital Costs at Different Dates of Construction of Car Parks per Car Space

	M.O.T., 1946 £	D. F. Orchard, post-war £	Nicholas, post-war £	London Working Party, 1952 £
Open-air single deck at ground level	3-44	Up to 60	30	—
Open-air multi-storey	—	120		
Enclosed multi-storey	150	225	225	944
Basement in building	—	—	205	—
Underground multi-storey ...	200-400	500	—	850

Source: See Note 2.

The differences in these figures reflect differences in design, date, the cost of construction per foot square and the area required for each car. One particular reason for the wide range of cost in multi-storey garages is the differing number of cars that can be accommodated in a given space when the cars are either mechanically parked, or parked by staff drivers or by their owners.

(*f*) (*g*) *Interest on Capital During Construction, and Profit.* While a private developer of car parks would allow for both these, a local authority would probably allow for neither.

(*h*) *Disposal Expenses.* These would not arise except where the authority leases sites for use as parking places, under powers in the Restriction of Ribbon Development Act, Section 16 (3).

II. Annual Costs

(*j*) *Return on Capital.* This would not arise.

(*k*) (*l*) *Loan Repayment and Interest.* Loan charges would be taken on the total capital cost.

(*m*) *Depreciation.* This is not provided for.

(*n*) (*o*) (*p*) *Occupation, Ownership and Operating Expenses.* Where an authority is operating a parking place it will consider its occupation, ownership and operating expenses together; they are hardly separable. On the simplest of surface car parks there will be a contribution in lieu of rates and the cost of maintenance and repairs. On the other kinds expenses will vary with the type of parking place and its size. In underground garages expenses might arise on wages, salaries, holidays with pay, superannuation, insurance; depreciation of ventilation plant, lighting, fittings, furniture and equipment; stationery; heat, light, power (gas and electricity), heat (solid or oil fuel); minor maintenance, repairs and decoration; uniforms, certain minor repairs to damaged cars, household goods, travelling expenses, telephone and other miscellaneous items; water rate; overhead and central office expenses; contribution in lieu of rates.[2] The operating cost per car day, which is the unit often taken in calculations, will thus vary with the kind of park and also with the number of days in the week and number of hours per day that the place is used. Post-war figures have been quoted ranging from 0·6s. for a surface car park at Windsor to 1·8s. for a multi-storey car park and 4·5s. per day for the suggested London underground car parks.[3]

III. Money Yield

Apart from the income that might be obtained in running a garage or service station on the site, the yield would be from charges for parking. There are no government grants. To estimate the income knowledge is required of the number of days in the week and the hours per day that the place will be open; and a forecast is needed of the use that will be made of it in terms of the number of cars that will park and their average length of stay. To this must be applied the intended charge which will range from nothing to say 2s. 6d. per day.[4] This will lead to average income per car space per day which can be related to the average running cost for the same unit.

IV. Financial Appraisal

The most suitable test is to relate the expected annual income to the total annual expenses, to see whether the parking place will operate at a profit or a loss (method (G)). A loss is frequently experienced for car owners are rarely charged an economic rent for parking in cities; they would rarely use parks were such charges made when free street parking is possible.[5] Any estimated loss can be compared to rate resources (method (H)).

Alternative Forms of Parking in Large Town

In the centre of towns where there is competition for land, and where car parks must be carefully located if they are to attract motorists to use them, authorities often cannot find enough land for the amount of parking required. They must then consider the erection of multi-storey car parks, and the financial calculations for alternative schemes on a particular site. This was the problem

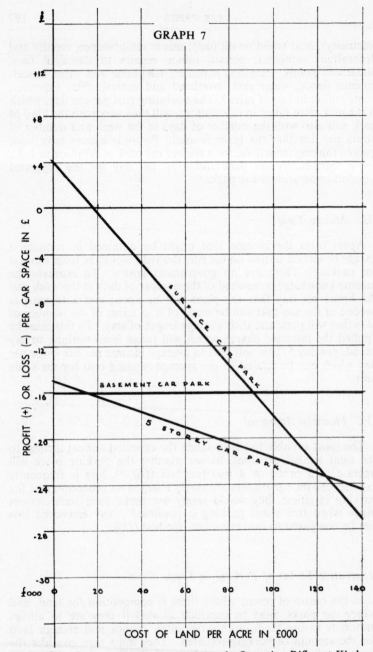

GRAPH 7

Net Profit or Loss per annum per car space in Operating Different Kinds of Car Parks on Different Value Land

analysed in the City of Manchester Plan, 1945, in terms of the cost of construction and operation per car space provided. Three types of car park were studied. Table 26 gives the relevant estimates.

TABLE 26

Comparative Construction and Operating Costs (excluding Land) and Income for Different Types of Car Park on 1-acre Site

	Five-storey car park covering three-quarters of site	Basement car park	Surface car park
Number of cars accommodated	600	160	180
	£	£	£
Initial cost of construction	135,000	33,000	5,400
Loan charges over 30 years at 3¼ per cent	7,425	1,820	300
Operating costs:			
Wages	2,382	596	596
Light, heat and rent ...	1,638	840	140
Rates	3,500	940	260
Schedule A*	975	260	100
Total annual expenses ...	15,930	4,456	1,396
Less Annual income at 4s. 6d. per car per week	7,020	1,870	2,110
Loss or profit in 1-acre site	(L) 8,910	(L) 2,586	(P) 714
Loss or profit per car ...	(L) 15	(L) 16	(P) 4

Source: See Note 2.

Note: * This ownership expense is not normally included in operating costs.

The table shows that on the figures taken the loan charges on construction costs are just about balanced by income in the five-storey and basement car park, so that in these, even ignoring the cost of land, the operating costs represent sheer loss. There is a profit, however, on the surface car park because construction costs are low.

The cost per car for land on a given site is not the same for all kinds of car park because of the differing number of cars they accommodate per acre of site. The profit or loss per car, taking land cost into account, for five-storey and surface car parks is seen in Table 27; the basement car park is not included since the land was assumed to cost nothing for parking purposes.[6] The comparative profit and loss on all schemes is shown in Graph 7.

TABLE 27

Comparative Costs of Land per Car Space at Varying Land Costs for Different Types of Car Park; and Net Profit or Loss per Annum per Car Space in Operating

Cost of Land	Five-storey garage 600 cars Loss in Table 26: £15 per car/annum			Surface car park 180 cars Profit in Table 26: £4 per car/annum		
	Annual cost of land	Net loss		Annual cost of land	Net profit	Net loss
10,000	0·7	15·7		2·2	1·8	—
20,000	1·3	16·3		4·4		0·4
30,000	2·0	17·0		6·6		2·6
40,000	2·6	17·6		8·8		4·8
50,000	3·3	18·3		11·0		7·0
60,000	4·0	19·0		13·2		9·2
70,000	4·7	19·7		15·4		11·4
80,000	5·2	20·2		17·6		13·6
90,000	5·9	20·9		19·8		15·8
100,000	6·6	21·6		22·0		18·0
110,000	7·3	22·3		24·2		20·2
120,000	8·0	23·0		26·4		22·4
130,000	8·7	23·7		28·6		24·6
140,000	9·4	24·4		30·8		26·8

Source: See Note 5.

At the figures quoted, surface car parking is run at a profit when the land costs less than £18,000 per acre and at a loss when it costs more; but the loss is smaller than that of the basement car park, even when the site of this is assumed to cost nothing, until the land cost is about £90,000 per acre, or of the multi-storey garage until the land cost is about £125,000 per acre. Furthermore, where the choice is between basement and five-storey garage, there is smaller loss on the garage where land cost is below about £16,000 per acre even though the site of the basement car park is assumed to cost nothing.

Calculations such as these enable decisions to be taken as to the form of car parking to be adopted. With a given number of cars to provide for, if ample land were available for surface parking it would not pay, at the figures quoted, to build a basement car park instead of a surface one until the land cost £90,000 per acre, nor to build a five-storey garage instead of the other two kinds, until the land cost £125,000 per acre. Where ample land is not available for surface car parks, the more common situation in practice, the extra cost of providing for a given number of cars in basement and multi-storey garages, above the cost of provision in surface car parks, can be calculated; and also the land cost at which one or the other kinds of non-surface parks would be most economical.

Pooling Costs and Yields

In the central business area of a town car parking is usually considered as a whole. It is useful, therefore, in such an area not merely to test individual schemes but to pool costs and yields for all. If this is done the total land cost would be common to all possible schemes, and alternative costs of construction and operating only would need to be examined. If, for example, 12 acres of land were available and 3,000 cars to be provided for, it might or might not be cheaper in construction and operating costs to use two acres for five-storey parks (1,200 cars) and 10 acres for surface parks (1,800 cars), rather than all the 12 acres for two-storey parks (at, say, 250 cars per acre each).

CHAPTER 15

COMPREHENSIVE RE-DEVELOPMENT

Re-development Before 1939—Powers for Post-war Re-development
—Re-development Under the 1947 Act—Grants Under the 1947 Act
for Comprehensive Development—Grants Under the Town and
Country Planning Act, 1954—Financial Statement for Re-develop-
ment—Adaptations of Statement for Financial Appraisal—Recon-
struction in West Hartlepool—Exercise 3 : Re-development for Housing
Under the Housing or Planning Acts.

Re-development Before 1939

THE RE-DEVELOPMENT of towns has been continuously going on.
Owners of buildings have pulled down and replaced them, individually or in groups, when they have found it necessary or profitable
to do so.[1] Owners of large estates have re-developed comprehensively when ground leases have fallen in. Local authorities have
cut new streets through outworn property and carried out associated
re-development, have cleared slums and re-developed with flats,
have built markets, abbatoirs, bus stations, municipal offices and
have often carried out or attracted re-development on adjoining
land. The re-development that was proceeding in this way before
1939 was not generally co-ordinated in accordance with a plan, and
was also not measuring up to the amount that was needed to adapt
the older parts of our towns to current conditions. There were
several reasons for this. The interest of private enterprise in
re-development was limited only to what was commercially profitable; and the powers which were available to local authorities for
the purpose were inadequate, as was also the financial assistance by
central government.

Powers for Post-war Re-development

During the war the government envisaged extensive post-war
reconstruction in war-damaged and other areas, and in 1941 it
asked the Uthwatt Committee, among other things, to " advise, as
a matter of urgency, what steps should be taken now or before the
end of the war to prevent the work of reconstruction thereafter being
prejudiced."[2] The committee examined the methods of re-development which were then available in the Town and Country Planning
Act, 1932, and Housing Act, 1936, and found them both lacking
for this post-war task. Their conclusion was that " the simplest
and only effective method for achieving the desired results is to
confer on the planning authority compulsory powers of purchase,
much wider and more simple in operation than under existing
legislation, over any land which may be required for planning or

other public purposes "; and they recommended new and extensive powers of compulsory purchase over developed land and also the tackling of the financial difficulties of re-development.[3]

In the Town and Country Planning Act, 1944, the Coalition Government accepted many of these recommendations. It gave powers to local authorities to buy areas of extensive war damage for the purpose of re-development as a whole, or other land for the relocation of population or industry or the replacement of open space consequent upon such re-development, for dealing with conditions of bad layout and obsolete development and for other planning purposes. It made grants available towards the cost of certain of these acquisitions. It gave powers for the erection of any kind of buildings or works on land so acquired, provided there were no other people able and willing to carry out the development. (This proviso was subsequently removed in the Town and Country Planning Act, 1947.)[4] With the granting of these powers there went the intention that authorities would lease the land so acquired to private developers as necessary, and so carry out their re-development both under planning and lease control.[5]

This Act was an emergency one to facilitate the expected large-scale post-war reconstruction. Many authorities obtained powers to purchase areas of extensive war damage; and one, Birmingham, about 1,000 acres of obsolete property. But comparatively little re-development took place. The 1944 Act was replaced as a re-development measure by the 1947 Act and the system under it. This made re-development part of a comprehensive planning system, and introduced a more realistic approach to it, one which took more account of likely economic resources. Under this Act considerable progress has in recent years been made in rebuilding bomb damaged areas to a new layout as more capital investment resources for rebuilding have become available.[6] Little has been done in the rebuilding of areas of obsolete property as the shortage of accommodation, and high cost of building, prohibit the demolition of property which is at all usable.

Re-development Under the 1947 Act

A local planning authority can initiate the development of any area by defining it as an area of comprehensive development in the development plan; that is an area which in their opinion should be developed or re-developed as a whole for the purpose of dealing satisfactorily with extensive war damage or conditions of bad layout or obsolete development, or for relocating population or industry or replacing open space in the course of the development or re-development of any other area, or for any other purpose specified in the plan.[7] In practice it is found that areas can be defined for any development which should be carried out as a whole. Areas can be defined, therefore, for both development and re-development on comprehensive lines, and both are treated in the same way under the Act. In this chapter we shall have regard primarily to re-development.

What constitutes re-development as a whole is not defined and a common-sense interpretation is used. The merging of ownerships to form new sites, or the alteration of a street pattern, are examples of comprehensive development; a modest street widening which leaves unchanged the adjoining uses and ownership boundaries is not.

In defining an area of comprehensive development, the size of the area to be defined and its boundaries are not always simple matters to assess. Since fairly specific plans have to be prepared to 25-in. scale, and this cannot be done too far ahead of actual development, the area is limited in practice to work which will be carried out in 10 to 20 years. But planning proposals are prepared not only for the defined area but also for such additional land which with it comprises an area which should be planned as a whole. For submission to the Minister the proposals can be shown on a combined comprehensive development area and supplementary town map (see page 16). In submitting, the Minister's approval is asked for the proposals and also for the defined area as one of comprehensive development for the stated purpose. When this is secured re-development can be started. The agency primarily responsible for carrying out the re-development is the local authority, not the local planning authority; that is, the council of the county borough or county district in which the land is situated. Other authorities, including a county council, can, however, take part.[8]

It does not follow that the local authority will acquire following definition, for it may be that the re-development as visualised can be secured by agreement with prospective developers. If the authority wish to acquire, however, it can either continue the procedure it has initiated under the 1947 Act, and apply for the Minister's authority for it to acquire any land within the defined area, or contiguous or adjacent thereto, which it has designated in the plan as subject to compulsory purchase;[9] or it can buy land within or without the defined area, whether designated or not, under other public or private Acts, for purposes for which it has powers to acquire under those Acts. It follows that where it wishes to acquire within, contiguous or adjacent to the defined area, for purposes for which it has no powers other than in the 1947 Act, for shopping or factory development, for example, it must do so under the 1947 Act after designation. Where land belonging to the authority is conveniently situated in relation to the defined area, and is no longer required for the purpose for which it was bought, it can be used for re-development as though acquired under the 1947 Act; or put more formally, appropriated out from the original service and appropriated into the re-development service of the authority.[10]

An authority normally proceeds to re-development by preparing a programme of land acquisitions which is related to the programme of works. The land is acquired, or appropriated in, as and when needed in advance of initiating the works. If it is bought too early the time is lengthened during which loan charges are paid for land which is perhaps being put to no use; and if it is bought too late the works will be held up. The prudent authority thus proceeds normally by buying land in parcels of a shape and size which are convenient for the construction of roads and services soon after possession is obtained. As soon as they are ready for building, sites are sold, or leased or appropriated to another service; an authority has no power under the 1947 Act to carry out works for any functions for which powers exist under another statute, so that for such works to take place the land in the re-development service must be appropriated to the relevant service or the authority.[11]

Re-development under the 1947 Act is therefore much wider in scope than re-development of slum areas under the Housing Act, 1936. It is not confined to clearance areas in mainly residential areas, nor to the rebuilding mainly of dwellings, but embraces much wider powers of acquisition, development and disposal.[12]

Grants Under the 1947 Act for Comprehensive Development[13]

The 1947 Act provides for grants from central government to local authorities undertaking certain kinds of comprehensive development: that is, the re-development as a whole of areas of extensive war damage, or of bad layout or obsolete development; for the relocation of population or industry or the replacement of open space arising out of such re-development; or the bringing into use of derelict land, that is land which is incapable of reasonably beneficial use in its existing state, and is likely to remain so indefinitely.[14] The purpose of the grants is to assist authorities where they need to acquire land at high cost, as, for example, in a built-up area, or need to carry out expensive works in preparing land for development, as on derelict land, and are not able to recoup themselves in the new values which are created. The grants are towards the full cost of acquiring and clearing land during the initial period when the land is made ready for development; and subsequently, for the remainder of the 60-year period over which loans for re-development are generally repaid, towards any loss on such land, that is, towards the excess of cost of acquisition and clearing over the value of the land for its new use. The grants are thus not paid towards the provision of major roads, services, buildings or other works. Such works will be carried out by another service of the authority, and will earn the appropriate exchequer grant, if any, of that service.

In areas of extensive war damage the grant is 90 per cent for the initial grant period (five years with a possible extension up to eight years) and 50 per cent for the balance of the 60 years. A grant period normally starts one year after a compulsory purchase order has been confirmed. In areas of bad layout and obsolete development there are four possible scales of grant, as in Table 28, depending on the relative wealth of the authority. The measure of this is the average rateable value per head of population in the area of the authority compared with the average of similar authorities.

TABLE 28

Scales of Grant for Comprehensive Development in the 1947 Act

Grade scale:—	Initial period	Intermediate period	Final period
I	80	50	50
II	70	50	40
III	60	40	30
IV	50	30	20

Source: *Explanatory Memorandum on Grants Regulations*, Appendix D.

Note: The final period normally starts at the 12th year of grant period, and between this and the initial period, as above, is the intermediate period.

Where there is relocation of population or industry, or replacement of public open space in connection with re-development, the scale of grant would be the same as for the associated re-development. This would be paid to an importing local authority carrying out relocation in connection with re-development. Grant for the acquisition and clearing of derelict land is also paid on this scale.

The payment of grant is made subject to the conditions " (a) that there shall have been submitted to the Minister such information as to the proposals of the local authority for the layout and re-development of the land as the Minister may require in order to enable a comparison to be made between the annual return to the authority from the carrying out of the re-development and the annual equivalent of the cost thereof; and (b) that these proposals shall have been approved by the Minister with the consent of the Treasury as being likely to result in an annual return and an annual equivalent such as are mentioned in the foregoing paragraph which are reasonable in relation to one another having regard to the circumstances of the land and the requirements of a proper layout and re-development."[15] The information referred to in (a) is a financial statement, which is designed to show what the estimated profit or loss on the scheme will be, and therefore the grant liability (see page 208-9). Grant is not in fact paid on this statement, but on the actual deficit as shown each year in a memorandum account, the Re-development Capital Account, which is kept by the authorities.[16] Both the statement and the account relate not to the whole comprehensive development area but to parts of it called " re-development units." These are usually areas of a shape and size which can be developed and disposed of forthwith, perhaps an area covered by a single compulsory purchase order.

Grants Under the Town and Country Planning Act, 1954

The 1947 Act's grants system has been modified in the 1954 Act and a new scheme will come into operation during 1955. Sections 93 and 95 (1) of the 1947 Act, which deal with grants for re-development, and also Section 94, which deals with planning grants for other purposes, are replaced by Section 50 of the 1954 Act, which provides for one comprehensive grants scheme for all planning purposes. The new scheme will involve new regulations to replace those described here. Section 50 of the 1954 Act states that the regulations will provide, inter alia, for grants towards the cost of land acquired or appropriated for purposes of the regulations, towards other compensation, towards the clearing or preliminary development of land. Instead of the varying percentages formerly paid the grant will in general be an annual one of 50 per cent of cost, or of excess of cost over receipts, but for land acquired for public open space the Minister may agree to pay up to 75 per cent. See Appendix III for an account of the 1954 Act grant scheme.)

Financial Statement for Re-development

The financial statement which is submitted to the Minister under the 1947 Act was designed primarily for the purpose of giving estimates of that part of the cost which would fall on the re-development service, and so indicating government liability for grant. It can also be used, with adaptation, as a method of appraising the finances of any re-development scheme. It will therefore be useful to describe it instead of our standard statement; and to draw attention to the adaptations which are necessary if it is to be used for financial appraisal of schemes. It is reprinted here.

APPENDIX C

Statement required under the provisions of return from the carrying out of redevelop

Local Authority...

for { * an area of extensive war damage
     * an area of obsolete development or bad lay-out
     * derelict land

                              * Delete whichever is inapplicable.

I. Estimate of (a) capital costs of acquisition and clearing and (b) capital values of appropriations or transfers to other accounts and of disposals, except transfers of land in respect of which rent will be receivable (See Note 1).

Capital costs of acquisition, appropriations and transfers in, and of clearing			Capital values of appropriation or transfer to other accounts and of disposals, except disposals of land in respect of which rent will be receivable		
Item	At end of fifth year of grant period	At end of twelfth year of grant period (See note 5)	Item	At end of fifth year of grant period	At end of twelfth year of grant period (See note 5)
1. Acquisition of land (including land acquired from Government Departments and other local authorities) (a) Compensation for acquisition (excluding acquisitions of operational land from statutory undertakers) ... ... (b) Compensation for disturbance (c) Compensation to statutory undertakers	£	£	6. Sales of land, e.g., to Government Departments, religious bodies, statutory undertakers 7. Land appropriated or transferred to other accounts and services of local authority:— (a) Housing Account ... ... (b) Education Account ... (c) Highway Account ... ... (d) Other accounts and services	£	£
2. Land appropriated or transferred from other accounts and services of the local authority (a) Housing Account ... ... (b) Education Account ... ... (c) Other accounts and services			8. Sales of land to other local authorities:— (a) Housing Authority (name) (b) Education Authority (name) (c) Highway Authority (name) (d) Other authorities		
3. Other costs of acquisition (see Appendix A)			9. Premiums on land disposed of under lease, e.g., for industrial and commercial development ...		
4. Clearing of land (see Appendix B)					
5. Total capital costs ... ...£			10. Total capital value of appropriations, transfers and disposals ... ...£		

NOTES.

1. The statement should be prepared on the basis of the valuation for acquisitions, appropriations, transfers and disposals to be used for the purposes of the grant scheme and set out in the Memorandum (including the review provisions where relevant in the case of the position at the end of the twelfth year) except that (i) the figures for ground rents (item 13 (d)) should be the annual income which it is estimated will be receivable, calculated in accordance with paragraph 4 below, and (ii) the figure for rack rents (item 13 (a)) should be the annual rents estimated to be receivable from standing property acquired (see item 1 in Appendix F).

2. The annual equivalent in item 12 and notional loan charges in the statement in note 4 below should be calculated on the basis of a loan repayable in 60 years on an equal annuity basis, with interest at the rate fixed by the Treasury for such loans by the Public Works Loan Commissioners.

3. Separate statements should be submitted in respect of each redevelopment unit or area of derelict land, and also separately in respect of any " overspill " area associated with the redevelopment unit.

Section 95 (1) (a) to show the annual ment and the annual equivalent of the cost

Redevelopment Unit..Compulsory Purchase Order No.   (   )

II. Statement of the annual equivalent of (a) the difference between the estimated capital costs and the capital values of appropriations or transfers to other accounts and of disposals and (b) the estimated annual return by way of rents.

	At end of fifth year of grant period	At end of twelfth year of grant period (See note 5)
	£	£
Capital costs of acquisition and clearing (item 5 in statement I) ... *Less* capital value of appropriations, transfers and disposals (item 10 in statement I)		
11.*Excess of capital cost over capital value (deficit)* ... ... Excess of capital value over capital cost (surplus)		
12. Annual equivalent of item 11 (see note 2) ... ... *Deficit* *Surplus*		
13. Rents per annum (see notes 1 and 4) (a) Rack rents of properties not demolished for redevelopment ... (b) *Less* provision for repairs, insurance and management		
(c) Net rack rents ... . (d) Ground rents		
(e) Total rents ((c) plus (d))		
14. Estimated annual deficit or surplus, being the amount *Deficit* in item 12 minus or plus the amount in item 13 (e) *Surplus £*		

* Delete whichever is inapplicable.   Signed..Chief Financial Officer

.....................................Date

NOTES—*continued*

4. The figures to be inserted in item 13 (d) should be the net return after allowing for site development costs borne by the local authority but not eligible for grant. Details of the calculation should be inserted below.

	At end of fifth year of grant period	At end of twelfth year of grant period (See note 5)
	£	£
Gross ground rents per annum ... ..., ... *Less* notional loan charges (see note 2 above) on the estimated site development costs (£) to be borne by the local authority		
Net annual return as stated in item 13 (d) ... ...£		

5. Where the local authority decides to have a general review of ground rents at a later date than the end of the twelfth year (see paragraph 18 (c) of Memorandum) the figure to be inserted should relate to the review date and the heading of the columns should be suitably amended.

The statement is prepared for a limited area only, the re-development unit, so that for each comprehensive re-development area there may be more than one statement. The boundary of the unit may be quite arbitrary in relation to the proposals, perhaps excluding islands of standing property in respect of which the compulsory purchase order has not been confirmed.

Each statement relates to all proposed uses in the unit, both private and public, and in the public uses, both remunerative and non-remunerative. It will also relate to uses, such as part of a traffic road, which are not complete in themselves; and to others, such as public buildings, which are complete.

The statement is in two sections. Part I deals with capital sums. It estimates the difference between (a) the capital costs of acquiring and clearing the land and (b) the capital values which can be realised on transfers of land to other services of the authority, to other public bodies and also by way of premiums on land disposed under lease. In Part II this difference is converted to its annual equivalent in loan charges and these are related to the estimated annual rents. By this means the annual deficit or surplus can be estimated.

The statement asks for the ultimate financial position to be shown, that is when all property will have been acquired and all development completed. This, it is reckoned, will have taken place at the end of the twelfth year of grant period. The statement also asks for the position at the end of the fifth year of grant period. By this time, it is reckoned, the work of acquisition and clearing will have been completed, and the land will have been transferred to the various developers for construction.

Part I (a), Capital Cost

The capital cost of acquisition and clearance (items 1-4) are similar to items (a), (b) and (c) in the summary of capital costs in Chapter 10: the cost of acquisition and of the legal and physical preparatory work to be done. Item 1 relates to the cost of acquisition under compulsory purchase formulæ, and item 2 to the value of land which is already owned by the authority and is appropriated to its re-development service. This is taken at existing use value or " if that use is of such a nature that there is no general demand or market for land for that purpose, at the value of the land for adaptation to its best other use."[17] Item 3 deals with what we have called the legal costs of site preparation, and also the legal costs of acquisition, professional fees and the expense of raising loans.[18] Item 4 relates to clearing, that is the physical preparation of the land to make it available for re-development; clearing includes not only demolition and clearing away, but also the removal and levelling of spoil heaps on derelict land, removal expenses and filling of excavations.[19] There is no provision for interest on the capital which is to be lying idle, or profit, or disposal expenses.

Part I (b), Capital Values

Where land in, adjacent or contiguous to an area of comprehensive development is acquired by local authorities, or is appropriated into the re-development service, the authorities dispose of it in one of two ways. They sell sites to government departments, statutory undertakers and other local authorities, and transfer them to other services of the authority; but they normally lease to private developers. They were originally debarred from selling, or leasing for more than 99 years, to private developers except in exceptional circumstances: for example, to religious bodies; but while this no longer applies, in practice they continue to lease to private developers.[20]

Part I (b) of the statement estimates the prices to be obtained from such sales, appropriations and transfers (items 6-8); and also, to keep all capital items together, the premiums on land to be disposed under lease to private bodies (item 9). The sales and appropriations are at formula value;[21] and this, incidentally, is the value on which any exchequer grant for new local authority uses is calculated where such grant is related to the land cost. (See page 222).

The effect of formula values on the cost of different local authority services can be seen by considering, for example, a new school site and public open space which are created on the site of what was once valuable property. Their new values in the statement will be, respectively, that for residential purposes and one quarter of that for residential purposes. The re-development service will in consequence show a loss, while the local authority's education and open space services will acquire sites at much less than what they would have paid under their appropriate Acts. Alternatively a site for municipal offices might be proposed on land which was originally slum, and in consequence cheap to acquire. The new value to be paid by the municipal office service would be that for a comparable commercial use, which would be higher than the acquisition cost. In this way the values current at the time of acquisition are written down or up to new values which are based, according to formula, on the new uses; and the financial losses and gains in creating new land uses out of old ones are attributed to planning.

Where this takes place in a county borough, the initial cost to the authority of acquiring and clearing the land must be the same whether the land is bought for school, open space or municipal offices under the Planning Acts and appropriated to other services, or whether it is bought direct under other powers and the values of the property in question, at the time of acquisition, are carried forward as the cost of the new use; a loss on one service is a gain on another. But the final cost to the rates of the authority may be different, depending on the amount of the exchequer grant which is paid towards acquisition under these different powers. An example which illustrates this is examined below (page 218). Where expensive land is acquired, however, for re-development by a county district council, and is transferred to a county council for a school, the county district re-development service will show a loss, and the county education service a gain, compared to what would have happened had the land been acquired by the county under the Education Acts.

The total of I (b) shows, apart from the premiums, the new capital values of sites which are to be used for public development. The difference between the totals in I (a) and I (b), that is the surplus or deficit on the acquisition and clearing of land and making it available for private development, is transferred to Part II. This difference is usually a deficit and represents the capital sum on which the loan charges must be recouped by rents if there is to be no loss. In order that this net capital cost can be compared with annual income in rents it is necessary either to convert the capital cost to its annual equivalent, or to capitalise the rents. The former course is chosen (item 12); and, irrespective of the way in which the authority proposes to borrow its money for the purpose, the statement provides for the annual equivalent to be calculated as loan charges over 60 years on an annuity basis, with interest at the current Public Works Loan Board rate.

The estimated income is divided into the net rack rents from the usable standing properties which are bought; and ground rents (item 13). Where revenue producing standing properties are included and are not to be demolished, the statement will reflect any difference between the loan charges on acquisition costs and the actual net rents which will be received. Since most standing properties will be bought to show a rate of return higher than the current Public Works Loan Board rate, the statement will show a profit margin on such acquisitions and so minimise the deficit on the scheme. In contrast, a comparison of capital values would not show any profit or loss in the acquisition of standing property, where the property is to be retained in its former use.

Ground rents are estimated on the basis that the necessary estate development works are in existence. Where these have yet to be provided, the loan charges over 60 years on their cost is deducted from the estimated ground rents to arrive at the net values which will be realised. Where major works such as trunk sewers or principal traffic roads are to be provided by the authority because of its functions, of a kind which an estate developer would not normally provide, their cost is not deducted. Their cost is therefore assumed to be borne by the appropriate service of the authority, and perhaps by other government grant.

The statement closes with the estimated annual deficit or surplus that can be expected at the stated times (item 14). A percentage of this gives the likely amount of grant that will be needed.

Adaptations of Statement for Financial Appraisal

We will now consider the adaptations of Appendix C which are necessary if it is to give a financial appraisal of comprehensive re-development.

The boundaries chosen for a re-development unit may be so arbitrary that a surplus or deficit on it may have no significance; this is one reason why in paying grants the surplus and deficit on successive units are in fact pooled. It is preferable to prepare calculations for a combination of units which make up an area which is reasonable for the purpose; perhaps the area of comprehensive development itself or some other.

A unit or combination of units will often include some development which is remunerative and some which is not. The final balance draws no distinction between the two, one surplus or deficit being estimated to cover both. As we have seen, however, the testing of remunerative and non-remunerative development must be quite different; and separate statements are therefore required for each. The division of the statement into Parts I and II, it is true, goes some way towards this in abstracting from the acquisitions, in items 6-8, the capital values of the new public uses which are created. It does not go the whole way, however, since the capital costs of these uses are not compared with the new values, the losses or gains on them being included in the total which is carried forward to Part II; and secondly since in the total of I (b) there may be premiums for remunerative uses.

The unit or combination of units may, moreover, include parts of a principal traffic road or open space which can only be tested as a whole and not in parts, as can groups of shops or offices. These should also be separated out.

In Part II are included rack rents for buildings which are acquired and not demolished, whereas the remainder of the statement deals with the new values created in the acquisition and clearance of land only. There is thus included in one statement the surplus and deficit from both property acquisition and land development. The true result of the land development is thus obscured.

It follows from this that instead of the one test for the scheme which is included in Appendix C (the comparison of annual yields with loan charges on a 100 per cent loan, resembling our method (G)), alternative tests will be necessary for different aspects of the scheme. For a comparison of capital cost and capital values of new public uses our method (A) could be used; of cost and yield on commercial development methods (A), (B), (C) could be used; for the deficit or surplus on the scheme method (H) could be used. In all tests account should be taken not only of the effect on the Re-development Account but also, where appropriate, on any other accounts of the authority (see page 211).

GRAPH 8

Reconstruction in West Hartlepool. Proportion of Total Loan Charges Borne Each Year of Loan Period by Ground Rents, Specific Government Grant and Rates

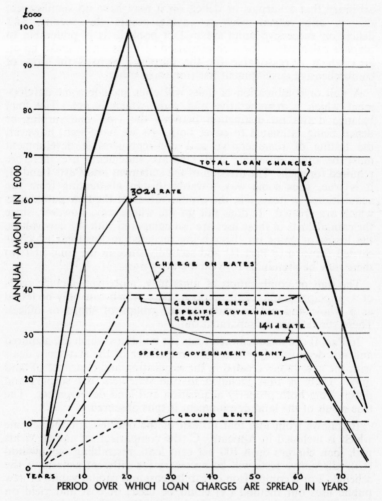

Source: From figures supplied by Borough Treasurer, West Hartlepool.

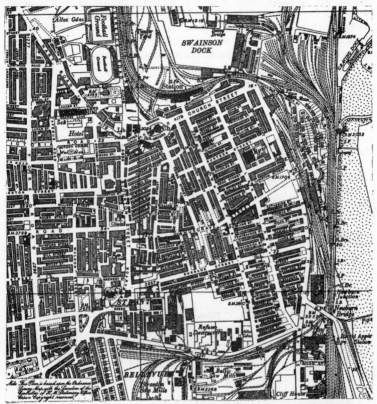

FIGURE 3.—*Map of Central Area of West Hartlepool as Existing*

Reconstruction in West Hartlepool

Estimates for a reconstruction scheme at West Hartlepool, which would take at least 20 years to implement, have been published in full.[22] They are summarised here because such estimates are rarely published. The West Hartlepool Development Plan, 1950, following the advisory plan of Mr. Max Lock, includes among its proposals the demolition of a built-up area outside the central business area and the provision there of sites for a new shopping and business centre, in replacement of the existing one, and for new public buildings. (Figs. 3 and 4.) Estimates were made of the cost of acquiring the necessary land and buildings, of clearance, of constructing development roads and sewers, of building a new cross-town road and improving the existing north-south road, and of the yields, the ground rents and the transfer prices, that would be obtained for the sites to be used for commercial and municipal services respectively. The costs of buildings for educational, housing, public buildings and welfare services were ignored on the grounds that they would have been incurred without any plan.

I. Capital Costs. Acquisition of Land, Site preparation, Site Works. The estimated total capital cost under these heads amounted to about £2 million of which £1,400,000 was for purchase of land (excluding that for local authority purposes), compensation for removal and disturbance, £50,000 for demolition and £300,000 for roads and sewers in the new central area. It was assumed that roads and sewers would take 10 years to carry out, that the scheme

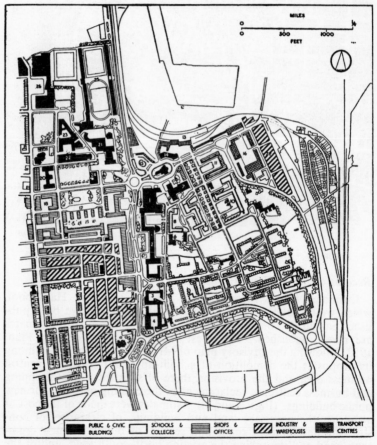

FIGURE 4.—*Plan of Re-development Scheme for West Hartlepool*

would take 20 years to complete, that expenditure would be evenly spread throughout the period and that loans would be raised for each job as it was started, the final loan being raised 16 years after the scheme was begun.

II. Annual Costs. For calculating the loan charges an interest rate of 4 per cent was taken, and loan periods of 60 years for the purchase of land, 20 years for the construction of roads and 30 years for construction of sewers. No other annual costs were considered.

The loan charges were not calculated on the total capital expenditure on the development when completed. The more realistic approach was adopted of staging the expenditure, and estimating the total amount of loan charges to be paid year by year from the inception of the scheme to the time, 76 years afterwards, when the loan charges would be fully repaid.

III. Annual Yields. The yields from the scheme would be the ground rents for the shops, offices, warehouses, etc., which would reach a maximum of £10,000 per annum in the 20th year, and grants under the Town and Country Planning Act, 1954, at 50 per cent of the annual loss on acquisition and clearance throughout the period. The balance would be met out of the rates except for any contributions to be made by exchequer equalisation grants. It was assumed that this would be continued on the current basis of 25 per cent of net rate expenditure (that is after deducting for specific grants).

IV. Relation of Cost to Yield. The method adopted of testing the effect on the rates can be seen from the following summary of total cost and yield over 76 years:

	£	£
Total loan charges		4,633,410
Less total ground rents	665,000	
Less total government specific grants	1,646,555	
		2,311,555
Charge on rates		2,321,855
Average annual charge on rates		30,551

For the purpose of the calculation a 1d. rate product of £2,000 was assumed throughout the period, somewhat more than the 1954 product of about £1,800, no attempt being made to gauge the effect on rateable value in the town of future development. The average annual charge on the rates for 76 years would therefore amount to 1s. 3d. If one-quarter were offset by exchequer equalisation grant it would leave an annual average rate of about 1s. to be found by the Council.

The actual rate expenditure (that is before deducting for exchequer equalisation grant) in any one year during the period would vary from the average. The degree of variation is indicated in Graph 8, and also that in the loan charges, ground rents and the specific government (planning) grants.[23] The rate expenditure would rise to a peak in the 20th year, when it would amount to a 2s. 6d. rate, and then fall to 1s. 3½d. in the 30th year and 1s. 2d. in the 40th year. During this period rate expenditure would be more than planning grant on acquisition and clearance for the roads and sewers would be paid off with no contribution from planning grants. From the 40th year rate expenditure would be equal to grant, and both would start falling in the 60th year to finish at ⅜d. in the 76th. Thereafter there would be a net income represented by the ground rents, and after 99 years by rack rents if the property still stood.

EXERCISE 3: *Re-development for Housing Under the Housing or Planning Acts*

The Housing and Planning Acts are intended for different purposes, and upon these purposes and the circumstances of the case will depend the decision whether land will be bought under one or the other. In some cases a particular piece of land might be bought under either. Whichever Act is used the cost of the scheme will be much the same; but government grants may not be, and in consequence the proportion of costs that have to be borne by rates and occupiers. This will be illustrated by comparing the calculations for an imaginary housing re-development scheme where land is acquired under (A) the Housing Acts or (B) the Planning Acts.

Fig. 5 shows a site of poor-class housing, part slum and part low standard, with some business property. The area is 12.6 acres to the boundary of the adjoining roads and streets. Fig. 6 shows how it is to be re-developed as a whole, the new uses being:

	Acres
Strip adjoining road for widening to 80 ft. (Class I)	0·6
Open space	2·8
Housing (to which is added half width of road 0·2 acres, for net density purposes)	9·2
Total	12·6

The proposed housing accommodation is as follows:

117 five-storey flats with 351 habitable rooms (average dwelling is 3 habitable rooms)

109 two-storey houses with 436 habitable rooms (average dwelling is 4 habitable rooms)

226 dwellings   787 habitable rooms (average density 84 habitable rooms per acre)

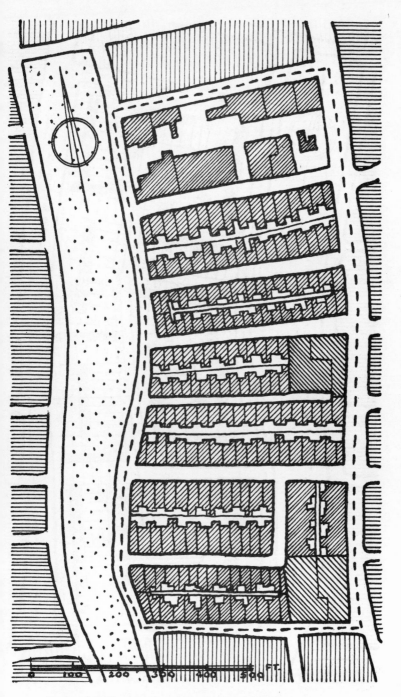

FIGURE 5.—*Plan of Area for Re-development—Exercise* 3

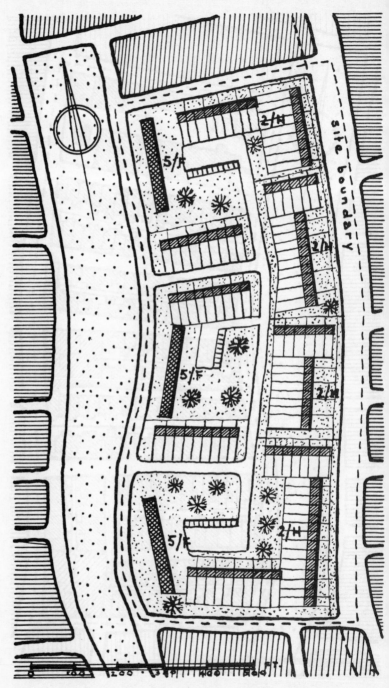

FIGURE 6.—*Plan of Re-Development Scheme—Exercise* 3

I. Capital Costs. (All works include fees, legal expenses, etc.)

		£	£
(a)	Acquisition:		
	Already bought after compulsory purchase order in clearance area	15,000	
	Compensation for new acquisition	113,000	

		£
Of which—Acquisition	86,000	
Disturbance	20,000	
Legal expenses ...	7,000	

£113,000

		£	£
(b)	Legal preparation of site	8,000	
			136,000
(c)	Physical preparation of housing site (clearing) ...	17,000	
(d)	Site works on housing site:		
	Services	9,000	
	Roads...	18,000	
			44,000
(e)	Buildings:		
	109 houses at £1,600	174,000	
	117 flats at £2000	234,000	
			408,000
			£588,000

(A) Acquisition Under Housing Acts

Land Cost. The total cost of the land acquisition and legal preparation of the site is divided up between the different accounts of the authority as follows:[24]

	£
Strip adjoining road A	10,000
Open space	30,000
Housing	96,000
	£136,000

Housing Service

Capital Cost. The capital cost of the housing scheme is therefore £588,000 *less* £40,000 (appropriated out)   = £548,000

Subsidy (1952 Act). (See Chapter 12). For subsidy purposes the land is clearly expensive and it is necessary to know the cost of site as developed.

	£
Acquisition	96,000
Clearing	17,000
Roads and services which are allowable in cost of site as developed, say	19,000
	£132,000 or £14,200 per acre.

House subsidy: Per house from exchequer	£53 14s. 0d.
Per house from rates	£17 18s. 0d.

Flat subsidy:

The notional acreage is $\frac{351}{787} \times 9 \cdot 2$ acres $= 4 \cdot 1$ acre.

The notional density is $\dfrac{117}{4 \cdot 1}$ = 28 flats per acre.

The notional cost of site is $\dfrac{35}{28} \times £14,200 = £17,700$ per acre.

Subsidy, exchequer: £66 15s. 0d. per flat + £10 10s. 0d. for lifts = £77 5s. 0d.
Subsidy, rates: £22 5s. 0d. per flat + £5 5s. 0d. for lifts = £27 10s. 0d.

II. Annual Costs

		£	£
(k) (l)	Loan charges on total capital cost of £548,000 at 4 per cent for 60 years (4·4 per cent) ...		24,100
(n)	Occupation expenses (rates ignored): repairs and maintenance, say £8 per house, £16 per flat	2,740	
(o)	Ownership expenses: supervision and management, say £4 per house, £8 per flat	1,370	
			4,110
			£28,210

III. Annual Yield

	£	£	£
Annual exchequer contributions:			
House, £53 14s. 0d. each...	5,850		
Flat, £77 5s. 0d. each	9,050		
		14,900	
Annual rate contributions:			
House, £17 18s. 0d. each...	1,950		
Flat, £27 10s. 0d. each	3,220		
		5,170	
			20,070

	£
To be found out of rents (excluding rates) or from additional rate contribution	£8,140

(B) Acquisition Under the Planning Acts

Summary of statement following Appendix C of Grants Memorandum when land fully developed.

Planning Service

		£	£
(a)	1. Acquisition of land:		
	(a) Compensation for acquisition	86,000	
	(b) Compensation for disturbance	20,000	
	2. Land appropriated from Housing Account ...	15,000	
(b)	3. Other costs of acquisition (£7,000 + £8,000) ...	15,000	
(c)	4. Clearing of land	17,000	
	5. Total capital costs		153,000
	7. Land appropriated to:[25]		
	(a) Housing	29,400	
	(b) Highways	6,000	
	(c) Open space	2,600	
	10. Total capital value of appropriations		38,000
	11. Excess of capital cost over capital value deficit		115,000
	12. Annual equivalent of item 11 at 4 per cent for 60 years = 4·4 per cent per annum		5,050

If the authority is assumed to be on scale II the government will pay 40 per cent on this through most of the period, that is £2,200 per annum, leaving £2,850 to be found by the authority.

Housing Service

Capital Cost. The capital cost of the housing scheme is therefore £588,000 *less* £136,000 *plus* £29,400   = £481,400

Subsidy (1952 Act).   Subsidy payable on new land value of £29,400.

The cost of site as developed is:

		£
Appropriation		29,400
Less clearing[26]		17,000
		£12,400
Add expenses of clearing, roads and services which are allowable for subsidy calculations, say		36,000
		£48,400 or £5,250 per acre.

This is still expensive land for both houses and flats.
Exchequer house subsidy: £33 9s. 0d.
Exchequer flat subsidy:
The notional acreage and density as before.

Notional cost of site is $\frac{35}{28} \times$ £5,250 = £6,550 per acre.

Subsidy = £57 0s. 0d. plus £10 10s. 0d. for lifts.

II.   Annual Costs

		£	£
(k) (l)	Loan charges on capital coat of £481,400 ...	21,300	
(n) (o)	Occupation and ownership expenses as for the Housing Act scheme	4,100	
			25,400

III.   Annual Yield

Annual exchequer contribution:—

		£	£
House, £33 9s. 0d. each		£3,640	
Flat, £67 10s. 0d. each		7,890	
			11,530

Annual rate contribution:—

		£	£
House, £11 3s. 0d. each		£1,210	
Flat, £24 5s. 0d. each		2,840	
			4,050
			15,580

To be found out of rents (excluding rates) or from additional rate contribution   9,820

Summary—Distribution of Total Annual Cost of Scheme When Completed:

	Exchequer	Rates	Rents	Total
	£	£	£	£
Housing Acts				
Housing	14,900	5,170	8,140	28,210
Highways*	550	180	—	730
Open space†	—	2,200	—	2,200
	£15,450	£7,550	£8,140	£31,140‡

	Exchequer	Rates	Rents	Total
	£	£	£	£
Planning Acts				
Planning...	2,850	2,220	—	5,070
Housing	10,840	3,860	9,820	24,520
Highways*	330	110	—	440
Open space†	—	190	—	190
	£14,020	£6,380	£9,820	£30,220‡

* Highways: Exchequer grants of 75 per cent, loan period 20 years at 4 per cent, annuity = 7·3 per cent. The exchequer would pay a capital grant on this, but the annual equivalent is taken for comparison purposes.

† Open space: No exchequer grant assumed. Loan period 20 years at 4 per cent, annuity = 7·3 per cent.

‡ These totals differ because the amounts taken at 60 years and 20 years loan period in the two alternatives differ.

In this example, therefore, the tenants as a whole would have to find a greater contribution in rent towards total cost, if acquisition were under the Planning and not Housing Acts, to the benefit of both exchequer and rates; and the highways account and open space account would benefit too.

It must not be assumed that the results of using either Act will always be similar to this result from an imaginary example. There are clearly so many possible variations that a generalisation is difficult. But it was stated in 1952, from experience throughout the country, that " Generally, experience up to the present has shown that where re-development is almost entirely for housing and education it is in the financial interest of the acquiring authority to proceed by compulsory purchase orders under the Act applying to those services."[27]

CHAPTER 16

TOWN DEVELOPMENT

Various Methods of Housing People From Congested Areas—Town Development Act, 1952: The Authorities Concerned : Participation by Authorities in Town Development : Additional Powers Relating to Land : Financial Contributions : Estimates for Grant Purposes —Exercie 4: Estimating the Cost of Town Development.

Various Methods of Housing People From Congested Areas

WHERE there is insufficient land within the boundary of a local authority for it to provide dwellings and ancillary development for its current and expected population, it can proceed to house these people outside by one or more of several methods. It can seek boundary extension; and this has been successfully pursued by many authorities of recent years, despite the obstacles to this method, for example by Worcester, Dudley and West Hartlepool County Boroughs. It can acquire land adjoining, or some distance from, its boundary where it acts as developer, collecting the exchequer housing subsidy, and paying the rate fund contribution, the county and district councils providing their respective facilities and services.[1] In this way the London County Council has built its satellite towns around London, Manchester at Wythenshawe and Liverpool at Kirkby. It can make arrangements for a county district council to provide dwellings in its area for families from the overcrowded town, the county district paying the rate fund contribution, collecting the exchequer subsidy, and providing the services. In this way the West Lancashire Rural District Council provided dwellings at Aintree and Maghull for people from Mersey-side, and Preston Rural District for people from Preston County Borough.[2] In London or Glasgow it can arrange with one of the new town development corporations to house its people.[3] Another method has been pioneered in Lancashire, Cheshire and Staffordshire where the congested county boroughs nominate tenants and perhaps agree to pay the housing rate subsidy for a period of 10 years, the county district council provides the dwellings and district services and facilities, the county council provides its own services and facilities and also gives financial and professional assistance to the county district. Under these arrangements overspill population from Salford has been housed in Worsley, from Manchester in Whitefield, from Preston and Wigan in Leyland and from Wolver-hampton and other Black Country towns in Wednesfield, Seisdon and Sedgley. Lancashire County Council has not confined its assistance to county districts to this kind of case. It has also given professional assistance to county districts which have built dwellings for overspill population, and financial assistance to the cost of district services where a county borough has built in a county district.[4] Finally, since 1952, authorities can use the Town Development Act. The London County Council, Birmingham, Manchester and other large towns have been pursuing negotiations for overspill schemes under this Act with many reception authorities.[5] Among the first schemes to be promised government grant under the Act were those for the expansion of Bletchley, Buckinghamshire, from 11,000 to 21,000 people, and for Ashford, Kent, from 25,000 to 50,000 people, both with the participation of the London County Council; and for Swindon from 46,000 to 69,000 people with the participation of the London County Council and Tottenham Borough Council.

Town Development Act, 1952

This Act was passed in order to facilitate the arrangements which were already being made for housing overspill population, and to provide an additional method, for a small number of largish schemes rather than for the country as a whole, whereby " large cities wishing to provide for their surplus population shall do so by orderly and friendly arrangements with the neighbouring authorities."[6] This method, in brief, is for the necessary development to be carried out in a county district by the council of that district, either alone or with the participation of other interested local authorities, with the assistance of the additional powers in the Act and financial contribution from government. Such development is defined in the Act as " town development " when it will have " the effect, and is undertaken primarily for the purpose, of providing accommodation for residential purposes (with or without accommodation for the carrying on of industrial or other activities, and with all appropriate public services, facilities for public worship, recreation and amenity, and other requirements) the provision whereof will relieve congestion or overpopulation elsewhere."[7] This definition of town development is fairly narrow; popularly the term means any form of town expansion. In this chapter the narrower meaning will first be used in describing the Town Development Act; and we will return afterwards to the wider meaning for an example of financial calculations. We will use " Town Development " for the former and " town development " for the latter meaning.

The Authorities Concerned. The authorities primarily concerned are the council of the town which cannot house its population, the exporting authority; and of the county district which is conveniently situated to receive population from one or more exporting authorities, the receiving district.[8] In addition to the exporting authority others may participate in the Town Development: the council of a county district which is not a receiving district, the council of the county in which the Town Development or part of it is carried out, and any joint water or sewerage board.[9]

Participation by Authorities in Town Development. A participating authority may assist in Town Development in one or both of two ways: by financial contributions, or by taking part in the actual development. The methods of financial assistance are considered below. As to co-operation in development, a participating authority can enter into an agreement, which must receive the Minister's consent, with the receiving district to carry out development works.[10] Where a receiving authority is unable or unwilling to enter into an agreement, any authority which is eligible to participate in its Town Development may apply to the Minister for an order setting up the machinery for Town Development with the assistance of participating authorities.[11] Two or more county borough or county district councils may ask the Minister to set up a joint body which will represent them as participating authorities in Town Development.[12]

In carrying out development a participating authority can act either as principal or as an agent of the receiving authority. Acting as an agent, the authority could, for example, prepare plans and layouts, put works out to tender, supervise progress, erect dwellings using direct labour, or do any works which the receiving authority could. As a principal, an exporting authority could, in the county district, carry out any works for which it has normal local government powers in its own area. On completion of the works they and the debt are transferred to the receiving authority; where the exporting authority act as agent they may retain the property and debt for a period of years. County councils are vested with the powers of county borough councils for the purpose of carrying out works in a receiving district. County Councils may thereby become housing authorities for the purpose of Town Development; but it is not intended that they own and manage the houses they build.[13]

Additional Powers Relating to Land. Where land in a county district is required for the purposes of Town Development, the receiving authority may be authorised to buy it compulsorily even though it is not designated as subject to compulsory acquisition in a development plan; or any other local authority may be so authorised, if the Minister thinks it expedient after consultation with the receiving authority and appropriate county council.[14] Where land is thus acquired for Town Development, the authority has in relation to it the powers of disposal, appropriation and development which are given in Sections 19-20 of the 1944 Act as amended by the 1947 Act.[15] (See Chapter 15). Where land is acquired in connection with Town Development it can be appropriated for planning purposes provided it will be used for the purposes of Town Development.[16]

Financial Contributions. The expense which falls on a county district when housing overspill population is made up of the rate contribution for the houses and the cost of county district facilities and services for the new population. Very often the new rateable value which is created will not produce sufficient rate income to balance this expense. This is because so much of the new development is in relatively low rateable value dwellings which do not produce sufficient rate income to balance the cost of the local authority services they give rise to. Just what rateable value is necessary to meet this cost depends on local circumstances. In 1945 it was stated that " It is impossible to say with precision whether such [i.e., working class] houses pay their way . . . but it has been roughly estimated that the rates paid by the occupier of a house of less than about £30 rateable value are unlikely to cover the cost to the rates of the services which he and his family enjoy."[17]

Some figures published for the Worsley Urban District scheme for housing Salford overspill illustrate this. Had Worsley received no financial assistance in providing 4,000 dwellings and residential facilities for an overspill of 14,000 people from Salford, it would have been faced with the need, it has been estimated as follows, to levy rates to produce an additional £36,274 per annum (1950 prices).[18]

	£	£
District council services	45,126	
Less capitation grants	9,395	
To be borne by district rates		35,731
Housing rate fund contribution (at £5 10s. per annum in 1950) ...		22,000
		57,731
Estimated rate income from new development at 1950/51 rate ...		21,457
Total expenditure from district rate		36,274

Since the product of a 1d. rate in 1950-51 amounted to £564 this estimated expenditure would no doubt have been sufficiently heavy to deter Worsley from carrying out the development. The actual burden would in fact have been heavier than the figures suggest because there would have been disproportionately heavy expenditure in the early years before much new rateable value had been established.

In order to enable people to be transferred from Salford to Worsley, Lancashire County Council gave professional and technical assistance to Worsley and also a financial guarantee in the following terms: " (a) that until the annual rate income from development specifically provided for Salford overspill population meets the annual outgoings incurred by Worsley in the provision of the development, the county council will pay to the urban district council the annual local authority subsidy for each house erected; (b) that until the annual rate income meets the annual outgoings, the county council will financially assist the urban district council in providing services for the Salford overspill development to the extent necessary to prevent the urban district council suffering any financial loss; and (c) that in receiving financial assistance as above, the urban district council will not be placed in a better financial position than that of the average county district."[19]

A similar scheme was devised by the Staffordshire County Council who agreed to contribute to local authorities 6/11ths of the statutory rate fund contribution for each house provided in accommodation of overspill population; and a further annual payment, where necessary, to limit to a rate of 1s. 0d. in the £ the total amount falling on to the district council rates in respect of such housing. Contributions could also be made towards the provision of services; and technical and administrative assistance could be given where necessary.[20] Other county councils are following this lead.

In addition to making financial contributions to the district councils the county councils have to find the cost of their own; services for the incoming population. For the 14,000 people expected at Worsley, for example, it was estimated that the county services would cost the county £41,200 per annum, after deducting specific and exchequer equalisation grants, but that the estimated rate income would be only £33,900.[21] And it has been estimated that the rate income from the 4,200 houses built by the London County Council at Oxhey, Hertfordshire, barely covers the cost of education. By the time when 2,700 of these houses had been built, the rateable value per head on the estate was only £4 12s. 9d., as compared with the county average of £7 19s. 9d., yet there were 260 school children per thousand of the population compared with 130 per thousand in the county as a whole. In consequence the annual rates payable on the houses to the county (£30,000) was about equal to the county expenditure on education alone (after deducting specific grants, there being no equalisation grant).[22]

Partly as a result of the investigations for these schemes it became generally realised that for population movement to be successfully carried out more financial assistance from the government was necessary, as well as additional powers for local authorities. The Town Development Act was the result, and schemes which were previously started are being pursued under this Act. The financial assistance provided for in the Act is of two kinds; as between local authorities, with the Minister's approval, and from the exchequer to local authorities.

An exporting county borough or county district can contribute towards the expenses of the council of a receiving district which are incurred in the carrying out of Town Development, and can make conditions for ensuring that it will secure the intended relief from congestion or over-population;[23] and can also contribute to the expenses incurred by any authority participating in the Town

Development: for example, to a county council which provides the necessary county services.[24] In particular it has been suggested that it pay the housing rate fund contribution to receiving authorities for a period of 10 years for each dwelling provided for, and occupied by, a family nominated by them.[25] A receiving or participating authority can also contribute to the expenses incurred by a river board or drainage authority.[26] County councils can make contributions under their general powers.[27]

A local authority under these powers can, with the Minister's approval, contribute to another authority's expenses for any kind of Town Development; the exchequer, however, will make contributions to Town Development only if certain conditions are satisfied. These are that it is Town Development as defined in the Act; that it is on a substantial scale in the light of the size and resources of the receiving district; that congestion or overpopulation will be relieved in a county borough, or the County of London, or a county district in an area of continuous urban development adjacent to the County of London, or another big centre of population, or a county district outside the county in which the development is to be carried out.[28] The effect of these conditions is that the Act will facilitate any Town Development to relieve a congested area by providing the additional powers which have been described, but exchequer help will be confined to moves of population which are substantial and over some distance. In interpreting " substantial " the Minister will have regard to the size of the development in relation to the population of the receiving area, the direct relief given to the receiving area, and the speed at which congestion will be relieved by development; five to seven thousand people may be substantial in some cases. With regard to the distance, exchequer help is designed to assist the difficult move which hops over intervening country and not, for example, transfers within a county. In practice only a minority of overspill schemes qualify for exchequer grant.

The Minister can make contributions to receiving districts, or to participating county councils other than London, towards expenditure on any of the following: (a) annual rate fund contribution for houses, (b) acquisition of land for development, (c) site preparation, (d) provision, extension or improvement of main water supplies sewerage and sewage disposal, (e) contributions to water undertakers to obtain supplies and (f) contributions to river boards or drainage authorities.[29] He does not normally expect to contribute towards expenditure under the first three heads, since housing subsidies already cover them and any necessary further assistance should come from other authorities. But there might be occasions for his doing so, as where the cost of an industrial estate, or of sites for private enterprise housing which are provided for the incoming population, present a rate burden in the early years. It is on the expenditure in the last three heads that assistance is most likely to be given.[30] There is thus no contribution towards the provision of local authority services for the new population, or for building new traffic roads or county schools or for shifting industry from the congested area.

The Minister's contributions to participating county boroughs and county districts, and the London County Council where participating, is limited to expenses incurred in the provision of services under the last three heads, and also on the acquisition of land for any of these services.[31]

The grant is that required to get the job going, when the local authority carrying out the development can show that it cannot meet the burden without some assistance. It is settled in each case by the government in negotiation with the exporting and receiving authorities concerned and with the county councils. No formula was laid down for the amount of grant as it was realised that the circumstances of each scheme would differ so: the capital expenditure, the loss, the resources of the authorities, the benefit of relief to overcrowding. But after some experience the Minister stated in 1955 that, after the 10 years or other period for which the exporting authority had agreed to pay the annual rate fund contribution on dwellings, he would meet the whole or part of the contribution for a further period, as he thinks appropriate, where there would otherwise be an unduly heavy burden on local rates. He would furthermore pay a uniform grant of 50 per cent towards the cost of extending sewerage and water services, which have been found in practice to be one of the main items in Town Development schemes.[32]

Estimates for Grant Purposes. Before agreeing to pay grant the Minister requires from the receiving authority provisional estimates showing the financial consequences of the Town Development.[33] The kind of information which is required includes estimated costs of the capital expenditure which will arise from the Town Development, over each of the first three to five years, on works for water, sewerage and sewage disposal, on site acquisition, roads and services for commercial and industrial development, and on town services; and also a forecast over the whole period of development, or the first five years whichever is shorter, showing for each of these kinds of development, and also for housing, the product of a 1d. rate and also the net annual rate burden. This forecast would take account of loan charges on capital expenditure, services for the existing and imported population, the income received from these services, equalisation grant and capitation payments. A forecast of probable trends for the ensuing five years, for both capital costs and rate position, is also asked for, wherever it is possible to provide it, since an estimate looking 10 years ahead is necessary if the full flavour of the scheme is to be grasped.

EXERCISE 4: *Estimating the Cost of Town Development*

These grant estimates relate to Town Development in the statutory sense, are gradually made only for those schemes which, it is hoped, will satisfy the conditions as to payment of grant, and are designed to bring out the expenses on which the Minister is prepared to pay grant and to show the effect on the rates of the receiving district. Estimates for town development, in the wider sense, are required also by any local authority where town expansion is proposed without prospects of grant under the Town Development Act, as when, for example, it is estimating the financial implications of development plan proposals. It will be more useful for us to consider one of many possible methods for estimating the cost in such a case. The same method and approach will apply for all kinds of town development; and it can be adapted as necessary to estimating for statutory Town Development.

The method and approach are illustrated by examining imaginary estimates for an imaginary scheme of extension of a town, an urban district of 45,000 people, an important market centre in a county of 600,000 people (Fig. 7). The town's central shopping area is used also by a rural population of 35,000 people. Housing is required for 27,000 people in the period of the development plan, to meet the following needs:

Natural increase of population	3,000
Persons that cannot be re-accommodated in re-development areas...	6,000
Planned immigration from another part of the region	18,000

Of this, 4,000 people will be accommodated on various sites around the town, and 23,000 are to be housed with full neighbourhood facilities on 1,000 acres on the southern edge of the town, within the urban district boundary. A 70-acre industrial area is to be provided for about 3,600 manufacturing workers who might be expected to arrive with the incoming people. (Fig. 8).

The development in the neighbourhoods can be summarised as follows:

1. Improvement of Class I road, by widening throughout its length, and construction of main streets, some of which will be Class III roads.

2. New trunk sewer to join existing sewer.

3. Housing for 23,000 people—20 per cent in flats and 80 per cent in houses. With the dwellings there will be provided all minor streets, garages, small open spaces and play spaces. There will be about 6,800 dwellings, 1,800 of which will be built by private enterprise on sites leased from the urban district council.

5. Nursery, infant, junior and secondary schools for approximately 370 children per age group.

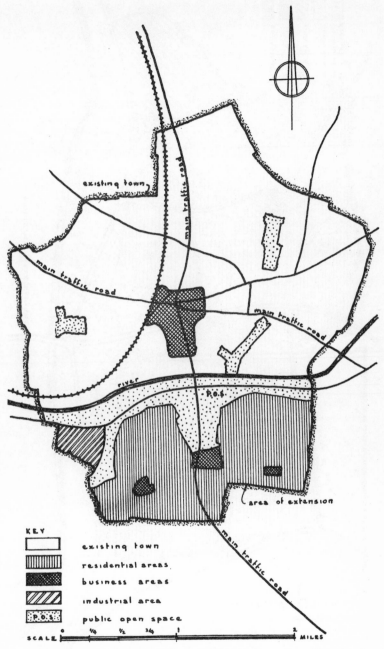

KEY

☐	existing town
▥	residential areas
■	business areas
▨	industrial area
P.O.S.	public open space

SCALE 0 ⅛ ½ ¾ 1 2 MILES

FIGURE 7.—*Sketch Plan of Area of Town Expansion—Exercise 4*

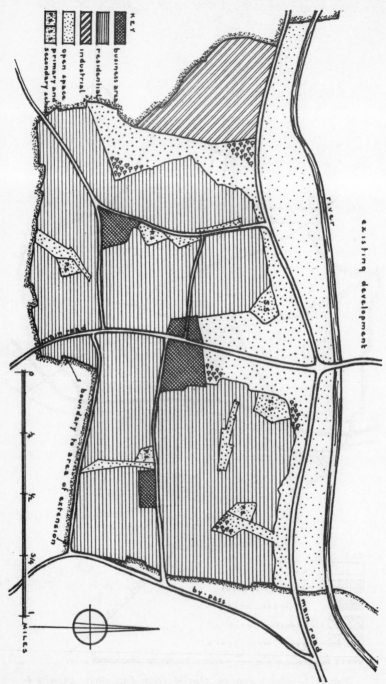

FIGURE 8.—*Plan of Neighbourhood Layout for Scheme of Town Expansion—Exercise 4*

				TOTAL		
				1,000		

'hurches

Ch.	U.D.	C.C.	Govt. Grant	Govt. Developt.	P.E. and Church	TOTAL
(23) £	(24) £ 198,000	(25) £	(26) £	(27) £	(28) £	(29) £ 198,000
10,000	(51,000)	39,000		2,000	10,000	
	1,901,000	200,000				2,101,000
100,000	9,090,000	850,000		20,000	7,400,000	17,360,000
	(60,000)	(126,000)	186,000			
110,000	11,118,000	923,000	186,000	22,000	7,410,000	19,659,000
	506,780	46,830				
	111,300	155,000				
	53,000					
	394,200					
	2,500	2,000				
	(133,000)	(113,900)	246,900			
	35,380	85,930	246,900			
						156,100

facing page 235

Fields, etc.	Allotments	Factory Area		Public Buildings		
	30	70		20		
M.O.E.	U.D.	U.D.	P.E.	Library Com. Cen. U.D.	Health Centre C.C.	Com. Cen. Health Cen. M.O.E. M.O.H.
(16) £	(17) £	(18) £	(19) £	(20) £	(21) £	(22) £
	4,000	10,000		2,000		
				(14,000)	4,000	
	1,000	140,000	1,000,000	10,000	50,000	
40,000		1,000,000	1,000,000	80,000		20,000
				(20,000)		
40,000	5,000	1,150,000	1,000,000	58,000	54,000	20,000
	80	40		50	50	
	4·18	5·05		4·66	4·66	
	200	58,080		2,700	2,340	
	100	4,000		6,000	2,000	
		10,000				
	200	70,000				
				500		
					(2,200)	2,200
		(17,920)		8,200	2,140	2,200
	100	3,500	3,500	600	400	

TABLE 29
Estimates for Extension of Town " X "

Shopping, Offices, Cinemas, Service Industry, Post Office			Nursery, Primary and Secondary Schools			Playing Parks
30			90			16
U.D.	P.E.	P.M.G.	U.D.	C.C.	M.O.E.	U.D.
(9) £	(10) £	(11) £	(12) £	(13) £	(14) £	(15) £
6,000			15,000			30,000
(2,000) 160,000		2,000	(30,000) 10,000	30,000		80,000
	1,800,000	20,000		800,000		10,000 (40,000)
164,000	1,800,000	22,000	(5,000)	830,000		80,000
20			60	50		40
7·36			4·42	4·66		5·05
12,070			(220)	38,680		4,040
1,000			200	150,000		12,000
25,000						
				2,000 (110,000)	110,000	2,000
(11,930)			(20)	76,680	110,000	14,040
	8,000			5,000		

Routes and Streets		New Trunk Sewer	Dwellings, Minor Streets, Small Open Space		
		—		550	
	M.O.T.	U.D.	U.D.	M.O.H.L.G.	P.E.
	(4) £	(5) £	(6) £	(7) £	(8) £
			121,000		
,000		100,000	1,300,000		
,000			8,000,000		4,500,000
,000)	126,000				
,000	12?,000	100,000	9,421,000		4,500,000
		30	60		
6		5·78	4·42		
,810		5,780	416,400		
,000		1,000	85,000		
			18,000		
			324,000		
,700)	1,700		(133,000)	133,000	
,110	1,700	6,780	26,400	133,000	
			90,000		45,000

redit.

Description of Works	Principal Traffi... Main S...	
Acreage		50
Agency	U.D.	C.C...
No. (1) Capital Cost	(2) £	(3... £
1. Acquisition of land ...	10,000	
2. Adjust for land appropriations and sales ...	(5,000)	5...
3. Site Works	100,000	200...
4. Buildings...		
5. Adjust for Capital Grants		(126...
6. Total Capital Expenditure	105,000	79,...
7. Period of loan—years ...	20	2...
Annuity at 4 per cent interest...	7·36	7·...
Annual Cost and Yield		
8. Charges on loans to be raised	7,730	5...
9. Plus ownership, occupation and operating expenses (no rates in Columns 6 and 18) ...	2,000	3...
10. Less income from rents— Ground		
11. Less income from rents— Rack		
12. Less income from charges		
13. Adjust for specific grants		(1,...
14. Net annual cost or gain to local authority and Government Departments (except for capital, exchequer equln. and capitation grants)	9,730	...
15. New rateable value created...		

NOTE: The figures in brackets are not a cost but a c...

6. One central and two smaller business areas consisting of minor streets, shops, offices, service industry, cinemas and post office and depot.

7. A library, community centre, health centre and churches.

8. Playing fields and parks of 7 acres per 1,000 people.

9. Allotments of about 1-⅓ acre per 1,000 people.

10. Factory area for the 3,600 incoming manufacturing workers.

The following estimates are devised:

(A) To show what the total capital cost of the scheme will be and what proportions will be borne by the different agencies, and also what the net annual cost of the development will be to the local authorities;

(B) To enable tests to be made in order to decide whether the scheme will be financially satisfactory.

For simplicity only the ultimate position will be considered, that on completion of development but before any loan period has expired. Acquisition under the Housing Acts is assumed.

(A) Capital and Net Annual Cost of Scheme

The urban district council will acquire all the land but will not carry out all the works itself. It will put in the trunk sewer and main streets for the whole area, relying on the county to carry out the improvement of the Class I road and to contribute towards the cost of the Class III roads; it will carry out all the development in the residential area (dwellings, minor streets, small open spaces), in part of the factory area (minor streets, open space, factories), and in part of the public buildings area (library, community centre); it will do all the work for the playing fields, parks, and allotments; it will provide the minor streets in the business areas and remaining part of the factory area, leasing all sites to private developers except for one site which it will sell to the Postmaster-General for a post office and depot; it will sell sites provided with frontage roads and services to the churches and to the county for schools and health centre. Not all the work for which the urban district council will be responsible will be carried out by the housing committee; other committees might, for example, develop the playing fields and parks, the allotments, sewer, library, community centre and factories.

Since there are so many different agencies involved in the scheme, and the calculations for each are not uniform, it is necessary for us to consider each class of development separately. Table 29 has been devised to assist in this. It has been designed to show how the capital costs for each class of development is broken down into the net annual cost falling upon each of the authorities. Each line of the table will be considered in turn.

Capital Costs

Lines 1 *and* 2. *Acquisition and Disposal of Land.* The urban district council will acquire at compulsory purchase value (see page 140 ff.). This is estimated at £198,000, averaging £200 per acre.

Where land is to be sold by the urban district council to other authorities, the Postmaster-General or the churches, or to be appropriated from the committee which acquires it to other services, it will be transferred at a formula price. This price will not be based on a pro rata calculation of the average price per acre for acquisition, but may be related either to the price that would be payable by the purchaser under a compulsory purchase (see page 80) or to the actual cost of acquiring the site transferred plus the cost of any improvements made on the site and the cost of providing road frontage thereto (see page 149). Line 2 shows the adjustment for sales to the county council, Postmaster-General and churches: the formula prices of the sites are logged against them and the same amount credited to the urban district council.

Line 3. *Site Works.* The costs of principal traffic roads, main streets and the trunk sewer are not allocated to the different kinds of development, but appear as an item on their own.

It is assumed, for simplicity, that minor streets would be constructed by the urban district council in all areas, whether they erect all buildings or lease or sell sites.

Line 4. *Buildings.* The cost of all buildings are shown, indicating the agency which is responsible. In the cost of building is included that of the access roads which would be constructed with the buildings by the county, General Post Office and church, and also of the car parks and service roads within curtilages which could be constructed by lessees.

Line 5. *Adjust for Capital Grants.* Capital grants are made for classified roads, the playing fields, and community centre. In this line the amount of grant is logged against the Ministries of Transport and Education and deducted from the capital cost for which the urban district council or county council would be responsible.

Line 6. *Total Capital Cost.* The total capital cost of work will amount to £19,659,000, divided among the different parties as follows: —

	£	Percentage
Urban district council	11,098,000	56.4
County council	943,000	4.8
Government grants — Ministry of Education, Ministry of Transport	186,000	0.9
Postmaster-General	22,000	0.1
Churches	110,000	0.6
Private enterprise	7,300,000	37.2

Annual Costs

Lines 7 and 8. *Loan Charges.* These are shown only for the local authority development. The loan periods for different kinds of work in each section of development might vary, but for simplicity a single period is assumed for each section. Annuities are calculated at 4 per cent; the multipliers are shown.

Line 9. *Expenses of Occupation, Ownership and Operation.* Where ground rents would be received, for housing, business and industry, there would be expenses of ownership; where rack rents would be received, for dwellings, allotments and factories, there would be expenses of ownership and occupation (rents are taken exclusive of rates); there would be maintenance expenses for the principal traffic roads, main streets and sewer; and occupation and operating expenses for the schools, playing fields, parks and public buildings. There would be, in addition, maintenance and lighting of all minor streets; this is allocated between the areas.

Lines 10 *and* 11. *Ground and Rack Rents.* These lines show the expected yield in ground and rack rents.

Line 12. *Income from Charges.* Where the authority would use land and buildings for their functions, they would sometimes be able to make charges for their use by others. An allowance for this is shown.

Line 13. *Specific Annual Grants.* There will be annual exchequer subsidies for housing (1952 Act subsidies are taken), grants for schools and health centre, and towards the maintenance of classified roads. The adjustment for this is shown.

Line 14. *Net Annual Cost or Gain to Local Authorities and Government Departments Except for Capital, Exchequer Equalisation and Capitation Grants.* The annual costs in lines 8 and 9, less the income received in lines 10 to 13, give the net annual costs to the urban district, county and government departments (who would also pay the capital grant in line 5) before the equalisation and capitation grants are considered. The net cost to the urban district council is about £35,000. The non-remunerative services (the main streets, sewer, playing fields, library and health centre) show a loss of about £36,000, the housing a loss of £26,000 (that is the rate subsidy contributions of £44,000 which must be met in the Housing Revenue Account, against which, as far as the rate position as a whole is concerned, is offset £18,000 of ground rents for building leases); the remunerative shopping and factory areas show a profit of about £30,000; the cost of the allotments and profit on disposing of the school site are small. The county council cost is much greater, about £86,000, which is made up of deficits for the non-remunerative classified roads, schools, and health centre, the school expenditure being the predominant. In contrast, the capital costs of the urban district council are much higher, as was noted above, than those of the country council.

Line 15. *The New Rateable Value Created.* This shows an estimate of the new rateable value which will be created: that is £156,000. In addition there will be the other new rateable value that will be generated, mainly in the central area, through the arrival of 18,000 immigrants in the town. This would be difficult to estimate: an increase of £5,000 is assumed. The total increase in rateable value would be thus £161,000, or £7 per head of the population to be housed.

Off-site Local Authority Services

To the costs of development in Table 29 must be added those occupation and operating expenses, for local authority services and facilities for the new population, which are not provided as part of the new development, and not shown in the table. For example, in the county there would be fire, local health (home helps, health visiting, day nurseries, ambulances, etc.), town and country planning, police, registration of births, etc., civil defence, higher education, care of children, vehicle licensing, probation. And in the county district there would be car parking, cemeteries, etc., rate collection, refuse collection, registration of electors, sewerage and storm water disposal, swimming baths, administration of various bye-laws, inspection of food and drugs, factories and shops inspection, and museums, etc. Estimates of these costs will be made from records of unit costs of these services. (See page 154). We will assume 30s. per head for the district services and 40s. per head for the county, totalling £80,500 per annum for both.

(B) Testing of the Scheme—Potential Rateable Value and Rate Income

The town expansion which we have been considering is part only of the development and re-development in both the urban district and the county as a whole, and its financial implications cannot be fully considered in isolation from all the development plan proposals. But in practice it may not be possible to consider the development for the whole county, or even for the whole county district, at one time and some method is required of testing the effect of a town development scheme on its own.

The purpose of the estimates for statutory Town Development is to establish the actual burden that will fall on the county district rates, so that the measure of necessary grant can be ascertained. For this it is necessary to forecast the effect of exchequer equalisation and capitation grants. It is not simple to do this. The amount of the future exechequer equalisation grant for the county depends on its future average rateable value per head of weighted population compared with the future average for the country as a whole. The amount of capitation grant depends on the total amount of exchequer grant paid. The distribution of the exchequer equalisation grant and capitation grants between the county districts depends on their relative rateable values and populations. Because of the difficulties of forecasting various assumptions must be made, such as that the income from exchequer equalisation grant will amount in future to the same proportion of rate-borne expenditure that it does at the time of estimating; or that the exchequer will pay equalisation grant to the county at the same rate in the £ on its future rateable value as it does on its current rateable value; or that capitation grant will continue to be paid at the same amount per head as it is currently.

The tests to be described do not have as their purpose the establishment of the actual burden that will fall on the rates. Their purpose is rather to see whether the expenditure that will fall upon the rates as a result of the new scheme will be balanced by the rates obtainable from the new rateable value to be created, or whether it will in part have to be met from rates on existing property. These tests can be made without introducing the non-specific grants: that is by considering what we can call " gross " rate expenditure. This is the total expenditure that would fall on the rates after allowing for specific grants, but if there were no exchequer equalisation or capitation grants and no source of income other than rates or grants. The " gross " rate is the rate that would be levied to meet this expenditure. The current gross rate expenditure and gross rate are taken to be as follows:

	Urban District			County		
Population	45,000			600,000		
	£	s.	d.	£	s.	d.
Rateable value	325,000	0	0	4,200,000	0	0
Rateable value per head	7	4	0	7	0	0
Product of 1d. rate	1,350	0	0	17,500	0	0
Gross rate expenditure	157,000	0	0	3,300,000	0	0
Gross rate expenditure per head ...	3	10	0	5	10	0
Gross rate in £	9	7		15	8	
Combined gross rate in £ of urban district council and county council...				25s. 3d.		

The tests can be considered either from the viewpoint of the county district or the county council or both combined; we shall consider only the first. In doing so we must make some assumption about the amount of the county expenditure which will fall upon the urban district. This expenditure, if it is for general county purposes as opposed to special county purposes (which is charged to particular district councils only since it is particularly for their benefit) will be distributed throughout the county according to rateable value. Only a proportion therefore will fall upon the urban district. But in addition the urban district will need to find its share of the general purpose county expenditure that will be taking place in other parts of the county. This share can only be estimated by considering all expected expenditure in the county. An assumption will be that the amount of the total county expenditure that will fall on the urban district council will be equal to the actual county expenditure on the scheme; that is, that the distribution of new general county expenditure will follow roughly the distribution of the total of existing and new rateable value combined.

Test 1.   The new rateable value per head that will be created by the new development can be compared with the current rateable value per head.

New rateable value	£161,000
New rateable value per head	£7 0 0

This is rather less than the current rateable value per head in the urban district (£7 4s.) but the same as that in the county as a whole.

Test 2.   The gross rate income that would need to be levied per head of the new population to pay for the town expansion can be compared with the gross rate income currently levied per head in the urban district by both authorities.

Gross rate expenditure on scheme (line 14 of table):

Urban district	£35,380
County council	£85,930
Add cost of off-site local authority services and facilities,	
urban district and county council	£80,500
	———
	£201,810
Expenditure per head for 23,000 people	£9 3 0

This is the same as the gross rate income currently levied of £9 3s. per head of urban district population (i.e., £3 10s. by the urban district plus £5 13s. by the county council (£7 4s. × 15s. 8d.)).

Test 3.   The new gross rate expenditure that will be occasioned by the town expansion can be expressed as a gross rate in the £ of the new rateable value, and this compared with the current gross rate in the £; or alternatively the gross rate income from the new rateable value at the current gross rate in the £ can be compared with estimated net expenditure on the new scheme.

New rateable value	£161,000
Total cost of scheme to local authorities as in Test 1	£201,810
Combined gross rate that would need to be levied...	25s.

This compares well with the current gross combined urban district and county council rate of 25s. 3d. so that the scheme would not call for additional rates to be levied on existing rateable value.

Summary of Tests.   In short, therefore, on the assumptions made, when the scheme is completed the new rateable value that is created should produce enough income to both authorities to meet the additional cost of the scheme without calling upon ratepayers of existing property to pay a higher rate on account of the scheme. But the assumptions must be recalled: the effect of exchequer equalisation and capitation grants is ignored, and the new general county expenditure will follow roughly the distribution of the total of existing and new rateable value. The actual effect on the urban district and county council may therefore be different.

During the carrying out of the scheme, as we saw in Chapter 15, losses could be expected while construction was being carried out in advance of rate income being obtainable.

CHAPTER 17

NEW TOWNS

The Establishment of New Towns—Objects and Powers of a New Town Development Corporation—Acquisition of Land—Disposal of Land—Financing of Development Corporations—Ministry Approval of Plans—The Corporation is a Unique Kind of Developer—Relation of Cost to Yield in Corporation Development—Financial Statement—Local Authority Development in a New Town.

The Establishment of New Towns

THE POST-WAR administration accepted the establishment of new towns as one method of housing people. The Reith Committee in consequence was asked to consider the " general question of the establishment, development, organisation and administration that will arise in the promotion of the new towns in furtherance of a policy of planned decentralisation from congested urban areas, and in accordance therewith to suggest guiding principles on which such towns should be established and developed as self-contained and balanced communities for work and living."[1]

The New Towns Act, 1946, providing for the creation of new towns by Development Corporations, was passed having regard to the Committee's recommendations; and 14 new towns, each with its own Corporation, were established in Great Britain, after land was designated for their sites by the Minister of Town and Country Planning or Secretary of State for Scotland.[2]

Objects and Powers of a New Town Development Corporation

The objects and powers of the Corporations are clearly defined in the 1946 Act. They are " to secure the laying out and development of the new town in accordance with proposals approved in that behalf under the following provisions of this Act, and for that purpose every such corporation shall have power to acquire, hold, manage and dispose of land and other property, to carry out building and other operations, to provide water, electricity, gas, sewerage and other services, to carry on any business or undertaking in or for the purposes of the new town, and generally to do anything necessary or expedient for the purposes of the new town or for purposes incidental thereto."[3]

These powers appear to be limitless, but they are not. Corporations are not rating authorities. They do not displace the local authority or the statutory undertakers who are operating in the area designated as the site of the new town; and these retain all their normal powers, duties and functions except for the special arrangements to be described. In order to exercise any of their powers the corporations must obtain specific authority: of Parliament, for example, when they wish to carry on any utility or transport undertaking,[4] or of the Minister of Housing and Local Government, who acts for other interested departments, when they propose to acquire land or carry out any development. They can obtain capital only by way of advances from this Minister.[5] They must observe all the building and street bye-laws, and other laws relating to the control of development, except that where the Minister has approved its Master Plan and made a Special Development Order freeing it of the necessity a Corporation does not need permission from local planning authorities.[6] Corporations furthermore have the right to make observations to the local planning authority on all development applications in their designated areas.[7]

A new and sudden concentration of people can clearly place a great strain on local financial resources. Corporations are therefore permitted, with the Minister's consent and Treasury concurrence, to contribute to the expenses of any local authority or statutory undertaker, which are incurred in the performance of any of their statutory functions in relation to the new town.[8] They can also make special arrangements with authorities and undertakers as to sewerage and water. Where, for example, county districts have insufficient resources to provide the necessary major sewerage system and works, Corporations have been authorised by the Minister to become the sewerage authority for their designated areas, the former sewerage authority contributing to the Corporation's expenses out of its rates. For similar reasons three Corporations have been constituted by the Minister as water authorities and they are empowered to charge water rates, or for bulk water supply, to recoup their expenditure.[9] Corporations may also provide such municipal services as open spaces, community halls and street lighting where the local authority is unable to do so; and may also make contributions towards the cost of new traffic roads which will serve their needs and which would normally be made by the highway authority with M.O.T. grant.

A Corporation may transfer any of its assets upon agreed terms to a local authority or statutory undertaker, with the consent of the Minister and concurrence of the Treasury.[10] When the purposes for which a Corporation has been set up have been achieved, the Minister may wind it up and transfer its assets to the appropriate local authority and statutory undertakers. Payment will be required for the assets. Any surplus money will be paid to the exchequer and any deficit defrayed out of public funds.[11]

Acquisition of Land

Corporations may acquire, by agreement or compulsorily, any land within the designated area, or land adjacent to that area which is required for the development of the town, or any other land required for the provision of services for the town.[12] The compensation code is the same as for public authorities.[13] Just as though they are local authorities carrying out re-development under the Town and Country Planning Acts, 1944 and 1947, Corporations are obliged to offer accommodation, as far as it is practicable, to persons who were living or carrying on business or other activities on land which they have acquired.[14] And they must find other residential accommodation for persons displaced by acquisitions and can contribute to their removal expenses; they can obtain possession of rent-controlled premises; they can, upon acquisition, interfere with easements and other rights in land, extinguish highways and private rights of way, and rights as to apparatus of statutory undertakers; and can use and develop consecrated grounds, burial grounds and open spaces.[15]

Disposal of Land

Corporations can dispose of land as they consider expedient for securing the development of the town. They were originally debarred from selling the freehold or granting a lease for more than 99 years, other than in exceptional circumstances; but this requirement has now been relaxed, and they may with the Minister's consent sell sites, or land and buildings, outright.[16] In practice, sales are made to local authorities, statutory undertakers and government departments; there have been few private sales. The prices of transfers to public bodies are negotiated between them and the Corporation, the maximum price being market value for the new use, or, where the new use is one for which there is no market, the value according to formula. The value for educational land, for example, is value with planning permission for residential purposes; and the value for public open space, allotments and detached school playing fields is value for agricultural use.[17] Other sales are at market value, except for subsidised houses the sale prices of which are governed in the same way as those of houses sold by local authorities. (See page 161.)

Financing of Development Corporations

As stated earlier, Development Corporations are entirely dependent on the government for their financing and have no other powers of borrowing at all. They receive advances, as required for their work, from the Minister " to defray expenditure properly chargeable to capital account, including provision of working capital."[18] Parliament voted £50 million for this purpose out of the Consolidated Fund in the 1946 Act and a further £50 million in each of the New Towns Acts, 1952, 1953 and 1955. Advances are repayable on terms fixed by the Minister with the approval of the Treasury, the current terms requiring repayment by annuity over a period of 60 years at the Public Works Loans Board rate which is current at the time of borrowing. The Corporation is liable for interest and repayments from the date of loan. There is no suspension of interest payments even during the period when works are unproductive; but repayments of principal during this period may be suspended for a period up to five years. No Corporation, however, takes advantage of this arrangement.

With regard to expenditure which is chargeable to revenue the Minister may make grants which are not repayable.[19] It is under this power that the Minister pays to Corporations the equivalent of the annual rate contribution on subsidy dwellings, where this is not receivable from a local housing authority, and also 50 per cent of the net revenue deficiency suffered by the Corporation during its first year and 25 per cent of that in the following year.

Ministry Approval of Plans

Development Corporations are responsible to the Minister of Housing and Local Government for the exercise of their powers. He may give directions to Corporations restricting the exercise of the powers or requiring that they be exercised in any specified manner. The Corporations prepare and submit annual reports and accounts, in a prescribed form, to the Minister;[20] and also submit each year capital and revenue budgets for the forthcoming year and programmes of capital works to be carried out in the forthcoming three years.

It is necessary for Corporations to obtain the Minister's approval to their development proposals, the Minister consulting with the local planning authority, any other local authority who appear to him to be concerned, and with other departments.[21] The Minister must also examine the economics of these proposals since it is a condition of making advances that these " are likely to secure for the Corporation a return which is reasonable, having regard to all the circumstances, when compared with the cost of carrying out those proposals."[22] In general, the Minister's approval is in three stages. At the outset he approves the Master Plan for the whole town, although this is not provided for in the Act. At the second stage he approves large-scale proposals, for perhaps the town centre or a whole neighbourhood or industrial area; and at this stage he requires sufficient information to consider the broad financial implications of the proposal, and therefore asks for estimates of capital and annual costs and of profit or loss, with the reasons for any estimated loss. Third-stage approval arises when advances are requested for sections of work that are to proceed; and with their applications the Corporations submit more detailed financial information under the following headings as appropriate:

Estimated Capital Cost. Land, site development, construction fees and salaries, interest on capital during construction, landscaping, other items.

Estimated Revenue Account. Interest charges on capital cost and depreciation, repairs and maintenance, management supervision and insurance, voids, subsidies, contributions, ground or rack rents, other items.

The Corporation is a Unique Kind of Developer

From this account it is seen that a Corporation is a unique kind of developer. It has the powers of a public body in acquiring land, and its facilities in obtaining 100 per cent loans, on the same terms as local authorities are able to borrow from the Public Works Loans Board, for repayment over a period of 60 years. It is subject, however, to the law relating to development and to close scrutiny of its development by government.[23] It is forced to exercise and pay for certain functions which normally adhere to local authorities and statutory undertakers; and while it may receive contributions from them when doing so, it can levy no local rates although it can charge water rates where it is a water authority. It starts its operations with no assets and in its early years must borrow to meet revenue expenditure. But, after a few years, revenue is expected to exceed expenditure, and it is hoped that on completion of the town the Corporation's assets will be worth more than their cost. It can expect, as any developer can, that authorities and undertakers will carry out their statutory obligations; but it cannot compel them to exercise their powers, although it can where necessary be authorised by the Minister to take over their water and sewerage powers. To stimulate the carrying out of development by authorities and undertakers it can, with the Minister's consent and Treasury concurrence, make financial contributions to them. Its pecuniary relationship with local authorities is thus not that of the normal developer and is a matter of local negotiation for which there are no general formulae; and while there are no centrally stipulated rules for this relationship any agreement is subject to the Minister's approval, and any contribution from a Corporation to a local authority or statutory undertaker needs, in addition, Treasury concurrence.

Relation of Cost to Yield in Corporation Development

Arising out of its unique position as a developer a Corporation has a unique financial problem in relating cost to yield. Unlike a private developer it carries on many different kinds of development, many of which are non-remunerative in themselves; and in relating cost and yield it is primarily concerned with the new town as one financial unit and not with individual sections of it. Unlike a local authority it is not primarily concerned with non-remunerative services and facilities which must be paid for out of rates and taxes; and it can look forward to the completion of its enterprise in the relatively near future when, on its being wound up, the total values which have been created can be measured against the total capital cost which has been incurred.

Because it is concerned with the whole town as a financial unit the Corporation will bear in mind throughout its life the estimated cost and yield for the town as a whole, that is total values and total costs. During its life, however, it must prepare broad calculations for sections of development as they are designed, and more detailed calculations for smaller sections as they are carried out. This is necessary so that the Corporation can consider the financial implications of the section in question before deciding to go ahead; and also to satisfy the Minister when submitting schemes to him that a reasonable return is being obtained.

Before considering the relationship between cost and yield for the town as a whole it will help us to consider it for five different kinds of corporation development, for each of which the yield will come from a different source, and the testing of cost and yield will be accordingly different.

(1) For commercial and industrial development the yield is by way of market rents or sales, either for sites which are improved and leased or for buildings which are let at rack rents. The considerations affecting the testing of cost and yield are those described for remunerative development by public bodies. Capital value can be related to capital cost, method (A), although these values will rarely be realised in the market since the properties are normally let at ground or rack-rents. A more suitable method is the relating of money return to capital cost, (B), keeping ground rents and rack-rents separate; but an appropriate rate per cent is not easy to determine since the conditions of the Corporation as developer are so different from those of a private developer operating in the market.[24] Method (C) is also suitable, the relation of money return to the expected yield on investment, but the appropriate per cent for the latter is difficult to determine, as in (B). None of the methods which take financing into account are applicable except (G), which relates money yield to annual loan charges.

The Corporation may obtain a yield from another source which is not development: the acquisition and letting of standing buildings. A profit may ensue because of the comparatively low interest rates at which the purchase price is borrowed compared with the rate at which purchase is made. To obtain a true test it is necessary to keep these transactions separate from those of development.

(2) Where trading undertakings, such as the supply of water, are operated by the Corporation, alone or in conjunction with another undertaker, the yield will arise in the specific charges which are made. There is usually only one test for such undertakings: the yield by way of charges in relation to the full annual costs of operation. Housing carried out by the Corporation in a new town can be regarded as a trading undertaking for the purpose of testing cost and yield. A Corporation has no rate fund on which to draw; and it is required to charge rents which will balance the cost of housing.

(3) Corporations might provide minor services such as local open spaces, public car parks, small community halls and industrial estate canteens. These may be non-remunerative in themselves, or remunerative as where specific charges are made for the use of the halls or car parks. They are usually for the specific use and benefit of an industrial, commercial or residential part of the town; and for testing purposes their cost and any yield can be included in the testing of that part.

(4) Where local authorities, government departments, statutory undertakers and *ad hoc* bodies need to carry out their functions in the New Town, the Corporation may sell sites to them at a transfer price which is based on formula. These sites have the benefit of major roads and services; and the developers would normally provide minor streets, services, paving and planting, etc., as part of the development they carry out. The test of the Corporation would be method (A), the relation of capital cost to value, which in this case would be the formula transfer price. Where virgin land is improved such transfer prices may amount to a writing up in value, with a capital profit, rather than the writing down which so often occurs when re-development takes place.

(5) Finally, there are the major non-remunerative services, the sewerage works, traffic roads, major open spaces and central car parks. These works are provided for the benefit of the town as a whole, or for large parts of it. They would normally be undertaken by local authorities, when the cost would come out of the rates and, sometimes, government grant. One test, therefore, is method (H) the annual subvention in rates that will have to be found by the local authority when the works are eventually transferred to them. This, however, does not assist in testing the projects from the Corporations' viewpoint. They may receive some contribution towards the cost from local authorities, but this apart the yield is contained in the general yield which the services make realisable, the prices and rents referred to in (1) to (4) above. The actual amount of the yield for the major services which is realisable from different sites or areas cannot be estimated or calculated.

In preparing calculations for the execution of individual sections of development certain difficulties arise when testing their cost and yield. Since the shape and extent of each section is selected to comprise an area which can be reasonably planned and developed as a unit, it will often contain various kinds of development whose yield will come from different sources. A town centre which is designed as a whole, for example, will contain development of each of the five groups which have been described. The costs and yields in each of these groups must be separated out if they are to be tested by the appropriate methods.

To summarise the foregoing, if the town as a whole is considered from the Corporation's viewpoint the cost and yield on the second and third groups might be expected to balance roughly; there should be a surplus from yield over costs on the first and third; the fifth would be all cost with little yield. It is thus out of the surplus on the first group, the remunerative development, that the cost of the major works in the fifth group, sometimes called " general development expenses," must be met, as must also any other expenditure, sometimes called " other development expenses," which is similar in character in that it cannot be specifically allocated to particular sections of development, cannot be charged against a specific income, and is particularly heavy in the initial years of a new town's growth. Examples are the contributions to local authorities and statutory undertakers, preliminary expenses such as the cost of surveys and investigations for the preparation of the Master Plan, the provision of hostels for building labour which does not live in the town, the cost of administrative offices, salaries and establishment which cannot be allocated to specific development.

While a Corporation may estimate at the outset the amount of these expenses and the surplus that it would need to earn on the remunerative works in order to balance them, it cannot be sure till the town is completed that it will in fact cover them. It is important therefore that it should throughout its life keep down its cost of construction and maximise its yields, in other words aim at the maximum surplus, consistent with the high standards of development expected of it and with its responsibilities as a public body. In order to guide it in obtaining a sufficient surplus to cover costs the Corporation will charge to the capital cost of each section some contribution towards those general and other development expenses. The result is that if yields are in fact obtained to cover these costs, the Corporation will, over the years, accumulate at least sufficient to balance the cost of these expenses which are necessary for building the town as a whole.

Any such charging must be by some arbitrary formula. One which is used by Corporations is to add some percentage, perhaps five to ten, to the capital cost of each section of development, the actual percentage being based on the estimated total of the general and other development expenses expressed as a percentage of the estimated total cost of development which is to be charged.[25] Another is to charge such a percentage not on cost but on the estimated value that would be realised in the new use. Another is to charge a fixed sum per acre of development over the town; and yet another is to charge such a sum per acre with the more remunerative uses taking a heavier share.[26]

Financial Statement for Corporation Development

We have already considered the money return that can be expected for the different kinds of development, and the methods of testing its relation to capital cost. We will only briefly consider capital and annual costs.

I. Capital Cost

The calculations for capital cost are similar to those for other public bodies, and there is little difference between those for the five different kinds of development. These will all be considered together.

(*a*), (*b*) *Acquisition of Land and its Legal Preparation.* As we have seen, corporations work with the same legal powers and are subject to the same compensation code as other public bodies.

(*c*), (*d*), (*e*) *Cost of Site Works and Buildings.* Corporations need to carry out both civil engineering and building works. Where it is necessary to separate out the costs of works falling into one or other of the five kinds of development, it is sometimes necessary to make allocations of the cost of roads and services between different kinds, as where a street in a town centre has public buildings on one frontage and shops on another.

(*f*) *Interest on Capital During Construction.* A Corporation incurs this as a cost, and it is included in the items of estimated capital cost for the purpose of obtaining advances from the Minister. As to whether the yield should cover this cost it can be argued that it should do so for the five classes of development which have been described. Where sites are sold, capital value should cover the item; where remunerative development is let the yield over the life should recoup it; where non-remunerative development is carried out its total cost, including this item, is a charge which should be covered by yield from the remunerative development.

Whatever the proper course for development calculations, however, in the formal accounts of the Corporation this interest is charged to revenue and not capital. This has the effect of increasing revenue expenditure and reducing capital expenditure accordingly; and in the early years of the new town, when rents are low compared with expenditure on construction, of increasing correspondingly any annual deficiency. This has been criticised as giving a false picture in that it shows exaggerated revenue deficiencies when the New Town is forging ahead.[27]

(*g*) *Profit.* An allowance for profit is not included in the estimates of capital cost submitted for advances. It is clearly out of place in the calculations relating to non-remunerative development and also where sites are transferred at formula value, since the formulae take no account of it. There is a case, however, for including profit on remunerative development. This is comparable to private enterprise development, and even though Corporations might still develop if there were no profit, they should be able to obtain yields which cover an allowance of profit for risk bearing; they should therefore include profit in capital cost when testing cost and yield under method (*A*). Such a test enables the Corporation to ensure that its development is comparable at least with the efficiency, measured by capacity to earn profit, of successful private enterprise developments.

(*h*) *Disposal Expenses*. Since most of the development carried out by a Corporation is not for their own occupation they have expenses of disposal.

(*i*) *Staff*. All the Corporations have a staff who supply the professional and other services occasioned by different stages of the work, and many also pay fees to consultants. The expenses of this staff are allocated, where practicable, to the appropriate works. The administrative costs which cannot be so allocated are included in " Other Development Expenses."

II. Annual Costs

(*j*) *Return on Investment*. This does not arise since all money is borrowed from the government.

(*k*), (*l*), (*m*) *Interest on and Repayment of Loan and Depreciation*. Development Corporations tended in their early years to follow local authority practice and allow for loan charges but not depreciation, the loan charges being calculated on an annuity or sinking fund basis for 60 years at the Public Works Loans Board rate which was current at the time of calculation. The Ministry subsequently required Corporations in their formal annual accounts to write down all capital assets except land, over a period of years appropriate to the asset, on the annuity basis at the Public Works Loans Board rate current at the time of calculation. The periods of years for this purpose were prescribed by the Ministry. It is 60 years for most new buildings, and for property which is bought a period corresponding to its expected life. Site works are not written off if the local authority is to take them over. Corporations have moved towards this practice in their development calculations. They thus follow private enterprise development calculations except that Corporations take interest at Public Works Loans Board and not market rate and invariably, and not exceptionally, allow for depreciation on the asset.

(*n*), (*o*) *Occupation, Ownership and Operating Expenses*. These will be of the same character as discussed for development in earlier chapters, but the kind of expense will vary considerably with the different classes of development, and with the terms of disposal where the Corporation do not occupy. In certain cases there will also be operating expenses, as where the Corporation runs a water undertaking.

Local Authority Development in a New Town

We have discussed the relation of cost and yield solely from the viewpoint of a Corporation. Local authorities, government departments and statutory undertakers will also carry out development in the new town and will need to consider the relation of their cost and yield.

The development carried out by local authorities will be non-remunerative in the main. The financial calculations will be similar to those discussed in earlier chapters except that the contributions to and from the Corporations will need to be included. The cost incurred may be very heavy in relation to rate resources. It has been suggested that in one new town the local authorities might contribute about 15 per cent of the total capital expenditure, and of this about one-third would be met by specific government grant.[28] New rateable value to produce income for this expenditure would be slow in coming about in the early stages of the town's growth. But on the other hand authorities will often have the benefit of new rateable value without having had to carry out all the works that would normally be expected of them before attracting such rateable value. The burden and benefit to the rates will fall not only on the particular county districts of the designated area but also, through the county council, over the county as a whole.

From this it is seen that the development of a particular section of the town, or indeed of the town as a whole, may have certain financial implications for the Corporation, others for the particular county district and yet others for the remainder of the county.

PART IV

BALANCE SHEET OF DEVELOPMENT AND PLANNING

INTRODUCTORY

In any proposal for development there are numerous and varied implications, some of which will mean a benefit and some a loss to various people other than the developer. When he is considering whether or how to develop, or which of alternative schemes to adopt, a developer might not take account only of the kind of financial appraisal described in Part III. He might also take account of some of these other implications of the proposed development; but he would rarely consider it his duty to take all of them into account. In other words, he might take account of some but rarely of all social costs. A public developer would consider more of the social costs than a private one, but also might not consider all.

In illustration Chapter 18 takes five imaginary but typical cases of development and itemises their implications. These are examples of a development balance sheet. In each case are suggested the items which a typical developer would consider to be his concern, and which he would not, and the persons upon whom the losses and benefits arising from the item would fall. In each case are picked out the losses and benefits which could be measured in money terms.

In making a decision on a development proposal or programme a planning authority might also list and weigh up these implications, particularly where the issue is complex. It might, that is, prepare a planning balance sheet. But it will not necessarily have the same viewpoint as the developer, nor consider just the same implications, in reaching a decision. It will usually consider more of the social costs but might still not consider all. To help it reach a decision the planning office should define the items as clearly as possible and measure the losses and benefits, where possible in money terms. Methods of doing this are not well advanced but, in illustration of the approach, methods of measuring four of the items in the cases in Chapter 18 are described in Chapter 19. Some problems that arise in weighing up the items in the balance sheet are discussed.

Since the planning authority takes into account social costs in reaching a decision on proposed development, the decision will often apportion these costs between the developer and the community in a way that would not have obtained without the exercise of planning powers. This is discussed, and leads on to a discussion on the costs and gains of planning.

CHAPTER 18

PRIVATE AND SOCIAL COSTS IN DEVELOPMENT

The Development Balance Sheet—1. A Large Factory in a Residential Area—2. Ten Acres of Private Enterprise Housing Away from a Town—3. The Extension of a Town Within its Boundaries—4. The Widening of a River Bridge—5. The Widening of an Existing Trunk Road or the Building of a By-pass—Private and Social Costs in Development.

The Development Balance Sheet

THE FINANCIAL appraisal of schemes, which we discussed in Part III, would assist developers or operators in deciding whether and how to develop, and which of alternative schemes to adopt. Such a financial appraisal, however, would not always be conclusive in the mind of a developer for there might be, and often would be, implications other than financial ones which he would consider in making decisions. For example, whereas a property company deciding to build shops on a traffic road would be influenced solely by cost and yield, a local authority in considering whether to build such shops would also be influenced by the possible effect of the vehicles, which would be attracted, on the existing flow of traffic or on the safety of prospective shoppers. And whereas the typical private owner of an area of sub-standard housing would re-develop it if it paid him to do so, a local authority would acquire it and re-develop, even at a loss, because of the danger to health of the occupants. Even a local authority, however, does not take into account, in deciding whether or not to develop, all the implications of its development proposals. There are housing authorities who would reclaim derelict land at considerable expense rather than build on good agricultural land which could be easily developed. Others would not consider it their concern to do so. It has therefore been found necessary to urge authorities to incur some additional cost in selecting poorer housing land where it will enable them to keep off good agricultural land.[1]

In any proposal for development there are thus numerous and varied implications, both financial and non-financial, some of which will mean a benefit and some a loss to various people other than the developer. In making their decisions developers would take account of some of these implications but rarely all; and in similar schemes some developers would take into account more than others. All the implications of a particular development proposal or programme, whether they will be taken into account by the developer or not, can be listed in what we have called above (page 11) a development balance sheet. For the imminent proposal it is possible to define the implications more precisely than for one which is in the future, but the same considerations apply to both, and in this chapter no distinction is drawn between them. In illustration we shall describe five imaginary but typical cases of development and list their implications, differentiating between those which would concern a typical developer and those which would not, and indicating upon whom the losses or benefits arising from the implications would fall. The items are not exhaustive but are indicative of those which would arise in such cases.

Some of the implications can be well expressed in both physical and money terms, as where the new water service main that would be required to serve a proposed factory can be described as 600 yds. of piping which would cost £1,000 to lay. Some can be better expressed in money rather than physical terms, as where the amenity that would be created by a new park for adjoining houses can be described as increasing the value of the houses by £50 per annum. Some can be expressed only in physical terms, as where the traffic that would flow on a road can only be described by its volume or weight. Some cannot be expressed at all in physical or money terms, as, for example, the potential improvement in health and welfare to adolescents in the provision of 100 acres of new playing field, or the injury to children of living in high density flats rather than houses. Those costs which can be measured in money terms have been called tangible or economic ones, and those which cannot, intangible or social.[2] In our cases we shall pick out the items which can be measured in money terms; and in illustration of how this measurement is done four particular items are selected for elaboration in Chapter 19.

Case 1.   *A Large Factory in a Residential Area*

An industrialist is considering building an engineering factory on a one-acre site in the inner part of a large city. The site is vacant, having formerly been occupied by a mixture of slum houses and workshops which have been demolished by the owner under a clearance order. It is part of a predominantly residential area, mostly comprised of houses built about 1890, which it is not expected to re-develop in the period of the development plan, and which the plan has allocated to residential use.

The financial appraisal would tell the industrialist whether the investment is worthwhile: for example, whether the rental value of the premises would afford a return on capital cost which would compare favourably with that from other possible kinds of investment; or whether the capital cost compares favourably with what he would need to pay for other such premises. This is only part of his financial calculations. He would also need to consider whether his operating costs, for example of labour and transport, will be reasonable in relation to selling price. This calculation will often be more important than the first since rental costs are often a small part of an industrialist's total costs. To many industrialists these calculations would be conclusive, and, if unfavourable, would defeat the project. Other industrialists might have a wider horizon, as where the particular enterprise was part of a larger undertaking, and they might go forward in the face of an estimated loss on the development in question alone, if the other parts of the undertaking would benefit by the production in the proposed factory.

The industrialist would probably not take account of any other implications. One would be the loss of residential amenity that would be suffered by people living in the area—in less pleasant surroundings, in greater noise and smoke, in nuisance from additional heavy traffic on the doorstep. It would not be possible to measure this loss in physical terms; but some financial measure might be given in the prospective diminution of rental value of the dwellings or reduction in rating assessments. This would be a measure of the financial loss to occupiers and owners of residential property and to the ratepayers as a whole. Another implication would be the loss or gain to other industrialists and to the economy as a whole, which would result from his increased production. These would be measurable in money terms if the necessary data could be obtained, but they probably could not. Another item would be the introduction of additional lorries into the residential area, perhaps leading to increased road accidents, particularly among children playing in the streets, and to the need for increased policing to safeguard against such accidents. It would be difficult to estimate in advance the possible number of accidents, but if such an estimate were made it would be possible to place a money value on them (see Chapter 19). The cost of such accidents would not fall upon the industrialist but upon the sufferers, the insurance companies, premium payers, hospitals, etc.; and the cost of policing would fall upon ratepayers and taxpayers, but on the industrialist only insofar as he is one of these.

Case 2. Ten Acres of Private Enterprise Housing Away from a Town

A private developer wishes to provide 100 houses for sale on 10 acres of good farmland in a county district just outside a small county borough. The site is well away from schools, shops and other housing. There are other sites nearer the centre of the town which are on poorer agricultural land. No main sewers are available and cesspools would be used. Water mains are laid in the Class III road on which the site abuts. Gas and electricity mains are some distance away and feeder mains would be necessary.

The financial appraisal would tell the developer whether he can expect a suitable profit on the sale of the houses; and on this alone will rest his decision to proceed. His interest, and financial appraisal, would be limited to this site. He would take account of none of the following items except insofar as they were reflected in the capital cost of, or the yields from, the development.

The gas and electricity boards would be called upon to provide mains. They would recoup their abnormal expenditure in special charges because the site is isolated from other consumers. The quantity of labour and materials involved could be measured in physical or money terms; and also the amount of the charges that would be necessary.

A demand would arise for public transport between the site and the town. An existing transport service may be made more profitable from the additional custom, or perhaps a new service may have to be operated at a financial loss. The prospective profit or loss could be estimated.

The occupiers of the dwellings would have lengthy journeys to the shops, entertainment centres, places of employment and schools. The cost of these journeys, which could be measured financially, would add to their living expenses.

It might be that the Class III road connecting the site and the town would need improvement at bends, or additional waiting bays for buses, and also more frequent surfacing than formerly. This would throw additional capital and maintenance expenditure on to the county borough, the county council and exchequer. The county would receive in compensation some new source of rate income, but not the county borough. The estimated costs and rate income could be measured financially.

Additional local government services would need to be provided, partly by the county and partly by the county district: the collection of refuse, the emptying of cesspools, policing, street lighting, schooling, library, etc. The cost of the services might be disproportionately high because of the isolation of the site, and might not be balanced by the new rate income that would accrue to the county and district, so that some of the cost of the new services would be spread over the county and district ratepayers as a whole. This could all be measured financially.

There would be loss of amenity to the townspeople in having the open country pushed further away from their doorsteps, and to any local residents whose views and surroundings would be transformed from open fields to houses. Such losses cannot be measured; but they might be reflected in a reduction in rental, market and rateable values of the properties concerned. The loss would be borne not only by the occupiers of property, but also by its owners and by the ratepayers as a whole.

The occupiers of the dwellings would have homes and the country's stock of dwellings would be added to.

There would be the loss of 10 acres of good farmland; and instead of its potential produce, wheat, milk or beef, there would be the vegetables, fruit and eggs from gardens. The farmer would suffer an upset since he would be deprived of that particular means of livelihood, as would his employees. The landowner would gain in being able to realise development value. The community would lose in that the potential farm produce would be replaceable in home-grown food only by higher costs of production on other land, or in foreign food only by exporting more of our national product, both leading, other things being equal, to higher prices at home for food. As against this the community would benefit in that more of its land than before would be cultivated in gardens by labour whose cost would not be charged to the cost of food production. These losses and gains could be measured financially (see Chapter 19).

Case 3. The Extension of a Town Within its Boundaries

For our third case we will take the example worked out in Chapter 12: the comparison by a housing authority of four alternative schemes for housing a population of 56,000 people within the boundaries of a county borough, each scheme having a different net density for re-development. For comparing such alternative schemes the implications for each can be fully listed, or merely the differences in the implications. The former is necessary where, for example, knowledge of the full implications of each scheme or of any of its aspects is required; the latter where it is accepted that the 56,000 people must be housed and it is the density and location only of dwellings which is to be decided. We will make an examination of differences.

The financial appraisal, not only for the dwellings as outlined in Chapter 12 but also for ancillary development, would tell the authority which scheme would be cheapest in capital and annual cost, and the proportion of cost in each scheme which would be borne by exchequer, rates and tenants. In making its decision the authority would also be influenced by the other expenditure that the scheme would cause to fall on the rates. For example, less expenditure by the authority in providing schools, open spaces, community buildings, libraries, etc., would probably be required with the greater concentration because more people could make use of the facilities which existed in the centre, and also less expenditure would be required to run the municipal services of the authorities, the policing, refuse collection, street cleansing, gully emptying. With the greater spread there would be greater cost on new and improved principal traffic roads and also higher costs in maintaining, cleansing and lighting the new roads. It might be, however, that the new mileage justified the use of vehicles and plant which were not previously economical in use, so reducing the average costs of maintenance, etc., throughout the town.

The authority might or might not take into account also the following implications. The more the town spread the more capital expenditure would be required of the gas and electricity boards.

But even in the most expensive scheme it would not follow that the cost per unit of producing the extra gas or electricity would be more than the cost per unit before expansion, and that all current consumers in the locality would thereby need to face an increase in charges. It might be that because of the way in which the existing mains were distributed, or because the existing works had latent capacity, the additional consumption would enable the undertaking to reduce its cost per unit for any of the schemes. This could be calculated.

The bus services on the roads would also probably cost most per head of the population with the greater spread; but here again the result could only be judged in relation to the economies of the existing services. The additional dwellings in any scheme might, for example, be located where new customers used a section of the service previously running at a loss.

In the high density scheme the occupiers of dwellings on the inner sites, including families with children, would have the disadvantage of living in flats on a congested site. In the lower density scheme more of these people would be living on the outskirts where they could, if they wished, have family dwellings; and the remainder would have pleasanter living conditions in the inner areas because of the lower density there.

The lower density schemes would spoil the amenities of more open country than would the higher density schemes, with the greater spread of the town into the countryside. They would also sterilise more agricultural land, but would give rise to more production from houses, gardens and allotments. This could be measured financially (see Chapter 19).

Case 4. The Widening of a River Bridge

A town of about 75,000 people, a county borough, has grown up on both sides of a river. On each side there live roughly the same number of people; but on the east side there is the principal business area and on the west the main industrial area. In consequence there is a considerable flow of traffic in each direction across the single bridge connecting the Class I road on both sides of the river. The bridge is in good condition, but is too narrow for the amount of traffic, and so there is delay. The accident rate is low. It is proposed to widen the bridge and double its traffic capacity. It is thought that there should result no increase in the number of accidents through the speed-up of vehicles.

No income could be expected so that the total expenditure on construction and maintenance, without any offset, would be shared by the county borough council and Ministry of Transport in the ratio of 1 : 3. The financial calculations would show the annual cost that would need to be found out of rates and taxes.

The relief of congestion in the bridge approaches would have certain results, to all of which both the authority and Ministry would normally have regard in deciding to carry out the improvement. There would be an improvement in amenities for persons living and working in the vicinity, in less noise from stationary and slow-moving traffic on the bridge approaches, in less petrol fumes and in less obstruction to pedestrians and vehicles wishing to use the adjoining premises and streets. This would be difficult to measure money terms. Less time would be spent by the police in keeping the approaches under observation and sorting out the traffic. This could be measured financially. There would be a saving of time by the persons using vehicles as the traffic speeded up; and also a saving in the running costs of vehicles arising from fewer stops and starts and higher average speed of travel. These could be measured financially (see Chapter 19).

Case 5. *The Widening of an Existing Trunk Road or the Building of a By-pass*

A trunk road which carries a great deal of long-distance traffic passes through the principal business street of a market town which is a municipal borough. The street is too narrow to carry the traffic, and in consequence there is congestion in the street, danger to the pedestrians who come to shop, difficulties of circulation and parking for the local vehicular traffic, particularly on market day, and noise, throughout the day and night, of lorries passing through. The road also goes through two pleasant villages some two and five miles from the town respectively. Here there have been many accidents and there is considerable noise and nuisance. The alternatives are being considered of widening the trunk road throughout, or of building an eight-mile by-pass to town and villages, whereupon the existing road would become Class II. It is estimated that a substantial amount of the through traffic would use the by-pass. This is another case where the differences between the implications of the proposals can be listed.

The financial calculations would show the cost of carrying out the works and maintaining them, against which there would be no offset by way of income. The widening would probably be less expensive in engineering works than the construction of a new major road through open country, currently estimated at £200,000 to £250,000 per mile, but would be more expensive in compensation for land acquisition and disturbance. The proportion of the cost falling on each of the highway authorities would, however, not be the same in each scheme. Since either the widened or new road would be a trunk road, the Minister of Transport would be responsible for 100 per cent of the cost, in either scheme, of construction and maintenance. Should the by-pass be built, therefore, the Minister would pay in addition 60 per cent of the cost of maintaining the existing route; should the road be widened the local highway authorities would from then on pay nothing at all for maintaining this route.

In making their decision the highway authorities would in addition take account of all the following considerations.

It would not be practicable on widening to re-develop all the adjoining property to ensure that none of it had access to the widened road, so that parts of the widened road would continue to be used for both fast traffic and access to buildings. This would slow up the through traffic, since stopping and waiting vehicles would reduce the effective capacity of the carriage-way. The new route would have none of these disadvantages, since the adjoining frontages could be kept free from development and access permitted only from other principal traffic roads or main streets at intervals. The resulting difference in traffic capacity could be measured.

The widening of the existing road through the town and villages would result in more accidents than if a proportion of present and future traffic were diverted on to the new road. This could be measured in money terms (see Chapter 19).

The widening would destroy the pleasantness of the villages and the character of the market town, whereas the by-pass would leave them physically undisturbed. The widening would ensure into the future the increasing flow of heavy traffic through the town and villages, and so aggravate the current unpleasantness for the people of the town and villages which is caused through their living on a heavy-traffic route. This could hardly be measured in money terms.

If the new road were built there would be a loss of agricultural land and a possible disturbance by severance to farming operations. These could be measured in money terms. There would also be a loss of trade among shopkeepers in the town and villages. This could be estimated in money terms. Should the existing road be widened there would be a loss of assets in the buildings that would be destroyed and loss from interference with trade and production. These could be measured in money terms, and would be reflected in the cost of acquisition.

Finally, there would be savings in time and running costs to vehicle users that would come about through the construction of the by-pass. These could be measured financially (see Chapter 19).

Private and Social Costs in Development

In this chapter we have drawn a distinction between the prospective losses and benefits, financial and otherwise, which would accrue to a developer on the completion of his scheme, and which he would accordingly take into account in deciding his scheme; and those which would accrue to other people, and which he might or might not take into account. This distinction can be made in terms of what the economist refers to as " private and social costs and benefits."[3]

Private costs or benefits relate to all those money losses incurred or gains received by any particular producer or entrepreneur for any economic activity which he is considering at any one particular time. Social costs or benefits are the losses or gains to other people or enterprises which arise from the economic activity, where these people receive no payment from the producer for the loss or make him no payment for the benefit. (This meaning of the term " social costs " differs from that introduced earlier, page 255; we shall from here employ only this second meaning.) Social costs (losses) arise, for example, where helicopters cause considerable interference through noise with living and working conditions around helistops, or where a cement works causes dust to settle on surrounding property so making living conditions unpleasant and washing bills heavier. Social benefits (gains) arise where a property company replaces old and decrepit buildings with new offices and thereby helps to improve the amenity of the town, and so benefit others, or where a department store buys adjoining land for a car park for its customers and so enables other motorists to find parking places more easily.

When a producer or entrepreneur, or a developer or operator, is contemplating some economic enterprise he will estimate his costs and also his benefits. If he is solely interested in the financial outcome of the one enterprise, as our house builder in Case 2, he will take account only of private costs and benefits. If his enterprise is part of a larger undertaking he would take account too of some of the social costs. The industrialist in Case 1 might do so and the local authority in Case 3 would do so, for it would need to consider not only the housing development in question but its relation to other housing schemes. If the producer, entrepreneur, developer or operator is a public body it would also have regard to social costs and benefits because of its responsibilities. The highway authorities in Cases 4 and 5 would take into account the saving in cost to motorists of the schemes and their effect on amenities. The local authority in Case 3 would consider the social benefits in better health that would come from the alternative schemes and their impact on the operation of public services. Even public authorities will not, however, necessarily have regard to all social costs in carrying out their functions. One of the reasons for town planning is that it leads public authorities to have more regard for social costs and benefits than they otherwise would do. We shall discuss this in Chapter 19.

CHAPTER 19

THE PLANNING BALANCE SHEET

The Planning Decision and Planning Balance Sheet—Methods of Measuring the Losses and Benefits of Development in Money Terms—1. The Loss to the Community of Agricultural Land and its Potential Produce—2. The Cost to the Community of Road Accidents—3. The Losses and Gains in Vehicle Operating Costs from Building Fast Traffic Routes—4. The Savings to Users of Vehicles Through Relieving Congestion—Preparing the Planning Balance Sheet—Law and Custom, and Private and Social Costs—Land Planning and Private and Social Costs—The Costs and Gains of Planning.

The Planning Decision and Planning Balance Sheet

THE PLANNING office will need to consider a development proposal or programme on a variety of occasions, as for example when consulting with developers and others in the preparation of a plan, or when considering whether or not to give permission when a formal application is made, or when giving advice on an informal approach by a developer. The decision will in many cases be straightforward and require little deliberation. Where, for example, a new road through a built-up area has been fully investigated and justified by the highway authority, its construction is expected within 10 years and considerable compensation has already been paid in protecting the line, little hesitation is required in resisting a substantial building on the route. Other cases are not so simple, however, as where a school authority and mineral operator are competing to take over good farmland. In such cases some careful weighing up in the planning office of the implications of the development proposal, or of alternative proposals, is necessary. In this chapter we shall deal with the approach to this and some of the problems that are met.

In weighing up the implications the planning authority's viewpoint is not necessarily identical with the developers'; as discussed in Chapter 3, its horizon of interest is always wider and it has different objectives. It will accordingly take into account implications that the developer would not consider to be his concern in making his decision. But it will not necessarily take account of all implications; it will consider some but not all social costs.

Those implications which the planning office will consider can be listed, just as described in Chapter 18, with the costs or losses on one side and the benefits or gains on another, so that these, and their incidence, can be seen in relation to each other. This will facilitate the reaching of a planning decision. This listing we will call the drawing up of a planning balance sheet. From what has been said

of the possible divergence between the viewpoints of a developer
and a planning authority, it is apparent that for a particular proposal
or programme the items in the planning balance sheet will not always
be identical with those in the development balance sheet.

In its drawing up, the items in the balance sheet should be sharply
defined and expressed as quantities to the greatest possible extent.
It makes for greater clarity and precision when considering farmland
to speak in terms of its capacity to produce " A " gallons of milk or
" B " bushels of wheat per acre rather than of it being good, medium
or poor agricultural land, for these quantities, when compared with
norms, give an actual measure of the loss that development of the
farm would entail; and of a road having " C " accidents per mile,
or carrying " D " vehicles per hour at the peak, rather than its
being dangerous or congested, for these quantities, when compared
with norms, are a measure of the defect that requires to be remedied.
Many items, the intangibles, cannot be so expressed in quantities
and must be described in qualitative terms; the unpleasant smells of
a tannery, the nerve-racking noise of revving engines, the unpleasant
impact on the eye of shoddy materials in a building.

Where practicable the losses and benefits should be measured in
money terms, for it then becomes possible to compare certain items
which might otherwise not be susceptible of comparison. If, for
example, the alternatives were being considered of establishing
traffic lights or building a roundabout, at an intersection now
controlled by the police, it would be possible, in money terms, to
compare the current cost to a local authority of policing with the
expected annual costs of construction and maintenance of the
traffic lights or roundabout.

*Methods of Measuring the Losses and Benefits of Development in
Money Terms*

Methods of measuring the losses and benefits implied in a
development proposal in money terms are not yet well advanced.
In illustration of the approach to method four typical items which
are included in the cases described in Chapter 18 are selected
for elaboration. In measuring the losses and benefits it is important
to define their incidence, the persons or bodies on whom they will
fall, since this will affect the standard of measurement. The loss of
farmland, for example, to the community is measured by the value
of the crops that it could produce, but to the farmer by the loss of
livelihood and to the owner by loss of rent.

1. *The Loss to the Community of Agricultural Land and its Potential
    Produce.   Cases 2 and 3*

The loss to the community of 10 acres of good farmland in Case 2
can be assessed in various ways. Some examples are the acreage of
land of a particular agricultural quality or rental value; the number
per acre of livestock that has been kept, or the gallons of milk or

bushels of wheat that have been produced, over recent years; the
farm's gross output, that is the money value of this produce in
wholesale prices, or total farm revenue; the farm's net output,
that is the net money yield to the farmer for his produce, or total
farm revenue after deducting for purchase of livestock, feeding
stuffs and seeds.[1] It is past net output due to agricultural operations
on farms which is commonly used to indicate their potential
productivity. This productivity varies with the type and size of
farms as Table 30 shows.

TABLE 30

*Productivity of Farmland in England and Wales, 1949-50: Measured Gross and
Net Output per Acre*

(a) *By Type of Farming*

Type of Farming Group	Gross Output £'s per acre	Net Output £'s per acre	Net Output as Percentage of Gross Output
1. Grass types:			
Mainly dairying	32·5	22·1	68
Dairying and mixed ...	32·7	24·0	73
Mixed livestock (upland)	15·1	10·4	69
Mixed livestock (lowland)	22·2	13·8	62
All grass types	25·4	17·5	69
2. Intermediate types:			
Mixed farming with substantial dairying ...	31·0	21·5	69
General mixed farming ...	30·4	21·8	72
Corn, sheep and dairying	25·0	19·0	76
All intermediate types ...	28·9	20·9	72
3. Arable types:			
Heavy-land arable ...	24·7	19·4	79
Light-land arable... ...	26·8	20·5	76
Arable and mixed farming with alluvial arable ...	47·0	36·1	77
All arable types	31·6	24·4	77
All type groups (excluding specialist)	28·1	20·3	72
4. Specialist types:			
Market garden—Southern and South-western ...	96·9	86·2	89
Market garden—Wales ...	49·0	40·7	83
Kent hops, fruit and vegetables	68·2	61·0	89
Poultry	236·6	91·4	39
All type groups	28·7	20·9	73

(b) *By Size of Farm*

Size of Farm in Acres				Gross Output £'s per acre	Net Output £'s per acre	Net Output as Percentage of Gross Output
0- 50	...	...	...	...	47·2	31·2	66
51-100	...	...	...	...	33·3	23·3	70
101-150	...	...	...	...	28·4	20·7	51
151-300	...	...	...	...	28·5	20·6	72
301-500	...	...	...	...	27·2	20·1	74
Over 500	...	...	...	...	24·8	19·0	77

Source: Ministry of Agriculture and Fisheries, *Farm Incomes in England and Wales*, 1949-50, Tables 32-35, and see Note 3.

For comparison with these figures it is of interest to note an estimate of the potential productivity of the agricultural land which was shown for development in the initial development plans, within town map areas or likely to be used outside such areas for other purposes such as open cast mineral working. The average gross agricultural output per acre in 1949-50 of this land was thought to be £34·3, and average net output £28·7.[2] This is somewhat higher than the average figures for all types of farming shown in the table, no doubt because these were for output averaged over the whole of England and Wales, including the poorer uplands, while the development shown in development plans will take place in the main in lowland Britain, on farmland of medium quality which produces a diversity of crops.

Column 4 of the table also shows why net and gross output are not indicative of the same aspects of a farm's potential productivity. The same gross output on two farms might require different inputs of livestock, feeding stuffs, etc.[3]

Farmland taken over for housing is not, however, entirely lost to production of foodstuff since it can be expected that some proportion of it will be used for growing garden vegetables and fruit. A pilot survey to establish facts on this was carried out in 1951, over more than 600 gardens covering about 55 acres in suburban London.[4] It was found that while the area under crops varied in individual gardens, in those of houses at densities between 6 and 14 houses to the acre it tended to be relatively constant, ranging from 80 to 40 sq. yds. per house; that gardens with the largest areas under vegetables were found on the soils which could be worked the easiest; that 14 per cent of the area of plots as a whole was used for food crops; and that the area under food crops in council house gardens was more than double that in the private gardens. In another survey, of council housing sites throughout Somerset in 1953, it was found that at densities between 7 and

12 houses to the acre the land used for food production, vegetables, fruit and poultry runs varied erratically between 350 and 150 sq. yds. per house; while at densities between 12 and 20 houses to the acre it fell gradually from about 200 to 100 sq. yds. per house.[5] In order to eliminate some of the variables in the 1951 pilot survey, a further survey was carried out in 1953 over 2,000 gardens in inter-war local authority housing estates, in Bristol, Doncaster, Hull, Southampton and York.[6] The same survey methods were used in all towns. It was not found practicable from the results to establish a mathematical relationship between density and the proportion of plot cultivated, but it was found that the size of plot cultivated did fall with increasing density, and quite sharply between 8 and 12 houses to the acre. The 1951 survey was supported in one respect: over all the gardens about 14 per cent of the total area of plots was used for food production.

When farmland is taken for housing, therefore, only a small proportion of the former agricultural land is kept in food production. The gardens do not, however, produce the same kind of food as farms. Farmland can produce a variety of crops, including meat and cereals; gardens normally produce fruit, vegetables and poultry. In money terms the value of this garden produce is much higher than that of farms. Table 30 illustrates this: the average net and gross output of land devoted to market garden, or hops, fruit and vegetables, or poultry, is much higher than that devoted to grass, arable or mixed farming. It has been suggested, in fact, that the value of the produce from the gardens of an acre of land developed with houses at around 12 to the acre is, at retail prices, £67 10s. per year; and while there are no figures comparable to those in Table 30 for the retail value of farm produce, it has also been suggested that the retail value of the produce on an acre of average farmland would also be about this figure. In other words, if an acre of average farmland is replaced by houses at open densities, the retail value of the foodstuff grown will be about equal that from the farmland which has been taken; or, if we accept the figure of 14 per cent (1/7th) which is noted above as the proportion of the total area of plots, in housing at varying densities, which is devoted to garden produce, then about 1/7th acre or 700 sq. yds. of garden devoted to food produces in retail value as much as the average acre of farmland.[7]

By using these figures we can show how to estimate the measure of the loss of agricultural produce that would result from any of the four alternative schemes for housing 56,000 people, which were worked out in Chapter 12 and used for our Case 3 in Chapter 18. Table 31 sets out the appropriate figures, showing the actual position for Scheme A, that with the maximum average density, and comparing with this in lines 1-11 the differences occasioned by the extra spread in each of Schemes B, C and D. Line 12 of table shows the actual and not differential position for each scheme.

TABLE 31

Comparison of Loss of Agricultural Produce in Four Schemes in Case 3

		Total Scheme A	Excess over Scheme A in		
			B	C	D
		Acres	Acres	Acres	Acres
1.	All land taken on outskirts	954	128	300	368
2.	Agricultural land, say, 90 per cent of 1	859	115	270	331
3.	Land used for houses on inner land*	—	37	125	183
4.	Land used for houses on outer land*	413	67	153	187
5.	Total land used for houses	413	104	278	370
6.	Area of gardens devoted to food production (14 per cent or 5)†	58	15	39	52
7.	Allotments on outskirts included in gross acreage§	46	7	17	21
8.	Total of allotments and of gardens devoted to food production	104	22	56	73
9.	Net loss in food-growing land (line 2 minus line 8)	755	93	214	258
10.	Garden and allotment acreage (line 8) multiplied by 7 to allow for increased value of produce ...	728	154	392	511
11.	Net loss in agricultural produce (line 2 minus line 10)	131	−39	−122	−180
12.	Actual net loss in agricultural produce for each scheme	131	92	9	−49

* Lines 3 and 4 are obtained by dividing the number of habitable rooms in houses in each scheme (Chapter 12) by 60, the net density.

† The area in 5 includes not merely plots but that for roads, etc., which are included in the net density acreage. For simplicity 14 per cent of this is taken in both inner and outer land.

§ 1·5 acres per 1,000 people living on outskirts.

On these figures, Scheme A, which spreads least, would absorb 859 acres of agricultural land which would be offset by 104 acres of food-producing land in gardens or allotments. Scheme D, which spreads most, would take a further 331 acres (39 per cent) in agricultural land, but only 34 per cent more when this is offset by the additional 73 acres that would be producing food in gardens.

The picture is very different, however, if the food production is considered in terms of its estimated retail value rather than in terms of acres. In Schemes A and B there would still be a net loss of food production, to the extent of the agricultural produce that could be grown respectively on 131 and 92 acres of farmland. But in Scheme C the retail value of the farm food would be about the same before and after the houses were built; and in Scheme D there would be a net gain in food production amounting to the produce that could be grown on about 50 acres of farmland.

In our example, therefore, in terms of acreage the greater the spread the more land goes out of cultivation. But in terms of food production the greater the spread the more food is produced and, incidentally, there is devoted to food production a greater amount of labour whose cost is not charged to the national income.

Our example has been given to illustrate method. Additional factors may have to be considered in analysing a particular case. In our discussion, for example, we have ignored the possibility that the new housing might be in fact displacing market garden and not arable land. This may come about either directly, as where the housing site is a market garden, or indirectly, as where it is reckoned that the increase in the number of gardens under cultivation will result in a decrease in demand for market garden produce, and in consequence the substitution of farming for market garden land. There also needs to be considered the possibilities of a generous provision of allotments for flat dwellers near their homes. For example, if 36 houses were built at 12 houses to the acre they would take 3 acres of land of which, say, 0·4 acres (14 per cent) would be devoted to producing food. But if instead 36 family flats (three, four and five habitable rooms as in our example) were built at 200 habitable rooms per acre, and the 0·4 acres provided nearby in addition for allotments, they would take 1 acre. Both schemes would result in the same garden produce, and the flat scheme would leave in agriculture 2 acres of land which would, in the house scheme, have gone into lawns, flowerbeds, roads, etc.

2. *The Cost to the Community of Road Accidents* (*Cases* 1 *and* 5)

Traffic accidents result in loss in having injured persons kept from work and others looking after them, in killing people who have a contribution to make to the community, in destroying capital assets and in the misery and suffering of the victims and their dependants. It is possible to measure in money terms all these losses except the last. It has been estimated that road accidents between 1935 and 1938 in Great Britain cost the community in this way about £60,000,000 per annum at pre-war money values, and that the same number of accidents in 1946 would have cost £100,000,000.[8] In these figures are included the loss of income through human injuries, including fatal ones, amounting to about nine-tenths of the total; the damage to vehicles, including the cost incurred through inability to use the unrepaired vehicles; the damage to birds, animals, fences, walls, etc.; and the cost of administration in police attention, and legal and insurance costs. From this data it has been estimated that " on average, at present prices [1949] each serious, including fatal, accident costs about £1,230, each slight injury accident about £54, each non-injury accident £18. The economic cost of each fatality is £1,900, of each serious injury £1,020, and of each slight injury £30."

Where it is possible to guess from accident records the number of accidents that would be averted by a particular improvement, the data in these estimates can be used to place a money value on the prospective saving. By their use it has been estimated that a roundabout costing £8,000 at Warrington Road, Golborne, Lancashire, by reducing the average number of accidents per year by 2-6, would save £1,485 per year; and an improvement to cross-roads at Singleton, Lancashire, at a cost of £280 has reduced the average accident rate per year by 2·33, so saving £1,656 per year. Six other improvements carried out at a total cost of £53,000 resulted in a reduction in the number of accidents from 58 to 22 per annum.[9]

3. The Losses and Gains in Vehicle Operating Costs from Building Fast Traffic Routes (Case 5)

The costs of operating a vehicle may be divided into running costs which are incurred while the vehicle is on the road; and fixed or standing charges which must be paid whether the vehicle is running on the road or not.[10] Running costs depend on the number of miles that are covered, and vary with the speed, and with the amount of stopping and starting that arises, for example, from congestion. Fixed charges are spread over the time the vehicle is operating, independently of its speed.

In Case 5, vehicles which travelled on the by-pass instead of on the old route would incur heavier running costs as they would be travelling faster, for at uniform speeds running costs are lowest for speeds of about 20 m.p.h. and increase as speeds depart from this. But as against this they would save the running costs incurred on the old route in stopping and starting. For a particular journey their fixed charges would be less since travelling time would be saved. Whether at higher speeds there would be heavier or lighter running costs, and how much saving there would be in fixed charges, would need to be calculated according to the circumstances.

This kind of calculation was made by a committee which set out to show that the building of motorways would result in a saving of vehicle operating costs.[11] They investigated a particular stretch of trunk road, between St. Albans and Coventry, which is heavily used by industrial traffic and which would be relieved by one of the motorways included in the Minister of Transport's 1946 programme. They took a 24-hour census; and in the absence of an origin and destination survey they assumed that 90 per cent of the heavy goods vehicles would use the motorway (2,059), as well as 60 per cent of the light goods' vehicles (875) and an uncertain amount of other traffic.

The committee then compared the total operating costs (running costs and fixed charges per mile) for these kinds of vehicles (3-ton and 5-ton light petrol engine and 10-ton and 13-ton heavy oil engine) for the speeds they might have on the motorway with those for the average current speed on the existing route (24 m.p.h. for the lighter vehicles and 16 m.p.h. for the heavier). In all four cases the optimum speed on the motorway was 40 m.p.h. and the theoretical savings compared with costs on the existing route were:

Light petrol engine, 3 tons	...	...	...	1·06d. per mile (17·4 per cent)
Light petrol engine, 5 tons	...	...	...	1·11d. per mile (15·3 per cent)
Heavy oil engine, 10 tons	...	...	...	3·98d. per mile (32·4 per cent)
Heavy oil engine, 13 tons	...	...	...	4·25d. per mile (31·6 per cent)

These figures, multiplied by the number of vehicles, gave the theoretical savings in operating costs per mile run for light and heavy goods vehicles, to which was added 50 per cent to account for the uncertain amount of other traffic; some £15,000 in all per mile run. In other words, on these assumptions, if the motorway was the same length as the existing route, vehicle users would benefit by these amounts per mile.

4. *The Savings to Users of Vehicles Through Relieving Congestion (Cases 3 and 4)*

The calculation just described did not take full account of the savings in operating costs of vehicles, nor of the saving in time to drivers, through the avoidance of the congested conditions on the existing route. These will now be considered.

Time is lost to vehicle users through traffic congestion because the average speed of journeys is reduced. For illustration, in the autumn of 1950, mid-morning and mid-afternoon traffic on 36 miles of Central London streets averaged only 10·5 miles per hour, and was as low in some places as 5 miles per hour, 30 per cent of the journey time being spent stationary at intersections; while in five suburban London High Streets during weekday business hours the speed averaged 15-18 miles per hour.[12] Where a road improvement is aimed at relieving traffic congestion, the average amount of time that would be saved per vehicle can be gauged by comparing the estimated speed of traffic after the improvement with that which takes place before. The saving to the different classes of vehicle user would not be of equal significance in economic life. Persons going to and from work, shops and cinemas would save their personal as opposed to working time, and would have more time for leisure and less nervous strain from urban life. This could not be measured financially. Where the saving to vehicle users would result in more time being available for work of any kind connected with economic life, or less time spent on the same amount of work, the saving would appear in the decreased cost of production of goods and services. To obtain a measure of this saving it would be necessary to know what number of persons in vehicles currently using the road are engaged in economic processes, what time they would save, how it would be used and what the value of their output in this time would be. This would be impossible without close questioning of drivers and passengers. A partial and rough measure of the loss can, however, be obtained by abstracting from the total number of vehicles the number of commercial and public transport vehicles, by calculating the time that would be saved by their drivers, and by multiplying this by a money value per hour.[13]

Methods of estimating the saving in operating costs of vehicles that would come from relieving traffic congestion are being investigated, with many other aspects of this problem, by the Road Research Laboratory of the Department of Scientific and Industrial Research. Two results from their investigations are relevant here. Firstly, when particular vehicles were used in the same streets in Central London, in busy and slack periods, the journey speeds being roughly twice as fast in the slack as in the busy periods, the extra fuel consumption per mile in the busy period was as follows:[14]

Vehicle	Proportionate Fuel Consumption per Mile
	Busy hours/Slack hours
Small private car	1·37
Large private car	1·51
Goods vehicle (3 tons unladen):	
(a) Unladen	1·23
(b) Laden	1·30

Secondly, if a particular street intersection in London were improved for a capital cost of £7,750, the estimated annual money savings in fuel would be £130, in time of buses £640, and in time of goods vehicles £160, totalling £930. This would show a return of 12 per cent on the capital cost. In addition there would be annual savings in the time of the occupants of cars, and of passengers in buses and taxis, totalling some 11,600 man-hours.[15]

These measures of the cost of our present road conditions, and those described above, give point to the statement of Thos. H. MacDonald, U.S. Commissioner of Public Roads, that " We pay for good roads whether we have them or not, and we pay more for them if we do not have them."[16]

Preparing the Planning Balance Sheet

While the planning office is responsible for marshalling the relevant items in the planning balance sheet, it must rely to a great extent, for the measurement in money terms of the items themselves, upon developers and interests affected by the proposals and other expert sources. It should not be necessary in the office, when reliable estimates from developers and operators can be expected, to prepare estimates, for example, of the costs of building dwellings at different densities, of constructing different lengths of roads, of the productivity of different pieces of agricultural land, of the economics of alternative schemes for providing gas, electricity or bus transport, of the economics of building offices and shops. In the planning office there are necessary, however, the skills which are required to use such estimates, and to weigh them up.

The planning balance sheet is clearly not a balance sheet in either the individual or social accounting sense. The items are not all of a capital nature; the losses and benefits which accrue to various people and groups of people are considered, and not just those which accrue to a particular individual or company, as in private accounting, or to the country as a whole, as in social accounting; there may be double counting, as where in a proposal to take over agricultural land the loss to both the community and farmer are taken into account; there may be omitted certain implications of the proposal because the planning authority does not take account of all social costs. No simple balance can, therefore, be struck. It may not even be possible to strike a balance among all items which can be translated into money terms, for they may represent costs or benefits to different people. If, for example, when considering the alternatives of constructing a roundabout or traffic lights at an intersection, it was estimated that the roundabout would cost £200 per annum in construction and maintenance costs more than the traffic lights but would save motorists £200 per annum in time and vehicle operating costs, would it be true to say that for this scheme the cost balances benefit? Can £200 of the highway authority's expenditure, spread over taxpayers and ratepayers, be balanced against £200 of motorists' money, spread over the chance users of the intersection?

A similar difficulty arises where claims for the use of a particular piece of land are being balanced against each other as where, for example, a housing authority is considering either of two farms for development. The first is, say, on low-lying clay, with a net output per acre of £19 per annum and a rental value of £3; the second is well-drained gravel with a net output per acre of £29 per annum and a rental value of £5. The clay would require in drainage and development costs some £300 per acre more than the gravel. The authority would prefer the gravel as the cheaper and better site, but would be prepared to meet additional cost to keep off the better farmland. Faced, however, with the need to provide dwellings at low rents, it could not undertake too much additional expense. Can the planning authority, in balancing the claims of agriculture and housing, expect the housing authority to pay £300 more in capital costs to save potential produce valued at £10 of net output per acre per annum, or £2 per acre in rental value? And if not, at what point should it decide that the better agricultural land be given up for development rather than the poorer? Ignoring other possible considerations, such as the amount of capital sunk in the farms and their distance from centres of work and recreation, how are the money values of these items to be compared so that the planning decision can be made?

A necessary preliminary for comparison is either to translate the capital cost of the extra site works into annual terms, or to capitalise the difference in net product or rent. The former could be done, for example, by taking loan charges at current interest rates for local authority loans, or perhaps the market rate of return, if there is one, for investment in such works: that is £300 at, say, 4 per cent = £12. As to the latter, at the same rate per cent the difference in net product capitalised would equal £250, and in rent capitalised would equal £50. But are these figures comparable when calculated? From the housing authority's viewpoint the extra expenditure on works is an additional burden which must be borne by exchequer, rates or tenants. From the farmer's viewpoint the benefits of the extra farm produce will go to himself and the landlord. From the national point of view the extra expenditure on works is an unnecessary use of men and materials in the building industry; but it would, on the other hand, result in the need to import less food than if the better farm were used. The national standard of living would thus be affected, as some think adversely for " the improvement of standard of living can take place only if, as technique and economic conditions change, resources (land, labour and capital) are not deliberately impeded in their movement from uses which yield a small return of goods to those which yield a larger return."[17]

One suggestion for making the comparison referred to, that of the food replacement yardstick, has been put forward by Dr. G. P. Wibberley: will the loss of food resulting from the use of the better farm be more or less than what could be made up by investing the £300 per acre in the improvement of other agricultural land elsewhere or in the reclamation of unused land? If it is more, then the £300 should be spent on developing the clay land. If it is less, then the better farmland should be developed and some other land improved agriculturally by spending on it the £300 per acre not spent on the clay land.[18]

Figures quoted by Dr. Wibberley suggest that the loss of food resulting from the use of the gravel, £10 per annum per acre in net output, could not be replaced by spending the £300 capital, for each acre used for housing, in upgrading improvable upland farms. In 1949-50 these uplands had an average gross annual output per acre of £12 and average net output of £7·8, and it would take an annual expenditure per acre of £40 to upgrade the land to produce

£20·5 per acre gross or £13·3 per acre net. It would thus be necessary to improve nearly 2 acres of upland, at about £80 per annum, to replace the loss of £10 per acre in net output, an annual sum far in excess of the annual interest at, say, 4 per cent on the £300. But figures quoted by Dr. Wibberley and others suggest, however, that the £300 per acre might go a long way towards restoring to agriculture much land made derelict by mineral excavation, or to reclaiming coastal marsh or dunes.[19]

This line of reasoning can only be used in making a planning decision if in fact there is the intention of spending the £300, where it is not spent on works, on improving poorer land. All the while it is not, and there is no current machinery for allocating money in this way, it could not be listed as an implication of the development and brought into the planning balance sheet.

The same kind of problem (that is, the balancing of the claim of one use against another for particular land), with mineral-bearing instead of agricultural land, arose in the design of Corby New Town. The housing sites which were most conveniently related to the steel works and to the town centre were on land containing ironstone deposits, of which under each acre there was an average of 20,000 tons, worth about £13,000 to the industrialists.[20] If the housing were placed on the convenient sites this ironstone would be lost to the industrialists and the country, and would need to be replaced by deposits further away from the steelworks, which would be more expensive to haul over the longer distances. If the ironstone was not to be sterilised by building, less suitable housing land would have to be used which would involve increased development costs. The loss of ironstone and the extra development costs could be put in financial terms; but how could the value to the national economy, and to the industrialists and workpeople, of these deposits be compared to the extra housing costs that would be placed upon the exchequer, rates and tenants?

These difficulties illustrate how the weighing up of the items in the balance sheet, even where they can be reduced to money terms, cannot be simply done by striking a money balance. The reaching of a planning decision is facilitated, none the less, by defining as many of the items as clearly as possible, and where possible in money terms. For one thing, in making a planning decision, the losses or gains in money terms to particular individuals or sections of the community which would result from it can be more clearly defined and appreciated; for another, when benefit and cost are expressed in money terms they can most easily be related to each other and compared for alternative schemes.

Law and Custom, and Private and Social Costs

If the effect of land planning control is not taken into account, the incidence of the losses incurred and benefits received from a development project, that is the persons or bodies on whom they will fall, is decided by the law and custom of the country. For example, since the building bye-laws require adequate soil drainage of buildings, the cost of providing it falls clearly on the developer and consumer, and the community is saved costs that would otherwise arise through disease; private costs are more and social costs less than if there were no bye-laws. Law and custom is continually changing in this respect. Some examples will be given in illustration.

The social costs that arise through the excessive production of smoke in parts of some cities, for example of Manchester, Coventry and the City of London, are being transformed into private costs by the introduction of smokeless zones wherein, after a certain time from the passing of a private Act, all property occupiers in the zone must use smokeless fuel or adapt their apparatus so that smoke is no longer emitted. It is of interest that one authority decided not to introduce the smokeless zone precisely because they thought it would be too onerous on council house tenants to ask them to burn expensive smokeless fuel; the costs they thought, should remain social ones. Additional kinds of measures to reduce the total smoke in heavily populated areas by about four-fifths in 10 to 15 years were recommended in the Beaver Report on Air Pollution, and to implement many of the recommendations a Clean Air Bill was introduced in 1955.[21]   The Bill proposed that where a local authority declares a Smoke Control Area it shall pay seven-tenths of the cost of adaptations to any private dwelling in the Area (not being a new dwelling) which are carried out to eliminate emission of smoke, and that the exchequer will in turn pay four-sevenths of this. The costs of adapting these dwellings would therefore be partly social ones. Social costs which arise from the dereliction produced when ironstone is worked by open-cast methods are being partially transformed into private costs by the ironstone restoration fund. Into this exchequer, operators and landowners pay a fixed contribution per ton of extracted ironstone, the fund being used to secure costly restoration by meeting its excess cost over a standard rate per acre.[22] Part of the costs which arise from aeroplanes are social and not private as a result of the Order in Council providing that no manufacturer can be sued for noise nuisance from testing jet engines on airfields, and of the Crown accepting liability for compensating damage due to supersonic bangs.[23] Social costs which now arise from the traffic congestion caused by motorists parking in traffic roads in London should, it has been suggested, be transformed to private costs by preventing such parking and making motorists pay economic charges for parking off the streets.[24] The incidence as between landlord and tenant of the cost of dilapidation and waste caused by tenants, and of the benefit of improvements carried out by them, has continually changed with alterations in the law relating to landlord and tenant.[25] The Town and Country Planning Act, 1947, shifted the incidence of compensation for injury to, or acquisition of, development values in land in a locality from ratepayers to tax-payers; while the Town and Country Planning Act, 1954, shifted back from taxpayers to ratepayers the incidence for acquisition of development values which are established in claims.

In addition to changing the law Parliament can decide in other ways whether costs will be private or social. It can do so, for example, by taxation. A tax could be levied on smoke producers and the proceeds used to make good damage by smoke; or particularly heavy local rates could be levied on industrialists and other em-ployers in congested towns, and the proceeds used to carry out the street improvements which their traffic make necessary.

Land Planning and Private and Social Costs

We can restate the case for land planning in terms of private and social costs by saying that there is a need for public considera-tion of the social costs of development over and above the consideration they obtain as a result of the non-planning law and custom of the country. Experience has shown that if only private costs are considered in the carrying out of development, plus those social costs which private and public developers elect to consider, or are forced to consider because of this law and custom, then the result is not as good as it could be for the well being of the com-munity. This statement emphasises that it is not only land planning which is concerned with social costs of development but also the law relating to such matters as public health, property and taxation.[26]

The planning decision often results in an apportionment of costs between the developer and the community which is different from that which would have obtained without planning powers. In general, planning powers are used to supplement those of other public authorities in imposing requirements on developers, as we have earlier described, in order to turn social costs into private costs. Developers of new office buildings in the City of London, for example, are required under planning powers to provide car parks in their buildings, so as to reduce in some measure the social costs of traffic congestion and of providing for such parking at public expense. When used in this way planning results in an increase in private costs, which will be met by the landowner or consumer according to conditions in the market for new offices. But in securing planned development, planning often secures a reduction of private costs, as where a more compact expansion of a town leads to less cost to a local authority in providing sewers, or where industrial zoning leads to more efficient industrial production.

In short, therefore, land planning aims at a reduction in costs, both private and social, and at an apportionment between private and social costs which is in accord with current social conscience.

The Costs and Gains of Planning

It will be useful to close and in some measure to summarise this chapter by discussing the often formulated question of how to assess the cost of planning. There is no simple answer to the question since so much depends on the aspect that is being considered.

Most of the development which takes place in fulfilment of a plan would have taken place if there were no plan, although perhaps not quite in the same form, since planning ensures that development will take place in certain places rather than others, and in a planned rather than unplanned way. Planning, it can therefore be argued, costs nothing; or, rather, merely the cost of the salaries and establishment of the central and local planning staff, of their necessary materials and overhead expenses.

This gives too simple a picture. Planning may prohibit development on a piece of land altogether, or a particular kind of development in favour of another, or secure some changed form of development. In consequence, there may be losses or gains to individuals, certain sections of the community or the community as a whole. Planning, therefore, does cost somebody something, although taken over the years it should lead to less private as well as less social costs than would have been incurred without it. For while developers may lose in certain respects under planned development, they gain in others. It is only necessary to consider how sewerage, water, education and transport authorities would set about their programmes of development without a development plan for their areas, and with only their individual forecasts to guide them as to the likely development in those areas. With a plan they can plan ahead their works with much more confidence, and so avoid some of the costs of wrong anticipation, and of the over-provision and under-provision of services. The London Transport Executive must be in a better position in preparing its programme than was the pre-war London Passenger Transport Board which could obtain little guidance from plans in anticipating the direction and spread of suburban growth; and school authorities must be in a better position than those who in the 1930's provided insufficient school places for suburban growth in the early years and too many later on.[27]

It is sometimes argued that although planning decisions may increase the cost of development, the extra costs should not be attributed to planning, for developers must accept the economic and social framework which has introduced planning, and accept as normal the costs of developing in a planned way. What development might have cost without planning would then become of the same academic interest as the cost of a factory which did not incorporate the safety requirements and fireproof construction required by law.

It is an extension of this argument to include as one of the gains of planning the cost of not planning: the avoidable cost that would accrue if there were no thought given to securing orderly development. Planning can often prevent the erection of buildings on sites which are later required for some public purpose and, therefore, the expense of their subsequent demolition, and also the waste arising from the uneconomic layout of services or the unnecessary sterilisation of mineral-bearing land or farmland. In arguing for the use of town planning powers in 1914, J. S. Nettlefold pointed out, with other examples, that in the 10 years previous the City of Birmingham had spent £800,000 (pre-1914 money values) on street widenings, an expenditure which could have been avoided through foresight.[28] Planning can also help in preventing the deterioration of areas into slum and so help to avoid some of the cost to the public purse which is caused by slums. Studies of blighted and slum areas in American cities show that local and central government costs per head are above the average in such areas for such things as firefighting, public health, treatment of disease and policing. This is partly due to the poverty of the people in the area, which will not be remedied merely by land planning; but in part it is due to the effect of the poor physical conditions which might be. Fire hazard is increased; congestion of people and poor sanitary conditions facilitate the spread of infectious disease; dampness and lack of sunlight and daylight cause poor health; depressing home conditions and the lack of parks and playgrounds promote juvenile and adult delinquency.[29]

In avoiding prospective liabilities that can be avoided by the exercise of foresight, planning can be said to pay always, for " a city must pay for planning or lack of planning."[30] But since the liability that is avoided would sometimes fall on the individual, and sometimes on a local authority or the national income, it is relevant to ask " Whom does it pay?"[31] This question is relevant in considering certain costs which are always charged to planning but which, it can be argued, are not really the costs of planning. Firstly, there is the compensation payable for the reduction of land values because of planning restrictions. While the restrictions are imposed in the interest of planned development, the benefit of the restrictions falls on particular developers, owners or occupiers who do not contribute specifically towards the compensation. The prevention of building on agricultural land, for example, upon which there is an established claim for development value which must, in consequence, be paid, ensures a livelihood to the farmer, more home-grown food for the country and a bounty to other landowners who receive any shifted building value. The total costs to the community may be the same as if no plan were introduced, or even less; but planning is charged with a cost which is the result of private property ownership and the current state of social conscience with regard to compensation for property rights. Secondly, planning is inevitably charged with the cost of protecting amenity; but the cost of preserving a Georgian house or a clump of trees is really the price the community pays for protecting its heritage, and this could well be the responsibility of some Commission of Natural and Historic Treasures. In the absence of such a body the responsibility and cost fall onto planning. Thirdly, there is the cost which is charged to planning in the comprehensive re-development of war-damaged and obsolete urban areas. As we have seen, the principle behind the financial calculations for comprehensive re-development is for the planning account to bear the cost of writing down values where the cost of acquiring land is higher than that of the new values which will be created on it. This is really an accountancy convenience, and one which is welcome in divorcing new uses from land cost; but it can be argued that the total costs of land should be attributable to the particular new uses in question and not really to planning.

PART V

PROGRAMMES AND THE DEVELOPMENT PLAN

INTRODUCTORY

After the review in Parts II, III and IV of the factors which make for realistic programmes, Chapter 20 enumerates examples of development programmes which have been prepared for their own purposes by central and local government, other public bodies and private industry and trade. The characteristics of development programmes which are of interest in land planning are discussed. This leads in Chapter 21 to a description of the kind of programmes which planning authorities can reasonably seek from developers.

Chapter 21 discusses also the other programming work carried out in a planning office which leads to the plan being a programme for planned development. Six different aspects of the work are enumerated and described. Particular attention is given to the possibilities an authority has for testing whether the total volume of work in its plan is capable of being realised. The possibilities are examined for each of the five factors dealt with in Chapters 5 to 9. It is found that they do not exist for all the factors, but that tests can be devised in relation to the amount of local authority works, the land available for development and the amount of building and civil engineering labour that will be available for new construction in the locality. These tests are described.

CHAPTER 20

PROGRAMMES OF DEVELOPMENT

Examples of development programmes: Programmes and the National Budget, Programmes and local authority budgets, Programmes of ad hoc Bodies, Programmes in Industry and Trade—There are Programmes and Programmes—Flexibility of Programmes—Progressing of Development.

Examples of development programmes

DEVELOPMENT programmes are not required from developers merely for the purpose of development plans; as discussed in Chapter 1 they are prepared by them for their own purposes. We will give examples of such programmes and then describe some of their characteristics which are of interest in land planning.

Programmes and the National Budget. The Chancellor's annual Budget, being based on departmental estimates, is in part a statement of intended expenditure on all development which the Government will undertake directly, or will assist by way of grant in the forthcoming year. For the estimates to be submitted to the Treasury by the preceding November it means that in the discussions leading to them works are considered that may not be initiated for perhaps eighteen months ahead. These discussions are held against the background of programmes which look longer ahead than this; each year the departments also send to the Treasury their tentative forecasts of expenditure for the forthcoming three years, and discuss with them their investment hopes for at least two years, and in some cases perhaps five years, ahead. Furthermore, the departments in their discussions with *ad hoc* bodies or local authorities about the works which they sponsor must also look beyond the coming financial year to facilitate the smooth fulfilment of programmes. For example, since power stations may take three to five years to build, and often more, the Ministry of Fuel and Power will agree with the British Electricity Authority that additional capacity to a stated number of kilowatts can be brought into operation some five to six years ahead; and the Minister of Education in the autumn of every year agrees the programme for the forthcoming financial year with education authorities, and also a provisional programme for the following year: that is for work to start up to two and a half years ahead.[1]

Programmes and local authority budgets. Local authority annual budgets summarise the intended expenditure on development in the forthcoming year out of rate income, but often exclude such ex-

enditure which is not to be financed out of the rates, such as that
elating to trading undertakings. In the preparation of estimates
by the different departments, and discussions leading up to the
budgets, works are thus discussed which may be initiated up to
ighteen months ahead.

Some authorities carry out their annual budgeting against longer
erm forecasts of up to perhaps five years, and a local government
epresentative has suggested a 10 year budget.[2]   This longer
erm budgeting is on either a revenue or a capital basis. For the
atter, programmes of capital expenditure over a period are approved in principle by Council, forecasts being made of prospective
oan charges, maintenance and operating costs, and income. Other
authorities, while not preparing long-term capital budgets, make
heir annual revenue budget in the light of long-term estimates of
he liability for debt already incurred, expected exchequer grants,
expected expenditure on services and future rate product.

Before the war the Minister of Health on several occasions urged
upon local authorities the policy of making every year a survey of
heir probable capital commitments for at least five years ahead.[3]
By doing so. he suggested, they could take a reasonably long view
of their future requirements; could arrange their programme of
capital works in some order of priority to assist in securing smooth
progress of operations; could take advantage of periods when the
building industry was not otherwise fully occupied; and could assist
n attempting to stabilise employment in the building industry. The
Minister followed up, in 1938, by asking local authorities to prepare
a programme of capital works for the five years commencing April
1938.   The programme was to cover all kinds of local authority
works; and each project was to be enumerated with its estimated
cost, the amounts to be spent in each of the five years, the annual
charges on the loans it would be necessary to raise and the amounts
hat would fall on the rates.   After the war, to assist in economic
planning, this request was revived.   Local authorities were asked
o prepare programmes of capital expenditure, and also of expendi-
ure on the repair and upkeep of capital works, for the three years
beginning 1st April, 1946.   It was recognised that because of un-
settled conditions at the time authorities would find it difficult to
forecast expenditure for as long as five years ahead, but it was
hoped to be able to extend the period to five years later on.   It was
asked that the programmes be prepared in a realistic spirit; that is,
o take into account the great shortage of building materials and
abour and the excess of demand for them over supply.   In 1947
another three-year programme was asked for; but in 1948 no further
request for programmes was made when it was realised how much
n excess of the likely available capital investment resources were
he combined programmes of the authorities.   The request was

revived in 1954, for programmes from the larger authorities
schemes for the ensuing six to seven years (not housing or education
estimated to cost over £50,000 each.[4]

Local authorities before and since the war have also been en
couraged to prepare programmes for individual services. Three
year school building and improvement programmes were asked fo
in 1925 and 1931, and long-term education development plans i
1945,[5] Five-year slum clearance programmes were asked for
1930 and 1933; and the request for such programmes was renewe
in 1954.[6] Five-year programmes for the improvement of existin
main roads and the construction of new ones was asked for in 192
and 1935. A very ambitious ten-year road building programm
was announced by the Minister of Transport in 1946, and a mor
modest one, looking several years ahead, in 1953. In 1954 th
speeding up of this programme was announced, to the extent of tw
to three times the rate of expenditure envisaged in the 1953 pro
gramme, and a four-year programme and further speeding up wa
announced early in 1955.[7] In 1950 housing authorities were aske
to make arrangements " for the selection and acquisition of sites o
a planned basis and covering a forward period of at least thre
years," and were encouraged to make these arrangements in th
expectation that they could maintain for the coming three years th
rate at which they were currently building houses.[8]

Programmes of ad hoc *Bodies.* As has been indicated, *ad ho
bodies also prepare annual estimates and budgets against the back
ground of longer term programmes. For example, in 1950 th
National Coal Board published a fifteen-year programme whic
was designed to increase output, improve productivity and reduc
costs, and was based on estimates of the likely demand for each kin
of coal and the location of the demand.[9] In 1951-52 this programm
was considered in relation to that of the British Electricity Authorit
and Gas Council in an attempt to frame a national policy on the us
of fuel and power resources.[10] The B.B.C. prepare annually a three
four or five-year budget against the framework of a periodical te
year forecast of their long-term policy.[11] The Gas and Electricit
Boards periodically prepare a programme of contemplated work
for a period of three to five years ahead, and in 1954, as a basis fc
obtaining his approval to borrowing a further £1,300 million, the
submitted to the Minister comprehensive programmes of the likel
development in the industries up to 1960.[12] The Transport Com
mission published in 1955 its plan to spend £1,200 million over 1
years or so on modernisation of the railway system.[13] The Elec
tricity Authorities published in 1955 a programme for building 1
nuclear power stations at a cost of £30 million over the followin
10 years.[14] The Iron and Steel Board obtained Government ap
proval to the expenditure of over £250 million between 1953 an

958 for the modernisation and expansion of the iron and steel
ndustry, and in 1955 were already examining longer term issues,
ncluding investment for the 1960's.[15]

Programmes in Industry and Trade. Trading and manufacturing
oncerns have no uniform practice as to budgeting but they are led
o forecasting in a variety of ways. For example, several motor-
ar manufacturers announced long-term plans of expansion in 1954
n order to compete with rivals at home and abroad. A chemical
ompany may wish to buy land for future winning of minerals and
vill prepare perhaps 20 to 40 year plans to guide it in so doing.
Companies which go into the market for capital will need to devise
nd announce programmes of expansion in order to attract it. A
epartment store in a shopping street will prepare plans for extending
ts buildings as a guide to negotiations for buying adjoining property.
An industrialist, in buying or leasing a site on a new trading estate,
vill look ahead in order to decide how much land to take.

Firms vary enormously, in their size, the kind of goods or
ervices produced, methods of financing, kind of capital goods they
equire for their production or trade. The programmes they prepare
vill vary too, therefore, in the period these cover, in their detail
nd general character. Firms have, however, one thing in common:
hey rarely make public as much information about their pro-
rammes as do public bodies. They do not need to, and prefer not
o for business reasons.

Another general feature of the programming by industry and
rade is that whilst their long-term programmes are more difficult
o frame than those of public bodies, for they are coping with more
ncertainties, their short term programmes are often prepared with
reater precision. Their actual expenditure of money must be justi-
ed more carefully.

*here are Programmes and Programmes

While the term programme has been used to describe all these
precasts of intentions, aims and aspirations with regard to develop-
ent, it is clear that they are not all equally likely to be carried out.
rogrammes in annual budgets are most certain of implementation:
hey are " acts of will " and " directives to action,"[16] for money
ithin the control of developers will be spent by them within a
articular time in the initiation or continuance of works. The three-
ear housing programmes of local authorities are fairly certain of
eing carried out since government sanction to the buying of app-
opriate land, and authority for erecting the appropriate number of
ouses, are almost assured. Far from certain in their implementation
owever were the education development plans, the local authority
946-49 programme of capital works and the Minister of Transport's
946 road programme. These were also forecasts of intention; but

they did not take sufficient account of what in fact was likely to happen. They were not based on a realistic forecast of either the amount likely to be spent by government or of the capital invest ment resources that would be available. This was recognised by the Minister of Transport, when introducing the 1946 road pro gramme, when he stated " the rate at which it would be possible to initiate and proceed with work will depend on the priority which is found possible to give the different schemes as part of the tota investment activity of the country and in particular on a number o factors, including the availability of qualified technical staff and o suitable labour (which will vary in different areas) and the amoun of financial provision which can be made."[17] The 1955 road programme is far more certain of implementation since it has been prepared in relation to the exchequer grants that the governmen are prepared to pay, and there is not the same pressure on capita investment resources that existed in early post-war years.

Flexibility of Programmes

A programme is not a prophecy but a forecast of what is expected to take place. But no one preparing a programme can be sure of its implementation. However thoroughly it is prepared, and however closely it is attached to ascertainable financial and economic realities, its realisation may be frustrated in one or more of several ways; and over the past few uncertain years there have been so many cases of programmes going awry, even those implicit in annual budgets. This, however, is no argument against formulat ing a programme. To those local authorities in the thirties who resisted the Minister's pressure for programmes, because they found it difficult to look ahead, the reply came that the objection was " based on misunderstanding of the purpose of the estimate. The programme is not intended to be rigid except in its items for the current year. Its purpose is to serve as a guide and it should be revised annually at the time when the revenue estimates are under consideration."[18]

The implementation of programmes may be frustrated by the unexpected which requires their deferment, alteration or abandon ment. An economic recession may cause unemployment in one-industry town and result in the abandonment there of a housing programme and the reconstruction of a sewage works; or a revision in the line of a major road may alter the design of an adjoining resi dential area and perhaps lead to a change in the use of the land.

With the need for programmes on the one hand, and the possibi lity of having to alter them on the other, flexibility is required in the mind and purpose of the developer. He needs to formulate clearly the assumptions on which the programme is based and be able to recognise when changes in circumstances indicate the desirability or necessity of its revision or, perhaps, abandonment. A programme which is rigidly adhered to may be found to be point-less on its execution because of changed circumstances: the road, for example, that is built for traffic which has taken to a different route since the original traffic survey was made. There are, conversely, disadvantages in a programme being too flexible. If it is, the developer himself cannot proceed with working out the necessary details of construction, finance and organisation. His failure to do so may have its effect on other developers, as where the designer of a building, near the site for which runs the route of a projected main road, is forced to scrap successive schemes following changes in the line or elevation of the road. Flexibility therefore is desirable and essential; but there can be too much or too little of it. The necessary degree is difficult to generalise about; and there are certain kinds of programmes in which less flexibility is possible or permissible than others.

In every scheme there is a point at which it must be finalised and adhered to. This is the point of " no return," where it would be less expensive to adhere to the programme than to change it to some later alternative which comes to be preferred. It is the point familiar to all architects, engineers and surveyors concerned with the design of works. It is familiar, too, to the Coal Board who have stated: " Once a mining project has been started it soon becomes a definite commitment that can be abandoned only at a loss. But every project is flexible so long as it is in the planning stage."[19]

Progressing of Development

Those concerned in constructing works progress them as they proceed in order to see whether they are progressing as rapidly as visualised. In the same way developers can progress development programmes to see whether they are being fulfilled as visualised. Planning authorities can also progress the programmes implicit in their plans, and, as described in Chapter 2, are asked to do so on the occasion of the statutory review of their plans.

CHAPTER 21

PROGRAMMING AND THE DEVELOPMENT PLAN

Meaning of Programming—1. Co-operation with Developers in Preparing Their Programme—2. Independent Formulation of Programmes—3. Staging of the Programme—4. Testing for Limitations in the Total Amount of Work that Might be Carried Out in a Locality: Consumer Demand, Land, Building and Civil Engineering Industry, Opportunities to Invest, Finance, Summary.

Meaning of Programming

IN THE preparation and implementation of development plans the term "programming" is used to indicate at least six different kinds of work which are carried out in the planning office. These are (1) co-operating with developers in preparing their programmes; (2) formulating programmes independently of developers for incorporation into plans; (3) dividing the programme of works into plan stages (staging); (4) testing for limitations in the total amount of work that might be carried out in the locality and therefore that should be included in the plan; (5) indicating which development projects should be carried out first in the interests of the area (priorities); (6) improving the co-ordination or integration of works of construction (phasing). The fifth and sixth of these operations are included in the carrying out of the first four, and will be covered in our discussion of these four in turn. One general point will be made about these last two. The planning office can, because it must look at the area and its problems as a whole, contribute greatly towards the selection of priorities among works and their improved integration, but it has limited executive powers in actually securing that priorities are observed or integration is achieved. These are matters which are primarily decided by the development agencies themselves and by the government departments responsible for sanctioning works of public development.

(1) *Co-operation with Developers in Preparing Their Programme*

We saw in Chapter III that, as part of the preparation of a plan, the planning office is led to consult with prospective developers, as far as it is practicable, for information on their programmes, as far as these can be formulated, and to co-operate with them in the preparation of programmes. Having discussed the considerations which make for realistic programmes, and having reviewed some of the programmes that are prepared by developers for their own purposes, we can now consider what kind of programmes the planning office can reasonably seek from developers when preparing a plan.

(a) *Content of Programmes.* In Chapter 2 we saw that the information that would be sought from developers would not be in the detail which they employ for their own purposes, but generally would be in terms of the broad kinds of uses, their quantity, density and location. Sometimes greater detail would be sought so that the planning office could consider, for example, the fuller implications of a proposal, or of the phasing of different kinds of development. It would also find useful from developers, for the purpose of relating the sum of development programmes to the expected resources of the area, their estimates of the capital cost of works and the number of man-years in the building and civil engineering industry that they would absorb. For local authority development it would find useful an estimate of the relation of the needed rate expenditure to rate resources.

(b) *Likelihood of Programme Being Carried Out.* Very important decisions are made in relation to development plans, decisions affecting the country's economy and the livelihood and welfare of people. It is important, therefore, that a plan should be as certain as possible in its intentions; and it follows that the programmes upon which it is based should not be mere statements of aspiration but should be as certain as possible in the likelihood of being carried out. They should be based on what we have called the economics and financial calculations of development and operation.

Where forecasting is particularly difficult it may be practicable to obtain a programme based on the assumption that development in the future will take place at its current rate, or at the rate at which it has been taking place over past years; or at either of these rates but suitably modified to take into account factors which are likely to result in a change of rate. In the City of Manchester Development Plan, for example, the highway programme for 20 years was based on the expenditure of an 8d. rate by the city over these years, this being the amount raised for loan charges on highway development for land and works in pre-war years.[1] In many development plans the housing programme is based on a projection of the rate of house building current at the time of preparing the plan; in some cases it has been assumed that the rate would increase with increased productivity in the building industry, and in others that it would decrease as building on virgin land was replaced by building, after demolition, in built-up areas. This method involves some estimate of whether past or current experience will be repeated. It has the usual limitations of methods which project trends: it is not always possible to measure past achievements with sufficient precision; it is not easy to assess how circumstances have changed and will change, and how the changes will affect future development; the past may be no guide to the future. But it enables some justifiable programme to be put forward.

Where public bodies require government sanction in one form or another for their development, and assurances as to grant, they are not able to prepare programmes without some guidance from the departments as to what sanctions can be expected; and for this guidance to be given it means in effect that government programmes are also required. It would not be necessary for the programmes to be formally published. The purpose could be served by the departments' approval in broad terms of the developers' programmes. In approving them there could be no question of pledging grant since it is for Parliament to vote or refuse government expenditure year by year. Only an Act of Parliament can pledge the payment of government money in the future, and such an Act is likely to be passed only for the type of expenditure which is made for the Consolidated Fund Services. When, for example, Treasury representatives were asked whether highway authorities could be given a firm forecast over a period of perhaps five years of the minimum grant they would receive for maintenance and minor improvements, the answer came that " an absolute commitment to make certain sums of money available for a given purpose over a given number of years would restrict both the right of Parliament to vote expenditure year by year and the freedom of the Chancellor to draw up his annual budget."[2] But in the nature of things departments must be able to agree in principle that certain programmes should go ahead, and that government money will be forthcoming, for works that will be started in future years, in the expectation that future Parliaments will agree and not refuse to vote the necessary funds. This is implicit, for example, in the Minister of Transport's announcements of road programmes in 1953, 1954 and 1955 and of the Minister of Health's announcement of a three-year hospital building programme in 1955;[3] most of the money for these programmes will come from departmental votes.

(c) *Period of Programmes.* The programmes should be sought for the maximum period that developers can reasonably look ahead. This will, as we have seen, vary among developers. All will look ahead for the duration of their development process. Many will do so for longer periods for their own purposes, as discussed in Chapter 1: the mineral operators, large private-enterprise house builders, highway authorities, housing authorities, education authorities. Others will do so because they want the planning authority to reserve the land they wish eventually to acquire: the university, for example, thinking of its long-term extension on adjoining land. Except for the mineral operators and highway authorities, few would want to look ahead for more than 20 years.

(2) *Independent Formulation of Programmes*

We saw in Chapter 3 that the planning office may be called upon to formulate programmes itself, as where it fosters modified programmes or promotes new ones in attempts to stimulate and promote development, and where there are developers whom it cannot consult. In all this it will be guided by the same considerations it adopts when co-operating in preparing programmes. The office will also need to prepare programmes for the part of the plan period beyond the varying times for which the different developers wish to forecast. This arises because it is useful for development programmes to be available for a common period, so that the plan will represent what it is expected the area as a whole will broadly look like at a particular time ahead.

The term of the common period is not, however, simple to decide. It cannot be shorter than the duration of the development process for any substantial amount of development for, if it were, the programmes would consist largely of development which was already initiated, and the plan would lose point. It should not be the same as the duration of the normal development process, for a few years is hardly long enough to plan for in the life of a town. It should not be too long, for it is difficult to prepare realistic programmes for much longer ahead than the period of the development process; and there can be little confidence in plans which reflect completely uncertain programmes, or are based on no programmes at all, and which look ahead, in these swiftly moving times, to a day when conditions may be so different from what they are. Taking all these considerations into account a suitable common period is the 20 years for which the first round of development plans were prepared, although a little longer or shorter would be equally good.

In formulating programmes for the balance of the plan period authorities will be guided as far as possible by the considerations which make for realistic programmes. It will probably be necessary for them to use freely the method described earlier wherein past or current rates of development are projected.

(3) *Staging of the Programme*

We saw in Chapter 2 that development plan programmes are divided into stages, the first being for work that will be undertaken and substantially completed within five years of plan preparation. One reason for picking out this first stage is to make clear which development is imminent and fairly certain, and which is not. A period of five years is convenient for this purpose, although it equally well could be a little shorter or longer, for most developers can be expected to prepare fairly certain programmes for works which will be substantially completed within this period; in fact, this first stage of the programme shows works for most of which the development process will already have been initiated. This is not to say that either developers or the authority are bound by what is included in the first stage. Development plan programmes are not contracts between the authority and developers for the execution of works, and it must be expected that developers will wish to keep them flexible, to retard them or to depart from them if necessary. But too great a flexibility in a developer's programme is undesirable, as we have seen, for the developer himself; it is also undesirable because it unsettles other developers, and because it weakens the certainty of a plan. It may also result in a waste of time, energy and money in having the plan altered too frequently.   Although many changes in programmes can be catered for without formal alteration of the plan, because of the latitude afforded by its notation and the authority's freedom to give permission for development which is not in accordance with the plan (see page 21), a substantial change will require statutory modification of the plan; and for this local consultations will probably be necessary, passage through council, public inquiry and consideration by the Minister.

A second reason for staging the programme is to assist the plan's flexibility: to enable the authority to reconsider the later and more uncertain part of the programme in the review of the plan, which takes place at least once in every five years from its approval by the Minister. As part of this process the authority will make clear what the next ensuing five-year stage will be (see page 26). This is not merely a matter of selecting certain of the remaining works in the initial programme but also of reporting progress in consultations on programmes. Just as the first stage of a programme in a newly prepared development plan shows works for which the development process has already been initiated, so the next ensuing stage after review may show works to which the developers and planning authority are largely committed.

(4) Testing for Limitations in the Total Amount of Work that Might be Carried Out in a Locality

In Chapter 3 we saw that in its participation in the preparation of development programmes the planning office has one job which is quite distinct from that of any developer: the testing of whether there are likely to be any limitations which will prevent the carrying out of all the development which is proposed in the plan. It is this which is usually called the " programming of the development plan." There are two possible approaches.   The office might, instead of attempting to forecast, project past or current rates of development in the area and assume that development will proceed at the same or at a modified rate in the future. This can be done for the whole of the works in the programme or for major uses only. Alternatively, the office might attempt to forecast the consumer demand for, and economic resources that are likely to be involved in, the total programme and consider whether these are likely to be present.

The first approach is straightforward. It was used, for example, by the City of Leicester and County Borough of Preston in preparing their development plans; both measured, for comparison with the plan programme, the whole of their inter-war municipal development.[4] The approach has the weaknesses referred to earlier (page 289) of any attempt to project trends. We will discuss the second.

As we have seen, for development to take place at all there must be consumer demand for it; available land; enough capacity in the building industry; the opportunity to use the land and employ the industry, that is to invest; and, finally, the opportunity to borrow money. We will consider whether a limitation in any of these in a locality could limit the carrying out of a particular amount of work in the area of a local planning authority; and if it could, how the planning office would set about making the necessary test in order to see whether the limitation would operate in its locality.

(a) *Consumer Demand.* The total demand for development in a locality will come from both the individual and collective spending which will be done by a great variety of consumers living both inside and outside the area. This will clearly limit the amount of development which will take place. It is just not practicable, however, for any estimate to be made, even for a short time ahead, of the total of this demand for all development in an area; that is, how much of their future incomes the various consumers would be prepared to spend for new houses, schools, shops and open spaces, and all the other different kinds of development in a plan. It is practicable, however, to make a global check on the total of certain kinds of demand. This has been done for housing in the development plans as indicated above (see page 61). It has also been done for testing the total demand for industrial land. Estimates have been made, for example, of the total area that would be needed for new factories if a certain proportion of the expected increase in population were to be employed in manufacturing industry.

It is not so difficult, however, to estimate the demand at least for a few years ahead of one consumer which will pay for a large part of the development in a plan: the local authority. In the initial development plans, the City of Bath, for example, estimated that it would be responsible for 45 per cent of the total work in the first stage of its plan, and the City of Leicester and City of Nottingham that they would respectively be responsible for 46 per cent and 31 per cent of the total work in their plans.[5] The proportion of the total work carried out by local authorities is likely to be less in later plans, with the greater freedom of private enterprise, but it is bound always to be a substantial one.

In preparing their plans local authorities will often consider what the cost of their own programmes will be to them and whether they are prepared to levy the necessary rate income. An example is seen in the County of London Development Plan, 1951. The Council, after reviewing its past expenditure, decided on a total of £27 million per annum as the ceiling of its capital expenditure on new development within the county for the period of the development plan. In deciding this amount it had regard to the prospective burden on the rates of debt charges and maintenance costs, and also to the level of past capital expenditure and the likely limitations on the programme of the sufficiency of labour, materials and technical staff. This amount was then allocated between the different departments after consideration of their individual programmes.[6]

TABLE 32

Middlesbrough Development Plan. Summary of Capital Expenditure on Local Authority Works, and Methods of Meeting it.

Year		Total Capital Cost (1) £	Met by other Bodies and Persons (2) £	Met by Capital Grants (3) £	Met from Revenue (4) £	Met out of Loan (5) £
1	Residential	1,444,800	—	—	—	1,444,800
	Education	829,400	82,240	—	10,000	737,160
	Highways	37,000	10,000	13,500	—	13,500
	Sewerage	25,000	—	—	—	25,000
	Public Buildings	50,000	—	—	1,000	49,000
	Open Spaces	9,050	—	—	—	9,050
	Central Area	1,000	—	—	1,000	—
		2,396,250	92,240	13,500	12,000	2,278,510
2	Residential	1,444,800	—	—	—	1,444,800
	Education	556,520	28,260	—	8,000	520,260
	Highways	43,000	10,000	24,750	—	8,250
	Sewerage	50,000	—	—	—	50,000
	Public Buildings	62,000	—	—	1,000	61,000
	Open Spaces	10,100	—	—	—	10,100
	Central Area	1,000	—	—	1,000	—
		2,167,420	38,260	24,750	10,000	2,094,410
3	Residential	1,444,800	—	—	—	1,444,800
	Education	298,040	82,240	—	6,000	209,800
	Highways	48,000	10,000	19,000	—	19,000
	Sewerage	55,000	—	—	—	55,000
	Public Buildings	54,000	—	—	1,000	53,000
	Open Spaces	10,130	—	—	—	10,130
	Central Area	1,000	—	—	1,000	—
		1,910,970	92,240	19,000	8,000	1,791,730
4	Residential	1,444,800	—	—	—	1,444,800
	Education	358,000	32,160	—	6,000	319,840
	Highways	50,000	10,000	5,000	—	35,000
	Public Buildings	32,000	—	—	1,000	31,000
	Open Spaces	8,300	—	—	—	8,300
	Central Area	1,000	—	—	1,000	—
		1,894,100	42,160	5,000	8,000	1,838,940
5	Residential	1,444,800	—	—	—	1,444,800
	Education	459,480	37,230	—	6,000	416,250
	Highways	40,000	10,000	—	—	30,000
	Public Buildings	32,000	—	—	1,000	31,000
	Open Spaces	7,420	—	—	—	7,420
	Central Area	1,000	—	—	1,000	—
		1,984,700	47,230	—	8,000	1,929,470
	TOTAL	10,353,440	312,130	62,250	46,000	9,933,060

Source: *County Borough of Middlesbrough Development Plan* (1951), *Report on the Survey, p.* 85,

In Chapter 11 we saw how an authority would approach this problem of relating its potential financial resources to the estimated cost of its development and operation. Example of methods that can be used are seen in various development plans.[7] That used by the Borough Engineer and Borough Treasurer of Middlesbrough

TABLE 33

Middlesbrough Development Plan. Annual Cost to the Rates in respect of each Year's Programme of Local Authority Works showing Cumulative Effect.

Year	Service	Loan Charges (1) £	*Running Expenses (2) £	Total (3) £	Less Specific Grants (4) £	Net (5) £	Less Exchequer Equalisation Grant(½) (6) £	Net Rate Charge (7) £	Cumulative Rate Charge (8) £
1	Residential	200	6,550	6,750	—	6,750			
	Education	34,270	14,800	49,070	29,442	19,628			
	Highways	880	—	880	—	880			
	Sewerage	1,395	—	1,395	—	1,395			
	Public Buildings	2,532	2,100	4,632	1,196	3,436			
	Open Spaces	647	—	647	—	647			
		39,924	23,450	63,374	30,638	32,736	10,912	21,824	21,824
2	Residential	200	6,550	6,750	—	6,750			
	Education	24,328	10,160	34,488	20,694	13,794			
	Highways	662	—	662	—	662			
	Sewerage	2,790	—	2,790	—	2,790			
	Public Buildings	2,894	1,500	4,394	1,309	3,085			
	Open Spaces	721	300	1,021	—	1,021			
		31,595	18,510	50,105	22,003	28,102	9,367	18,735	40,559
3	Residential	200	6,550	6,750	—	6,750			
	Education	10,231	6,440	16,671	10,003	6,668			
	Highways	1,177	—	1,177	—	1,177			
	Sewerage	3,069	—	3,069	—	3,069			
	Public Buildings	2,622	8,600	11,222	2,116	9,106			
	Open Spaces	724	1,000	1,724	—	1,724			
		18,023	22,590	40,613	12,119	28,494	9,498	18,996	59,555
4	Residential	200	6,550	6,750	—	6,750			
	Education	15,120	6,600	21,720	13,033	8,687			
	Highways	2,168	—	2,168	—	2,168			
	Public Buildings	1,937	5,100	7,037	1,198	5,839			
	Open Spaces	593	900	1,493	—	1,493			
		20,018	19,150	39,168	14,231	24,937	8,312	16,625	76,180
5	Residential	200	6,550	6,750	—	6,750			
	Education	19,404	8,640	28,044	16,827	11,217			
	Highways	1,859	—	1,859	—	1,859			
	Public Buildings	1,937	7,100	9,037	2,197	6,840			
	Open Spaces	530	1,400	1,930	—	1,930			
		23,930	23,690	47,620	19,024	28,596	9,532	19,064	95,244
	TOTALS	133,490	107,390	240,880	98,015	142,865	47,621	95,244	

* Including Housing Statutory Contributions.

Source: *As Table 32, p. 86.*

will be discussed here in illustration. They estimated the rate burden of the first five-year programme of local authority works. The results are summarised in Tables 32-34.

Table 32 shows the estimated total capital cost in the period. not only of works but also of such items as school furnishing.[8] A loan for all the capital cost would not need to be raised; part of the cost of schools is met by the boards of management of aided and special agreement schools, and the cost of private street works is recoverable (Column 2); there are capital grants towards highways (Column 3); and a small amount of the cost, amounting to between a 3d. and 4d. rate, is met out of revenue (Column 4).

Except for housing, all the loan charges on loans in Column 5 of Table 32 would be met by rates or grants (Column 1 of Table 33). For housing, the contributions from tenants, rates and exchequer are assumed to meet the loan charges on capital cost and the cost of repairs, maintenance and supervision, leaving the loan charges on street lighting to fall on the rates. The housing rate fund contribution is included in Column 2 (running, or operating, expenses), with the cost of maintenance of public lighting, street cleansing, refuse collection and road maintenance. The running expenses for schools include the rates, upkeep of buildings, fuel, light, cleaning, salaries, etc.; for public buildings, they include wages, repairs and maintenance. For highways, sewerage and open space additional maintenance is assumed to be nil.

TABLE 34

Middlesbrough Development Plan. Annual Rate Charge in Respect of Local Authority Works, Showing Cumulative Effect

	Cumulative Net Rate Charge (Table 9, col. 8) (1)	Non-Recurring Revenue Expenditure (see note) (2)	Total Rate Charge in each year (col. 1 + col. 2) (3)	Estimated Rateable Value (Table VII) (4)	Equiv-alent Rate in the £ (5)	Annual Increase in Rate Charge (6)	Annual Net Increase in Rateable Value (7)
	£	£	£	£	s. d.	£	£
First Year ..	21,824	4,000	25,824	821,000	7½	25,824	18,000
Second Year ..	40,559	3,467	44,026	839,000	1 0½	18,202	18,000
Third Year ..	59,555	2,933	62,488	857,000	1 5½	18,462	18,000
Fourth Year ..	76,180	2,933	79,113	873,000	1 9¾	16,625	16,000
Fifth Year ..	95,244	2,933	98,177	889,000	2 2½	19,064	16,000
TOTAL ..						98,177	86,000

Note: The figures given in col. (2) are those shown in col. (4) of Table 32 after adjustment for specific grants and Exchequer Equalisation Grant.

The above Table shows:
  (a) That the Plan will cost the equivalent of an additional 4¾d. on the rate every year.
  (b) That the annual charge on the ratepayer will ultimately be equivalent to 2s. 2½d. in the £.
  (c) That the increase in rate burden is approximately 4d. in the £ in excess of the increase in rateable value generated by the Plan itself.
Source: *As Table 32, p. 87.*

Column 5 shows the net cost after deducting specific grants; and Column 7 the net charge to be met from rates after deducting one-third for exchequer equalisation grant, the same proportion of total municipal expenditure borne by these grants at the time the estimate was made.

The total rate charge in each year (Table 34) is made up of the loan charges and running expenses which would fall on the rates (Column 1) plus those small amounts of capital cost to be met from revenue (Column 2). This is expressed in Column 5 as a rate in the £ of the rateable value which, it is estimated, will exist in the ensuing years. This estimate is made by adding to the current rateable value of £803,000 an estimated annual increase (Column 7). This increase is calculated from the estimated rateable value of the proposed new dwellings, plus an allowance which is based on past trends for increase in the rateable value of other properties. Account is taken in the fourth and fifth year of the demolition of property on re-development. The notes to Table 34 summarise the result of the calculations.

(b) *Land*. The absence of enough suitable land which is readily available in an area will clearly limit the carrying out of programmes. The specific testing of the supply of land against demand for it is not, however, necessary, for it is inevitably introduced in any properly prepared plan. In the planning surveys the supply of land in the area would be considered and a picture formed of that which is suitable and readily available for development, including land which is built up and ripe for change; and that which is not because, for example, it should at all costs be kept free from building development (first-class farmland or land containing particularly scarce minerals), or because disproportionate expenditure is required to make it available for development (land made derelict through mineral excavation, or built-up land on which the property has long economic life). Against this picture of suitable land, and of its ownership, would be considered the requirements of developers, whose viewpoint on this we discussed in Chapter 6. In consequence there would evolve an earmarking of land in which would be reflected the planning authority's views on zoning, the location of uses, the uses which should prevail where there is competition, and all the matters we have considered in the balance sheet of planning. In this way the design of the plan would evolve.

In matching the supply of suitable land and the demand for sites regard must be had to the timing of development. For example, the developer who wishes to proceed forthwith will not be interested in land which will not be ripe for many years; and where a developer does not wish to proceed immediately it may be possible to introduce dual use of land during the plan period as where an old gravel pit is first used for tipping and then for open space. Regard must also be had to the requirements of a developer, as described in Chapter 6, and when he is steered from land he would prefer to other land this should be suitable for his purpose. Regard must also be had to existing and possible ownership. Where land is already owned by an industrialist for expansion there is a strong presumption in favour of its use by him; and where land is reserved for a particular use there is the presumption that an appropriate developer will be able to obtain the right to develop.

(c) *Building and Civil Engineering Industry.* We saw in Chapter 7 that the supply of firms, materials or professional skill is hardly likely to limit the total amount of work that can be carried out in a particular area; but we also saw that within suitably defined areas, such as the Ministry of Works zones, the number of operatives tends to remain fairly constant, as does therefore the amount of work that can economically be carried out by the industry in that area. A test can therefore be applied to such areas.

As we saw in Chapter 7, if it is assumed that the number of men who are employed on new work in such areas will remain constant, this number can be matched against the demands on the industry that will be made by a given programme of new works expressed in man-years: the number of operatives required over a given period of years. Refinements in the method can be introduced by assuming that the number of operatives will rise or fall with expected changes in total population; that the proportion engaged in new work will rise or fall; or that the output of the industry per man will increase through improved techniques and organisation[9].

This test of the total programme in a development plan was asked for in the 1951 development plans. There was to be shown a schedule of " the major works to be undertaken by local authorities and where possible by other developers, which will be necessary for the carrying out of the plan, including major clearing works, housing (both local authority and other), educational, industrial, commercial and other building works, and road, water supply and sewerage works." The schedule was to be divided to show the works in the first five years, and for the works there were to be noted the man-years that each class would absorb and, where possible, estimated cost. An estimate was required, too, of the labour resources in man-years likely to be available in the area for major building and public works construction.[10] Fig. 9 shows the results of the test for the County of Middlesex, indicating how the programme of works was geared to the expected resources of the industry. The diagram depicts the distribution of building labour which would be consistent with the proposals in the Development Plan during the 20-year period.

The need to relate the test to the area of plans, some of which were much larger than zones and some smaller, meant the introduction of a further assumption which was known to be unsound: that the number of operatives would remain constant in such areas, or in sub-divisions of such areas, which were unrelated to zones,

On this score, and because of the possibility of importing men to carry out work even in remote localities, and of the likelihood of labour migrating to the wealthier centres, and because it is by no means certain that the proportion of men engaged on new works in a zone will remain constant, and because it was wrongly inferred that the carrying out of the test amounts to a prophecy that either the programme would be carried out or that a larger programme could not be, the introduction of the test in the 1951 plans has been criticised as affording no useful guide to the size of plan programmes. But for its limited purpose, of helping to ensure that the contents of development plan programmes were not completely unrealistic, it has been successful. Just how successful it has been can be appreciated by comparing the modesty of their proposals in general with those in the post-war advisory plans which were prepared with no such test, and by realising that even so they probably contain more work than can be carried out in the plan period with the available resources.

The test was conditioned by the kind of statistics which were obtainable about the operatives and work executed in the area. When licensing was comprehensive the Ministry of Works knew a great deal about the current activities of the industry, for the contractor of each licensed job made a monthly return to them. They knew, among other things, from month to month, the number of building and civil engineering operatives which was currently employed by the contractors in each zone, and also the different kinds of works these were currently engaged on: maintenance and repair works on the one hand and new works of various kinds on the other. They also knew, as we saw in Chapter 7, the output of the industry, region by region, for the various kinds of new work expressed as money value produced per year per man in the Thirteen Trades. Such figures were supplied to many planning authorities for use in preparing their development plans. For example, Table 11, (page 98), shows such figures for England and Wales in 1950-51 and also for the South West Region. With the relaxation of licensing control the returns of contractors covered less and less of the work that was being carried out, and on the abandonment of licensing in November, 1954, no returns at all were obtainable. Since then, however, the Ministry of Works has instituted a system of obtaining quarterly returns from a sample of 15,000 representative firms in the industry, and an annual return from all firms. The return asks for the number of operatives employed at the time and the estimated value of building and civil engineering work of different kinds carried out in the preceding quarter. The figures will not be related to zones, nor will they be available month by month. Some modification in the technique of using this test will be necessary, therefore, for plans prepared from 1955 onwards.

FIGURE 9.—*Diagram Showing the Allocation of Labour to Works Between* 1951 *and* 1971 *in the County of Middlesex Development Plan* (1951)

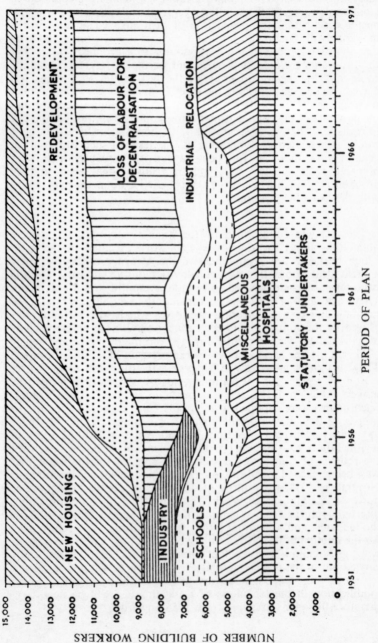

(d) *Opportunities to Invest.* In Chapters 4 and 8 were described the methods which have been used of recent years to fix a ceiling for the amount of investment in the country as a whole, and also to ensure that certain types of development should go forward rather than others. Investment resources as a whole were not, however, allocated to particular areas or localities by the government, not even to the different administrative regions of the country, although a production department may have allocated its own quota of a particular kind of investment among its regions. Even with central investment planning, therefore, should a local planning authority wish to know the amount of capital investment likely in its area it could receive no simple guidance, and could have no means of relating the total of the capital investment resources claimed by the developers in its locality to the total that was likely to be made available there.

Without central investment planning a developer can invest resources in development, given a site and the building industry, if he has command over enough money to use the site and employ the industry. There is no local limitation to the amount of money that can be employed for this purpose.

With or without central economic planning, therefore, no test of this kind can be applied.

(e) *Finance.* Finance is the most fluid of all the resources for development. The savings that make possible development in Birmingham might well come from anywhere in the world. There is thus no limitation of this kind on the total amount of work that can be carried out in a particular locality.

The amount of work to be carried out by a particular local authority might be circumscribed by lack of finance, however, when its indebtedness is high. As mentioned in Chapter 9, the Ministry of Housing and Local Government may, as loan sanctioning authority, place limits upon the amounts of loans that an authority can raise, should it consider that the authority has already too large a debt for its potential rate resources.

Summary. From this review it is seen that authorities can in general test the total requirements in their plan only against expected local resources in land and the building industry; and that a test can also be made of the likely ability of a local authority to pay for its own development. In any particular area, however, there may be a paramount limitation, in the kind of resources we have described or some other, which will circumscribe the total programme: in the amount of housing land, for example in a built-up area. In such cases the test should be devised for this limitation and it is hardly necessary to dwell on any others. Conversely, there may

be no point in testing for possible limitations in particular resources
of which the supply is clearly abundant. In the County of
London, for example, the building industry is likely to be able to
cope with any amount of work that developers will be prepared to
pay for. In short, there applies in this kind of programming the
maxim, which was culled from experience of a quite different kind
of programming, that of production in the recent war, that " the
golden rule of all planning is that it must be done in terms of the
scarcest of resources."[11]

PART VI

LAND VALUES AND LAND PLANNING

INTRODUCTORY

In the remaining chapters we will be discussing the economics of planned development from one particular aspect which is of particular interest to surveyors, that of land values. While only one aspect it touches upon the whole range of urban land use and land planning activities. In being related to land it is concerned with a common and fundamental factor in all development and planning. In dealing with values it is concerned with the use of land, for land values are the money values associated with the opportunity to use land in particular ways, either currently or in the future. In discussing this aspect, therefore, we will be reviewing much of the ground covered in earlier chapters; but this time we will be doing so in terms of land values.

Chapter 22 opens by referring to the economic and social forces which cause land to be used in particular ways, and cause changes in land use, and to the theories explaining the operation of these forces. It is suggested that many influences are at work, and it is accepted that " land utilisation takes place within three frameworks: the physical, the institutional and the economic." Part of the economic framework is the process described in Chapter 6 whereby it is the developer who secures the land in the market who effects the change of use in it to meet a demand. As a result land use becomes arranged in certain patterns in " response to the demands of consumers for the products and services of land." The proposition is discussed that if the market operated freely it would give rise to the best use of land from the community's viewpoint. It is suggested that, since the market does not and should not operate freely, land planning is needed.

The successful bid by a private developer in the market not only gives rise to a new use of land but also establishes its market value at that point in time. When uses change therefore the new land use and land value run together. But they are related at other points in time. The relation between land use and land value throughout the development and re-development process, and more generally, is traced. It is concluded that land values are a symptom and reflection of uses in land, of what is happening, has happened and is tending to happen to uses. A knowledge of values and of valuation, therefore, and of the forces which affect values, gives some insight into land use and land use changes. The chapter closes by describing some examples of land value maps as a preliminary to discussing their use for planning in Chapter 25.

Chapter 23 discusses the evolution of the statutory provisions for the payment of compensation or collection of betterment by public bodies, when the value of property is depreciated or enhanced respectively by certain of their actions. Such provisions existed before statutory planning was practised, and are not necessarily an integral part of a planning system. But some suitable compensation and betterment scheme is essential if planning powers are to be effectively used. The impact of the provisions on planning practice is therefore traced. The history of compensation and betterment provisions before 1939 is first outlined. The system existing in 1939 was found by the Barlow Commission to be hampering the progress of pre-war planning, and to be unsuitable for post-war planning by the Uthwatt Committee. The Coalition Government of 1944 made proposals for a revised system and these were largely followed by the Labour Government in Parts V to VIII of the Town and Country Planning Act, 1947. The 1947 Act system is described and its elements compared with the recommendations of the Uthwatt Committee and of the 1944 Government. The impact on planning practice of the 1947 Act provisions are described, and the reasons for their repeal. The revised provisions of the Town and Country Planning Acts, 1953 and 1954, are described and their implications for planning.

Chapter 24 introduces a discussion on the effect of a development plan on land values by considering what would happen to land values without a plan. It is suggested that these would not be stable but would rise or fall because of a variety of influences, to the loss or benefit of owners, and that a plan modifies or strengthens these influences. The possible effect of a development plan on land values is analysed, firstly by considering the effect on the values of individual properties of uncertainty and the different elements in a plan (that is of reservations for a public purpose, diagrammatic proposals and zoning); secondly by considering when the effect on land values takes place; thirdly by considering effects on land values in general. The effect on values of arrangements for paying compensation and betterment is not discussed; these do not so much alter values as the fortunes of the owners of the affected values.

The final chapter applies the discussion of the previous three chapters to suggesting how a knowledge of land values might be used to assist in the preparation and implementation of a plan for an urban area. The suggestions are made towards the furtherance of a technique; they are not a description of what has been generally practised in preparing development plans. The suggestions refer to the manner of using a knowledge of land values in analysing a town's problems and defects, in preparing and implementing planning proposals, and in the phasing of acquisition of land. This leads to a description of land value maps which might be employed in planning. The chapter closes by mentioning the difficulties of obtaining a knowledge of land values in a planning office and suggests that the assistance which is to be obtained must be provided by practising valuers who are closely in touch with the plan and sympathetic to it. This is not enough however. Just as it is aware of the place of land use, traffic flow, etc., in the preparation and implementation of a plan so should the planning office also be aware of the place of land values.

CHAPTER 22

LAND USE AND LAND VALUES

Economic and Social Forces Behind Land Use—Theories Explaining the Forces Behind Urban Land Use—The Market Process and the Best Use of Land—Relation between Changes in Land Use and in Land Value—Relation Between Land Use and Current and Potential Use Value—Use and Investment Value, Rental and Capital Value—Summary—Valuation—Land Value Maps.

Economic and Social Forces Behind Land Use

WHERE there is no planning control, it is by no means a matter of chance why towns and villages grow up in certain places rather than others, or factories settle in certain localities, or towns grow in a particular way, or similar uses group themselves together within towns; why, in short, particular pieces of land become used for certain purposes rather than others and a perceptible use pattern emerges. There is in this settlement of uses on land a certain orderliness of pattern and growth, certain tendencies which can be discerned, analysed and explained; and behind these tendencies are the social and economic forces which give rise to them. It is because these forces, when left to themselves, have led to such disastrous results in our towns and countryside that the need for town and country planning has been recognised, and the necessary powers introduced. But in the preparation and implementation of a plan it is essential to comprehend the existence of these forces, and of the pattern and change in land use that they are tending to produce, so that they can be adapted as necessary. The carrying out of a survey and analysis which leads up to a plan for a particular area assists in the understanding of the tendencies in that area, and of the extent to which their fulfilment is desirable, and in the framing of proposals with them in mind. As Sir William Holford has said in connection with the planning of central areas of towns, " Behind the physical form and outward appearance of the city are the economic and social forces which have brought the streets and buildings into existence. Any discussion on design must recognise this at the start, or remain purely subjective."[1] Sir William goes on to explain that design, nevertheless, has a function of its own.

Theories Explaining the Forces Behind Urban Land Use

Some explanation of the manner in which towns grow has been pursued by many students of urban society. Some have dealt with the town as a whole and others with particular uses or groups of uses within it.[2] Their theories have dealt with many different aspects: the location of towns, the manner of their growth, their ecology, that is " the spatial distribution of persons and institutions in the city, and the processes involved in the formation of patterns of distribution."[3] But it is only one aspect that is of interest here: the mechanics of the process of town growth and of the formation of its structure and pattern. The sociologist, geographer and economist have all speculated on this; and while each might agree on a description of what actually tends to take place, each attempts to explain the mechanics of the process particularly from his own viewpoint. To the sociologist, for example, it is the human being and his psychology which is the key to the process, his attitudes, interests, values, prejudices, likes and dislikes.[4] The geographer, on the other hand, while not suggesting that man's activities are dominated by nature puts emphasis on such things as relief, elevation, climate and geology.[5] Economists suggest that it is the economies which are to be obtained from using a particular piece of land, arising, for example, from its accessibility to people, its situation in relation to other pieces of land or to established uses or to established or potential channels of transportation or communication, which are the primary reasons for its becoming so used.[6]

The reasons why particular sites and parcels of land become used in particular ways by human beings, whether for urban or other purposes, cannot be explained completely from any one of these aspects; it is common experience that several kinds of influence are at work. When the line of a traffic road is decided, and accordingly the use of the land over which it is to run, it is because people wish to travel along the road; because of the levels of the land in question in relation to other land; perhaps because the land is already owned by a public authority; or perhaps because other land which would provide a better engineering line cannot be acquired, or is too expensive to acquire, or cannot be used because it is, in London, in a Royal Park. In some cases one particular kind of influence may be more important than in others; geographical considerations clearly predominate in deciding what land will be used for docks, while economic considerations are most important in deciding that other land will be used for factories. This is expressed in the conclusions of the American land economists, R. T. Ely and G. S. Wehrwein, as to the forces deciding the use of land of all kinds: " Land utilisation takes place within three frameworks: the physical, the institutional, and the economic."[7] By the physical framework they had in mind the laws of nature which would include geographical influences, climate, soil and topography. By the institutional framework they had in mind the practices, customs, traditions, laws, organisations and other institutions of human society which affect the use of land; examples are the recognition by society of private property in land and of public control over private property rights, the practices of financing institutions, such as the banks, and of local government and public corporations. Within their economic framework are the kind of influences we have been describing in this book, and also others such as the economic forces which affect the location of industry and of commercial and trading centres.

It can now be seen that in Chapter 6, in describing the way in which developers select sites, we were also describing the mechanics of the process whereby land use comes about within these three frameworks, in particular the economic framework. We saw that there are a variety of private developers all considering the sites that would be suitable for their purposes in area, in physical characteristics, location, relation to utilities (physical framework), and which they could obtain the legal right to develop in the way they wish (institutional framework), and making bids, at prices related to the proposed use, for the right to develop (economic framework). There are the owners and occupiers of land who are driven to leave it when their use cannot stand, as a cost, the bids of the developers or of those speculating in advance of development. There are the landowners considering whether to make their land available for development, and the prices at which they would be prepared to do so. As a result of competition, the developer who makes the highest bid for a particular piece of land, a bid which is sufficiently high to attract the landowner to sell and any occupier to vacate, would secure the right to develop it; the use of the land would then change to a new one, which would be associated with a new value. Public developers, we saw, take part in the competition with private buyers or lessees. But they do not secure the right to develop just because they can make a more profitable use of the site than other developers, and can in consequence afford to offer more; they do so because they elect to pay, in order to use the site, as much as others would pay.

If this process is visualised as taking place on all sites as development becomes due there is some explanation, primarily from the economic viewpoint, of the process whereby all kinds of urban growth takes place; why towns change and grow; and why in the centres of cities, the points of greatest accessibility and convenience, uses are found which can afford high land cost, and uses which cannot are pushed out. All the forces behind this process become crystallised in the development process on individual sites; and it is the market bid, if it is allowed to operate, which primarily decides which use is to come about. The similarity of the forces behind the decisions of the various developers gives rise to a " natural use zoning." As Ely and Wehrwein put it, " In response to the demands of consumers for the products and services of land, as expressed in price, land uses become arranged in certain patterns. Rent acts as sorter and arranger of this pattern"; and " the city is a living organism in which these elements [i.e., the various land uses] have arranged themselves according to the economic demands of the public."[8]

If the use of land is decided in this way it is apparent that planning control alone does not decide land use, although it is one of the important influences making for a decision. It can often be a decisive influence in preventing change in use, and also, when there are competing claims for land, in deciding in favour of one which cannot afford the highest bid.

The Market Process and the Best Use of Land

It follows that if the market operated freely the process we have described would generate a pattern of uses which would result from each parcel of land becoming used for what American valuers call its " highest and best " use: for that use which, it was estimated at the time of change, could extract the largest net return to the owner in money or amenities over a forseeable period of time.[9] It has been suggested, by Sir Arnold Plant, that where the market does operate freely " the uses of land which come about as a result of competitive rental bids for alternative uses [in a free market] give us the closest approximation to the preferences of the community. I know of no index of the right use of land which is safer, a less ambiguous guide to the community's wishes than the open market test."[10] And it has been suggested by R. U. Ratcliff that the " outgrowth of this market process of competitive bidding for sites among the potential users of land is an orderly pattern of land use specially organised to perform most efficiently the economic functions that characterise urban life."[11] It is suggested, in other words, that the freely operating market would give the kind of pattern that land planning seeks to achieve in seeking the best use of land, and so would reduce greatly the need for planning intervention. But, as Sir Arnold Plant continues in the above quotation, " Nevertheless, no one today believes that individual owners can always be recognised unfettered control over their land." This is because it is generally accepted that there are reasons why the market does not operate freely, others why it should not be allowed to do so, and others why it cannot be guaranteed to select the use which gives the largest net return. Out of these three kinds of reason has grown the need for land planning. We shall amplify them.

We saw in Chapter 6 some of the reasons why the market does not operate freely and why changes of use do not in consequence take place simply as a result of market bids. It is sometimes desirable, therefore, to intervene in the interests of planned development in order to ensure that particular land is developed when it might otherwise not be, and that land is available for a particular kind of desirable development. It may be necessary, too, on occasions to discourage the over-optimistic developer who has made too high a bid.

The market should not always be allowed to operate freely, and be permitted to establish uses by the highest bidder, because of the divergence of social and private costs. While the best return to the individual is often a guide to the best return to the community, often it is not. For example, a high value in a shopping site reflects the fact that it is highly accessible to many people and should, in the community's interest, be used for shops rather than for, say, housing; but where such a site is on a principal traffic road its high value will not reflect the social cost to the community that might arise from increased traffic congestion and accidents. And the high value for building of a flat piece of farmland reflects that it will require less capital expenditure on site works than a broken up site; but the high value will not reflect the social cost of using good agricultural land instead of the poorer land. And the relatively high value of a factory site in a decaying residential area would not reflect the cost to the other owners, and to the town, of the impediment which a new factory would be to ultimate re-development on planned lines. And the high value of an office site in the centre of a congested city reflects the fact that it is highly accessible for employees and business people; but the high value will not reflect the social cost implicit in the need for expensive improvements in the transport system which will be necessary to carry the growing number of employees to that centre. Planning must intervene, therefore, to minimise possible social costs, as we have discussed in Chapters 3 and 19.

While a freely operating market can within limits select the most profitable of various private uses it cannot, for the reasons discussed in Chapter 6, select the best of various public uses, nor indicate whether a public use is more valuable than a private one. The market can only indicate the land cost of establishing a public use on a site. It is necessary in planning, therefore, to decide upon some basis other than the market one whether land should be used either for commerce on the one hand, or a town hall, technical school or bus station on the other.

Planning powers must, therefore, be used to supplement market forces if the best use of land is to be achieved. But in the difficult task of making decisions on this the uses, and their associated land values, that would result from the operation of market process are a *prima facie* indication of the best use of land and of the cost, in terms of frustrating realisable values, of establishing uses other than those indicated by the market process. This indication can hardly be ignored. It is for this reason that a free market in land would be of great value for planning purposes. But for other reasons, as we shall see in Chapter 23, it inhibits planning if public authorities have to meet the full costs of compensation, for acquisition or injurious affection of development values, that would be indicated by a free market.

Relation Between Changes in Land Use and in Land Value

As discussed in Chapter 6, land use and land values will run together at the time when uses are at the point of changing through development. But development is a lengthy process, and while the new use and new value run together at this point they do not do so throughout the process. We will consider in illustration of the relation between changing land use and land value the typical transformation to built-up land of farmland on the outskirts of a town, and its eventual re-development. For simplicity we will, to begin with, define land value as its value for use; that is, the rental or capital sum which would be paid in the market for the current or potential use of the land. We shall assume for the moment that the capital sum is simply the capitalisation of the annual sum at a given rate per cent, so that rental and capital value are both related to use in precisely the same way.

While development is many years away the market value of the land will be based on its current use as farmland, and will reflect its fertility and condition. We shall call this its current use value. This is similar to value for rating assessment purposes: the rent that would be paid under certain stipulated conditions for current use from year to year; but it is not the same as existing use value, or restricted value of the Town and Country Planning Act, 1947, Section 61, which include some element of development value. In 1955 the current use value of farmland was of the order of £50 per acre on the poorer land and £500 per acre on the very best.

For some years before developers or speculators become interested in the land, and are prepared to make bids, anyone concerned with its value, for death duty purposes for example, would not be able to ignore the prospects of development. No one would know with certainty what the prospects were, or the point in time at which demand for the development would justify its being carried out. In advance of that point it would be possible only to make estimates as to when development will take place, what kind of development it will be, what costs and yields will result, and accordingly to arrive at a discounted value for the potential use. This we shall call potential use value. This is not the same as unrestricted value under the Town and Country Planning Act, 1947, Section 61, since this related to interests at a particular date (July, 1948) and to prices in January, 1947; nor is it the same as consent value of the Central Land Board since this was calculated for a particular development proposal, one not necessarily making the fullest use of the land.[12]

Whatever the difficulties of precise valuation, however, it would be undisputed that the potential use value of the land was more than its current use value for farming by reason of the potential value which could be realised on development. This potential value the Uthwatt Committee called " floating value," since it is by nature speculative. The hoped-for building may take place on the particular piece of land in question, or it may take place elsewhere; it may come within 5 years, or 25 years " . . . and it is impossible to predict with certainty where the ' float ' will settle as sites are actually required for the purpose of development."[13]

As the prospects of development come nearer, and the element of development value increases, that is the difference between current and potential use value,[14] the current use might or might not change in advance of the development. It will change, for example, where the farmer does not wish to continue cultivation because his crops and animals are being disturbed by townspeople, or because he knows that disturbance is fairly imminent, or because he is attracted by bids from developers or speculators which will enable him to buy another farm and show a profit. In these cases the use may change to accommodation land: a sports field, allotments or grazing pasture. The new current use value will increase to perhaps £100 to £150 per acre. The amount of development value would in most cases diminish; but it might increase on the best farming land where the new use had a lower use value than the old one.

As development comes nearer the competition among developers and speculators for the site will begin to show itself. Their bids will be based on the potential use value of the site at the time when it is expected that development will take place, discounted for the period which, it is estimated, will elapse before then. This competition may endure over years, and will be finalised only when works are begun. It is at this stage when the successful bid which is associated with an intention to develop decides the new use in the manner described; and the site attracts a market value which is associated with and reflects the intended use. This value, in 1955, might be of the order of £500 to £1,500 per acre for housing land.

When development is completed and the buildings are in use, new current use values are created which are associated with the new use of the land and buildings: that is with the rents that occupiers are prepared to pay for them. These new values are not always the same as those which were visualised by the developer when making his bid. They may be more or less. Where the cost of works, for example, has been sufficiently higher than was expected, or the yield sufficiently lower, the new site value, insofar as it can be separated out from the new joint value for land and buildings, may be less than the price paid for the undeveloped land.

For a period, most buildings continue to be used in the manner visualised by the developers. During this period the money prices which are offered for their use will fluctuate with variations in the value of money, and with variations in the supply and demand for the accommodation of which the buildings in question are a part. For example, when new suburban houses were built in such large quantities during the 1930's the prices of the older dwellings in the inner parts of our towns diminished. The current use of the dwellings remained residential, but their residential qualities were inferior to those in the new dwellings, and their use values diminished accordingly.

Many buildings go through their whole lives without alteration to adapt them for other uses; and others without change in the use for which they were designed. Their current use values will vary in the way just described. There will not always be a decline. In the central parts of big cities there are streets of terrace houses, erected for and originally occupied by members of the working classes, which have, because of their location, attracted middle-class occupiers and have increased in value. Many buildings, however, become adapted for a more profitable use before the end of their lives, and so attract new values which are above those associated with the uses for which they were designed. This may happen without much expense on works of adaptation, as, for example, in the Georgian and Victorian houses in our towns which have been converted to offices and places of business. In some cases considerable expense is necessary for adaptation, as where a large block of outmoded flats is converted into a hotel, or a terrace of Regency houses into flats, or a country house into a hospital. This kind of case is different in degree only to the last we need to consider: where buildings are demolished in order to re-develop a site more intensely or for a new use altogether. The owner of a departmental store may wish to expand and, not being able to buy an adjoining site, will demolish and rebuild with more space on his own site; or a freeholder to whom reverts an old dwelling-house at the end of a long lease may demolish and build flats on the site; or an industrialist might rebuild when his original buildings, or accumulation of buildings, hinder efficient production.

Where land and buildings are attracting a new use in this way, whether through adaptation of the buildings or following their demolition, it means that there is a potential use value which is above that for the current use; that there is a development value. This is similar in character to the development value which floats above undeveloped land in the way we have described. If it is to be worth the while of a developer to re-develop, the potential use value must be sufficiently above the current use value of the standing property. In other words, the potential use value of the site after demolition must exceed, at least by the cost of demolition plus loss through disturbance, the most profitable use value of the existing land and buildings; and this latter should not be more than the cost of an equally suitable site in the locality. Or the use value of the new development must exceed, by at least an allowance for developer's profit, the combined cost of the new buildings and works and the use value of the existing land and buildings. Until this point is reached the property as it exists has an economic life: it will be worth the owner's while to retain it in its current use, and re-development will not normally take place if left to private enterprise.[15] This suggests a reason why the levying of development charge in the 1947 Act can be said to have retarded re-development. It reduced any possible margin between the potential value which would fall to the owner of a property on re-development and the value which he enjoyed for the current use.

Many buildings become unusable for the purpose for which they were designed but can attract no other use which is of higher value than the original investment: the chapels and churches which have become superfluous through the falling off in worship and are usable only for stores, or the outmoded cinemas which are turned into garages for lorries. In these cases the new use is adopted in order to minimise losses.

Sometimes it is not worthwhile either to re-develop a property, or retain it in its current use, or find a less valuable use. This occurs when the property which has no development value becomes a liability instead of an asset, that is when the continuing expenses are likely to exceed any income that can be obtained for its use, and accordingly the property cannot be sold. This arises, for instance, with cottages of low rental value and in such poor structural condition that they attract sanitary notices. In England and Wales, to avoid payment of rates and so minimise expenses, an owner of such a property can leave it empty when it becomes vacant; but in Scotland, where empty property is liable for owners' rates so long as it is capable of occupation, it might have its roof removed in order to avoid them, and in the U.S.A. it might be demolished or boarded up to avoid local taxes.

These last two paragraphs help to explain, primarily from the economic viewpoint, some of the reasons why towns or parts of them stagnate or deteriorate. They stagnate where, for example, property is well adapted to its current use and no one will bid enough to attract the owner to give up the current use. And they deteriorate where properties cease to be usable for their current purposes, or the purpose for which they were designed, and so become used for less valuable purposes or become empty.

Relation Between Land Use and Current and Potential Use Value

We will now consider more closely the general relationship between land use and current and potential use value. Considering first current use values, these reflect the different values of land, or land and buildings, for use and enjoyment. Actual rents which are newly fixed in the market may truly reflect these values. In a study of 142 American cities in the 1930's it was found that a comparison of the rents of dwellings gave a general picture of their comparative residential qualities. Maps of each of the cities were prepared showing for each residential block the average rent of dwellings in it, and also such data as the density of dwellings, their age, their need of major repair, the proportion of the dwellings that were owner-occupied, that were used for commercial purposes, that had no bath, and the percentage of non-white people living in the block. A high degree of correlation was found between these conditions and the average rental value of dwellings in each block; and in each block the range of rents was found to be small, tending to cluster around the average. It was concluded that the actual rent paid for dwellings in these cities at that time was so sufficiently representative of the other housing conditions just enumerated, that a survey of rents alone could be used to make an analysis of the residential quality of different parts of cities where no other data were available.[16]

In this study it was possible to use the actual rents which were paid. But it is not where there is owner-occupation or long lettings; and it is not in this country because the rents of controlled dwellings cannot usefully be compared with each other or with those of uncontrolled dwellings. Where actual rents are not a true guide to current use values it may be possible to estimate them as is done in making assessments for rateable value. It is notorious that there has been in the past serious lack of uniformity in these assessments, as between different classes of property and different areas, while the general level of assessments has been below the levels of rents actually paid. For the purpose of comparing differential qualities relating to use and occupation of property, uniformity of assessment within one class of property and within one locality at least is necessary. It is too early to say to what extent this will be brought about in the revaluation for rating under the Local Government Act 1948.

Even were no money rents paid by occupiers, it would still be possible to visualise differential use values. If there existed, for example, nothing but peasant proprietorship of agricultural land, and no sales took place, there would still be different values for the potential output of different holdings. If all dwelling-houses were held on licence from the state without payment of rent there would still remain the differential residential qualities of the dwellings. In the absence of any guide given by rentals in such cases there would no doubt be found some other method of comparing these qualities.

Turning to potential values, these indicate that change in use is expected and also, broadly, the new kind of use to which, it is thought in the market, the land or land and buildings might be put in the future. They do not, however, so clearly reflect such potential uses as current use values reflect current uses. This is because they are related to prospects of development which are speculative; it is not known until development is fairly imminent on which sites the potential use will in fact settle, nor when it will settle nor the specific form the new use will take. Because of this, potential values are in practice more difficult to value than current use values; and out of this difficulty has arisen the controversy over the valuation of development values.

The Uthwatt Committee, accepting the view put forward by the Town and Country Planning Advisory Committee in 1939,[17] thought that the probability of floating value settling upon a particular piece of undeveloped land rather than any other was not capable of estimation. They concluded that where a large number of such pieces in a locality were valued long in advance of development, as might occur on public acquisition or when negotiating compensation for injurious affection, the sum of such probabilities would greatly exceed the actual possibilities of development in the locality: there would, in fact, be overvaluation.[18] This view has been challenged by those who, while accepting the existence of floating value, contend that the market value of a particular piece of land does take account of development probabilities and possibilities, and that by following the market overvaluation would be avoided.[19] There are two separate questions in this controversy. Firstly, does the market value of any piece of land reflect more than its share of the total development value in the area? And secondly, on acquisition, would a public authority pay more than this share? The first question has never been fully answered. There are some who contend that it never could be for, they say, the total of all development value in an area, as it exists at any one point in time, cannot be assessed. There are never, they say, sufficient market transactions in unripe land at any one time to reveal how developers assess the prospect of general development over a wide area and long period, and it is difficult, at a particular moment, to forecast the effect of early development on some sites on the prospects of successful later development on others. The valuations carried out over the whole country as a result of claims for loss of development value under Part VI of the Town and Country Planning Act, 1947, might have given some indication of the practicability of estimating, simultaneously, comparative potential values on a wide scale. They did not. This was because it was left to owners of land to claim and many did not; small claims were ruled out; valuations were prepared in order to negotiate claims; and January, 1947, the date for which the valuations were prepared, was a time when there was little prospect of private development. As to the second question, where land is fairly ripe market transactions should give a good guide to the price to be paid. But just because there are relatively few such transactions, and because these are likely to take place where prospects of development are more assured than not, it is argued that compensation which is based on them for land which is not ripe will probably tend to over-estimate development possibilities. This is likely, it is argued, if only for one reason: it is very difficult when negotiating for a public authority to establish that development will not fall upon a particular piece of land, and will not fall on it for some long period ahead. In the attempt to be fair to landowners, therefore, compensation is often awarded where true doubt exists as to the development prospects.

Whatever the difficulties, however, of preparing a picture of the development value for a whole area two things can be said. The existence of development values on sites heralds the informed opinion of the market that changes by development on them are due at some time, if they will be permitted by the planning authority. And trends in such values indicate trends in the prospects of such development.

Use and Investment Value, Rental and Capital Value

So far we have referred to values firstly as though they were always use values, and secondly as though capital values were always a simple capitalisation of rental values at a given rate per cent. But this is an oversimplification. On the first point, occupied property is often sold in the market for investment at an investment value different from its value for use. This occurs, for one thing, because in buying for investment it is the prospective income which is bought rather than the property. Similar properties, therefore, of similar use values may have different investment values. A freehold shop let on a short lease, with the prospect of increased rent at the end of the term, will fetch more than a similar property let at the same rent on a long lease. A rent-controlled house will fetch less than a similar house which is decontrolled. Furthermore, the investment value of a property may be affected by legislation which alters ownership rights, such as that controlling increases in rents or the selling price of new houses, although neither the use of the property nor its use value will be directly altered. On the second point, whereas the use value of a shop in a first-class position may be double that in a second-class position when expressed in rental value, it may be nearly treble when expressed in capital value simply because its rate of capitalisation is higher than that of the second-class shop. Or while rental values of properties may remain stable their capital values may change over a short period owing to changes in the market rate of interest for long-term loans, or the availability of loans from banks and building societies. A decreasing rate of interest will tend to increase property values, as will a relaxation of credit whereby would-be purchasers are stimulated and sales brought about more readily.

Similar properties with similar use values may therefore have differing investment values, which are invariably expressed as capital values. Similar properties with similar rental values may have differing capital values merely because their capitalisation rate differs. Capital values may change over a period in a manner unrelated to changes in use. The relation, therefore, between the land use and capital values of properties will not necessarily correspond with the relation between their land use and rental values. In attempting to find a relationship between land use and land values, therefore, in the manner we have described, it is simplest to employ use and rental values. The employment of other values makes for complication unless they can be suitably analysed to pick out the use value element this is not always easy.

Summary

This discussion has led to our principal conclusions with regard to land use and land values. We have seen the kind of social and economic forces which operate to bring about land uses and changes in use; and that these changes are associated with land values and changes in them. Just as uses and the trends in current and potential uses can be analysed, so can values and the trends in current and potential use values. The two are inter-related, although not in a simple way. Values are created and changed by the same forces that create and change uses: the " forces that create urban growths also create urban land values."[20] But values are affected in consequence of actual or expected changes in use and not directly by these forces.

Land values are not so much a tangible reality in themselves but rather a symptom and reflection of uses in land, of what is happening, has happened and is tending to happen to land use. There are, however, several different kinds of land values and each cannot be interpreted in the same way to indicate what is happening with regard to uses. Current or potential use values on a rental basis bear the closest relation to land use; changes in capital values, however, may reflect changes in spheres which have no direct relation to land use.

Valuation

The art and practice of valuation is largely concerned with the investigations for, and the expression of, an informed opinion as to what price would or should be offered or paid for property under certain defined conditions. These conditions can be very diverse, making it possible to have many different prices for the same property according to the conditions which are assumed. For example, the required price may be that which should be offered or paid for an immediate purchase or sale in the market: the valuation for exchange; that which the property might sell at if there were a forced sale in the future: the valuation for mortgage; the price at which a property owned by a person who has just died might have sold if offered at the date of his death: the valuation for probate; the rent at which a property might be expected to let from year to year under certain prescribed conditions: the valuation for rating.

The valuer does not decide what prices should be under the different conditions, but expresses an opinion of what would happen in the market under these conditions. Where transactions are carried out in the market in conditions comparable to those he has to assume he can readily test his opinion; and should market trends differ from what he forecasts, and shows signs of continuing to do so, he will adjust his opinions. Where no transactions are carried out, however, under conditions which are comparable to those they have to assume, valuers find themselves at a loss. They still have opinions as to the prices which would result in the market; but no means of testing the opinions. This is often the position with regard to valuation for compensation on compulsory acquisition, under the existing use value formula of the 1947 Act, of properties with development value. Since transactions for these properties rarely take place under the conditions stated in the formula it has become increasingly difficult to know whether the valuer's opinion reflects market conditions. Valuation then consists of making estimates which can rarely be tested; and such estimates may become very unreliable.

Since market prices are continuously changing for a variety of reasons a valuer needs to study them in order to keep himself informed. In doing so he knows that prices will fluctuate about a norm; and it is the norm in which he is interested, and long-term trends in values rather than short-term fluctuations. He is not puzzled when encountering the apocryphal auction records of five out of six identical interests selling for £X and the sixth for £$2X$, but guesses that there is something unexpected about the last sale which has no bearing on market value.

Keeping informed upon transactions in the property market is a more complex business than watching, for example, the stock market. For one thing, there are no comprehensive quotations each day. Sale prices at auctions are public knowledge, as sometimes are private treaty sale prices; but on the whole there is great reserve about rents and sale prices, the information on most of which is kept within the offices of surveyors, estate agents, insurance companies, local authorities, building societies, rating authorities and district valuers.[21] The last have the most comprehensive information since they are notified of all transactions in the country on which stamp duty is paid.[22] For another thing, a note of the transactions is not enough; an analysis of prices is essential. Similar prices may conceal variations in the interests in and rentals of physically identical units, and in the situation, structural condition, age and layout of non-identical units. For the analysis, details of the interests and an inspection of the property are necessary.

The valuer is not, however, content merely to watch and analyse market prices; he will know something of the conditions which influence and make up the market, understand its working and forecast what the market will do in response to certain circumstances. For this he must be in touch with the occupiers and users of properties and with the development process as we have described it. In understanding values he is thus comprehending the influences that affect them: and in doing so, as we have seen, the influences affecting town growth and change as a whole. He would acquire a deep comprehension of these influences if he followed the advice of the American, Richard M. Hurd, which was given some 50 years ago: " To look at the problem from the individual standpoint, in attempting to state the value of any single property, the inquiry would seek first, upon what forces does the city itself depend, how permanent are they, how diversified, are they strengthening and what is the resulting index figure, to wit, the rate of increase of the city's population; next, what are the characteristics of the section of the city in which the property is located, its past history, its present stability, its future prospects; what is the central strength of the property, how near the main center of the city or the various sub-centers of attraction; what is its axial strength, the quality, quantity and regularity of the passing travel, what is the character of building on the property as to suitability, planning, physical condition, prospect of changing utility, management, convertibility, gross and net income; at what prices have surrounding property been selling, are they rising or falling, and do they suggest any factors not yet taken into account; is the property liable to be injured or benefited by changes in the building laws; is there any special enterprise or strength on the part of the owner or of surrounding district likely to affect the property, what would be the probable effect of any inventions or improvements in transportation or the construction of buildings, and, finally what are the general commercial conditions as affecting the earning power of tenants, actual or prospective, and financial conditions affecting the capitalisation rate."[23]

Land Value Maps

Valuers use graphical methods of representing land values very little in practice; but there are examples of their use, chiefly foreign ones, for purposes other than land planning. These will be briefly described.

The simplest and commonest is the use of a map as an index of transactions. Where a sale price or rent of a particular property is known it can be recorded directly on a map, or in a file or card index under a reference number which is recorded on the map. This does not greatly facilitate comparison in values since the figures are not reduced to units.

Hurd gives maps which compare for the centres of many American cities the value of corners of street blocks (Fig. 10). The comparison is in terms of unit values, that is market (capital) value in dollars per foot frontage for a lot (plot) of average width and depth. This does not indicate actual values of properties but values of the plots should they be cleared and become available for development.

A similar map is given in Homer Hoyt's classic study of the relation between land use and land value in Chicago between 1830 and 1930.[24] This traces the growth of Chicago from a hamlet of log huts in 1830 to a metropolis of nearly 4,000,000 people in 1933, with a rise in value from a few thousand to five billion dollars. The map compares the values of the principal business corners throughout the city; the values are shown by the size of circles which are drawn to scale (Fig. 11).

In this Chicago study are three other land value maps which are of interest in showing methods of presentation. Fig. 12 shows the sale price obtained for acre tracts when Chicago was spreading in 1890-92. Since the tracts are of similar shape and size the figures can be used for direct comparison. Fig 13 shows the values of residential land in dollars per foot frontage in 1931, derived by the author from taxation assessments. Fig 14 shows the percentage increase in land values between 1918 and 1928, in three ranges. The biggest percentage increase took place in the areas of new settlement to the north and south of the town, and the smallest in the older areas where population declined.

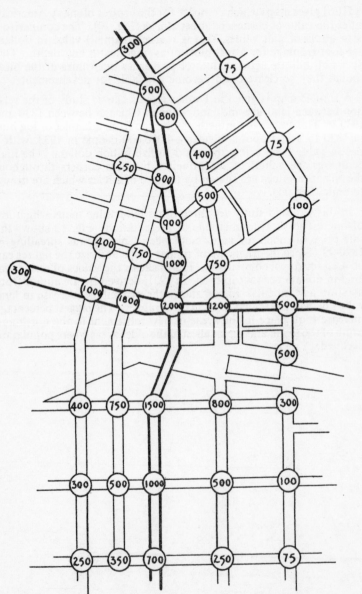

FIGURE 10.—*Diagram of Central Atlanta, U.S.A., Showing the Value of Corners of Street Blocks, in Dollars, at about 1900*

Source: *See note 23.*

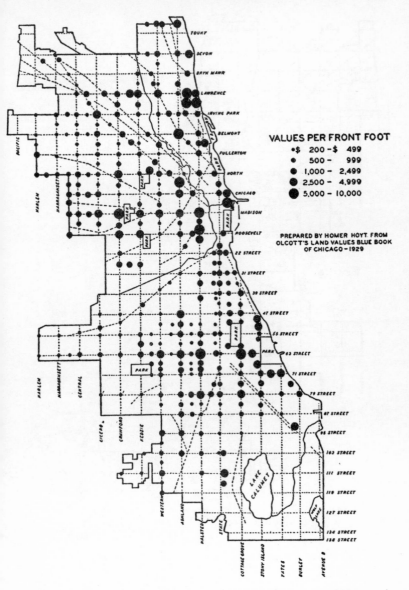

VALUES PER FRONT FOOT

- •$ 200 -$ 499
- •   500 -   999
- • 1,000 - 2,499
- • 2,500 - 4,999
- • 5,000 - 10,000

PREPARED BY HOMER HOYT FROM
OLCOTT'S LAND VALUES BLUE BOOK
OF CHICAGO - 1929

FIGURE 11.—*Map of Chicago Showing Land Values of the Principal Business Corners Outside the Loop,* 1928

Source: *See note 24.*

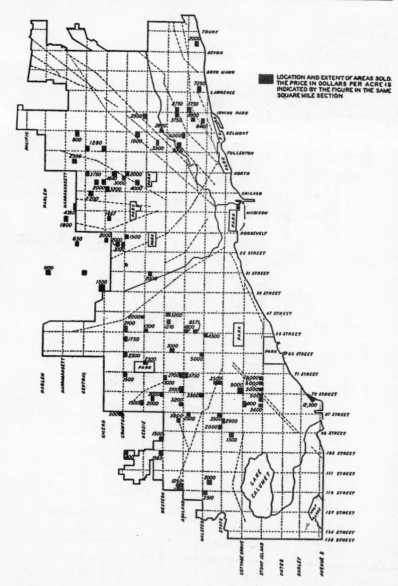

FIGURE 12.—*Map of Chicago Showing Land Values, 1890 to 1892, Indicated by Sales of Acre Tracts*

Source: *See note 24.*

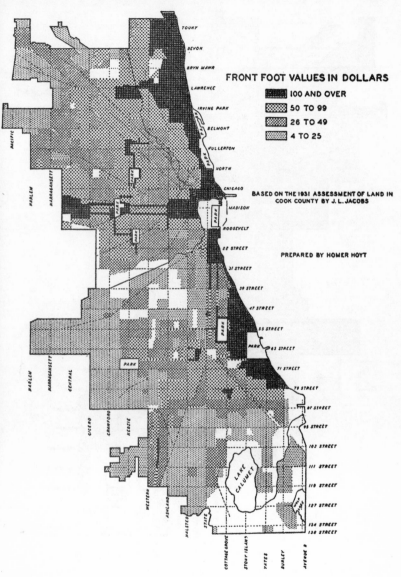

FIGURE 13.—*Map of Chicago Showing Residential Land Values per front foot,* 1931

Source: *See note 24.*

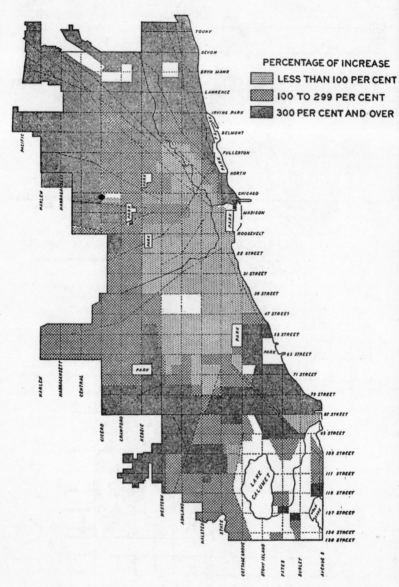

FIGURE 14.—*Map of Chicago Showing Increase in Land Values*
1918 to 1928

Source: *See note 24.*

Land value maps are prepared in some countries in connection with taxation or rating assessments. They facilitate the work of the valuers, assisting them to achieve some measure of uniformity in assessment, and are published to enable taxpayers and ratepayers to see that the assessments are equitable as between properties. Two examples will be described.

In Denmark public revenue is obtained in part from three kinds of tax on property: a tax on land value, on increases in land value and on improvements. For the purpose of assessment valuations are made of the capital value of the land (for the purpose for which it is best adapted if it were without its improvements) and also of the improvements (the difference between the total value of the property and its unimproved value). It is the value of the land which has, since 1920, been shown on land value maps. Before assessments are made for this, there is fixed a general level of values based on transactions. In the towns the unit of value is that per square metre of an imaginary plot of a standard depth of 30 metres (20 metres in some parts of Copenhagen) and this is shown for every street or part of a street (Fig. 15). Assessments of each actual plot are calculated from this unit value, allowance by formula being made for differing depths and for plots on a corner. In the countryside the unit of value is the hectare of an imaginary medium-size farm, and assessments of actual farms are calculated from this.[25]

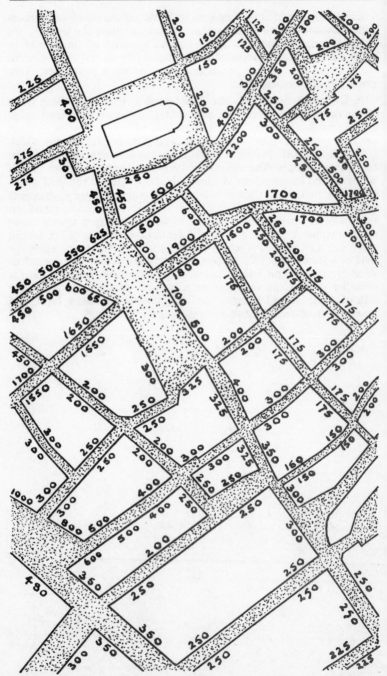

FIGURE 15.—Section of Land Value Map for Copenhagen, Showing Values of Land for Rating Assessments

Source: See note 25.

In the United States practice varies from State to State but there is ordinarily levied a general property tax on the capital value of property. For the purpose of assessment the land is usually valued separately from the buildings: the land as a site cleared of any buildings and used for the purpose for which it is best adapted, and the buildings at their cost of reproduction or replacement (that is their cost to provide if new, less depreciation, which is derived from standard tables). The sum of the values gives the assessment; this is the summation method of valuation. It is the land values which are shown on maps, and have been in New York since 1910. Fig. 16 is an example for Cuyahoga County, Ohio, where the unit value in the townships for land is the value per foot frontage of site to a depth of 100 ft. With the map are also published tables giving one of the many methods used by appraisers (valuers) in the U.S. of calculating from these unit values the values of plots of varying depths or of non-rectangular shapes, and of plots on corners.[26]

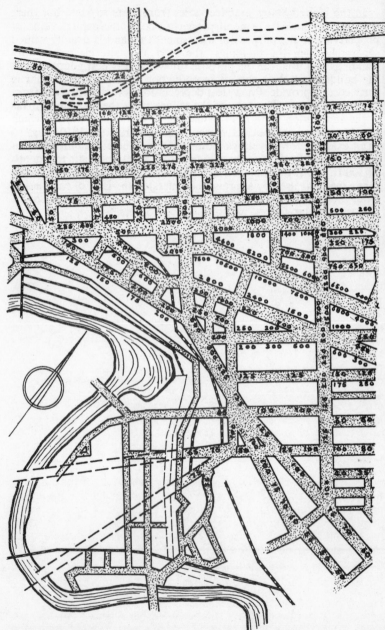

FIGURE 16.—*Section of Land Value Map for Cuyahoga County, Ohio, U.S.A., Showing Values of Land for Taxation Assessment*
Source: *See Note 26.*

CHAPTER 23

COMPENSATION AND BETTERMENT

The Compensation and Betterment Problem—History of Compensation and Betterment Before 1939—A. Compensation for Injurious Affection from Control Over the Use of Land—B. Betterment— (a) Betterment Proper—(b) Increase in Value Due to Community Influences—Proposals in Barlow Report, Uthwatt Report and 1944 White Paper—The Town and Country Planning Act, 1947, Uthwatt Report and the 1944 White Paper—A. Compensation for Injurious Affection Owing to Planning Restrictions—B. Betterment—The 1947 Act Financial Provisions and Planning—Reasons for Repeal of the 1947 Act Financial Provisions—The New Financial Provisions— The New Financial Provisions and Planning.

WHERE a private individual or body wishes to interfere with another's proprietary rights, and so perhaps diminish the value of the other's property, he can obtain no specific authority and must face legal action in respect of any damage done. Should he do something to improve the value of another's property, for example by building shops which attract higher values to adjoining land, he has no means, except by agreement, of obtaining any of the enhanced value. A public body, on the other hand, can interfere with proprietary rights on the specific authorisation by Parliament or a Minister; and the authorisation indicates the kind of damage to such rights which attract compensation from the body, and the formula for assessing its amount. Should the public body by its action improve the value of another's proprietary rights it is also sometimes authorised to collect for itself some, if not all, of the increase in value: of the " betterment."

Furthermore, it has on two occasions been the law of the country, but it is not at present, that the central government should levy a tax on all increments in the value of land (that is, of land independently of buildings) from whatever cause they arise. This has been based on the proposition that the community and not private owners should have the benefit of all or part of such increments since they result primarily from the existence and activities of the community (from for example growth and movements in population and increases in purchasing power) and only in part from those of landowners. The proposition has not led to a law providing for the community to compensate property owners whose values are depreciated merely by changes in its activities: by migration, for example, of people from one part of the country to another. The increase in land values due to these community influences is not normally termed betterment; for although this term is not used with precision it has generally come to be applied to " any increase in the value of land (including buildings thereon) arising from central or local government action, whether positive, e.g., by the execution of public works or improvements, or negative, e.g., by the imposition of restrictions on other land."[1] The term, therefore, does not include increases in value which result from action by central or local government which is not directed specifically to particular land: from, for example, the diversion by the Board of Trade of new industry to the development areas, or the subsidisation of particular industries such as agriculture or shipping.

It is difficult to distinguish in practice between the enhancement in value due to betterment proper and that due to more general causes; and between that part of the enhancement which is due to the manner in which a landowner or developer has used or created his opportunities, and that solely is due to community influences and which he passively receives. Partly in consequence of this the methods used by government in its attempt to collect the different kinds of increase in land value have become intertwined with each other. We must, therefore, consider all such methods. In practice, too, the usual methods of levying a tax on all increments in value, the rating and taxation of site values, become intertwined with the long-established practice of levying income tax and local rates on this practice here because it is simply a means of raising public funds. But we must note that these rates and taxes can be increased with any increase in the current use values of property, whatever the cause of such increase, and that they are lowered if the values fall.

The payment of compensation and the collection of betterment are thus, in brief, the means of making some financial adjustment between public authorities and landowners where the value of property is depreciated or enhanced by certain kinds of public action. The adjustment is not made in all cases where values are affected, there being differences in the nature and scale of the adjustment, the occasions when it is made and the methods of making it. The amount of depreciation will not in all cases therefore be offset exactly by the amount of compensation, nor the amount of enhancement by the amount of betterment; and nor will compensation that is paid always equal the betterment that is collected.

The depreciation or enhancement of values as a result of public action or control does not arise only as a result of land planning; in fact, as we shall see, financial adjustments of the kind described were made long before statutory planning was established. But the problem of paying compensation and collecting betterment has been particularly associated with statutory planning ever since it began in this country in 1909. A reason for this is that the exercise of planning powers results in much wider effects on land values than that of other earlier powers; and, as a corollary, the effective use of planning powers requires some appropriate compensation and betterment scheme. It is the relation of such schemes to planning that we shall primarily consider in this chapter. It is not sufficient for us merely to study the current scheme for compensation and betterment in Parts V and VI of the 1947 Act as amended by the Acts of 1953 and 1954. We must review the way the current scheme has evolved. In doing so we shall see that schemes, in their devising, must not merely provide for effective planning but also reflect the current attitude of Parliament and the current social atmosphere as to the relationship between the community and property rights, must be practicable in administration and have no undesirable effects on the economic and social framework.

History of Compensation and Betterment Before 1939

(A) Compensation for Injurious Affection from Control Over the Use of Land.

As we saw above (Chapter 11), whenever any interest in land is acquired by a public body compensation must be paid in law not only for the property taken but also for any injurious affection to other nearby land held by the same owner. It must also be paid for injurious affection to any other land the rights over which are interfered with by the construction of any works, even though no land has been taken from the owner. When, however, land is not acquired by a public body, but an interest in land is injuriously affected by public control over its use, and its value is depreciated, common law does not recognise the right to any compensation; as the Uthwatt Committee put it, any property rights that are lost " are destroyed on the grounds that their existence is contrary to the national interest."[2] The right to compensation in such circumstances is often, however, expressly conferred by statute.

With regard to existing buildings and existing uses the attitude of successive Parliaments has been fairly consistent in not permitting interference without compensation. Planning schemes under the Town and Country Planning Act, 1932, for example, had to secure that existing buildings could be renewed, maintained, reasonably altered and extended, and existing uses continued and reinstated.[3] This attitude was continued substantially in the 1947 and 1954 Acts although, as we shall see below, with not quite so much protection for the renewal of existing buildings. Exceptions to this attitude lie in the requirement that building bye-laws be observed whenever existing buildings are substantially altered or extended or their use materially changed; and that in smokeless zones existing fuel-burning apparatus should be altered to make it smokeless; and in the stipulation in the Town and Country Planning Act, 1947, that the right of the reinstatement of an existing building shall not include the right to reinstate one that does not conform to the building bye-laws.[4]

With regard to potential uses and values, and development values, there has not been this consistency and different Acts of Parliament have decided the matter in different ways. For example, compensation was payable for injurious affection following the introduction of a building line to roads and streets under the Roads Improvement Act, 1925, the prescription of a building line under the Public Health Act, 1925, and the adoption of a standard width for roads, and the restriction of building on classified roads, under the Restriction of Ribbon Development Act, 1935. It was not payable for injurious affection arising from the need to comply with building or street bye-laws made under the Public Health Acts. It was attracted for injurious affection arising from provisions in planning schemes under the Housing, Town Planning, etc., Act of 1909; but where a provision, with a view to securing the amenity of the area, prescribed the space about buildings, or their height or character, or limited the number of buildings to be erected, it was possible to avoid paying compensation. This principle, of avoiding compensation in certain cases, was extended in the Town and Country Planning Act, 1932. Under this Act compensation could also be avoided for provisions which, for example, prohibited or restricted building operations because they would be injurious to health or require excessive expenditure of public money on roads, sewers, water supply or other public services, or required accommodation for loading, unloading or fuelling vehicles intended to be used for business or industry. Furthermore, such provisions could have been introduced for any of the objects of a scheme (see Chapter 3, note 2) and not merely for securing amenity. But the amount of property in respect of which compensation could be avoided was limited because the Minister, before agreeing that it could be avoided, had to be satisfied that it was " proper and reasonable and expedient having regard to the local circumstances, taking into account (a) the nature and situation and existing development of the land affected by the provision in respect of which compensation is excluded and of neighbouring land not so affected; and (b) the interests of any person who would be affected by the provision in respect of which compensation is excluded."[5]   To what extent, in the face of this, planning schemes would have resulted in injurious affection without compensation is now difficult to say, because so few planning schemes were approved by 1939. But a pointer is given in the evidence to the Barlow Commission of the Ministry: " . . . the drinciple is already established that development which is contrary to the public interest may be prohibited without payment of compensation even though the prohibition may involve substantial loss to private owners."[6]

Another ground for excluding compensation, that of prematurity, which foreshadows section 20 (3) of the Town and Country Planning Act, 1954 (see page 346), was inserted in the Restriction of Ribbon Development Act, 1935. Under section 9 no claim for compensation for injurious affection under the Act would be entertained unless the claimant could show that the proposals for development at the date of the claim were immediately practicable, and that there was a demand for such development: in fact that the restrictions circumscribed the execution of development which was imminent.[7]

As public control over the use of land has steadily grown over the last hundred years it has been necessary to consider, with each infringement, whether or not and to what extent compensation for the loss of potential value should be granted by statute. There have been no formulæ for deciding these points. With the increase in public control over property rights, and the prospects of financial hardship to owners, there have been changes in the attitude of successive Parliaments, each influenced by the current social atmosphere as to the rights which property owners can be expected to yield up without compensation from the public purse. As the Uthwatt Committee put it, " . . . at what point does the public interest become such that a private individual ought to be called on to comply with a restriction or requirement designed to secure the public interest?" Taking the last hundred years in retrospect the Committee thought that the " history of the imposition of obligations without compensation has been to push that point progressively further on and to add to the list of requirements considered to be essential to the wellbeing of the community."[8] In other words, the cost of using land in the public interest has been transformed more and more into a private cost.

On the one hand Parliaments have had to avoid hardship to owners who would lose their property rights, a hardship which the affected owners find particularly unjust when others are permitted to retain the full value of their land. And on the other they have had to recognise that the loss of individual property rights is to the gain of, and essential to, the interests of the community; that there is a limit to the amount of compensation that can be found out of taxation; and that state interference today with property other than land may involve losses to some, and gains to others, on a large scale without any question of compensation.

(B) *Betterment*

The history of the attempts to secure some of the enhancement in value due to betterment proper on the one hand, and to general community influences on the other, are quite distinct from each other.

(a) *Betterment Proper*. Public action of a positive kind which increases the value of particular land has been taking place for centuries; and the attempts to recover for the community part of such increase have also been long practised, the first attempt having been made in an Act of 1427 empowering Commissioners of Sewers to levy a special rate on properties benefited by sea defence works. This method is partially one of recovering betterment and partially one of distributing the cost of public improvement among the occupiers or owners of those properties which are likely to benefit. It is not much used today in this country except in certain local Acts, in the levy of special rates (as, for example, by river and drainage boards and coast protection authorities) and in the recovery of the costs of making up private streets.[9]

An attempt to collect betterment was also made, under the name of " melioration," in the rebuilding of London after the Great Fire. The betterment was usually recovered as set-off against compensation.[10] This method has been included in many general and local Acts since the 19th century dealing with roads, housing and other public works (see page 192).[11] It does not appear, however, in the Lands Clauses Acts, Acquisition of Land (Assessment of Compensation) Act, 1919, or Town and Country Planning Acts.

Another method, already described (page 189), is that of " recoupment." This has not been popular with past Parliaments for general application, and has been mostly included in private Acts.[12] The wide powers of purchase in the Town and Country Planning Acts, 1944 and 1947, did permit of the principle being exercised, but the necessity of keeping down expenditure on acquisition under these Acts of recent years has reduced the possibilities of obtaining recoupment.

Negative restrictions on the use of land have also been imposed for centuries, but the first attempt to collect betterment on this account was under the Housing, Town Planning, etc., Act, 1909. Under this Act local authorities could impose negative restrictions in planning schemes on the use of lands, so enhancing the values of other land. The method used for collecting betterment was the " direct charge." Enhancement of value could also arise under a planning scheme as a result of public development, and a direct charge could also be levied to recover consequent betterment. These powers of collecting betterment were repeated in the Town Planning Acts of 1925 and 1932. This last Act empowered the authority to claim 75 per cent of the increase in value of property within 12 months of work being carried out, or of the coming into operation of the scheme; but the owners could defer claims until the enhancement in value was realised by, for example, sale, lease or change of use.[13] In practice betterment was very difficult to establish and collect. In all cash was collected in three cases under the 1909 and 1925 Acts, and not at all under the 1932 Act, although on a few occasions a claim for compensation was countered with a claim for betterment.[14] Negative restrictions on the use of land adjoining roads and streets have also been imposed in order to protect the line of proposed roads, as in the Public Health Act, 1925, section 33, or the Restriction of Ribbon Development Act, 1935, section 1; to control access to development along traffic roads as in the Restriction of Ribbon Development Act, 1935, section 2; to prescribe the lines of buildings along roads or streets or at junctions, as in the Roads Improvement Act, 1925, sections 4 and 5. All these Acts provided for betterment by way of " set-off " against any claim for injurious affection arising from the imposition of restrictions under them. Control under these Highway Acts is now superseded by planning control, under which there is now no provision for betterment. (See page 87 and page 347).

All these methods of collecting betterment were designed to recover increases in both existing and potential use values; there was no attempt to separate the two.

(b) *Increase in Value Due to Community Influences.* Proposals for the transfer to the community of private property in land have been made for centuries, and have recently been revived as regards rent-controlled property in the Labour Party election programme of 1955. As an alternative to land nationalisation, proposals have been made for the transfer to the community, by taxation, of privately owned land values or of increments in them; and it has often been advocated in this country that sites be rated to supplement or replace the rate income now collected from land and buildings. Arguments for this were put forward as early as 1775 in this country by Thomas Spence. Nineteenth-century inspirers of modern proposals were John Stuart Mill in this country and Henry George in the U.S.A. (Single Tax George). The reasoning behind proposals to levy taxes or rates on sites is both economic and political. Economists argue that land, or rather the economic rent in land, is a good source for taxes, because these would not be passed on to consumers, nor would they result in a curtailment of the supply of goods and services since they would not inhibit economic activity. Political grounds for the tax or rate are that economic rent derives primarily from the existence and activities of the community, and that it should be appropriated by them.[15]

Rates and taxes on site values are levied in other countries.[16] While in this country proposals for them have been debated almost continuously since 1885, site value rates have never been levied and site value taxes only for a short while.[17] This was in the Liberal Government's Finance (1909-10) Act, 1910, the only attempt to tax land values in this country which has actually resulted in money being collected. Four duties were introduced, of which only one the increment value duty, is strictly relevant here. This amounted to £1 for every £5 of increment value in land accruing after 30th April, 1909, and was to be paid on the sale of land, or on the granting of a long lease, or on death of the owner in the case of an individual, or at intervals of 10 years where a corporate body held the land. The value in question was the open market capital value of the site; in developed property this meant apportioning the total value between site and buildings. The legislation was complicated and raised many difficulties; the valuation was complex and was not expected to be completed before 1915. The agitated political controversies were, in retrospect, a rehearsal for those which have recently accompanied the financial provisions of the 1947 Act and its amendment.[18] After the 1918 war the position was inconclusively reviewed by a Select Committee of the House of Commons; and in the 1920 Finance Act the duties were repealed and the small amount of collected monies was refunded.

A second and more short-lived attempt at taxing land values was made in the Finance Act, 1931, by the Labour Government. The tax was to be at 1d. for each £1 of land value, this again being the open market capital value of the site free of improvement, based on a complicated valuation formula. The value of agricultural land was taken at its value for cultivation only, excluding any possible development value. Valuation was suspended under the 1932 Finance Act and the scheme itself abandoned in the 1934 Finance Act.

Among the attempts to levy site value rates was the Bill introduced by the London County Council, in 1901, in the attempt to supplement its normal income by a rate of 2s. in the £ on annual site value, the latter being defined to include development value. This was not successful. In 1938-39 the Council introduced another unsuccessful Bill proposing a similar rate in the £. The Government in 1907 introduced the Land Values (Scotland) Bill, following a successful private Bill from a Scottish member, for a rate of 2s. in the £ on annual value of land, which was defined as 4 per cent of the capital value of the cleared site. This Government Bill was amended by the House of Lords and never became law.

Proposals in Barlow Report, Uthwatt Report and 1944 White Paper

As part of its consideration of the distribution of industry and of the industrial population, the Barlow Commission reviewed town planning practice before the recent war. They received evidence to the effect that the difficulties being encountered by planning authorities, under the compensation and betterment provisions of the 1932 Act, were so great as seriously to hamper the progress of planning throughout the country, and they recommended, in 1939, the appointment of a body of experts to examine the question.[19] The Uthwatt Committee was accordingly set up in 1941 to " make an objective analysis of the subject of compensation and recovery of betterment in respect of public control of the use of land "; and they had to consider not only pre-war experience but also the needs of post-war reconstruction, and the steps that should be taken with regard to the problem to prevent the work of reconstruction being prejudiced. The Committee supported the findings of the Barlow Commission as to the difficulties experienced before the war with regard to compensation and betterment. In brief, these were that local authorities, as planning authorities, could not afford to pay for sterilising development value in land, whether by way of acquisition of land or compensation for injurious affection. They could not afford to do so because they received no financial assistance from the government and had to pay open market value, a value which was inflated when settling individual claims because of the difficulties of valuing floating value. Furthermore, the values which they paid for very often shifted to other land, but could not be recouped by the authority because the betterment provisions were ineffective; nor could any other betterment arising out of a planning scheme. And values which shifted to other land as a result of planning had often in turn to be acquired by the authority at market value. And since, in practice, planning authorities could not know their liability for their proposals until a scheme was made and claims were presented, their apprehension as to what this liability might be resulted in proposals being drawn which did little to restrict prospects of development, excepting where the authority intended to buy or where the Minister would agree that compensation need not be paid for injurious affection.[20]

The war-time Coalition Government did not fully accept the Committee's recommendation in the matter, and set out different proposals in 1944 which were largely followed by the Labour Government in the 1947 Act.[21] This has now been amended by the Town and Country Planning Acts of 1953 and 1954 on the lines foreshadowed by the White Paper of 1952.[22]

The Town and Country Planning Act, 1947, Uthwatt Report and the 1944 White Paper

We shall describe the provisions of the 1947 Act with regard to compensation and betterment. In doing so it will be useful to compare them with the apposite recommendations in the Uthwatt Report and the government proposals in the 1944 White Paper.

(A) *Compensation for Injurious Affection Owing to Planning Restrictions.*

(a) *Existing Use Values.* Where development was in existence in July, 1948, having been carried out in conformity with any planning control, or has since then been carried out in accordance with planning permission under the 1947 Act, it becomes an

authorised use. If the local planning authority requires the removal
or alteration of buildings or works which are so authorised, or the
discontinuance of any authorised use of land, it must pay compensation for depreciation in the value of the land and for disturbance.[23]
Where the depreciation results in the land becoming incapable of
" reasonably beneficial use " in its existing state, and it cannot be
rendered capable of such use by the carrying out of development
which the authority would permit, the owner can serve a purchase
notice on the authority requiring it to buy. The notice is sent to the
Minister. If he confirms the authority must buy, as though it
had in fact served a notice to treat for compulsory acquisition, and
must pay compensation on that basis.[24] Where a use is not
authorised, as, for example, where it has been carried out without
planning permission, no compensation is payable should the
authority require its removal; but the removal must be required
within four years of the development being carried out.[25]

Where any building was in existence in July, 1948 (or where
not in being on that date had been demolished since January, 1937)
or has been erected under a planning permission since July, 1948,
and permission is refused for its rebuilding, compensation is not
payable.[26] But an owner whose permission is refused can serve a
purchase notice on the local authority if he considers that the
property has become incapable of reasonably beneficial use in its
existing state.[27] This is passed to the Minister, who can grant the
permission applied for or can direct that some other permission
be given which will render the land capable of reasonably beneficial
use within a reasonable time. No compensation is attracted for
this. Or the Minister can confirm the notice, whereupon the
authority must buy as just described; but in doing so it need only
pay the site value for re-erection of the existing use as defined in
the Third Schedule of the Act (see page 341) if the development for
which permission was refused would have involved demolishing
the whole or most of the building.[28] An authority would thus appear
able to prevent the re-erection of a non-conforming or otherwise
obstructive building, without payment of any compensation, if
some other use of the site would be reasonably beneficial. In
practice, however, purchase notices can rarely be successfully resisted
under these conditions so that authorities are not able to do this
without payment.

The Uthwatt Committee considered the protection of existing
uses in the 1932 Act to have been too strong and favoured putting
a life on non-conforming buildings and uses; that is allocating a
period of years to it after taking into account " (a) the probable
effective physical life of the building having regard to its age and
condition, (b) its probable effective economic and income-producing
life, and (c) the degree and nature of the non-conformity." At
the end of the life the building or use could be made to conform

without compensation; and if this were done in advance of the expiration of the life the compensation payable would be assessed by reference to the remainder of the life still outstanding.[29]

The 1944 White Paper was not explicit in this matter of existing uses and buildings, but it can be assumed that no disturbance was intended without compensation.

(b) *Development Values.* In the 1947 Act development value is divided into two parts. The first is the value, for certain limited kinds of development, which is deemed to be part of the value of the land for its existing use. This development includes, for example, the use of the land, or land and buildings, for similar uses; the re-erection of demolished buildings; or the enlargement, improvement or other alteration of buildings, so long as the cubic capacity is not increased beyond 10 per cent or 1,750 cu. ft. in dwellings.[30] No development charge (this is described below) was payable on grant of permission for this development: and any valuation for compulsory acquisition, and on the confirmation of purchase notices, assumed that the owner would be allowed to carry out this limited development without development charge. In short, this part of development value was largely unaffected by the Act, just as existing uses and values were unaffected; and existing use value for valuation purposes under the Act was deemed to include this part of development value.[31]

The second part of development value is that which is in excess of the limited development value just described, and relates to what is called " new development " in Section 16 (5) of the Town and Country Planning Act, 1954. Such values were seriously affected by the 1947 Act for, on 1st July, 1948, they were taken over by the State which proposed to pay owners for them to the extent of £300,000,000. In promoting the Bill the government did not accept that landowners were entitled to compensation for their loss of development rights, taking its stand on the common law position with regard to development rights which was put forward in the Uthwatt Report, as described above (page 333). It recognised that hardship would be suffered by the owners of the rights and therefore provided this sum of £300,000,000 from which payments were to be made to owners of those rights which were depreciated.[32] The effect of this was that a local planning authority could, in controlling the use of land, affect development values without being called upon to pay compensation; and local authorities could acquire land at existing use values, that is without paying for these development values.

In order to frame a scheme for the distribution of the £300,000,000 the government asked for claims from those owners who considered that they possessed development value which had been taken over.

Development value for the purposes of the claim was to be calculated as the difference between the restricted and unrestricted value of the property, the former being its existing use value and the latter its value if the Act had not been passed. Both were to be calculated with regard to the physical state of the land and incidents of ownership, etc., as they were on the 1st July, 1948, but by reference to prices current immediately before 7th January, 1947, the date of the publication of the Bill. Small claims were not admissible.[33] The claims were made under Part VI of the Act and became known as Part VI claims.

The £300,000,000 was to be disbursed among claimants by 1953 in the form of government stock plus interest in cash for the period between July, 1948, and the date of payment. For some time no one could tell what proportion of any claim would be paid for land which was not agreed as " ripe for development " by the Central Land Board. Where it was agreed as ripe the claim was accepted as 100 per cent of the loss. The proportion became clear early in 1952 when a substantial number of the 820,000 valid claims had been agreed with the Central Land Board and it was announced that all the claims were likely to amount to between £345,000,000 and £350,000,000 and that the preferential claims, those for the ripest land, would amount to about £100,000,000. These agreed claims are called established claims in the Town and Country Planning Act, 1954.

The Uthwatt Committee recommended separate treatment for land lying outside built-up areas (subject to certain exceptions) and land lying within. For the former they recommended that the state acquire all development rights and pay for them fair compensation, by shares in a single sum, the General Compensation Fund, assessed globally for the whole country.[34] Their scheme was therefore similar to that in the 1947 Act, except that this related to development rights in all areas. For built-up areas the Committee recommended no such scheme. They thought that compensation should be paid for injurious affection because of planning restrictions, as under the 1932 Act; but compensation should be avoidable, the Committee thought, to a greater extent than under section 19 of the 1932 Act.[35]

The 1944 White Paper proposed that owners of both developed and undeveloped land which had development value on 31st March, 1939, would be entitled to compensation. Where rural land possessed little development value, claims for compensation would be met five years after the passing of the necessary Act. Claims for other land would be paid on refusal of permission to develop or re-develop. The amount of compensation was to be decided globally, after taking floating value into account, as suggested by the Uthwatt Committee. In computing these claims the White Paper visualised the exclusion of compensation which would not have been payable under the law at that time, that is, in particular, because of sections 19 and 20 of the Town and Country Planning Act, 1932.[36] No compensation would be payable for development value accruing after 1939.

(B) *Betterment.* The 1947 Act did not attempt to secure for the state or local authority any increases in the use values of developed properties, even increases which were the result of public action and which took place after the Act came into force. It was concerned mainly with development value which existed at the time the Act came into force, or which matured later, from whatever cause, on both developed or undeveloped land, and which owners wished to secure by carrying out development in accordance with planning permission. Where they did, since the State had taken over development rights it was necessary for the developers to repurchase them, and to this end they had to pay a development charge. Where an owner did not wish to secure the development value by development no charge was levied.

With certain exceptions, no development could be carried out without a development charge having been determined by the Central Land Board and its payment secured. The exceptions were that development included in the definition of "existing use" as described above, minor development which was exempted by regulations, and certain other kinds of development which were proposed on ripe land, or land held or acquired by local authorities and New Town Development Corporations.[37] The amount of the charge was left to the Central Land Board and there was no right of appeal. It was to be the full difference between the value of the land without the benefit of the planning permission which was sought (refusal value), and the value it would have with the benefit of the permission if no development charges were payable (consent value).[38] The Board could not differentiate between developers, so that there was no question of particular development being stimulated and other development discouraged.

It was thus proposed to compensate owners for the loss of their development rights as they existed in July, 1948, and at prices ruling in January, 1947, and then on some global rather than individual basis; and to assess development charge at prices ruling when the development application was made, and in respect of the difference that would be made by the permission to the value of the property, as it existed when the application was made. There was, therefore, except in ripe land, no identity between, on the one hand, the loss of development value in 1948 on a particular property or the amount to be paid on the established claim; and, on the other, the development charge which would be levied. It follows that only where the development charge was more than the established claim could it be said to represent betterment, and also that it was not necessarily " betterment proper," as described above, since in assessing the charge no attempt was made to decide the cause of the development value. The charge was levied whether the value arose from betterment proper or from general community influences.

Under the Uthwatt scheme betterment would have been recoverable in two ways. All undeveloped land was to be acquired by the state, when ready for development, at the value for its current use, the development rights being already owned. It would then be disposed of for development at a price or rent that would reflect the new use.[39] Betterment would be received where the price or rent exceeded the cost of acquisition of both development rights and the property itself. And in all land other than agricultural, including that developed after the scheme was started, increases in annual site value, from whatever cause other than that of certain recent expenditure by the owner, would be subject to an annual levy of, it was suggested, 75 per cent. An initial valuation was to set the datum, and a revaluation made every five years.[40] The Committee thought that their suggestions would make recovery of betterment by direct charge and set off no longer necessary, but that recoupment could continue.

The 1944 Act White Paper scheme was again very similar to that in the 1947 Act, proposing a betterment charge of 80 per cent on increases in value of land which could be realised on the granting of planning permissions.[41]

The 1947 Act Financial Provisions and Planning

It is generally agreed that the 1947 Act financial provisions largely removed the particular difficulties which were found to be hampering pre-war planning. Local authorities no longer had to meet the cost of sterilising the greater part of development values, whether by way of compensation for injurious affection or on purchase, since such rights were owned by the state and were to be paid for, as a whole, by the exchequer. In consequence plans were drawn more freely than before. The allocation of land for development could reflect the amount that would be needed over about 20 years and not simply all the land that had development value. And land for the business centre of a new town could be bought at agricultural value, and not at a value which reflected the intended development, so that the development corporation, and not the landowner, would receive the benefit of the development value which it had created out of its activities and out of public money. Furthermore, since the development charge was intended as a means of " holding the scales evenly between those who were allowed to develop and those who were not,"[42] planning authorities, in allocating certain land for development and restricting other land, could justifiably disregard any protest that the owners of the former were benefited while the owners of the latter were not. Let us consider three owners of three under-developed properties, each having equal development value and equal agreed claims. If one were permitted to develop, one not and the third were bought out by an authority at existing use value, the financial advantage of the first over the other two was offset by his having to pay a development charge amounting to the development value of his land. In practice, however, the amount of the charge was often not great enough to nullify his advantage altogether, and he was still left at least with his developer's profit.

The 1947 Act did not, however, remove all the difficulties facing planning authorities. They could not, except at very heavy cost, buy standing property for re-development, or secure the removal of non-conforming uses, despite the government grants made available under the 1947 Act. Nor could they, except by recoupment and increased rating assessments, obtain any of the betterment that resulted from their activities.

Reasons for Repeal of the 1947 Act Financial Provisions

The 1947 Act financial provisions have been amended not so much because they have hampered planning, but for various other reasons.[43] Firstly, the government decided that the payment of the £300,000,000 in 1953 would be undesirable since it would be inflationary in effect, and also because it would benefit many owners who had no case for compensation. Instances of such owners were those who had no intention of developing at all or for very many years, or those who could realise their development value only by a form of development which on current standards would be considered unneighbourly, or which would place an undue burden on the community. Secondly, the development charge had proved to be very unpopular because its basis and incidence were uncertain; and because payment in cash was often required of an owner even though he did not know when, and what proportion of, his claim on the £300,000,000 would be met. Thirdly, the development charge did not secure one of its important objects, that property should change hands at existing use values. Fourthly, it had adverse effects on the smoothness of the development process, as described in Chapter 6, and tended to retard re-development, as described in Chapter 22; these particular effects would probably have become more serious as building became more free.

The New Financial Provisions

In the White Paper of 1952 the government announced its intention of abandoning the compensation-betterment provisions of the 1947 Act, and, in brief, of not buying all development rights for £300,000,000; of abolishing the development charge; and of confining compensation to those owners whose development rights as they existed in 1948 were injuriously affected by planning decisions; and of not paying compensation to all these.

(a) *Compensation for Injurious Affection to Development Rights.*
The scheme to pay for development rights was abandoned in the
Town and Country Planning Act, 1953, section 1. The provisions
for compensation for injurious affection to them are in the Town
and Country Planning Act, 1954, Part II. Compensation is to be
paid only when loss is suffered, that is when, in general, the development of land is prevented or restricted under planning control.
Where permission is granted there is no claim. Where it is refused,
or granted subject to conditions, there is. For any particular piece
of land the compensation will be either the unexpended balance of
the established development value or the depreciation in the value
of the interest which is caused by the decision, whichever is the
smaller.

It is not intended to meet all established claims, even where loss
of development value is caused by refusal of permission or by
conditions attached to a permission. Compensation can be avoided
on various grounds, under sections 20 and 21.

At the one extreme, compensation will arise where permission is
refused for any development by way of building, engineering or
mining operations in, on, over or under land, except where the refusal
is on account of certain stated reasons. Then no compensation is
payable. These reasons are that the development would be premature either because of the order of priority indicated in the development plan for the area, or because of the existing deficiency in water
supply or sewerage services, or because the land is unsuitable for
the proposed development on account of its liability to flooding
or subsidence. At the other extreme, compensation will not be paid
where permission is refused for development which amounts merely
to making a material change in the use of buildings or land or to
the display of advertisements. In between these extremes two other
situations are catered for. Firstly, if permission is granted for
operations but conditions are imposed, no compensation is payable
for any conditions relating to density; layout; dimensions, design,
structure, external appearance or materials of building; provision
of facilities for parking, loading, unloading or fuelling of vehicles;
the use of any buildings or other land; the location or design of
any means of access to a highway (not including a service road)
or the materials used in its construction. Secondly, where permission
is refused but would be granted instead for any development which
consists wholly or mainly of the construction of houses, flats, shops
or office premises, or industrial buildings (including warehouses),
or any combination thereof, then no compensation is payable.

The adverse planning decision which gives rise to the claim will
be normally made by the local planning authority. The owner who
is injuriously affected will then make his claim within six months
to the authority, who will transmit to the Minister. The Minister
can review the planning decision and can modify it, after hearing the

authority and applicant as necessary. If an adverse planning decision is maintained, and compensation is due, it will be paid by the government.

The grounds just described for avoiding compensation are based on the precedent of section 19 of the 1932 Act (see page 334) but the effect may be very different in practice from that of the 1932 Act. Under this the possible effect on development values was clear to landowners when the scheme was approved by the Minister, since this was all to 25-in. scale and was fairly precisely interpreted in the scheme clauses, and the prospects of compensation being paid for damage could be forecast. Under the new provisions, the effect on development values will often not be known, because of the scale and flexibility of a plan, until a planning decision has been given and been reviewed by the Minister. Under the 1932 Act compensation was rarely avoidable where the scheme would in fact have substantially depreciated development values. Under the new provisions decisions will be given against the background of a plan which was drawn before the amendment of the 1947 Act, that is by an authority which felt free, because it had no liability for compensation, to depreciate the development values of certain land. It follows that compensation may often be avoided, on the various grounds described above, where in fact the plan has already depreciated values. For example, it might be possible to avoid a claim for compensation on a site on a traffic road, which has shopping value and an established claim, where permission is refused for shops but would be granted for dwellings.

(b) *Betterment.* In the 1952 Act development charge was completely dropped, and it is not proposed to put anything in its place. In giving his reasons for this, the Minister referred only to the betterment aspect of the charge, and not to its function in holding the balance between owners. He said " The truth is that the real purpose of the 1947 Acts was to facilitate planning in the modern world. They were planning Acts and not taxing Acts. They dealt with the intractable problem of how planning could be financed "; and " betterment may come into being, and if it does it will be taxed in quite a lot of ways under the ordinary taxation system of the country."[44]

The New Financial Provisions and Planning

It is too early to see how planning, as we have known it under the 1947 Act, will be affected by the new provisions, but certain possibilites can be visualised. Authorities are likely to be in the same position with regard to existing uses and values as under the 1947 Act. They will still be free of the cost of compensating for injurious affection to development values; but whereas under the 1947 Act they had no need to be influenced by the existence of claims for loss of development value, these may now influence them.

Firstly, local authorities will be faced with higher costs than previously on compulsory acquisition of certain sites, and in meeting certain purchase notices; they will now have to pay in addition to existing use value the unexpended balance of any established claim, including interest, but to offset this they will be relieved of the development charge they previously had to pay for certain kinds of development, and will often receive under the 1954 Act higher grants than previously. These additional factors may influence them to select certain sites rather than others for acquisition and development. Secondly, because of the abandonment of development charge, local planning authorities and local authorities with delegated powers, are now likely, in development control, to be more sensitive to the effect of their proposals, whether for acquisition or restriction of development, upon the fortunes of individual owners. The effect on owners of similar properties might be very different. Of the three owners in the example given above (page 344) the one bought out would be paid existing use value plus his established claim, including interest, the one who was refused permission would retain his existing use value and perhaps receive his established claim, while the first who was given permission would have the benefit of full market value. The adverse planning decision to the second owner would mean not only loss of development value but also, in certain circumstances, loss of compensation for it. The price paid to the owner who was bought out would be less than market value where development value of his property had increased substantially since 1947. It has been suggested, however, on this last point that there are factors within the Act which could inhibit price competition for potential building land, and thus tend to moderate disparity between open market and compulsory purchase value.[45] Cases will also arise where development values have not increased since 1947 so that compulsory purchase value will in fact be more than market value.

Authorities are also likely to appreciate more readily the significance of land values in the preparation and implementation of planning proposals. This appreciation was blunted by the provisions of the 1947 Act. Because of these it was too readily assumed that since the responsibility for the financial consequences of the effect of planning proposals on land values had been shifted to the state, these consequences could be disregarded, as could also the guide that land values can give to deciding the best use of land. These matters are discussed in Chapters 24 and 25.

As to betterment, local authorities are in the same position as under the 1947 Act, and can rely only on recoupment or increased rating assessments; but the exchequer will not have the betterment that could have been collected under the 1947 Act by way of development charges. It may be that there will in consequence arise further discussion on the possibility of collecting betterment, independently of planning machinery, by means of the taxation or rating of site values. This possibility was not considered by the Uthwatt Committee to be within its province;[46] and the majority of the Committee of Enquiry, which was set up soon after the passing of the 1947 Act, to consider the "practicability and desirability of meeting part of local expenditure by an additional rate on site values, having regard to the provisions of the Town and Country Planning Act, 1947, and other factors" reported against the rate mainly because of the now abandoned development charge provisions of the 1947 Act. Since these, they argued, ensured that the community received increases in development value, the only practicable basis of assessment for a site value rate was current use value, and this would not achieve any of the usual objectives of a site value rate. A minority did not, however, think that current use value was the only basis for assessment nor that the 1947 Act impaired the arguments in favour of a rate on site values.[47]

CHAPTER 24

THE EFFECT OF A DEVELOPMENT PLAN ON LAND VALUES

What is Meant by the Effect of a Plan on Land Values (A) What Would Happen to Land Values Without a Plan (B) The Effect of a Plan on Land Values of Individual Properties: Uncertainty, Reservations for a Purpose Which Will Involve Acquisition by a Public Authority, Road Schemes and Other Diagrammatic Proposals, Allocations of Land to Different Primary Uses (Zoning) (C) When Does the Effect of a Plan on Land Values Take Place (D) Effect of a Plan on Land Values in General.

What is Meant by the Effect of a Plan on Land Values

WHEN considering the effect of a development plan on land values attention is usually confined in practice to a fairly limited aspect of the matter. The effect is considered at the point in time when the plan is first published as one agreed by the local planning authority for submission to the Minister for approval, that is when it is placed on deposit for public inspection and, if need be, objection; the land values are those of individual properties, and it is to the financial consequences for the owners and occupiers of those properties that attention is paid and not the consequences, for example, for other owners or owners as a whole; and the matter is considered as though the plan has had a sudden impact on values on its publication and foreknowledge of the proposals, or apprehension with regard to them, have not already registered the impact. Before discussing the matter from this aspect in (B), we will consider as a background what would happen to land values if there were no plan (A); and later consider just when the effect of a development plan on values can be said to take place (C); and the effect of a plan on values in general (D).

(A) What Would Happen to Land Values Without a Plan

It is rather difficult for us to visualise today in this country what would happen to development and values without the presence of a plan and planning control. It is over 10 years since the Town and Country Planning (Interim Development) Act, 1943, introduced universal planning control in Great Britain and some 20 years since such control was widely applied under the 1932 Act; and with planning control there has always been in the background some plan, statutory or unofficial, changing or enduring, as the case might be, with regard to which the control has been exercised. This was recognised in making claims for loss of development value under Part VI of the 1947 Act. In estimating unrestricted value account had necessarily to be taken of what was likely to have been permitted under a pre-war planning scheme, or interim development control, and also of the compensation that might have been awarded to owners under the 1932 Act.[1]

But it is not difficult for us to see that without a plan towns would grow and alter in shape, and development and re-development would take place, as a result of the economic and social forces we have described. Some towns would change rapidly, others would stagnate and yet others would decline. Values would change or fail to change accordingly. Current use values would rise and fall, because, for example, of something fairly intangible like changes in fashion in residential areas; or because of something more tangible like the building of a new shopping centre which draws custom away from an established one, or the building of factories which depreciate the surrounding residential amenities and values. Such changes would probably be more drastic than those which are experienced where planning control exists. Development by public bodies would take place, after acquisition of land for which there would have to be paid the compensation stipulated by statute; and some of this development, as for example of railway stations, traffic routes and utilities, would greatly influence the direction of other development and of values. In effect, most if not all of the proposals of public developers which now appear in development plans would be made known and carried out under the appropriate statutes. Development and re-development would take place, and new uses and new values would be created, normally as a result of the highest bid. The most intense form of development that was economically profitable would be carried out on individual sites, subject to bye-law and similar control, so maximising their values and diminishing the opportunities for realising development value on other sites. Individual developers would not know, with any certainty, what was to be expected by way of development on sites adjoining theirs or in different parts of the town. They would not have the advantage of a plan which gives a general picture, and the only picture which is normally available, of development of all kinds which is likely to take place, of the periods within which the development can be expected, and of development trends which it is proposed to modify, suppress or divert. Without a plan there would be more cases than at present of values being affected by development which was never expected. There would also be shifts of values as where, for example, an otherwise suitable office site which had been spoilt by the erection of adjoining warehouse premises, and their heavy traffic, would lose its potential office value to the gain of another suitable site.

In short, the values of individual properties would not be stable, but would rise or fall because of a variety of influences. A plan modifies these influences or strengthens them, and adds to, detracts from or leaves unaltered, as the case might be, the increase or decrease in values that would have otherwise gone on.

(B) The Effect of a Plan on Land Values of Individual Properties

The effect on values of a plan is the effect of its different elements. These produce a different kind of effect according to whether they are reservations for a purpose which involves acquisition by a public authority; road schemes and other diagrammatic proposals; or allocations of land for different primary uses (zoning). Before considering these in turn, mainly in relation to the town map, we will refer to the effect on land values of two general factors: provisions for compensation and betterment, and the uncertainty which arises from the nature of a development plan.

We shall not, for the sake of simplicity, be dealing fully here with the effect on values of arrangements for paying compensation to owners for the depreciation of values or for the collection of betterment. These, as we have seen, do not so much alter the effect of the plan on values as the financial consequences to the owners of the values. A piece of land, for example, may lose its development value by being kept open as green belt. If it is subject to an established claim the exchequer will bear the loss or some part of it. If there is no claim the loss will fall on one or other private party, according to the circumstances and the provisions of Part I of the Town and Country Planning Act, 1954.

(a) *Uncertainty.*   A development plan has not the precision of a scheme under the Town and Country Planning Act, 1932. There is a certain flexibility in it, and in the exercise of the considerable powers of development control under it, as we saw in Chapter 2. In consequence, outside areas covered by comprehensive development area or supplementary town maps, the plan and written matter are not explicit about the authority's intentions with regard to each property. This leads to uncertainty in the minds of people as to the future of any property with which they are concerned; and the uncertainty affects values just as do the specific proposals in the plan. The uncertainty is increased, as is the effect on values, by genuine misapprehension as to the purpose and nature of a plan and what it is intended to convey.

Examples will be given below of uncertainty in relation to proposals in town maps, but it also arises with regard to comprehensive development area maps. To the owners of most property within it, definition of an area introduces certainty, even though it is unwelcome; the owners know, as everyone else does, that they may be bought out in a relatively short time. For the owners of some properties, however, there is uncertainty, as where the properties have been included in the area in order that a reasonable planning unit could be defined: properties of long life, for example, surrounded by others needing re-development, or whose inclusion has been necessary to make a suitable boundary. The approval of the comprehensive development area map by the Minister, with these long-life properties included in the defined area, gives the authority the power of applying for a compulsory purchase order after designating the land. But the power may or may not be exercised; and even if it is exercised the order may not be approved by the Minister.

Uncertainty of this kind is reduced if information is obtained from the local planning authority as to its intentions. This was seen when objections to development plans were withdrawn when the authority made clear its intentions in the form of undertakings that there would be, for example, no disturbance of a particular property for at least a stated period, or that its extension would be permitted. The objectors had not sought to obtain amendment of the plan, whatever the phraseology of the actual objection, so much as the clarification of the uncertainty, and the reduction of its adverse effect on values. Uncertainty of this kind will probably decrease as the years go by, as refusals and consents are given, as the Minister's decisions are obtained on appeal, as a knowledge of the authority's intentions emerge, and as the owners and users of property gain experience of what the plan actually means, and lose some of their apprehensions about it and some of their misapprehensions. Transactions will continue with greater confidence. Values may return to their former levels, or they may exceed them, and will tend to become more stable.

Uncertainty could be minimised, it has been suggested, by changing the nature of the development plan and including as proposals only those which are fully worked out to large scale, and to the carrying out of which the authorities are financially committed.[2] This could, however, amount only to a short-term programme, and hardly a plan. In achieving certainty in this way much would be lost that is in the interests of the area that is being planned: the looking ahead, the flexibility of approach, the review of decisions in changing conditions, the possibility of meeting the wishes of developers within a broad policy framework; in fact the benefits of a plan itself. In short, if there is to be land planning there must inevitably be some uncertainty; and it is likely that the development plan gives rise to less uncertainty than would be occasioned by other ways of preparing and presenting town plans. The need for relating the plan to a period and to resources means, for example, that proposals are not put forward which have no chance at all of realisation, but which would nevertheless, if put forward, affect values. The need to divide the programme into stages also assists in clarifying intention, for all concerned have a clearer idea of what to expect than from a plan without stages: the farmer at the edge of a town, for example, whose land is not to be used for housing in the first period of the plan. The defining of an area of comprehensive development produces relative certainty for owners outside the area. This must be selected to accord with the Act, and the five-year programme stages require that the proposals are carefully prepared. This makes for attention being given to virtually each property before it is included in a defined area. Finally, certainty is introduced by the statutory limitation on the Minister's approval of a designation map. For him to approve, the map must show property for acquisition only if it is required within 10 years, if urban, and within 7 years if agricultural.

Uncertainty is undesirable and should be avoided unless it is inevitable; it will be indicated below how uncertainty can be minimised in the preparation and implementation of development plans.

We will now return to the effect of the different elements in a plan on values of individual properties. We will see that a proposal will not necessarily affect the use and investment values of a particular property in the same way.

(b) *Reservations for a Purpose Which Will Involve Acquisition by a Public Authority.* The simplest cases to consider are those areas which are privately owned but are clearly intended for a specific public use involving public acquisition: the reservations, for example, for schools, open space, principal car parks and railway extension. Simplicity of effect arises in these cases because of relative certainty: firstly because the site will usually have been selected with some care in order that it can be shown with precision on a 6-in. map; and secondly because the implications of eventual public purchase are clearly appreciated. The effect will be most certain if it is known, from a programme or designation map, that the purchase will be fairly imminent. If it is not to be imminent the effect is less certain, since the scheme might take up to 20 years to come about, and might even not materialise; a public body is not bound to pursue its proposals. In some such cases values may not be adversely affected. The market, and occupiers of property, do not always have complete confidence in the stated aims of public authorities, and they may discount for a proposal which they think is so unrealistic that it is never likely to come about.

The use values to the occupiers of the affected properties will be diminished by the prospective disturbance, where this is expected to be fairly soon or where the time of intended acquisition is uncertain. The depreciation in value might be quite small where the properties have users who habitually take premises on short tenancies, as for example have certain types of flats in times when there is no housing shortage. But the use value to occupying industrialists or shopkeepers is more seriously diminished if their use seems likely to be disturbed.

Exchange values, whether for the purposes of occupation or investment, will probably be more seriously affected, even in those cases where the owner can look forward to compensation at full market value at the time of acquisition. For one thing purchasers are reluctant to buy, either for occupation or investment, property which is likely to be compulsorily acquired at some later date; and it is made difficult for them to buy because banks, building societies, etc., are reluctant to lend on such property. For another, the owner himself similarly finds it difficult to borrow money on the property, money which may be required to finance a move to another site, and so is disposed to accept a lower price. For another, when public acquisition of property is threatened there is a natural tendency for occupiers and owners to have less interest in it than before, and for it to deteriorate in consequence and to become less valuable. Any reduction in value resulting from these factors may lead to compensation on eventual acquisition being lower than market value at the time the proposal is made known, for if the acquisition takes place after many years the negotiations for compensation must reflect the lowered value. It is for this reason that land ought not to be threatened by proposals unless these are reasonably firm; land values should not be undermined unnecessarily. This was recognised in the Town and Country Planning Act, 1947, section 51 (3), with regard to land designated in a plan. It there states that where interests in such land are valued for compulsory purchase no account shall be taken in calculating its value " of any depreciation in the value of such interests which is attributable to the designation ".

Development value, which is to be prevented by the reservation from settling on land, may shift to other land where the demand for the use is capable of being satisfied, and where the planning authority would permit the value to be realised. The shift cannot be traced precisely. It will become palpable in the enhanced prospects of development on this other land compared to what would have been the prospects before the plan was published.

In some cases owners of development value which will be acquired on purchase cannot look forward to compensation at market value for the loss of their development rights. This arises where the unexpended balance of the established claim for such rights, the measure of the compensation, is less than their value in the market.

The threat of public acquisition of particular property today therefore may depreciate its value. This is in contrast to the position in the last century and early part of this one. Then owners often welcomed the prospects of being bought out by a public authority because, for various reasons, they received generous compensation. Speculators often, in fact, bought up property on the line of road improvements in the expectation of profit. On the then existing arrangements for compensation the Scott Committee of 1918 reported: " It has become notorious . . . that the sums paid for the acquisition of property for public purposes, not only in contested but also in uncontested, cases, have for many years past been in many cases excessive."[3]

Reservations for public use may influence values of adjoining land. A simple example is the proposal for a public open space which would increase the use value and investment value of dwellings adjoining, and also the development value of adjoining sites for dwellings. Another example is the reservation for a car park or omnibus station which would probably have the opposite effect on residential values because of possible injury to amenity. In such a case, or where a site is allocated to a wholesale market, a new railway station or municipal offices in an established residential area, the diminution of residential use value may be accompanied by an increase in development value. A retail or wholesale market, for example, will attract shopkeepers, restaurants and service industry to serve the people who would congregate there. A site for a new group of public buildings might attract a demand for office use.

New commercial development values which settle in this way will sometimes be entirely new to the area, as where a new retail market attracts new shoppers to the town. Sometimes they will be floating development values which are already present, as where the trends in development of a central shopping area are diverted to the fringes of a new bus station. Or it may be that the new values will replace current use values which are made to decline by the new reservation, or made to decline more rapidly than they otherwise would have done.

(c) *Road Schemes and Other Diagrammatic Proposals.* Where the property that will be required for a road scheme is clearly indicated, as it might be where a new road is to run between two existing parallel streets, the property so shown can be said to be specifically reserved, and the values will be affected in the manner described. This is the exceptional case, however; most of the road proposals shown on town maps are diagrammatic, and do not attempt to indicate the property that will be affected by them. For example, when an existing road is picked out on the map as a principal traffic road, by two parallel lines of constant width, these do not purport to show the intended width of the road or the side on which any widening will take place; in fact no widening or improvement may be intended. Or when a new principal traffic road is shown by such lines, although it is more often than not carefully plotted from larger scale plans it is again diagrammatic. When therefore the road is built, a slight deviation of line may affect properties away from the plotted road line, and leave some undisturbed which appear to be affected on the town map.

Not only is what is shown little guide to what will happen in practice, but in diagrammatic road proposals there is much that is not shown. Firstly, proposed roundabouts and similar improvements to junctions are not normally mentioned in the written matter to the plan, and no attempt is made to delineate their extent on the town or programme map, even though considerable acquisition may be entailed. Secondly, it is not known how much acquisition and re-development there will be outside the road line where a new road cuts across developed property. The uncertainty in such a case is considerable because it is not known whether the authority will carry out the work by acquiring only what is needed for the road, or whether it will initiate comprehensive development for the purpose of dealing with the frontage land. Thirdly, town maps do not show roads of less importance than trunk and principal traffic roads; in some towns therefore proposals for the widening and improvement of important streets, which have been designed in detail, are left out of the plan.

Road proposals were presented in the initial set of plans in this way because there was not the time to carry out the detailed surveys necessary to finalise all new road schemes, nor was it thought desirable to attempt this, and present detailed plans to the public, too long in advance of the work being carried out. It was hoped that objections and discussions could be postponed until more detail had been worked out and construction was imminent. Nonetheless, and perhaps unavoidably, it introduced great uncertainty; and apprehension has led to the claim that the values have suffered in all properties that might conceivably be affected. An authority has often found it possible to reduce such uncertainty by producing some of the larger scale schemes upon which the diagrammatic proposals have been based. This happened at development plan inquiries where, to meet objections, authorities often produced detailed plans to justify their diagrammatic road proposals. The discussion in detail at the inquiry has had to be fully considered in detail after the inquiry by the government departments concerned. In most cases the result has been a clarification of the authority's intention, and an increase in certainty, even if the objector did not always succeed in having the offending road line altered.

Comparable in its effect on values with diagrammatic road lines, but probably creating more uncertainty still, is the symbol indicating approximately where in a built up area there will be a school reservation when more details have been worked out. Since the symbol conveys the intention to reserve a school site in its vicinity on the plan, occupiers and would-be purchasers of property in the vicinity, of the kind that might attract an acquiring authority, naturally have their minds exercised in the matter, so affecting values.

(d) *Allocations of Land to Different Primary Uses* (*Zoning*). The elements in a plan which are most complex in their effect on values, and which affect the greatest number of properties and the greatest amount of value, are the allocations of areas to be used primarily for residential, industrial, principal business, shopping, civic, cultural or other use. Such areas are drawn with a fairly wide brush on a town map, since the map is intended to be a broad statement of intentions and to show only a few primary uses. It follows that the authority's intentions with regard to the development of particular properties are not precisely indicated, and indeed often cannot be formulated until development applications are submitted. The plan will thus give a *prima facie* indication of the effect of the allocations on values of particular properties, but in many cases the effect can only be seen when the authority gives its decision on an application or the Minister does so on appeal. It is the *prima facie* indication in the plan that we will discuss.

The simplest case is the allocation to a primary use of fully developed land whose current use accords with the primary use and of which no re-development is proposed. The effect will be to make more certain the use and occupation of the property, since continued use without interference by a public authority is assured, as is the exclusion of inharmonious surrounding uses. Use values and investment values will be stabilised, and will be enhanced through the greater certainty.

There will often be properties whose current use does not accord with the primary use of the area within which they fall; they will be non-conforming. Here uncertainty is introduced. The uncertainty is less in certain cases than others. For example, where an old and dilapidated factory is being used for a noxious trade in a residential area, action by the authority to close the non-conforming use is much more likely than where there is a modern and substantial factory in the rear of a shopping centre. Where the primary use would *prima facie* permit of a more profitable use in the non-conforming properties than their current one, as, for example, where houses come within an industrial area, the market values of the non-conforming properties would be increased, since any development value for the more profitable use could be exploited by the owners. But the use value for dwellings in such an area will diminish, since there is no future for that use and there is the likelihood of inharmonious uses being introduced. Where the non-conforming uses are " zoned down " in value the position is different. Where, for example, factories are included in a proposed residential area, the owners will not re-develop for the lower value use, and action by the authority will be required if the factories are to go. The authority may in fact intend that the factories will stay indefinitely, since they do not conflict with surrounding uses, but in such a case the use and investment value of the premises will diminish if only because of the uncertainty about possibilities of expansion.

As to development values in general, where land, whether virgin or built-up, has development value and is allocated to development, this value will be capable of realisation. If it is not so allocated then it will not, and its potential use value will be lowered. Even if it is allocated for development, it might be for a use which is less profitable than some other for which there is a demand, and its value will be lowered.

Sometimes land which has development value, an obsolete housing area or business area, is intended for development or re-development by a public authority, for housing, factories, shopping, etc. The development value will not, therefore, be realisable by the current owners, and they will be in much the same position as owners whose property is subject to a reservation which will involve acquisition by a public body, as already described.

Of interest to those concerned with potential use and development values will be not only the uses which may be permitted, but also the density of use, particularly in business areas. If there is the demand, higher density will mean a higher development value. If the values flowing from a high density in business areas can be realised on a particular site, and a lower density only is permitted, the development value of the site is diminished.

(C) When Does the Effect of a Plan on Land Values Take Place?

It is natural that the effect of a plan on values is considered at the time it is put on deposit. Not till then is it certain what proposals the local planning authority will adopt; and then is the occasion for owners and occupiers to consider the effect of the plan on their properties, to decide whether or not to object to the Minister, and the grounds on which an objection can be made. While, however, the publication of a plan is a significant event, it is really the climax of one process and the beginning of another. The effect on values is felt long before this climax is reached. The authorities will have been working on their plans for many years, and some of their proposals will have remained unchanged since, for example, they were included and published as part of pre-war statutory schemes or advisory plans. Others will have been introduced into the development plan for the first time, but they will have been discussed in committee and council and with other interested authorities, referred to in council minutes, brought out at inquiries into refusals of planning permission, made known to owners and developers who had made informal inquiries, or submitted formal applications for permission to develop, or made searches as to title on purchase. In some measure a knowledge of various proposals will have got about among the public and those interested in property, and will have influenced purchasers, tenants and mortgagees, and so affected values. Values which had been so affected would fluctuate were there later changes, as where proposals are ommitted from development plans when it becomes appreciated that they are unlikely to be achieved within the period of the plan.

There is thus probably little that is new in development plans when they are published, little that those concerned with property could not have discovered in preceding years had they been so minded. But the publication of the plan and the ensuing public inquiry by the Minister does in itself have its effect on values. An opportunity is given of studying all the proposals so that the comprehensive effect on values can be seen; the proposals which have been selected from among the many that have been discussed are picked out so that uncertainty about tentative proposals is removed and their effect made clear; opportunity is given for attempts to secure clarification of uncertainty; the preliminary skirmishes are fought in the eventual disputes over compensation; the prospects of development in the future, and perhaps distant future, are discussed at the inquiry and the intentions of the planning authority are made clearer; perhaps more information is obtained about proposed public development.

(D) Effect of a Plan on Land Values in General

The effect of a plan on land values in general, that is from the viewpoint of owners and occupiers as a whole, is partly gauged by a summarisation of its effects on individual properties, as described above. If all the properties in the town were considered individually this general picture would emerge; and it would be found that losses on some would be accompanied by gains on others. But this is part only of the general effect, for we have not considered above those proposals in a plan which affect values of properties although they do not directly impinge upon the properties in question. Some instances will be given.

Firstly, there are those proposals which affect the basis of current values in the town. Where a plan, for example, allocates land for substantial expansion by immigration of people, and these are likely to come, use and development values in the central business area will increase in expectation of the increased purchasing power. Conversely, where a town is thriving industrially, and is attracting immigrants to work and live in it, a plan which aims at stopping expansion by immigration, by allocating insufficient land to meet the demand for houses and factories, will result in an increase in the development value of particular sites but probably in a diminution in the total development value for dwellings and industry. It will probably result, too, in an increase in the current use values of residential property as this becomes scarce in relation to demand by immigrants; these will not stop coming to the town just because of the plan. Effects such as these are seen on the edge of metropolitan London as a result of the implementation of the policy of restricting the growth of London. Another example arises where a by-pass road, by threatening to divert traffic and people from a particular town centre, also threatens the trade, and therefore the values, of the shops in that centre. This kind of threat is often based more on apprehension than reality; but there are cases where it would be real, and where it would undermine values. Another example is where a plan proposes to permit the manufacture of cement quite near a well-established seaside town, so that visitors to the town will be discouraged and shopping, entertainment and hotel interests will suffer, and the values which are based on them.

Secondly, there are the broad effects of density zoning. Limitations upon the intensity of development, both for residential and commercial use, make possible a shifting of development value on to other land where the demand for such use can be satisfied. If a town is to expand at an average net residential density of 50 habitable rooms to the acre it follows that more land will be required than if the density were 70 habitable rooms to the acre; more land acquires development value. This was an argument used by Sir Raymond Unwin in his battle for lower densities.[4] He showed that it would take, on the then current trends, 146 years to re-develop for commerce the 44 square miles of blight in central Chicago, 187 years if there were re-development for residential use at 100 families to the acre, and 18·7 years at 10 families to the acre. He argued from this, and from similar figures for the 61·7 acres of vacant land in New York City, that it would pay landowners as a whole to accept a plan which envisaged the low density and low value development, because more of them would obtain development value even though individuals had their land values depreciated. To the landowners as a whole this is an unanswerable argument; to the individual landowner, hoping for some of the commercial value to settle on his land, it is unacceptable, as Sir Raymond recognised when arguing for lower housing densities.[5] It is an argument which could be employed in favour of reducing the density of business use in rebuilding a city centre where there are fears that there will not be enough demand to take up the amount of business floor space that existed previously. But were this done there would probably be successful purchase notices, and the compensation on the land so acquired would probably be above the values that could be realised on resale or letting, for it would be difficult to prove that values were in fact falling; and where values were increased on the fringes, through the lowering of the average density, the betterment, in the absence of purchase for recoupment, would flow to private pockets.

Conversely, if the amount of land allocated for development is small enough in extent to force high densities it follows that the development value on that land will tend to be increased through the more intense use; it might also result in monopoly conditions being introduced which would permit of particularly high prices or rents being asked and high values being established.

Thirdly, there is the effect of over-zoning: the allocation to a use of more land than the long-term demand justifies. Where there is significant over-zoning, values on particular pieces of land may be reduced; there will be more choice of land for developers so that owners in competition will need to reduce prices. But it will not necessarily result in a reduced average intensity of development over the whole area, and in consequence reduced average development values. Developers will still proceed to build at a density which they find profitable and not at any lower density. It is the demand for development which determines the value in this case and not the supply of available land. The over-zoning of developed residential land for business and industrial use, through optimism about the demand for such uses, may have the effect of diminishing current use values if tight development control is not exercised. Once a few sporadic new businesses or factory premises are permitted the residential amenity of the dwellings is diminished, as is their use value. In some properties the development value for the new use will compensate for the fall in the current use value, but not in all. This optimistic over-zoning of developed areas for a more profitable use in the United States has contributed to the growth of blighted areas, those where current uses and values are undermined and new uses and values do not arise, and " where it is not profitable to make or maintain improvements "; or " those sections of a community where, as a result of social, economic, or other conditions, there is a marked discrepancy between the value placed upon the property by the owner and its value for any uses to which it can be put, appropriate to the public welfare, under existing circumstances."[6] The effect there of over-zoning has been aggravated through the practice of basing local tax assessments on potential values which tend in turn to follow zoning. Owners might have to pay unduly high taxes on dwellings whose current use values are undermined by loss of residential amenity.

Fourthly, although a plan cannot decide that development value will settle on a particular piece of land rather than on other land, it can strongly influence where it will settle. Where houses, for example, will be as successfully sold or rented on one piece of land as another, and there is little difference in the costs of development, then development value can be led to settle on the land allocated in the plan for residential purposes. Where a central shopping area can equally well extend along one of two streets, the introduction of a traffic route cutting across one of the streets may well force the development values to settle in the other street. But such values cannot always, or entirely, be shifted. In Sir Arnold Plant's words: " There is no economic law as to the conservation of value."[7]

Where very attractive housing land which has development value is not so allocated, and less attractive land is, the latter will probably have development value but not so much as could have been realised on the former; or where sites on a town centre, having unique value for business and shopping because of their location, are allocated to car parks or open space, their development value will not be fully recreated on adjoining sites which are allocated to business use, and may not be recreated at all. In short, two plans may allocate the same acreage of land for particular uses, and one will be fully implemented and not the other; and even were they both fully implemented as visualised, one might result in more value and general utility, being created on development, than the other.

CHAPTER 25

LAND VALUES AND PLANNING FOR AN URBAN AREA

Land Values in the Development Plans—How a Knowledge of Land Values Might be Used in Planning an Urban Area: The Analysis of a Town's Problems and Defects, Preparation and Implementation of Proposals, Phasing of Acquisition—Land Value Maps in Planning —Obtaining and Using Information on Land Values.

Land Values in the Development Plans

THAT a knowledge of land values might assist in the preparation of a development plan is apparent because of their close relationship to land use. Little guide is afforded, however, to the manner of their employment for the purpose in the regulations and circulars dealing with the preparation of the initial development plans. Their only reference to the matter is the request that in the written statement should be included an estimate of the cost of acquiring land which is designated within an area of comprehensive development.[1] There is no request, for example, for information on current land values, or the effect on them of the plan, for the consideration of land values in preparing proposals, for estimates of land acquisition costs where public acquisition of non-designated land is involved. And a perusal of the written analyses for plans will show that although many authorities do consider acquisition costs, there is in general no more than a passing reference, if that, to the subject of land value among the full consideration that is given to such matters as land use, traffic flow, density, housing conditions, employment and education.

It is not that the considerations concerning land values and land cost are considered unimportant in planning, either by central government or local planning authorities. Some regard has certainly been paid to them in the preparation of most plans, even though this has not been based on formal survey and analysis. That there has been this regard, even though attention has not been drawn to it, is probably due, for one thing, to land values being directly related to and symptomatic of other things which are more familiar in planning. In having regard to these, regard is also had to land values. The answer to which of two pieces of land will make the better housing site, for example, will have been sought in terms of such things as elevation of the ground, aspect, nature of the soil and convenience for transportation services; and the same answer would have been reached as if it had been sought in terms of land values. For another thing, the need to consider the practicability of achieving proposals in about 20 years has led an authority, where the cost of a proposal would fall on the public purse, to have regard to cost in terms of land acquisition before finalising proposals; and even if specialist valuation advice has not been sought there has been some general knowledge of the property values in the town and where it would be expensive to acquire.

That the regard for land values has not been more pointed has been due in part to the atmosphere created by the 1947 Act. In offering a solution to compensation and betterment, it tackled the problem of the financial adjustment between landowners and government where planning proposals affected land values. To many, however, it appeared to make unnecessary any consideration of land value at all, in the sense in which we have been discussing it, in the preparation and administration of plans. It has also been due in part to the practical reasons we have discussed earlier. In contrast to such matters as land use, the age of buildings, population, employment and traffic, it is difficult to obtain for planning purposes comprehensive information on land values, to make an analysis of any such information and of trends in values, or to devise some graphical representation of the information and its analysis which can be readily related to other aspects of the survey and analysis. There is, in short, difficulty in obtaining, and no established technique for using, a knowledge of land values in the preparation of a plan. What is said in this chapter must be regarded as a contribution towards the furtherance of such a technique, and not the description of one which is generally employed.

How a Knowledge of Land Values Might be Used in Planning an Urban Area

A. *The Analysis of a Town's Problems and Defects.* The current use values of land, or land and buildings, are related to their differential qualities which give rise to rent in land. This suggests that a comparison of such values would throw light on these differences in qualities. For example, a comparison of current use values would assist in the division of a central shopping area into the different groups of shopping which make up such a centre: the groups of stores, multiples, local traders, high quality shopping and of the fringe shopping which is really of a neighbourhood character. Or a study of the differences in current use values for similar uses throughout a town would help to throw light on the qualities which the users of land and buildings value in them and in their location, and for which they are prepared to pay, and which a plan might try to create and enhance. This would supplement what can be learned from land use maps about the structure, shape and working of the town in the same way as does information on accommodation density, floor space index and the age and condition of buildings.

It does not follow that the higher land values are always associated with desirable qualities. They may result from good or bad conditions from the town's point of view. High shop values may be associated with highly accessible and convenient shopping sites; but also with intolerable congestion. High residential values per acre may be found in slums because of the overcrowding of people in them. Particularly high values for houses have of recent years been associated with their exceptional scarcity in relation to demand. In these and other cases high values result from defects which a plan might aim at remedying.

Interest in the structure, shape and working of a town is not confined to obtaining a static picture on each occasion that a survey is carried out; it extends to comprehending the trends in change and movement within the town which are taking place all the time, even though slowly. This comprehension is advanced by, among other things, a study of the wishes and interests of developers when they make informal inquiries or formal applications for permission to develop. It will be assisted by an awareness of changes and trends in current use and development values. For example, movements of trading activity from and within the central shopping areas of towns have been quite common, often resulting, as at Southampton and West Hartlepool, from an extensive suburban spread which has made the historic shopping centre inconvenient for the new residential areas. Such movements in trading are reflected in the higher rents which forward-looking traders are prepared to pay in certain places, and in the increase there of development values, and in the reduction in rents which are asked for in other places. The trends in trading are reflected in trends in value.

Such shifts in shopping centres have been comparatively gentle in this country, and it is not to be expected that anything as violent will occur here as has happened in this connection in the U.S.A. But experience there illustrates the point. The congestion of people and traffic in central shopping areas has become so intense in certain towns that it has become possible to divert a substantial amount of potential custom away from the centre to new out of town regional shopping centres which permit of shopping in comfort to those who are prepared to use motor cars for the purpose. Examples of such centres are Thirlington near Washington; Clearview near Princeton, New Jersey; Middlesex at Framingham, Massachusetts; and Northgate near Seattle. A knowledge of trends in use values in such a case might give warning of impending change. As it has been stated with regard to American conditions, " The stability of a retail business section is most endangered when rental values have reached their highest level. The pressure of population that causes values to increase in such a section tends, in time, to destroy accessibility by congestion and to reduce the security on which the values depend."[2] If despite the warning it were not practicable to stimulate remedial measures in the old centre, the warning might be sufficiently timely to enable the planning authority to ensure that the new development took place in a planned manner.

In a similar way the study of trends in use values might help to illuminate what is taking place in most of our big towns by way of dispersal of people, business and industry from their centres. Whatever the cause of the dispersal, it results in a falling off in demand for accommodation in the central parts of the towns, and an increase in demand in other parts. This again is a process which takes place slowly; but the effect on values is illustrated by recalling what happened on the occasion of dispersal, following bombing in the recent war, of people and business from central parts of towns. Large dwellings outside the central part of the town suddenly were in demand for business use, so increasing their use value above former levels; other dwellings in the town dropped in value as people left it for safer areas.

Where the current use values of land and buildings are much below the potential use value of the land if it were cleared, it means that the land in question is under-developed and that full use is not being made of its potentialities. In the normal working of the development process a private developer would seek in such circumstances to redevelop in due course; but it is in the general interest if the planning authority can anticipate the move, can be ready for the re-development proposal, and perhaps arrange for its initiation, speeding up or implementation. A knowledge of values may be a guide in this, perhaps a better guide to the likelihood of re-development than the physical appearance or age of buildings which has often been the only criteria in preparing a life of buildings survey. In a similar way a knowledge of values may indicate when non-conforming factories are approaching the end of their economic life and, therefore, when it is reasonable for a development application for extensive renovations to be refused because it is timely for the factory to be removed to another site.

A knowledge of whether buildings are coming to the end of their economic lives is of value in considering the ever present problem of widening traffic routes. Where a substantial amount of property on such a route is becoming ripe for re-development it is reasonable to expect that improvement can be achieved within a reasonable time merely by requiring the new buildings to be set back to a new line; but where little property on the route is approaching ripeness it will be known that any improvement in the next decade or two can be achieved only by re-development. This knowledge should lead either to re-development proposals where the widening is urgent, or perhaps to a search for an immediate alternative to the road widening.

A knowledge of values may also be of help in considering the future of areas of mixed use, particularly those areas of transition around the centres of towns in which are found dwellings, shops, factories, warehouses and other uses. In deciding the primary use to which such an area should be allocated in a plan, regard is normally had to the uses which predominate, to the need for protection from other inharmonious uses of those which do not predominate, to trends in uses and to the difficulties of zoning against rising development values. A study of trends in current use and development values may also help in making the decision. If, for example, a housing area has been invaded by business uses, which have sought to take advantage of low land cost, it is common practice to zone up to the higher values. If, however, there is little development value in the area, an authority might be encouraged to resist further business use and to allocate it for residential purposes.

In zoning on the fringe of a central area regard must be had to any need for the expansion of the central business area because, for example, of expected population changes. A knowledge of development values would supplement other means of gauging whether there is really the demand for such expansion; the existence of development value in the land would mean that developers are willing to back their judgment with money that such demand exists. Furthermore, where it is recognised that the additional land should be allocated in the plan, the existence of development values will indicate the direction in which the business area will most easily grow.

Finally, it will be recalled what was said earlier of a person informed of values: that his knowledge is not based entirely on the records of sales, but also on familiarity with the different sections of the community from whose activities land values derive. For example, the estimates of whether development value for shops exists on a certain site is based, in part, on a knowledge of the habits of shoppers, since it is upon this kind of knowledge that shop developers and shopkeepers will rely before embarking upon development. In other words, in acquiring a knowledge of a town's values there is also necessarily acquired a great deal of other knowledge which may be useful in analysing its problems.

B. Preparation and Implementation of Proposals. The regard for land values in the preparation of proposals might arise in many different ways; and this regard will be needed throughout the preparation of proposals, and not merely at one stage or when the plan is completed.

In formulating proposals their effect on different parts of the town should be considered, and not only their impact on the specific properties which are affected. Will, for example, a proposed industrial zone or sewage works affect the residential amenities of nearby dwellings and the potential residential amenities of nearby building land, or a proposed bus station or market the livelihoods of certain traders? These and other questions should be asked and answered, and it should be considered whether the consequences are desirable. It is not necessary to do this in terms of land values, nor is it always simple or possible to do so, but often a consideration of the effects in terms of land values will assist. For the reasons given earlier it does not follow that a diminution in land values is always to be avoided or resisted; it might be necessary if defects in the town's structure or pattern are to be remedied. But where there must result a diminution or destruction of potential values, a knowledge of land values will assist in the earmarking of land whereon the loss in values might be fully re-created.

As we have seen, land values can be depreciated merely because of uncertainty, and it is not possible in planning to avoid uncertainty altogether. But there is nothing to be gained by introducing avoidable uncertainty, since it is unnecessarily harmful to trade, industry and welfare generally; and it may incidentally delay or frustrate the very development required to realise the plan. A knowledge of land values can be used to frame proposals so that uncertainty is not unnecessarily created.

Where use values of properties are decreased substantially by a plan there will probably follow a consequential decrease in their assessment for rates, and a loss of potential rate income. A knowledge of values is essential if authorities are to be warned of this. It does not follow that a loss of rateable value must or can always be avoided, for just as high values may need to be undermined so may high rateable values. The existence of a thriving town centre is no good reason for discouraging the growth of a competitive district centre in a growing town. The high rateable value per acre which comes from high density housing is no reason for obstructing re-development which will reduce that density. The loss of rateable value which would follow the movement of industry should not prevent the attempt to transfer employment with population when providing new housing on the outskirts of a town. Sometimes, in such cases the loss of rateable value in one part of the town may be compensated for by new rateable value elsewhere. But very often the new values would be in another local government area; and, local government finance being what it is, planning authorities are perhaps tempted to formulate proposals which will result in exporting to another local authority the minimum of new rateable value.

Also of importance is the creation of the maximum use value and rateable value from any new development, consistent with good design. It is possible, for example, to house ten thousand people and by poor design to provide no sites which will attract high value houses, or successful shops or business, whereas another design would provide for such sites. A town map does not decide the kind of layout; but, in its preparation the foundations are often laid for good layout and the consideration therefore arises at this stage.

In allocating land for a particular use in a town map it is often envisaged that development or re-development will be undertaken by private developers, or that they will participate in it. Whether or not they are likely to act in the manner envisaged is, often, difficult to say. A knowledge of land values can assist in gauging the likelihood. For example, if land which has no development value is zoned for business or industry there can be a *prima facie* inference that it will not " go," that the development will not take place if left to private enterprise. A knowledge of values can, therefore, provide a useful check against over-zoning.

Where alternative possible locations are being considered for a use which relies on private enterprise to bring it about, it may be that the use could derive more advantage from the location and accessibility of one area than another, and yet meet the needs of the town in either. Shops, in particular, are very closely tied to location. It is in the interests of neither public nor traders, nor of rateable value, to attempt to steer them to a site which is inferior for the purpose, while a better shopping site is allocated for a use, such as public buildings or car park, which is more flexible in its location; in other words, to fail to create the maximum value, including rateable value, consistent with good design. A knowledge of values will assist in avoiding this. It may go further in pointing to the particular sites which will most readily attract developers.

In considering the development or re-development of business areas, a knowledge of the height, intensity and volume of building that is likely to be undertaken is needed when delimiting zones. These are not likely to be uniform throughout the area, but will vary with demand for space, the cost of building, location and land cost. A knowledge of values can assist in forecasting the height, intensity and volume that will be in demand. It does not follow that the plan should follow this demand, for it might lead to poor daylighting, congestion of vehicles, excessive concentration of people, inadequate arrangements for car parking and unloading of vehicles. But if defects such as these can be avoided there is no reason why developers should not make as intense a use of sites as they find economical and practicable.

It does not follow from this that a plan should reflect merely what private developers will find profitable to do. But as indicated in Chapter 22, the " highest and best " use of land that would result from market operations is a *prima facie* indication of its most efficient use, and this is reflected in its value. And, furthermore, where it is hoped that private developers will carry out certain development it is necessary to try and gauge what can be expected from them. If it is concluded that they would not implement the development, it would be necessary, in order to get it, to stimulate it in one way or another. This arises where the social benefit, that is, the public gain, to be derived from development is high but the private cost is also high, perhaps too high for the development to be undertaken by a private developer. For example, an authority may wish to see used for industry land which has been made derelict by surface working of clay. A knowledge of values would underline, if not reveal, the fact that the expense of reclaiming the land to make it suitable for building would exceed any prospective yield, or the cost of acquiring alternative land for industry. This means that to secure the use of the land for industry it would be necessary for the authority to acquire and reclaim the land themselves, and lease at a rent which did not cover expenditure. Or where an authority wished to see a part of its business area re-developed, but learned that the margin between current and potential use value was insufficient to induce private developers to undertake the work, some stimulus of market forces would be called for. Alternatively, the authority might be led to realise that it was because of the restrictions which they were imposing on the amount of floor space that private developers would not re-develop, and be led to permit a higher floor space index to encourage re-development. A third instance might arise, in the business area just referred to, where the authority wished to see certain heights of building, in order to give architectural scale, and found that developers did not wish to build up to these heights because demand was lacking for space on the upper floors. To achieve their heights the authority would probably have to acquire the land and let at reduced ground rents. A knowledge of land values would forewarn them of this, and enable the cost to them of their proposals to be measured. Such knowledge could also be used to influence the architectural design of proposals at an early stage so that their scale could be adjusted to what was likely to take place, and the situation avoided in which the architectural conception could not be realised except by forfeiting income in rents. The need for early discussion in the evolution of a scheme, on this and other points, between the planning and valuation officers of an authority, has been illustrated by W. K. Shepherd in his account of the re-building of the bombed centre of Plymouth.[3]

We have left to the last the three matters of greatest familiarity wherein a knowledge of land values assists in the consideration of proposals: the cost of land acquisition for public development and the yield from it; the liability for compensation; and the possibility of betterment.

A knowledge of values and valuation is essential for estimates of the cost of acquisition of land by public authorities; and such estimates are necessary to ensure that the cost to an authority will be within its financial resources. But not only can alternative proposals be costed in order to select that which is financially most attractive to the authority, but a knowledge of values will assist in the selection of sites, and in the definition of their boundaries, with a view to minimising costs. For example, in siting a school in a built-up area the cheapest properties can be selected for acquisition, consistent with good location, and the cheapest line for a new road among alternatives which have a satisfactory engineering and architectural alignment. This line is often not simple to decide in a built-up area. To make the best choice it is necessary to have not only the details that can be obtained from maps and inspection, for example the size and shape of parcels and the structural condition of the properties, but also others which must be obtained from owners, for example the trades carried on, the factors which would give rise to a disturbance claim, the various interests in the properties and the extent of ownerships which would influence possible claims for severance and injurious affection. These other details might not be available when the estimates are being made on proposals, becoming known only when notices to treat are served. It is necessary therefore to make assumptions as to the likely trade disturbance and the nature of the interests, and also as to whether it will be cheaper to buy part of properties or to buy the whole, or to pay the cost of setting back shops along a street to be widened or to buy the whole site and re-develop. For the making of such assumptions a considerable experience of values and valuations is required: the appearance of buildings alone can be very deceptive.

Where an authority acquires for re-development, particularly for comprehensive re-development, a knowledge of values is also necessary in order to estimate the yield so that this can be related to cost. And it can furthermore be of help in designing proposals: in deciding, for example, when building a new road through a built-up area, whether additional land, and how much land, should be bought for recoupment; or what height and volume of building can be expected; or what types of development will or will not produce a yield which is commensurate with the proposed expenditure.

On this last point surveyors must rely primarily on their experience. But experience is not always a guide to the yield that can be expected on novel kinds of development. This is illustrated by the controversies that have arisen at the design stage of precinct shopping centres, that is centres into which shoppers' vehicles will not be able to enter. Such centres may eventually produce values which are as high as, or even higher than, values in conventional centres; but at the design stage no one really knows whether they will or not. In consequence, traders are often doubtful about the prospects of trade in such a centre, and are unwilling to offer as high rents, on what amounts to an abnormal speculation, as they would in a conventional centre. If there is to be a speculation, they argue, the backers of the new kind of development should pay for the risk, by accepting lower rents, and not they. These likely reactions of traders and developers would be pointed out by the surveyor at the design stage, and he would advise as to the loss in rental income or capital value that might be expected from pursuing the precinct design, and as to modifications necessary to minimise this loss. But his experience might be little guide.

As to compensation, as we saw in Chapter 23, that for depreciation of existing use value is payable by a local planning authority, and that for loss of development value by the government. In both these cases the decision which gives rise to the claim is not made in the preparation of a plan but after a development application is submitted to the authority. Since, however, what is proposed in the plan, and the deliberations that lead up to the making of it, will have some bearing on the development control decisions that will be made, the scale of financial liability implicit in the proposals can be considered in their preparation. It is not a simple matter, however, to estimate at this stage the probable compensation liability on the Treasury for depreciation of development values. The total possible liability is given in the actual amounts of the established claims; but as already described (page 346) compensation is to be paid only when loss is suffered, and then not in all cases; and when it is paid it will not be the actual amount of the claim but that part which has not been written down by permission already given or by payments already made.

With regard to betterment, we have seen that there is only the possibility of recoupment remaining to authorities if they are to attempt to secure any of the rise in values that might come about as a result of the plan. Recoupment can only be successful as a means of recovering betterment where the land to be acquired is carefully decided upon. The price must be reasonable; the new values to be created must be sufficiently in excess of the cost of their realisation; and the time that will elapse before yields are received must not be so long that loan charges on idle capital exceed any profit. To make decisions on all this a knowledge of land values is essential.

C. Phasing of Acquisition. Where substantial acquisition of land is proposed by an authority a knowledge of land values is essential for the preparation of an acquisition policy and programme. We have already mentioned the relating of the acquisition cost to what the authority can afford. This will influence the size and staging of the programme.

Another problem arises in the timing of acquisition. Where land is to be developed or re-developed the property which is most ripe should be acquired first. Where land will not yield income until developed by the authority its too early purchase is unwise (see page 205), but where there is standing property to be demolished early purchase may be profitable (see page 152). These considerations apart, the likely effect on land values of the new development may influence the timing of acquisition. Where the nucleus of a shopping centre exists, for example, and it is being expanded for the arrival of additional population, if it is ever intended to buy out the original shops it is preferable for the authority not to wait until the values of the old shops are increased by the new population. If they do there will occur the reverse of recoupment: the acquisition of values after they have been increased by the new development. Conversely, if values are falling in an area it will be imprudent to buy earlier than necessary in that area.

In practice, authorities have not had the freedom to follow their best interests in this matter. They are in general discouraged from buying in advance of requirements; there have been the postwar restrictions on capital expenditure for purchase of land by public bodies; and purchase for recoupment by authorities is not generally favoured. Under these conditions, it is ironical that authorities who might have wished to defer purchase of particular properties have been forced to buy them because of successful purchase notices under section 19 of the 1947 Act, when applications to rebuild have been refused because of the authority's eventual intention to acquire and re-develop as a whole. This has particularly affected the war damaged towns who have, in total, spent several millions in this way. The City of London, for example, had, by December, 1953, spent some £2,300,000 on buying for re-development but had been forced to spend £5,000,000 in addition on section 19 acquisitions. And in Manchester, where the total cost of all blitzed sites in the central area of the City is estimated at £1,800,000, before much progress in rebuilding the sites had been made the Corporation had spent £1,000,000 on them because of purchase notices.[4] In some cases the service of numerous purchase notices has been anticipated by the purchase of large areas in order that the authority could avoid having to acquire single properties at a time. Because of the relative paucity of building licences and the restrictions on road works, it has not been possible to develop the land; but loan charges on its purchase price have had to be met.

Land Value Maps in Planning

In all planning work it is necessary to present graphically, even in some simple form, as much as possible of the data that is being used. This is done not only to record it, and to relate it to other information which is being analysed, but to avoid the misapprehension that often results from the attempt to retain all relevant considerations in the head and merely to impart conclusions.

There have, nonetheless, been very few attempts to show land values graphically, largely because of practical difficulties which we have discussed.

This chapter, and indeed Part VI as a whole, can be briefly summarised by suggesting the kind of land value maps which might be of use, if prepared and interpreted by valuers, in the preparation and administration of development plans. The suggestions follow from what has been discussed in this chapter. They are only tentative since they have not been tried in practice to any extent.

Current Use Values. Two kinds of map would be of interest The first would aim at showing the comparative cost of disturbing different groups of property in different parts of the town. For this purpose the map would show, for the built-up area, the average current use value, per acre of curtilage, for groups of similar properties. It would be prepared by totalling the current use values for a block enclosed by streets, or part of a block, and dividing by the acreage of curtilages.

It would be a large undertaking to prepare such a map specially for planning purposes, and recourse might be had to the new rating valuation. Although this reflects use value in its literal sense, and not as defined for compulsory acquisition purposes in the 1947 Act, it would be a guide to areas of high existing use value. A map on these lines was included in an Advisory Plan for the City of Bath[5]. For street blocks in the central area the average rateable values per acre of land were shown. The values ranged in eight steps between 1s. to 1s. 6d. per yard square and 21s. to 24s. per yard square. (Fig. 17.)

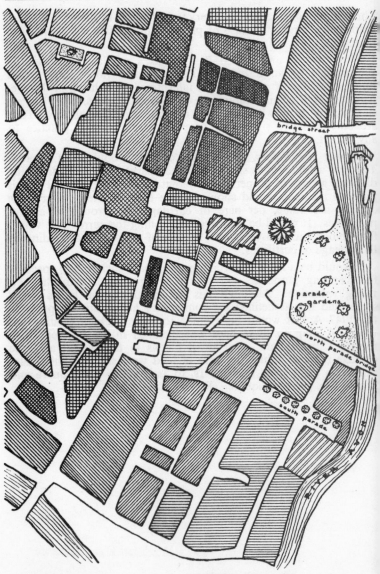

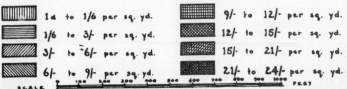

REFERENCE TO RATEABLE VALUES

▦	1d to 1/6 per sq. yd.	▦	9/- to 12/- per sq. yd.
▦	1/6 to 3/- per sq. yd.	▦	12/- to 15/- per sq. yd.
▦	3/- to 6/- per sq. yd.	▦	15/- to 21/- per sq. yd.
▦	6/- to 9/- per sq. yd.	▦	21/- to 24/- per sq. yd.

SCALE   0   100   200   300   400   500   600   700   800   900   1000   FEET

FIGURE 17.—*Sketch Plan of Central Bath, Showing Rateable Value of*
Source 14: *See note 5.*   *Blocks of Property per Acre*

The second map would aim at giving depth to the land use map in particular problem areas where detailed investigation would be useful. For individual properties, or groups of properties having similar size and value, maps showing the value per unit of floor space might be prepared. Single-storey shops could be compared, for example, in value per foot frontage or foot square or even, in complex areas, per foot square of the front zone: the front strip of a shop, that is perhaps 15 to 25 ft. in depth, where the maximum value is considered to lie and from where value falls off towards the rear of the shop. Multi-storey buildings with different uses on the various floors might need to have each floor and use shown separately. For the purpose of this map the rating valuations would be most appropriate since it is literal use value that is required.

Development Values. A useful map would be one indicating, in transitional or under-developed areas, where there was inadequate utilisation of sites and the possible existence of development value. For this purpose current use values of properties per foot or yard square of their sites could be plotted for individual properties, or for groups having similar site areas and uses, so that any low site utilisation would be revealed. The rating assessments would again be appropriate.

Information on development values as they existed in 1947, with the appropriate restricted and unrestricted values, is available in the 1947 Act Part VI claims for a great part of the development value in the country. This information must be treated with reserve since the valuations do not, as do rating valuations, have a consistent or uniform basis, and they are not necessarily available for all properties having development value. The plotting of the established claims and their amounts should be of interest however in suggesting where there was development pressure at that date, and the reduction of the agreed figures to a unit basis would reveal how intense the pressure was. Such a map would also show where the price for public acquisition might be higher than existing use value. Whether or not it would be higher would depend, *inter alia*, on how much of the established claim has been written down.

A map giving potential values has been suggested for gauging the effect of planning or development proposals on values as they exist before the plan takes effect.[6] The value referred to is not the current use value or development value but the market value of land, if it could be developed for the best possible use, after discounting for the time necessary for this value to emerge. In built-up areas all land is visualised as cleared of buildings. The values at a given date would be indicated graphically by means of contour lines, (isovals), each line joining points where the land is considered to be, either currently or after the proposals have taken effect, of equal value. The isovals delimit areas within which the land value lies between those values indicated by figures on the bounding isovals. A figure of 100 might represent either £100 per foot square or £100 per foot frontage of a plot of standard depth. (Fig. 18.)

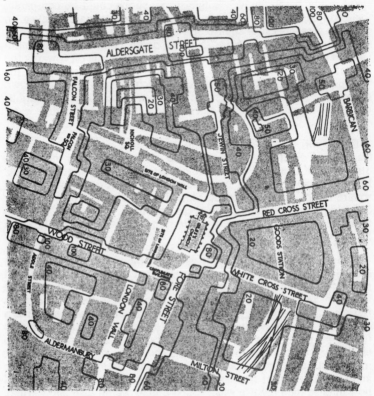

FIGURE 18.—*Plan of Barbican Area, City of London, Showing Suggested Isovals*

Source: *See Note 6.*

Trends in Values. Trends in current use or development values are more difficult to show graphically than the position at any time because the valuations for different dates must be on some comparable basis. It will not be possible for this reason to compare the new rating valuation with the pre-war one.

A map comparing values at different dates is shown in Fig. 13. A comparison between values in 1914 and 1923 in Manhattan Island, New York, is shown in the Regional Survey of New York and its Environs, by means of two separate maps.[7] It is the assessed value of the land for taxation purposes which has been taken: the unit-value of the site in dollars per foot frontage, on an imaginary plot 100 ft. deep, the sites being imagined free from buildings and available for development for the best use (see page 329). The total assessed value of the land in the Borough of Manhattan during those years increased by 6 per cent; and the maps show where values remained stationary, and where they rose and fell. Values are shown, average over street blocks, in these ranges in dollars: 6-25; 26-100; 101-200; 201-500; 501-1,000; 1,001-5,000; over 5,000.

Obtaining and Using Information on Land Values

The information on land values that is required, if it is to be of assistance in the preparation of a plan, can be summarised from the preceding discussion as:

(a) current use values and development values of land, or land and buildings, at any particular date, and

(b) trends in such current use and development values at all times.

This information is not recorded in any form which is particularly suitable for planning offices. Some information is available as to the relative, but not the actual, current use values of land and buildings in the rating and Schedule A assessments; and it can be expected that the new assessments are on a more uniform basis; and therefore more helpful for the purpose, than the former ones. Some information is available about development values as they existed in 1948, in the claims that were made, and in the details of the negotiations about them, under Part VI of the 1947 Act. Apart from this, as we saw in Chapter 22, knowledge of values exists in the offices of district valuers, surveyors, estate managers, estate agents, of property companies, dealers and investors, and of building societies, insurance companies, etc. Only some of this information is published, as for example in auction records and in the reports of cases heard by the Lands Tribunals, but most of it is confidential and kept in reserve. Information and knowledge of trends in values, which are perhaps more important in planning than the actual values themselves, exists only in the experience and records of those offices which are continuously concerned with values.

Even if the figures were available a mere knowledge of them would not be sufficient for the purpose. What is wanted is a skilful and informed breakdown of the figures and interpretation of trends, so as to give the information which would be of use in the preparation and administration of the plan. The breakdown and interpretation would have to be fairly scientific, and this kind of analysis of land values is not simple. This all suggests that the assistance which is to be obtained on land values must be provided by people expert in their understanding, capable of their analysis, and knowledgeable of the values and their trends in the locality for which the plan is being prepared; by those who retain the opportunity for remaining in touch with values and the operations which give rise to them; and by those who are also closely in touch with the plans and familiar and sympathetic with its objectives, problems and proposals. As things are, such specialist help with regard to land values can come only from an independent surveyor advising the authority for a retainer or fee, the estate or valuation officer of the local or local planning authority, or the District Valuers of the Valuation Office.

This problem of how specialist assistance can best make its contribution to planning is not peculiar to this question of land values; it arises where there is a contribution to a plan from economists, geographers, landscape architects, sociologists, engineers and others. It raises the hoary question of whether planning is best done by a team of specialists or, along more traditional lines, by specialist land planners with the collaboration, as required, of the other specialists. We will not debate this question here, but just consider current planning practice. Assistance with regard to land values from any of the specialists mentioned will fit in well enough with this current practice whereby development plans are prepared and implemented in the main by specialist planning officers in the employment of local planning authorities, and whereby they call upon specialist help from within and without the authority's staff as required. It is not enough, however, for the planning officer merely to have the assistance. It is traditional in his training that he is sufficiently aware of the skills of all who contribute in planning for him to neglect none of them in preparing and implementing a plan; that he knows when and how specialists should be invited to assist, what particular contribution they can be expected to make, and how to co-operate with them to the best advantage. There is thus also a need for the planning officer to be aware of the place of land values in the preparation and implementation of a plan, just as he is of the place of traffic flow, sewerage capacity, population growth and employment. This awareness must be part of his approach; it must influence the technique of land planning.

APPENDICES

APPENDIX I

THE CONTENT OF DEVELOPMENT PLAN MAPS

The following items might appear on the maps under which they are listed. In town maps and county maps those above the line must be shown and those below are to be shown if applicable. See *Town and Country Planning (Development Plan) Regulations,* 1948 (S.I. 1948, No. 1767), and *M.O.T.C.P. Circulars* 59, 70 and 92.

COUNTY MAP

Areas comprised in Town Maps already approved or presently submitted. Within these areas, the following areas are to be shown:—
Existing industrial areas.
Areas proposed for industrial development.
Existing built-up areas other than industrial areas.
Areas proposed for development other than industrial development.
Principal roads.
Location of areas for which Town Maps will be prepared at a later date.
Location of areas for which Comprehensive Development Area Maps are already approved or presently submitted.
Location of areas for which Designation Maps are already approved or presently submitted.
Boundaries of areas designated or proposed to be designated under Section 1 of the New Towns Act, 1946.
Settlements other than those referred to in items (i) (a) and (b) and (ii) of this Part where the following facilities are to be provided or are existing:—
Primary school(s).
Health centre.
Community centre.
Water-borne sewerage system.
Secondary school(s).
Trunk roads.
Roads linking towns and other settlements where there will be facilities such as secondary schools, an industrial centre or the larger shops, to the trunk road system or to each other; and roads of comparable importance.

Land for railway purposes.
Railway passenger stations.
Waterways, whether docks, harbours or inland waterways of traffic importance.

Areas allocated for securing:—
(i) surface mineral workings other than coal;
(ii) underground mineral workings other than coal.
Surface areas for the winning of coal, or for collieries.
Areas for the deposit of refuse or waste materials including industrial waste.
Large areas for service department or other government purposes, other than those included in other items of the notation.
Airfields.
Large water works or reservoirs.
Large sewage disposal works.
Areas for local authority smallholdings.
Large areas for local authority or statutory undertaker purposes, other than those included in other items of the notation.
Areas of great landscape, scientific or historic value.
National Parks as defined by the National Parks and Access to the Countryside Act, 1949.
Nature Reserves as defined by Section 15 of the National Parks and Access to the Countryside Act, 1949.
Areas of special scientific interest notified to the local planning authority by the Nature Conservancy in accordance with Section 23 of the National Parks and Access to the Countryside Act, 1949.

Areas of outstanding natural beauty for which orders have been confirmed under Section 87 of the National Parks and Access to the Countryside Act, 1949.

Ancient Monuments.

Areas where facilities are to be provided or maintained for holiday camping.

Areas, not otherwise shown, which are intended for the working of minerals other than coal.

Large areas for industrial use, including land for docks and wharves, other than those included in item (i) (a) of Part II.

Areas held or to be held for public open spaces.

Areas intended for open spaces not open to the general public, such as club golf courses, private grounds or playing fields, allotments, cemeteries, etc.

Hospitals and other establishments with large grounds.

Routes which are the subject of approved proposals relating to a long distance route under the National Parks and Access to the Countryside Act, 1949.

Woodlands under the control of the Forestry Commission or subject to a dedication covenant or tree preservation order.

Other land covered by water.

Boundary of Local Planning Authority's area.

TOWN MAP

Areas comprised in Comprehensive Development Area Maps already approved or presently submitted.

Location of areas for which Designation Maps are already approved or presently submitted.

Areas primarily for industrial use.

Areas primarily for principal business use (i.e., offices and wholesale warehouses) for the town as a whole.

Areas for shopping use in town centre or main district centre.

Areas for groups of buildings for civic, cultural or other special uses.

Areas primarily for residential use.

Shopping centres (i.e., other than the main town or district shopping centres).

Trunk roads.

Other principal traffic roads as the road framework for the town as a whole.

Principal car parks.

Stations for public vehicles.

Land for railway purposes.

Railway passenger and goods stations.

Waterways, whether docks, harbours or inland waterways of traffic importance.

Wharves, depots and land for use with such waterways.

Primary schools and grounds attached thereto.

Secondary schools, colleges and other educational institutions with grounds attached thereto.

Areas held or to be held for public open spaces.

Areas for open spaces not open to the general public, such as club golf courses, private grounds or playing fields, allotments, cemeteries, etc.

Areas allocated for securing:—
(i) surface mineral workings other than coal;
(ii) underground mineral workings other than coal.

Surface areas for the winning of coal or for collieries.

Areas for the deposit of refuse or waste materials including industrial waste.

Large areas for service department or other government purposes, other than those included in other items of the notation.

Airfields.

Water works.

Sewage disposal works.

Areas for local authority smallholdings.

Large areas for local authorities' or statutory undertakers' purposes, other than those included in other items of the notation.

Areas of great landscape, scientific or historic value.

National Parks as defined by the National Parks and Access to the Countryside Act, 1949.

Nature Reserves as defined by Section 15 of the National Parks and Access to the Countryside Act, 1949.

Areas of special scientific interest notified to the local planning authority by the Nature Conservancy in accordance with Section 23 of the National Parks and Access to the Countryside Act, 1949.

Areas of outstanding natural beauty for which orders have been confirmed under Section 87 of the National Parks and Access to the Countryside Act, 1949.

Ancient Monuments.

Areas where facilities are to be provided or maintained for holiday camping.

Areas, not otherwise shown, which are intended for the working of minerals other than coal.

Hospitals and other establishments with large grounds.

Routes which are the subject of approved proposals relating to a long-distance route under the National Parks and Access to the Countryside Act, 1949.

Woodlands under the control of the Forestry Commission or subject to a dedication covenant or tree preservation order.

Other land covered by water.

Boundary of Local Planning Authority's area.

COMPREHENSIVE DEVELOPMENT AREA MAP

Boundary of the area defined as an area of comprehensive development.

Business zones:—
Shopping.
Office.
Wholesale warehouse.

Residential zone.

Educational zone, including grounds and playing fields attached to schools and colleges.

Recreational and Public Building zone.

Industrial zones:—
Light Industrial.
General Industrial.
Special Industrial.

Trunk roads.

Principal traffic roads, other than trunk roads.

Streets forming the main internal framework of residential, industrial or principal business areas.

Areas held or to be held for public open space.

Open spaces not to be open to the public, such as private grounds or playing fields, club golf courses, allotments, cemeteries, etc.

Car parks.

Stations for public vehicles.

Land for railway purposes.

Woodlands.

Land covered by water.

Other particulars or proposals of importance not mentioned above.

Any part of the map sheet which is not to form part of the Development Plan at the 1/2,500 scale.

Boundary of the
(a) Local Planning Authority's area;
(b) Local Authorities' areas, when these come on the map.

SUPPLEMENTARY TOWN MAP

This will largely follow the Comprehensive Development Area Map.

APPENDIX II

County Borough of Preston
SUMMARY OF MAIN PROBLEMS REVEALED BY THE SURVEY AND PROPOSALS CONTAINED IN THE PLAN.

Problems	*Proposals*
Intermixture of industrial and residential uses.	Zoning proposals in Town Map.
Shortage of Playing Fields.	Town Map shows 83.11 acres of additional public open space, some of which can be used for games and also 39.75 acres of future school playing fields.
Need for improved access to land in Ribble Valley and preservation of agricultural land.	Ribble Valley included in open space system for the County Borough.
Shortage of local open spaces in central areas.	Winckley Square Garden to be designated as public open space.
Need for allotments in certain areas.	To be provided in detailed layouts of estates.
Preservation of buildings of historic and architectural interest.	Buildings in Statutory Lists to be preserved.
Land required for re-location and modernisation of industry.	Trading Estate, Longridge Road, Extension to Dock Estate.
High percentage of old, obsolete and unfit property. Extensive slum clearance needed, amounting to 11,500 dwellings.	Clearance of 1,530 dwellings. Estimated building programme 1951/1977 of 6,398 dwellings comprising:—
Need for 3,364 additional dwellings to reduce overcrowding.	Replacement of unfit dwellings . . . 1530 (390 within County Borough).
Need for 1,504 additional dwellings to accommodate natural increase of population.	For natural increase and relief of overcrowding . . . 4,868. (800 within County Borough).
Acute shortage of land for development.	Land within County Borough for 1,190 dwellings accommodating 4,165 persons. Land required outside County Borough for overspill of 18,228 persons (5,208 dwellings).
Overbuilding of sites in Town Centre.	Modern layout as and when redevelopment occurs.

Problems	*Proposals*
Preston as a regional centre needs sites for modern public buildings.	Sites to be reserved or later made available as a result of redevelopment proposals.
Need for extension of Markets.	Proposals to safeguard the necessary land.
Urgent need for car parks and improved rear access roads to commercial buildings.	To be provided as redevelopment occurs. Temporary use of vacant and cleared sites.
Urgent need for a new 'bus station.	Temporary station on land mainly owned by Corporation, later to be incorporated into permanent scheme.
Owing to its geographical situation, Preston has exceptional road traffic problems of more than local concern. There is urgent need:— (a) To relieve pressure of through traffic. (b) To relieve congestion in town shopping centre.	Reservation of land for proposed north/south by-pass road. Construction of central by-pass (inner ring road). Other road improvements.
Urgent need for a comprehensive school building programme.	Reservation of sites for new schools and extensions within County Borough. Other schools outside County Borough by agreement with Lancashire County Council.
Sites required for clinics and Health Centre.	Sites to be made available.
Public utility services require extending to serve land needed for industrial and other development. Extensions to Gas Works.	Proposals for extension of services. Negotiations to continue concerning Gas Works and Savick Valley Sewer.

Source: *Development Plan for the County Borough of Preston* (1951), Written Analysis, p. 20.

APPENDIX III

THE SUBSIDY SCHEME IN THE HOUSING SUBSIDIES ACT, 1956

Background of new scheme

As mentioned on page 162, in 1956 the Government introduced an entirely different subsidy scheme for new dwellings to be built by local authorities, new town development corporations and housing associations. For local authorities acting under the Housing Acts and development corporations under the New Towns Acts the scheme will apply to those dwellings for which a tender or estimate for constructions was accepted on or after 3rd November, 1955. For housing associations (including Development Corporations when acting as such) it will apply to those dwellings erected under arrangements made with local authorities on or after the same date.

The Minister in introducing the Bill explained that the new subsidy scheme was part of a wider policy which would also tackle the interrelated problems of rent control and local government finance[1] and that it had two main objectives. Firstly, it was intended to reduce the total amount of exchequer subsidy which would be payable on future dwellings. This was being done because the rents of a large number of council houses were being subsidised to a greater extent than the financial circumstances of their individual tenants required and the subsidy to which the Government was committed on existing dwellings provided, he thought, a margin which could be properly used for financing some part of the future housing programme. Secondly it was intended, by introducing differential rates of subsidy for dwellings provided for different purposes, to stimulate the provision for particular purposes, particularly for rehousing people living in slums.[2]

As to the first objective, the amount of Exchequer subsidy being paid each year for local authority permanent dwellings is very substantial. For 1955-56 in England and Wales it was estimated at £47 million, about £34 million more than in 1945.[3] Furthermore, the annual commitment will go on increasing as more local authority dwellings which attract subsidy are added to their existing stock (about 2.6 million at the end of March, 1956)[4] unless the rate of increase in commitment is smaller than the rate of falling off in subsidy payments under pre-war Acts. There is not much immediate relief to be expected from this; the subsidies for the 1.16 million pre-war local authority dwellings fell from £14.4 million in 1945-56 only to £11.5 million in 1955-56. Therefore if the annual commitment is to be reduced substantially the rate of subsidy must be reduced for any addition to the new local authority dwellings which have been built in England and Wales since the war. This is proposed. The new subsidies are not intended to be enough therefore, as were those under the Housing Acts 1946-52, to make up the difference at current prices between the average annual costs of a new dwelling and a notional rent.[5] This difference has increased over recent months rather than decreased, because of the rise in building costs and interest rates. In illustration of the latter, the rise of P.W.L.B. rate between Feb., 1955 and Jan., 1956 from 3¼ to 5 per cent has meant an increase in loan charges or £10.7 per annum on a capital cost of £1,000. If earlier practice had been followed therefore the new subsidies would have been increased rather than decreased.

Since the subsidy will not make up this difference an authority can, if it decides to build, do one of three things to bridge the gap. It can attempt to obtain sufficiently high rents for the new dwellings; it can draw on its rate income; or it can spread the load over the tenants of its existing houses, where it has an adequate pool of them, by raising rents, particularly low rents. The Minister favoured the last method and therefore suggested that the exchequer subsidy being paid on existing houses provided a margin for financing some part of the future house building programme.

The Act relieves local authorities of their obligation to make the statutory rate contribution for each dwelling which receives the exchequer subsidy, but they can make a contribution from the general rate fund to the housing revenue account if they think fit (section 8(1)). The result is that authorities will have to contribute from the rates to balance the housing revenue account only if it shows a deficiency in any year. If they choose to raise rents therefore any resultant saving will benefit the rates; any saving they made previously did not necessarily do so (see page 170).

As to the second objective, that of differential subsidies, the following table and Graph 9, which are based on section 3 of the Act, show how the annual contribution for each dwelling (for sixty years from its completion) will vary with the purpose for which it is provided. The table applies to dwellings provided by local authorities and new town development corporations, but can be applied by the Minister to dwellings provided by housing associations (section 3(4)).

These subsidies are paid for dwellings built on sites which are not expensive, i.e., which cost less than £4,000 per acre. Where expensive sites are used a separate additional subsidy is paid (see page 394).

The table shows that dwellings which are in blocks of 4 or more storeys (and not 3 or more as under the former scheme) will attract a higher subsidy even if not on expensive land. It shows too that blocks of differing heights will now attract differing subsidies to reflect the increase in cost as storey heights increase. For each storey above six an increase of £1 15s. 0d. per flat per storey is allowed to reflect the increased cost of building with increasing height. A bigger increase (£6) is allowed between 4 and 5 storeys to reflect the practice of putting lifts in the higher blocks, and a yet bigger increase (£12) between 5 and 6 storeys to reflect the need to use framed construction for all blocks of 6 storeys or more.[6]

These figures show that the difference between the subsidy for flats and houses in the new scheme is generally not so great as it was under the 1955 scheme. Where flats are to be provided for general needs or slum clearance they will attract £10 more than houses when 4 storeys high, rising to £35 more when 10 storeys high; and when provided for overspill they will attract £8 to £33 more. Under the old scheme many flats did not attract the extra subsidy, as they were not on expensive land. But where they did this was £23 17s. 0d. more if there was no lift, and £34 7s. 0d. more for a flat of 4 storeys or higher with a lift. If however the general needs subsidy is dropped for houses but not flats (see next para.), then the difference would be higher for this class of provision (i.e., £20 when 4 storeys high rising to £45 more when 10 storeys high).

The Subsidy Scales for different purposes

As shown in the table, the subsidies will be paid for three distinct purposes: 1 general needs, 2-3 slum clearance and 4-7 certain kinds of overspill.

1. The lowest scale of subsidy is for dwellings provided for general needs. This is not defined but can be taken as any purpose, including the relief of overcrowding, other than what may be broadly called slum clearance or overspill, as described in items 2-7 of the table. For houses and flats in 2 or 3 storeys the subsidy will be £10, and for flats in 4 or more storeys it will rise from £20. This house subsidy for general needs the Government has stated its intention of discontinuing at a later stage, perhaps in a year or so.

Purpose	Subsidy			
	Dwellings (other than flats in 4 or more storeys)	Flats in 4 storeys	Flats in 5 storeys	Flats in 6 storeys or more
1. Provided by local authorities for general needs, i.e. any purposes other than those specified in 2-7 of this table.	£10 per annum	£20 per annum	£26 per annum	£38* per annum
2. Provided by a local authority for the purposes of slum clearance or redevelopment under Part III of the Housing Act. 3. Provided by a local authority for the purpose of re-housing persons coming from camps or other unsatisfactory temporary housing accomodation.	£22 1s. per annum	£32 per annum	£38 per annum	£50* per annum
4. Provided by the local authority of an expanded town under the Town Development Act 1952. 5. Provided by a local authority for persons coming into their area to meet the urgent needs of industry. 6. Provided by the local authority of a congested or overpopulated area in some other area as part of a scheme of large scale development of "new town" character. 7. Provided by a development corporation of a new town.	£24 per annum	£32 per annum	£38 per annum	£50* per annum

* The subsidy is increased by £1 15s. for each storey in excess of six.

GRAPH 9

*House and Flat Subsidy Scheme for new dwellings under Housing Subsidies
Act, 1956—annual exchequer contribution per dwelling*

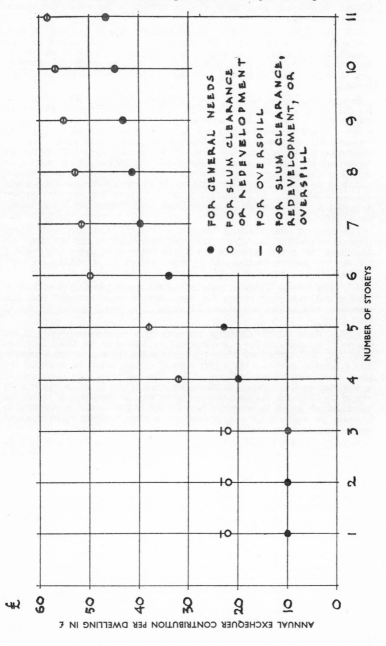

It will pay £10 in the interim in order to avoid making the transition too abrupt. It has not announced what it intends to do about the general needs flat subsidy.[7]

2-3. For houses provided by a local authority for the purposes of slum clearance or redevelopment or for rehousing persons from camps or other unsatisfactory temporary housing accommodation, the subsidy will be the same as the 1955 scheme general standard amount of exchequer contribution, that is £22 1s. 0d. For flats in 4 or more storeys it will rise from £32 per annum.[8]

Section 11(1) of the Act prescribes the kind of dwellings which will qualify for the higher slum clearance subsidy. They are dwellings for the people displaced as a result of the demolition of insanitary houses, the closing of whole or part of any building for sanitary reasons, or the dealing with Housing Act clearance or redevelopment areas (see page 160). The displacement of people from any house in a clearance area will attract the higher subsidy, and from any house in the five redevelopment areas submitted to the Minister before November, 1955, but only from unfit houses, and those so arranged as to be congested, in any redevelopment areas which are submitted later. In Planning Act areas of comprehensive development it is only the displacement of people from unfit houses which will attract the higher subsidy.[8]

The kind of unsatisfactory temporary housing accommodation whose removal will attract the higher grant will be decided by the Minister. He has stated that it will extend to the Nissen hut type of temporary dwelling but not to post-war prefabricated houses except those erected on open spaces.[9]

4-7. For certain kinds of overspill development, flats in blocks of 4 storeys and more will attract the same subsidy as if provided for slum clearance, and houses will attract £2 more. The overspill may be one of four kinds.

Firstly, there are the dwellings provided by a receiving authority in the course of a scheme of town development, as defined in the Town Development Act, 1952, carried out wholly or partly within the area of that authority. For a scheme to attract the higher subsidy it does not have to attract the town development grant (see page 229). The higher subsidy is payable to a receiving and not exporting authority because the latter is expected to regard its overspill dwellings in the same way as dwellings it builds for general needs within its boundary, whereas the former cannot be expected to increase the rents of its own population in order to keep down those of people coming from outside.[10]

Secondly, and for similar reasons, the higher subsidy will also be paid where dwellings are provided by a receiving authority for the accommodation of persons coming from outside its area in order to meet the urgent needs of industry. It will be paid only in special circumstances. For example, the industry must be one of national importance, such as coal mining; it must be in the national interest that the development take place, and therefore that the authority not be deterred from building houses; and the influx must represent a big proportional increase in population.[11]

But it is an exporting authority of a congested or overpopulated area which will attract the higher amount for the third kind of overspill, the carrying out in some other area of a scheme of comprehensive development similar in character, but not necessarily equal in size, to the building of a new town under the New Towns Act, 1946. Reasons for this are that such a scheme involves at the outset considerable unremunerative expenditure which is not directly connected with meeting housing need, and the Minister wishes to encourage overspill development which includes all the facilities of a new town, including opportunities for work.[12]

GRAPH 10

House and Flat Subsidy Scheme for new dwellings under Housing Subsidies Act, 1956—annual exchequer contribution per acre for expensive sites.

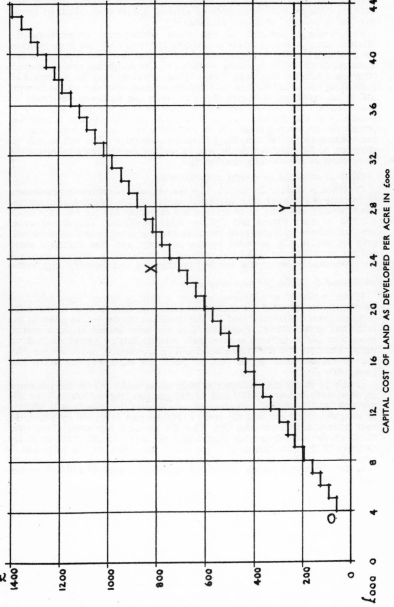

Finally, the higher overspill subsidy will be paid to new town development corporations when they are not acting as housing associations because they have no comparatively large pool of existing houses over which to spread any loss of subsidy on future dwellings.[13]

For dwellings provided by new town development corporations the Minister can pay annual grants in addition to his subsidy (see page 184) and for dwellings provided under approved schemes of town development he can make contributions to receiving districts or to participating county councils other than London (see page 230). These payments may be in respect of a dwelling which has become occupied by a tenant who was on the housing list of an exporting authority, but for whom the authority has made no contribution. In such a case the Minister is now entitled, where he is satisfied that the dwelling has been provided for the purpose of relieving congestion or overpopulation in an exporting area and has been used for the purpose, to recover something from the authority. This will be half his payment, or £4, whichever is the less, in each of the ten years following the completion of the dwelling (section 9).

Additional subsidies in special circumstances

Provision is made under section 5 for the Minister, in certain circumstances, to increase the subsidy to a particular authority, for dwellings for general need or slum clearance, to an amount not exceeding £50 for flats in a block of four or more storeys and £30 for other dwellings. The circumstances are that there is an urgent need for more housing accommodation which will only be met if it is provided by the authority, and that authority could not do so unless the additional subsidy is forthcoming, without imposing an unreasonably heavy rate burden, or charging unreasonably high rents.

Additional Subsidies for expensive sites

Under section 6 an additional subsidy is paid as before when subsidised dwellings are provided on expensive sites, but this is now to be quite separate from the subsidy paid for the dwellings themselves, as given in the table and graph above. Expensive sites are now defined as those costing more than £4,000 per acre as developed, whether flats or houses are built on them. The cost of a site as developed will be ascertained, in accordance with the Second Schedule to the Act, in much the same way as before (see page 165).

Graph 10 shows the exchequer subsidy to be paid. Where the site costs, as developed, between £4,000 and £5,000 per acre, the subsidy will be £60 per acre for 60 years (O). As the cost of site rises the subsidy will increase at the rate of £34 per acre for every £1,000 or part of £1,000 by which the cost exceeds £5,000 per acre (X). The £34 per acre represents about two-thirds of the loan charges on £1,000 at 5 per cent over 60 years, or three-quarters of the loan charges at 4 per cent. But where an expensive site of more than £10,000 per acre as developed has no flats at all of 4 storeys or over then the rate of subsidy will be that applicable to a site of £10,000 per acre and no more (Y).

APPENDIX IV

THE SCHEME FOR REDEVELOPMENT AND OPEN SPACE GRANTS UNDER THE TOWN AND COUNTRY PLANNING ACT, 1954, SECTION 50.

The Revised System

As mentioned on page 207, a revised planning grants scheme was fore-shadowed in section 50 of the Town and Country Planning Act, 1954. The scheme was introduced by Regulations and outlined in an Explanatory Memorandum.[1] It had effect from 14th April, 1955, except that on certain expenditure incurred before that date grant will continue to be paid at former rates. For example, where the purchase of land in areas of extensive war damage was authorised before 26th February, 1954, the 90 per cent grant for the initial period of five to eight years will be continued. We will ignore these transitional provisions and describe the new scheme. It will be seen that it is very similar to the old one, but is simpler and incorporates certain lessons from experience.

Redevelopment grant will be paid as before towards the redevelopment of areas of extensive war damage or bad lay-out or obsolete development, and the bringing back into use of derelict land. It will also be paid towards the acquisition of land for other planning purposes. These are not defined, but would include the re-location of population or industry or replacement of open space arising out of redevelopment, which are no longer specifically mentioned as attracting grant, and also a variety of acquisitions which previously attracted grant under section 94 of the 1947 Act. But whereas under the former regulations grant for providing open space was payable as part of redevelopment grant it is now payable under separate provisions. It will be towards expenditure incurred under any enactment on public open space, provided no other exchequer grant is payable in respect of the expenditure.

Redevelopment Grant

The grant is paid towards the same kind of expenditure as before (on acquisition and clearing of land) and in addition on the cost of " preliminary development ". This is defined in section 50 (4) of the 1954 Act as " the carrying out of any work preparatory to the development of the land for the purposes for which it was acquired or appropriated, or work comprised in the initial stages of such development ". It will cover roughly the provision of land drainage, estate roads, sewers and services, but not major works which would be carried out by another service of the authority, and would earn the appropriate exchequer grant, if any, of that service.

The differential rates of grant, as between different kinds of redevelopment, different authorities and different periods, is dropped. A flat rate of 5 0per cent is paid in all circumstances.

Open Space Grant

Grant is paid towards expenditure on the acquisition, clearing and pre-liminary development of land, but not on the lay-out of the open space or planting. This may attract grant from the Ministry of Education. Pre-liminary development will include the filling of excavations, the stabilisation of subsidence areas and works of land drainage or culverting streams or ditches, other than works which are the responsibility of a drainage authority or river board.

The rate of grant will, in general, be 50 per cent of the notional annual loan charges on the total expenditure, calculated on the annuity basis for a 60 year loan at the current P.W.L.B. rate. But the Minister may agree to pay a higher rate, not exceeding 75 per cent, on a particular scheme, on the condition that the total expenditure by the authority on public open space in the year in which the scheme is undertaken exceeds a certain amount. This total expenditure is taken as the notional annual loan charges, on the basis just described, on the expenditure of that year. Where this equals or exceeds the product of one-tenth of a penny rate the condition is satisfied. The level of the higher rate will be determined as follows, according to the relation of the rate levied by the acquiring authority in the year of expenditure to the average rate levied in England and Wales.

Where the rate in the £ of the acquiring authority is:	The rate of grant will be:
More than 2/- above the average rate for England and Wales...	70 per cent.
Up to 2/- above the average ...	60 per cent.
Not more than the average ...	50 per cent.

plus, in each case where the loan charges exceed the equivalent of $\frac{1}{2}$d. rate, an additional 5 per cent for each $\frac{1}{2}$d. or fraction thereof above the first, up to a maximum of 75 per cent in all.

For a county council the rate poundage will be the average rate poundage of all country districts in the county; and for a parish council, the rate for the county district in which it is situated.

Financial Statement

An authority is still required to submit a financial statement for each grant unit and for the same purpose. These units, however, are to be larger than before. Their size and boundaries should, the Explanatory Memorandum suggests in para. 2 (2), be determined " with reference to the manner and stages by which the physical operations involved will be carried out, e.g., so that road and sewer works to be done in a single contract are included in one grant unit rather than apportioned artificially between two or more units." It goes on to suggest as suitable an area that can be redeveloped in a period of ten years.

The form of Statement has been revised and simplified, and asks for the figures relating to the ultimate position only, that is on completion of development, and not for an interim one too. It appears as Appendix A to the Explanatory Memorandum and is reproduced here. We will describe it as we did Appendix C of the former memorandum. It will be seen that it will need adaptation in the same way as the former statement, if it is to be used for the financial appraisal of a comprehensive development scheme.

The Statement is in two sections. The first details the capital cost of acquisition, clearing and preliminary development; and the second the value of the land for new uses after and upon completion of redevelopment. This enables the capital loss or gain to be struck. The annual equivalent of the loss or gain, which is the indication of grant liability, can then be calculated.

The cost of acquisition and clearing (items 1-3) are similar to items (a) (b) (c) and (d) in the summary of capital costs in Chapter 10: the cost of acquisition, of the legal and physical preparatory work to be done, and of roads, sewers and services. Item 1 relates to the cost of acquisition under compulsory purchase formulae, and includes what we have called the legal costs of site preparation, and also the legal and professional costs of acquisition. These are described in Appendix B of the Explanatory Memorandum. Item 2 relates to the value of the land which is already owned by the authority and is appropriated into the redevelopment service. The value for appropriation will be normally on the basis of existing or prevailing use (see page 149) subject to the qualification that where land to be appropriated is in an area in which comprehensive development has already begun, there should be excluded from the value any increase or decrease in value attributable to the comprehensive development already carried out or proposed (*Explanatory Memorandum,* para. 3). This attempt to exclude "betterment" or "worsement" resulting from, or implicit in, the redevelopment scheme, applies only to the values for appropriation. Item 3 relates to clearing and preliminary development; what we called physical preparation and site works in Part III. The meaning of *clearing* is amplified in Appendix C of the Explanatory Memorandum, and of *preliminary development* in Appendix D. There is no provision for interest on the capital which is lying idle, or profit or disposal expenses.

Items 5-7 list the new uses of the land, with subdivisions for sale to public bodies, appropriation to other services of the authority, and development by private developers. The value of standing buildings which are not being demolished is included. The land will be valued on the basis set out in Appendix E of the Explanatory Memorandum; a summary will be given. Trunk roads and classified roads will be valued on cost of acquisition, excluding compensation for severance or injurious affection disturbance and legal or other expenses; in other words, the highway service will bear the cost of the property itself and Ministry of Transport grant will be paid towards this, while the redevelopment service will bear the other compensation and expenses and planning grant will be paid on this. Other roads will be valued at nil; the redevelopment service will bear their whole cost. Public open spaces will be valued at nil, i.e., grant will be paid on the actual cost of acquisition, clearing and preliminary development. Whereas land for roads and public open space will be valued on cost, the following will be valued at the market value for the proposed or notional use, as the case may be. Land for housing or education will be valued at residential use; for municipal offices, depots and car parks at comparable commercial use; for public buildings and works at the prevailing use of contiguous or adjacent land; for allotments at agricultural use; for industrial and commercial development at those uses; for operational purposes of statutory undertakings and for government offices, depots or other buildings at comparable industrial or commercial use or, if there is none, for prevailing use on contiguous or adjacent land. In these cases, except for local authority housing, the land is valued with the benefit of new road works and sewers to be constructed, and existing ones to be retained, in, or adjacent to, the redevelopment area. In local authority housing, where the roads and sewers are to be constructed under housing powers, the value will be taken without their benefit.

Item 9 gives the tests of the scheme. Firstly, in 9 (a) and 9 (b), the difference between capital cost and values is struck, to give capital loss or gain, which is expressed as a percentage of the total capital cost. This is similar to our test (*A*). Secondly, in 9 (c), the annual equivalent of the capital loss or gain is calculated. This is the basis on which grant will be payable (*Explanatory Memorandum,* para. 4). Each year the annual equivalent of the value of land appropriated, developed or disposed of by the authority (plus net rents of property not appropriated, developed or disposed of) will be deducted from the annual equivalent of loans on acquisition clearing and development (plus expenditure from revenue). The grant basis is 50 per cent of the balance. The annual equivalent will in all cases be taken as the loan charges on the annuity basis at the current P.W.L.B. rate for a period of 60 years (which is the loan sanction period for all expenditure attracting grant) irrespective of how the authority finance the work. This test does not correspond with any of ours described in Chapter 10, nor is it comparable with that in the former Appendix C, which resembled our test (*G*). Thirdly, in 9 (d), the product of a 1d. rate is asked for, so that the annual equivalent of the loss or gain can be related to rate resources. This corresponds with our test (*H*).

APPENDIX A.

TOWN AND COUNTRY PLANNING ACT, 1947.

Estimate of the cost of redevelopment for purposes of grant under Section 93

Name of local authority...

Identity and acreage of redevelopment area..

....

Estimated cost of acquisition and clearing

1. **Acquisition**   £   £
   (a) compensation for the acquisition of land, other than operational land of statutory undertakers...
   (b) compensation for disturbance in respect of (a)
   (c) compensation for acquisition of operational land of statutory undertakers ...   .
   (d) miscellaneous expenses of acquisition ...   ...
   (e) land already acquired under Section 19, etc., at cost including miscellaneous expenses   ...

       Total acreage and cost of acquisitions......acres

2. **Appropriations**
   (a) land to which Section 82 applies   ...   ...
   (b) other land   ...   .

       Total acreage and value of appropriations
                ......acres   ...   ...

3. **Clearing and preliminary development**
   (a) clearing   ...   .
   (b) preliminary development roads and sewers:
       (i) under S. 20 of 1944 Act ...   .
       (ii) under other powers ...   .
   (c) other preliminary development ...   .

       Total   ...   .

4. **Total acreage and costs**   ......acres ...   ...   £

Estimated acreage and value of land including standing buildings not being demolished, for new uses after redevelopment.

5. Land for sale to—
    (a) other local authorities   ...   .
    (b) statutory undertakers   ...   .
    (c) government departments   ...   .

    (d) Total sales   ...   .

6. Land for appropriation for other services of the
    authority
    (a) housing   ...   .
    (b) education   ...   .
    (c) (i) classified roads   ...   .
        (ii) other highways   ...   .
    (d) public open space   ...   .
    (e) other services   ...   .

    (f) Total appropriations   ...   .

7. Land for development by private developers
    (a) shopping and commercial   ...   .
    (b) industrial   ...   .
    (c) housing   ...   .
    (d) other   ...   .

    (e) Total   ...   .

8. Total acreage and value of land ...   ...   acres £

9. (a) Estimated capital loss/gain on completion of
       redevelopment   ...   .   £
    (b) Percentage of (a) to the total cost of acquisition,
       clearing and preliminary development   ...   per cent.
    (c) Annual equivalent of capital loss/gain on 60
       year basis   ...   .   £   p.a.
    (d) Product of 1d. rate   ...   .   £

Notes

The District Valuer, on application supported with the necessary plans and information about the redevelopment proposals, will furnish a report of the estimated total cost of the acquisition, appropriation and disposal value of the land in the redevelopment area. The local authority should prepare its own estimates of the cost of clearing, preliminary development, and other expenditure not included in the District Valuer's report, giving brief particulars of the works and, in the case of preliminary development, the powers under which they are to be carried out. The District Valuer's report and the estimates should accompany the statement. Plans showing the area as it is and as it will be after redevelopment, and a brief report of the stages in which the redevelopment is to be undertaken and the time it is expected each stage will take, should also be furnished at the same time.

APPENDIX V

REVISIONS, 1956

This Appendix brings up to date certain details of the text in the light of events which occurred while it was being printed; it also introduces corrigenda to pages 3, 44, 106 and 186.

CHAPTER 1

Page 3. Table 1.

Corrigendum. In the source replace " Central Office of Information " by " Central Statistical Office."

Page 7. Line 42. Note 4.

The provisions in the *Air Corporation Act,* 1949, sec. 13, for exchequer grant to Air Corporations when necessary, expired on March 31, 1956. It is unlikely that they will be continued. (H.C. Debate, Vol. 548, col. 1672.) The Air Corporations will, therefore, no longer be classed as dependent.

Page 9. Line 22.

A time table for building a power station is given in the *Report of the Committee of Inquiry into the Electricity Supply Industry* (Herbert), Cmd. 9672 (HMSO, 1956), p. 22. For the station to come into commission in 1960 it is included in a tentative programme, and the site initially selected, in 1952. Site works will begin in 1956. Following this it is unlikely that the scheme will be dropped although it might be advanced or retarded. The Report also states (p. 21) that the Central Electricity Authority looks fifteen years ahead in its forecast of future plant requirements.

CHAPTER 4

Page 44. Line 45.

Corrigendum. Replace " European Economic Commission (E.E.C.) " by " Economic Council for Europe (E.C.E.)."

Page 150. Line 11.

In 1956 the Government found it necessary to cut capital investment in order to combat inflation. To do this it raised the Bank Rate, asked the banks and Capital Issues Committee to restrict credit, withheld loan sanction to local authorities for all but the most urgent works (see *M.O.H.L.G. Circulars* 10/56 and 11/56) and made the Treasury the sole source for Public Corporation long term borrowing. See also below under Chapter 9.

CHAPTER 5

Page 56. Line 44. Note 5.

This Select Committee met during 1955 but found that it could not carry out its terms of reference because they left " insufficient scope to make enquiries or to obtain further information regarding the Nationalised Industries which would be of real use to the House." H.C. Select Committee, *Special Report on Nationalised Industries,* Session 1954-55, H.C. Paper 120 (HMSO), p.v. The Government propose to set up a Select Committee with fresh terms of reference as follows: " To examine the reports and accounts of the nationalized industries established by statute whose controlling boards are appointed by Ministers of the Crown and whose annual receipts are not wholly or mainly derived from moneys provided by Parliament or advanced from the Exchequer." H.C. Debate, Vol. 552, Col. 1423.

Page 57. *Line* 30. *Note* 6.

In 1955 a Parliamentary Committee recommended that legislation be introduced to abolish town meetings and polls, since on balance they could no longer be justified. See *Report of Joint Committee on Private Bill Procedure*, Session 1954-55, H.L. Paper 14, 58; H.C. Paper 139 (H.M.S.O.), p. xxi.

Page 59. *Line* 33. *Note* 9.

The cut in subsidies provided in the *Housing Subsidies Act,* 1956, will not have this effect because the new subsidies apply to dwellings begun after the date of introduction of the Bill, 3rd November, 1955 (see Appendix III).

Page 66. *Line* 12.

See Page 113, Line 14, below.

CHAPTER 8

Page 106. *Line* 10.

Corrigendum. Replace " factories " with " industrial buildings and structures." See Note 8.

CHAPTER 9

Page 113. *Line* 14.

From 1956 Public Corporations which previously had borrowed in the open market were placed, provisionally for a period of two years, in the position of the National Coal Board. Except for short term capital they can borrow only from the Treasury (*Finance Act,* 1956.)

Page 113. *Lines* 35 *and* 40.

Following the Budget Speech of October, 1955, two important changes were introduced in P.W.L.B. practice. First, local authorities are no longer to borrow from the Board when they choose; the Board will lend only where they are unable to raise money on their own credit in the stock or mortgage market. Secondly, the Board's rates will not necessarily be those at which the Government can currently borrow; they will reflect instead the credit of local authorities of good standing in the market for loans of comparable periods (H.C. Debate, Vol. 545, Col. 215).

Page 115. *Line* 11.

In January, 1946, the P.W.L.B. rate for short periods was made higher than that for long periods. Graph 11, which extends Graph 2, p. 117, into 1956, shows the position.

Page 116. *Line* 38. *Note* 9.

The ceiling of £50,000 was reduced to £10,000 in 1956 by the *Control of Borrowing (Amendment) Order,* 1956, S.I. 1956, No. 358.

Page 118. *Line* 21. *Note* 10.

See also H.C. Debate, Vol. 548, Col. 2677.

Page 119. *Line* 15. *Note* 13.

The rate referred to in Note 13 was raised from April 1st, 1956, to 3½%. See *M.O.H.L.G. Circular* 68/55.

CHAPTER 11

Page 144. *Line* 45.

See Page 170, Line 40, below.

Page 146. *Line* 43.

See Page 113, Lines 35 and 40.

Page 155. *Line* 32.

The revised rating assessments have not resulted in any substantial difference in the total amount of exchequer equalisation grant, but revised

GRAPH 11

Various Rates of Interest, 1955-6

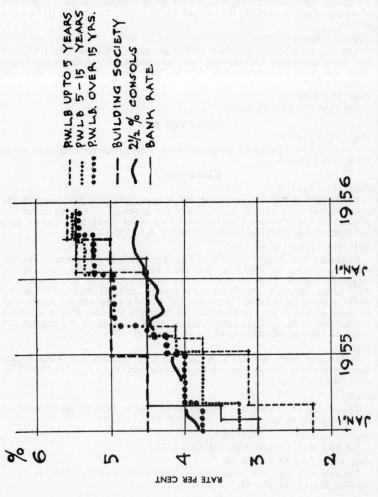

Source—As Graph 2

calculations under the formula have produced changes in the list of authorities who are entitled to it. In 1956-57, 53 county boroughs and 54 county councils will receive the grant. This will exclude 8 county boroughs and 2 county councils which did so in 1955-6 and include 6 county boroughs which did not.

Page 157. *Line* 45.

An analysis of the new assessments in a classification of uses which is comparable with that in Table 23 has not been published. The old and new assessments have however been compared on a different kind of use classification, as follows. It will be seen that domestic property bears a smaller proportion of the total than formerly, but shops and industrial a higher proportion.

TABLE 35

Analysis of rateable value as at December, 1955, in the new and old valuation lists.

	County Boroughs		County of London		Other Admin. Counties	
	New %	Old %	New %	Old %	New %	Old %
Domestic ...	45·8	56·5	29·2	42·1	57·9	67·1
Shops ...	17·7	13·8	16·5	12·9	11·6	8·3
Miscellaneous	28·4	22·9	46·3	35·7	20·6	15·5
Crown ...	1·4	2·1	3·6	6·2	2·8	4·4
Industrial ...	6·4	4·4	3·7	2·6	7·0	4·6
Freight—						
Transport ...	0·3	0·2	0·7	0·5	0·1	0·1
	100·0	100·0	100·0	100·0	100·0	100·0

Notes: New lists are those prepared by the Inland Revenue under the *Local Government Act*, 1948, and sent to the rating authorities in December, 1955. They will be altered following objections. Old lists are those prepared under the *Rating and Valuation Act*, 1925, and current in December, 1955.

Source: *Distribution of Rateable Values between different classes of property in England and Wales* Cmd. 9718 (H.M.S.O., 1956).

CHAPTER 12

Page 160. *Line* 41.

See Note 8 to Appendix III.

Page 162. *Line* 22.

The statutory obligation to pay rate contributions was removed in the *Housing Subsidies Act,* 1956, sec. 8. See Appendix III above.

Page 170. *Line* 3.

See Page 162, Line 22, above.

Page 170. *Line* 40. *Notes* 39, 40 *and* 42.

Rules (1), (2) and (4) are altered by the *Slum Clearance (Compensation) Act,* 1956. This provides:

Rule (1). If an unfit house is bought before 13th December, 1965, full compulsory purchase value will be paid instead of site value where an owner or member of his family was in occupation, or deemed to have been in occupation, on 13th December, 1955, and had bought the house between that date and the 1st September, 1939 (sec. 1). If an unfit house is occupied wholly or partly for business on the 13th December, 1955, or if not then for 10 years before its acquisition by the authority, and it is compulsorily acquired at any time after 13th December, 1955, the person entitled to the receipts of the business will have his interest, in such part as is used for business, compensated at full compulsory purchase value instead of site value, provided his interest is more than the tenancy for a year (sec. 2).

Rule (2). The Minister is given power to adjust from time to time the rate of the additional payment for well maintained houses (sec. 3). These payments are not available for houses or the parts of houses on which payments are made under sec. 1 or 2 above.

Rule (4). Compensation paid under sec. 2 in part replaces the ex gratia payments under sec. 44 of the *Housing Act*, 1936. But these will still be available to occupiers with an interest which is less than a tenancy for a year.

Page 183. *Line* 39.

With the abandonment of the statutory rate contribution, the *Housing Subsidies Act*, 1956, sec. 8 (2), provides that in future the payment will be instead one-third of the exchequer subsidy, or £8, whichever is the less. Any arrangements in force before 1st April, 1956, will continue.

Page 184. *Lines* 14 *and* 17.

See Page 183, Line 39, above.

CHAPTER 13

Page 186. *Line* 27.

Corrigendum. Replace " largely constructed " by " initiated on a large scale."

CHAPTER 16

Page 227. *Line* 47.

See Page 162, Line 22, above.

Page 230. *Line* 3.

See Page 183, Line 39, above.

Page 237. *Line* 37.

See Page 162, Line 22, above.

CHAPTER 17

Page 245. *Line* 9.

See Page 183, Line 39, above.

CHAPTER 19

Page 276. *Line* 34. *Note* 22.

A revised version of the *Explanatory Memorandum*, to reflect the *Town and Country Planning Act*, 1954, was issued in 1955. The standard rate per acre was fixed at £110 by S.I. 1955, No. 255.

Page 276. *Line* 43. *Note* 24.

This principle has been accepted by the Government in the *Road Traffic Act*, 1956. This authorises the designation of parking places on the highway, and the making of charges for parking there which increase with the length of time parked.

CHAPTER 20

Page 284. *Line* 30. *Note* 9.

The N.C.B. issued a revised programme for the following 14 years in 1956. See *Investing in Coal* (The Board), 1956.

Page 285. *Line* 3.

The Post Office issued its development programme in 1955. *Report on Post Office Development and Finance*, Cmd. 9576 (H.M.S.O.), 1955.

CHAPTER 22

Page 314. *Line* 28.

The abolition of owners' rates in Scotland was recommended in Scottish Home Department, *Report of the Scottish Valuation and Rating Committee* (Sorn), Cmd. 9244 (H.M.S.O.), par. 178. The abolition is provided for in the *Valuation and Rating (Scotland) Bill, 1956*, section 16. But a rating authority would still, if it wishes, be able to collect rates from an owner of unoccupied property where it is satisfied that he is allowing the property to remain unoccupied without good reason.

REFERENCES

List of Abbreviations used in the References in this Book

Statutes

H. Act	Housing Act
L.G. Act	Local Government Act
N.T. Act	New Towns Act
P.H. Act	Public Health Act
R.R.D. Act	Restriction of Ribbon Development Act
T.C.P. Act	Town and Country Planning Act
T.D. Act	Town Development Act

Ministries

M.A.F.	Ministry of Agriculture and Fisheries
M.O.H.	Ministry of Health
M.O.H.L.G.	Ministry of Housing and Local Government
M.O.L.G.P.	Ministry of Local Government and Planning
M.O.T.	Ministry of Transport
M.O.T.C.A.	Ministry of Transport and Civil Aviation
M.O.T.C.P.	Ministry of Town and Country Planning

Institutions

C.A. & E.A.I.	Chartered Auctioneers and Estate Agents Institute
I.M.T.A.	Institution of Municipal Treasurers and Accountants
I.Mun.E.	Institution of Municipal Engineers
I.T.	Institute of Transport
R.I.B.A.	Royal Institute of British Architects
R.I.C.S.	Royal Institution of Chartered Surveyors
R.S.A.	Royal Society of Arts
R.S.S.	Royal Statistical Society
S.C.T.	Society of County Treasurers
T.P.I.	Town Planning Institute

Miscellaneous

H.C.	House of Commons
H.L.	House of Lords
H.M.S.O.	Her Majesty's Stationery Office

Note: Where full particulars are not given of any source it has been mentioned earlier in the References.

REFERENCES

CHAPTER 1

[1] This list of use groups is taken from M.O.T.C.P., *The Re-development of Central Areas* (H.M.S.O., 1947), Appendix 1.

[2] *The Re-development of Central Areas*, Appendix 2, lists some 200 different kinds of building indicating in which use group they might be included.

[3] The classification follows that in Edward Goodman, *Forms of Public Control and Ownership* (Christophers, 1951), p. 19.   Only those bodies which undertake development are here mentioned; there are many others.

[4] Examples of self-financing corporations, with their dates of establishment, are North Scotland Hydro-Electric Board, 1943; National Coal Board, 1947; Transport Commission, 1948, and its 6 Executives; British Electricity Authority, 1946, and its 14 Area Electricity Boards; Gas Council, 1949, and its 12 Gas Boards; the 14 New Town Development Corporations, 1946-49; Iron and Steel Corporation, 1951; Independent Television Authority, 1954. Examples of dependent corporations are the Forestry Commission, 1919; the British Broadcasting Corporation, 1927; British Overseas Airways Corporation, 1939; the British European Airways Corporation, 1946; the 14 Regional Hospital Boards, 1946; United Kingdom Atomic Energy Authority, 1954.

[5] By the *T.C.P. Act*, 1954, sec. 33, where a prospective purchaser is told, upon his request by a local authority that any interest in land in its area which he wants to buy is not required by a public authority, and he buys or enters into a contract to buy within three months, any public authority buying compulsorily from him within five years must pay for the value of the land with any planning permission already granted and still in force at the time the purchaser was told, and not just existing use value plus established claim as written down, the normal compensation price under Part IV of the *T.C.P.* Act, 1947, and Part III of the 1954 Act.

CHAPTER 2

[1] The Act enables the Minister to set up a joint planning board for the areas of two or more county or county borough councils, but he has not used the power except for the area of certain of the National Parks which were set up under the *National Parks and Access to the Countryside Act*, 1949.

[2] *T.C.P. Act*, 1947, sec. 12 (2).

[3] *T.C.P. Act*, 1947, sec. 14 (1).

[4] *T.C.P. Act*, 1947, sec. 5 (1).

[5] M.O.L.G.P., *Progress Report: Town and Country Planning*, 1943-51, Cmd. 8204 (H.M.S.O., 1951), page 23.

[6] *T.C.P. Act*, 1947, sec. 12 (2) and 119 (1).

[7] *T.C.P. Act*, 1947, sec. 12 (2).   The groups of similar uses are defined in the *T.C.P. (Use Classes) Order*, 1950, S.I. 1950, No. 1131.

[8] *T.C.P. General Development Order and Development Charge Application Regulations*, 1950, S.I. 1950, No. 728. For a discussion on the meaning of development in the 1947 Act, see, e.g., R. E. Megarry, *Lectures on the T.C.P. Act*, 1947 (Stevens & Sons, 1949), page 13.

[9] By virtue of agreements authorised under *T.C.P. Act*, 1947, sec. 34, and *T.C.P. (Authorisation of Agreements) Regulations*, 1947, S.R.O. 1947, No. 2499.

[10] *T.C.P. Act*, 1947, sec. 10 (1).

[11] *T.C.P. Act*, 1947, secs. 26-29.

[12] *T.C.P. Act*, 1947, sec. 16.

[13] *M.O.T.C.P. Act*, 1943, sec. 1.

[14] For a list of government regional committees see Select Committee on Estimates, *Report on Regional Organisations of Government Departments*, Session 1953-54, H.C. Paper 233 (H.M.S.O.), Appendix 6 to Minutes of Evidence.

[15] *T.C.P. Act*, 1947, sec. 14 (4); *T.C.P. Act*, 1954, sec. 59; *T.C.P. (Erection of Industrial Buildings) Regulations*, 1949, S.I. 1949, No. 1025.

[16] *National Parks and Access to the Countryside Act*, 1949, sec. 12.

[17] *T.C.P. Act*, 1947, sec. 38, in general; *Mineral Workings Act*, 1951, sec. 16, in ironstone areas; *National Parks and Access to the Countryside Act*, 1949, sec. 89, in national parks; *Distribution of Industry Act*, 1945, sec. 5, in development areas.

[18] Compare the following by a county planning officer: " In discussing development by the Local Planning Authority itself, I come to a matter of some little delicacy, but as my experience has shown that the County Council or County Borough Council, as a developing authority, is seldom reticent if it considers that ' planning '—(generally used in a slightly derogatory sense)—is getting in the way, I think the other point of view should be put plainly, though, of course, without offence. Fundamentally this is a case of non-recognition by what may be called the Executive Department of the local authority of the duties which devolve upon it as the local planning authority. The responsibility for the right use of land does not cease because the user happens, also, to be the local planning authority and all the uses proposed by that body do not become right automatically. Surely the tests which are applied to anyone else's use of land by the Department especially established and equipped for the purpose should be applied to development proposed by the authority itself—if for no other reason by way of a good example." M. J. Hellier, " Control of land use in daily practice," *Journal I.Mun.E.*, Vol. 80 (1953), p. 326.

[19] For the form and content of development plans this account derives from *T.C.P. Act*, 1947, sec. 5; *T.C.P. (Development Plans) Regulations*, 1948, S.I. 1948, No. 1767; *T.C.P. (Development Plans) Amendment Regulations*, 1954, S.I. 1954, No. 933; *M.O.T.C.P. Circulars* 59, 70, 92 and 97; *M.O.H.L.G. Circulars* 48/54 and 9/55.

[20] Many authorities did submit, as part of their comprehensive development area maps, proposals for areas surrounding the comprehensive development areas, as suggested in *M.O.T.C.P. Circular* 59, par. 13. These maps are combined comprehensive development area and supplementary town maps, although not submitted under this name.

[21] *T.C.P. Act*, 1947, secs. 37, 38 and 45.

[22] The floor space index is the ratio that the amount of floor space that is or will be erected on a site bears to the area of the site, including half the width of adjoining streets. Plot ratio is the ratio that the same amount of floor space bears to the area of the site curtilage.

[23] *T.C.P. Act*, 1947, sec. 6 (1) and 6 (2), and *M.O.H.L.G. Circular* 9/55.

[24] By *T.C.P. (Development Plans) Direction*, 1954, made under *T.C.P. Act*, 1947, sec. 14 (3) (b), and S.I. 1950, No. 728. *M.O.H.L.G. Circular* 45/54 gives the Ministry's view as to what in practice represents a substantial departure from a plan.

[25] In particular *M.O.T.C.P. Circulars* 59, 70, 92 and 97.

[26] *Cf. M.O.H.L.G. Circular* 9/55.

[27] *T.C.P. Act*, 1947, sec. 5 (1), *M.O.T.C.P. Circulars* 40, 63 and 97.

[28] *M.O.T.C.P. Circular* 97, par. 2.

[29] Consultations on development proposals with certain public authorities are provided for formally. For a list of such authorities see M.O.T.C.P., *The Control of Mineral Working* (H.M.S.O., 1951), pars. 87-106; and see also *M.O.T.C.P. Circulars* 31, 65, 99, 100.

[30] *M.O.H.L.G. Circular 9/55.*

CHAPTER 3

[1] T.P.I.: Research Committee, " Memorandum on Programming and Cost of Development in Urban Areas," *Journal of the T.P.I.*, Vol. 38 (1951-52), p. 141.

[2] The objectives were defined in sec. 1 as: " controlling the development of the land comprised in the area to which the scheme applies, of securing proper sanitary conditions, amenity and convenience, and of preserving existing buildings or other objects of architectural, historic or artistic interest and places of natural interest or beauty, and generally of protecting existing amenities whether in urban or rural portions of the area."

[3] *T.C.P. Act*, 1947, sec. 5 (1).

[4] *Explanatory Memorandum on Town and Country Planning Bill*, 1947, Cmd. 7006 (H.M.S.O., 1947), par. 3.

[5] H.C. Debate, Vol. 432, col. 947.

[6] A guide to reasons behind planning decisions, and to planning objectives, can be seen in the Minister's published decisions on appeals to him against the planning decisions of local planning authorities. See *Bulletins of Selected Appeal Decisions* published periodically by H.M.S.O., and extracts from letters to the interested parties published regularly in *Journal of Planning Law, Estates Gazette, Builder*, etc. See also A. E. Telling and F. H. B. Layfield, *Planning Applications Appeals and Inquiries* (Butterworth & Co., 1953), Part II.

[7] M.O.L.G.P., *Town and Country Planning*, 1943-51, p. 91.

[8] *County of London Development Plan* (1951), Written Statement, p. 13.

[9] *M.O.H.L.G. Circular 58/51.* See also *Journal of Planning Law* (1954), p. 384 and (1955), p. 829.

[10] M.O.H.L.G., *Bulletin of Selected Appeal Decisions*, No. XI, par. 16.

[11] M.O.T.C.P., *Bulletin of Selected Appeal Decisions*, No. VI, par. 12.

[12] M.O.H.L.G., *Bulletin of Selected Appeal Decisions*, No. XI, par. 19.

[13] W. G. Holford and H. W. Myles Wright, *Cambridge Planning Proposals* (Cambridge U.P., 1950), p. 50. This aim was incorporated into the County of Cambridge Development Plan and has been approved by the Minister.

[14] *Report of the Committee on the Qualification of Planners* (Schuster), Cmd. 8059 (H.M.S.O., 1950), p. 19.

[15] Lord Goschen, quoted by Herman Finer, *English Local Government*, 2nd Ed. (Methuen, 1945), p. 21.

[16] I. G. Gibbon, " Some problems of local government," *Public Administration*, Vol. IX (1931), pp. 101 and 102.

[17] " First and Second Reports of the Policy Advisory Committee to the City Council on the survey of organisation and methods undertaken by the Organisation and Methods Division of H.M. Treasury," *Public Administration*, Vol. XXXII (1954), p. 80.

[18] H. R. Page, *Co-ordination and Planning in a Local Authority* (Manchester U.P., 1936), p. 315.

[19] H. R. Page, pp. 316-320.

[20] W. G. Fiske, " Planning Administration," *Proceedings of the Conference of the British Sociological Association*, 1953 (The Association), p. 4.

CHAPTER 4

[1] *Economic Survey*, 1947, Cmd. 7046 (H.M.S.O., 1947), par. 1.

[2] *Economic Survey*, 1947, par. 1.

[3] *Employment Policy*, Cmd. 6527 (H.M.S.O., 1944), Chap. VI.

[4] *Economic Survey*, 1947, par. 12.

[5] H.C. Debate, Vol. 536, col. 31.

[6] This relies on *Economic Survey*, 1947, pars. 8-29.

[7] Selections of these statistics are published annually by H.M.S.O. in *Annual Abstract of Statistics* and *National Income and Expenditure*, and monthly in *Monthly Digest of Statistics*. These refer to sources.

[8] For the types of building and civil engineering work (other than housing) sponsored by various departments see Economic Information Unit, *Industrial Building* (H.M.S.O.), Appendix I.

[9] For a list of such bodies and working parties see Central Office of Information, *Government and Industry* (H.M.S.O., 1948).

[10] *Government and Industry*, p. 7.

[11] At one end of the scale are the Soviet economic plans, " instructions which are compulsory for all managements and which determine the future course of the economic development of our entire country." This is " planning with a purpose." At the other extreme are " guess," " wish " or " dream " plans, where the planners are interested in gauging what is likely to happen but with which there is associated no intention to do anything to influence events. British planning is somewhere in the middle. See for a discussion on these and other kinds of economic planning, and for the source of this phraseology, John Jewkes, *Ordeal by Planning* (Macmillan, 1948), Chap. V.

[12] *Economic Survey*, 1947, par. 29.

CHAPTER 5

[1] J. M. Keynes, *The General Theory of Employment, Interest and Money* (Macmillan, 1936), p. 104.

[2] Many local authorities carry on trading activities which are not monopolies, often in competition with private traders, because they consider it to be in the interest of their areas. We have not described this as collective spending. Examples are swimming baths, concert halls, tennis courts, restaurants. Some unusual examples are the manufacture and sale of ice-cream in Sunderland, the sale, servicing and installation of radio sets by Fulham, Birmingham's Municipal Savings Bank, Oundle's trusteeship of the local cinema. For others see series of 15 articles on " Unusual Municipal Undertakings," *Telescope*, Vols. 3, 4 and 5 (1952, 1953, 1954).

[3] D. N. Chester, *The Nationalised Industries* (Allen & Unwin, 1951), p. 66. Some think, however, that the Boards should cover in their prices not the cost which is averaged over all production but marginal costs, that is the cost of producing supplies which would be additional to those being produced at any one time. *Cf.* the discussion from these viewpoints on the price that should be charged for coal in *Report of the Committee on National Policy for the Use of Fuel and Power Resources* (Ridley), Cmd. 8647 (H.M.S.O., 1952), Chap. IV.

[4] *Cf.* " How can one read the law without the sense that the central departments seem peculiarly to have been placed in the position of defenders of the consumer. There is no express clause to this effect in any of the statutes; but,

taken in combination, the various powers devolved to the departments in regard to the price, purity, regularity and quality of supply of a commodity instal them in such a situation." Herman Finer, *Municipal Trading* (Allen & Unwin, 1941), p. 83.

[5] The recommendation for this Committee was made in H.C. Select Committee, *Report on Nationalised Industries*, Session 1952-53, H.C. Paper 235 (H.M.S.O.), p. xii.

[6] There must be a reference back to the local electorate, via a town meeting or poll, when a borough or urban district wish to obtain powers in a private Act (*L.G. Act*, 1933, sec. 255 and Ninth Schedule). For example, the Manchester City Corporation held a town meeting in 1949 to gain support for its wish for private Act powers to build a new town for Manchester people at Mobberley in Cheshire; and the town meeting voted against it.

[7] J. R. Hicks and U. K. Hicks, *Standards in Local Expenditure* (Cambridge U.P., 1943).

[8] For a discussion on this aspect of grants see D. N. Chester, *Central and Local Government* (Macmillan, 1951), Chaps. VI-VIII. See also Appendix A of this for details of specific grants and also J. M. Drummond, *The Finance of Local Government* (Allen & Unwin, 1952), Appendix B.

[9] J. R. Jarmain, *Housing Subsidies and Rents* (Stevens and Sons, 1948), p. 97.

[10] Henry Brooke, " The Effect of Housing Subsidies on the Re-development of Central Areas," *Journal of R.I.C.S.*, Vol. XXXII (1953), p. 753; " Subsidies on Scottish Flats," *Town and Country Planning*, Vol. XXIII (1954), p. 473; F. J. Osborn, " How Subsidies Distort Development," *Lloyds Bank Review* No. 36 (1955), p. 25; " Housing Subsidies and Density in City Development," *Town and Country Planning*, Vol. XXIII (1955), p. 407.

[11] *L.G. Act*, 1948, Part I, replacing block grants in *L.G. Act*, 1929, Part VI. It is generally accepted that the exchequer equalisation grants scheme of the *L.G. Act*, 1948, has not succeeded in its main objective: the equalising of rate burden among authorities. *Cf.* A Research Working Party: " *The Effects of the Local Government Act, 1948, and other recent legislation on the Finances of Local Authorities* " (Incorporated Accountants Research Committee, 1954). The working of the scheme was officially examined in M.O.H.L.G., *The Report of the Committee Appointed to investigate the operation of the Exchequer Equalisation Grant in England and Wales* (Edwards) (H.M.S.O., 1953). The Committee made recommendations as to reform.

[12] Eric Shankelman, " Economic Forecasting in Great Britain," *Applied Statistics*, Vol. II (1953), p. 86.

[13] This kind of estimating has been carried out in the planning stage before building new shopping centres in the U.S.A. Sometimes these are larger in scale than those in our new towns. For a note on the methods of estimating in such cases see Geoffrey Baker and Bruno Funaro, *Shopping Centres: Design and Construction* (Reinhold Publishing Corporation, New York, 1951), pp. 196, 207 and 219.

[14] The method here outlined is given in Chester Rapkin, Louis Winnick and David M. Blank, *Housing Market Analysis* (Institute for Urban Land Use and Housing Studies, Columbia University, New York, 1953).

[15] *Cf.* for example W. A. Evatts, " Estimating the Gas Demand," *Gas Journal*, Vol. 266 (1951), p. 239, for the manner in which the expected additional gas demand was estimated for an additional population of 150,000 which was visualised in development plans. This population included that of four new towns in Hertfordshire. And *cf.* for an estimation of the demand for coal, National Coal Board, *Plan for Coal* (the Board, 1950), ch. III.

[16] *Financial Statement*, 1954-55 (H.M.S.O.), p. 4.

[17] Sir John Woods, " Treasury Control," *The Political Quarterly*, Vol. XXV (1954), p. 372.

[18] *Report of the Machinery of Government Committee* (Haldane), Cmd. 9230 (H.M.S.O., 1918), par. 14.

[19] *L.G. Act*, 1933, sec. 182.

[20] *Rating and Valuation Act*, 1925, sec. 12.

CHAPTER 6

[1] Alfred Marshall, *Principles of Economics*, 8th Ed. (Macmillan, 1920), p. 115.

[2] An exception to this is where a mineral undertaker can in certain circumstances apply to the High Court for a compulsory grant of working rights which does not convey a freehold or leasehold interest. See M.O.T.C.P., *The Control of Mineral Working*, p. 8.

[3] We have referred here only to the fee simple absolute. A freehold may be held for the life of its owner, or for the life of one or more other parties, or for as long as there is a line of succession in a particular family. In such cases it may be subject to particular restrictions which protect the rights of successors.

[4] For a brief discussion on this point in relation to land values see W. H. Rothwell, " Theory of Valuations: The effect of the Town and Country Planning Act, 1947," *Transactions of the R.I.C.S.*, Vol. LXXXXIV (1952), p. 37.

[5] Agricultural rents over the war years do not seem to have been fixed in free competition. In an investigation into the agricultural rents between 1938 and 1946 on about 1·66 million acres, that is about 10 per cent of non-owner-occupied cultivated land in England and Wales, it was found that whereas in 1938 the average gross rent per acre (i.e., contract rent plus interest on improvements) was 25s. 6d., in 1946 it had risen to only 27s. 6d. despite the increase in agricultural prosperity and fall in the value of money between these dates. In 1934-38 the proportion of owners' gross rents remaining after paying for maintenance, statutory charges and improvements was 38 per cent, but by 1946 this had shrunk to 20 per cent. These figures were average over the 1·66 million acres; those for individual farms would be different. See D. K. Britton, *An Enquiry into agricultural rents and the expenses of landowners in England and Wales, 1938 and 1946* (Central Landowners' Association, 1949).

[6] For a discussion on the principle of substitution see Marshall, *Principles of Economics*, p. 295, and on proportioning the factors of production see R. T. Ely and G. E. Wehrwein, *Land Economics* (Macmillan, New York, 1940), p. 113.

[7] H. T. Dorau and A. G. Hinman, *Urban Land Economics* (Macmillan, New York, 1928), p. 169; R. U. Ratcliff, *Urban Land Economics* (McGraw-Hill, New York, 1949), p. 354.

[8] In Marshall's words " and thus even the rent of land is seen, not as a thing by itself, but as the leading species of a large genus; though indeed it has peculiarities of its own which are of vital importance from the point of view of theory as well as practice." This other kind of rent he called " quasi-rent ". *Principles of Economics*, p. 340.

[9] See Chap. 10 for a fuller discussion on cost and yield. By cost is sometimes meant initial capital cost and sometimes both this and continuing annual costs.

[10] M.O.H.L.G., *Density of Residential Areas* (H.M.S.O., 1952), p. 51 and R. Nicholas, *City of Manchester Plan* (Jarrold & Sons, 1945), p. 268.

[11] *Principles of Economics*, p. 371.

[12] Dorau and Hinman, *Urban Land Economics*, p. 167, and R. U. Ratcliff, *Urban Land Economics*, p. 373.

[13] One of the weaknesses of the development charge provisions of the 1947 Act was not so much that they inhibited development as the transfer of land for development. Landowners on the whole, thinking that they were entitled to the development value, were not induced to make land available only for existing use value; and developers, in general, could not afford to pay a development charge and also a price which included development value. They could and did do so, however, where there was a high scarcity value for the finished development.

[14] It has, however, been suggested that all land has a " community value," which is " the power that land has to meet the needs of men living in community," and that community value, including that of land used or to be used for public purposes, is capable of being assessed in money terms. This value would be indicated by, but not necessarily be equal to, the market value of the land. See Bryan Anstey, " On the Nature of Value," *The Sociological Review*, Vol. XL (1948), p. 13, and also note 5 to Chapter 25.

[15] *Acquisition of Land (Assessment of Compensation) Act*, 1919, sec. 2, Rule 5.

[16] *T.C.P. Act*, 1947, sec. 45 (5) and *T.C.P. Act*, 1944, Fourth Schedule.

[17] *Central Land Board Circular* 3/51.

CHAPTER 7

[1] This account relies on Ministry of Works: Working Party Report, *Building* (H.M.S.O., 1950) and Ministry of Works: Report of the Committee of Enquiry, *The Distribution of Building Materials and Components* (H.M.S.O., 1948).

[2] Those statistics which are published appear in the *Monthly Digest of Statistics*, *Annual Abstract of Statistics*, the annual reports of the Ministry of Works, and *Ministry of Labour Gazette*.

[3] C. M. Kohan, *History of the Second World War, Works and Buildings* (H.M.S.O., 1952), p. 25; and Ian Bowen, " The Control of Building," *Lessons of the British War Economy*, ed. D. N. Chester (Cambridge U.P., 1951), p. 122.

[4] Select Committee on Estimates, *Report on Regional Organisation of Government Departments*, Appendix 6 to Minutes of Evidence.

[5] It is interesting to note that restriction of private building was contemplated even before the war, in 1937, to assist in bridging the gap between demands on the industry and its capacity, and attempts were made to find new sources of manpower and a way of determining priorities between the departments. C. M. Kohan, p. 17 and p. 462.

[6] *Training for the Building Industry*, Cmd. 6428 (H.M.S.O., 1943).

[7] British Productivity Council, *A Review of Productivity in the Building Industry* (The Council, 1954), p. 14.

[8] *Cf.* Table 3 and notes to Graph 1. But note the variations in firms of different size in Table 7.

[9] For example, *County Borough of Bolton Development Plan* (1952), Written Analysis, p. 151; *Isle of Ely County Council Development Plan* (1951), Written Analysis, p. 135; *County Borough of Gateshead Development Plan* (1951), Written Analysis, p. 84; *County Borough of Leeds Development Plan* (1951), Written Analysis, p. 123.

[10] For an example of an exercise of this kind see N. Dickenson and P. L. Benneworth, " A method of programming for a Town Map," *Journal of the T.P.I.*, Vol. 38 (1951-52), p. 62.

CHAPTER 8

[1] J. R. Hicks, *The Social Framework*, 2nd Ed. (Oxford U.P., 1952), p. 15, from which the terminology in the following paragraph is also derived.

[2] *Cf.* J. R. Hicks, Part IV.

[3] For an explanation of the terms used see Central Statistical Office, *National Income and Expenditure*, 1946-51 (H.M.S.O., 1952), pp. 3-13, and also the succeeding annual publications *National Income and Expenditure*.

[4] "The Corpse in the Capital Market," *The Economist*, Vol. 166 (1953), p. 375.

[5] It has been pointed out that if the Gas Board had based depreciation in 1952-53 on replacement cost, and so set aside £32-34 million, they would have shown a trading loss of £16 million; but as they based it, in accordance with normal accountancy practice, on historical cost, and set aside £14·4 million, they showed a profit of £2·3 million. Paul Bareau, *Municipal Journal*, Vol. 61 (1953), p. 2320.

[6] For periods adopted by the Gas Council and British Electricity Authority for their assets which are acquired after vesting date see The Gas Council, *Second Report and Statement of Accounts*, 1951 (H.M.S.O.), par. 187 and Appendix 11; and British Electricity Authority, *Second Report and Accounts*, 1949-50 (H.M.S.O.), par. 355 and Appendix 43.

[7] *Cf. L.G. Act*, 1933, secs. 195 and 198, Eighth Schedule. The maximum loan period for local authority development is generally 60 years, although the period for land for housing, allotments and smallholdings is 80 years. Maximum loan periods in practice for particular kinds of development are buildings in general 30 years; dwellings 60 years; laying out of paths, cemeteries, recreation grounds 30 years; construction of roads, streets and footpaths—depending on kind of construction—4 to 20 years; sewers and sewage works 30 years; tree planting 20 years; airfields 15-30 years. For periods agreed under local authorities' local Acts see A. B. Griffiths, *Municipal Capital Finance* (Chas. Knight, 1936), Appendix I. For periods agreed for water undertakings, and for various gas, electricity and transportation undertakings before nationalisation, see Herman Finer, *Municipal Trading*, p. 134.

[8] The current allowance is an initial allowance of 10 per cent and an annual write down of 2 per cent on the reducing balance method, for a period of 50 years. See *Income Tax Act*, 1956, sec. 16. The relief is afforded to industrial buildings and structures as widely defined in *Income Tax Act*, 1952, sec. 271. "Industrial" includes transport, storage, mining, agriculture.

[9] *M.O.H. Circulars* 185/45 and 144/46, and M.O.H., *Annual Report*, 1947 (H.M.S.O.), p. 195.

[10] M.O.H., *Annual Report*, 1929-30, p. 131.

CHAPTER 9

[1] The discounted value of £100 in three months at 2 per cent is £99 10s.; that is £99 10s. will accumulate to £100 in three months at 2 per cent.

[2] In government accounts a distinction is made between receipts and expenditure which are "above and below the line." Receipts above the line come from taxation resulting from the budget; expenditure above the line is made out of this taxation. Expenditure below the line is that for which the government have power to borrow; included in it are loans to local authorities via the Public Works Loan Board, and advances to the New Town Development Corporations and the National Coal Board. Receipts below the line are interest, loan repayments and borrowings earmarked for such expenditure.

[3] *L.G. Act*, 1933, sec. 215.

[4] *Local Authority Loans Act*, 1945, sec. 1, which was allowed to lapse in 1952.

[5] *L.G. Act*, 1933, secs. 205-214.

[6] *L.G. Act*, 1933, sec. 204, and Regulations.

[7] *H. Act*, 1936, sec. 122.

[8] *Local Authorities Loans Act*, 1945, sec. 8.

[9] *Borrowing (Control and Guarantees) Act*, 1946, and *Control of Borrowing Order*, 1947, *S.R.O.*, 1947, No. 945.

[10] *Memorandum of Guidance to the Capital Issues Committee*, Cmd. 6645 (H.M.S.O., 1945), par. 1.

[11] For example *Memorandum of Guidance*, Cmd. 6645; *Special Memorandum to the Capital Issues Committee*, Cmd. 7281 (H.M.S.O., 1947); H.C. Debate, Vol. 486, col. 152; Vol. 494, col. 326; Vol. 537, col. 204; Written Answers, Vol. 470, col. 295.

[12] Those used to valuation tables might note that under this method the loan charges are the reciprocal of the years' purchase for the Present Value of £1 over the corresponding number of years in the Single Rate Valuation Table.   In illustration:

Present value of £1 per annum for 20 years at
  4 per cent Single Rate   = 13·59 years' purchase
Reciprocal of this = 1/13·59   = 0·07358
Annuity (Principal and interest) for the repayment
  of a loan of £1 over 20 years   = 0·07358

[13] Where local authorities set up sinking funds for various purposes the maximum rate at which they are deemed to accumulate is prescribed by the Minister. Currently it is 3 per cent. See *M.O.H.L.G. Circular* 12/52.

[14] *Financial Statement*, 1954-55 (H.M.S.O.), pp. 4 and 8.

[15] Figures such as these are obtainable from *Archer's Loan Repayment and Compound Interest Tables* (Shaw and Sons). The figures in the sinking fund column are obtained by deducting from the total interest payable the interest that would be earned on the sinking fund.

CHAPTER 10

[1] M. E. Holander, " The General Design Problems of Hospitals," *Journal of R.I.B.A.*, Vol 61 (1954), p. 493.

[2] For particulars of professional and legal fees mentioned here and below see E. G. Robinson and L. B. Keeble, *Development of Building Estates* (Estates Gazette, 1952).

[3] The procedure for this is in the *Highways Act*, 1835, secs. 84-92, or the *T.C.P. Act*, 1947, sec. 49.

[4] The procedure is in *Law of Property Act*, 1925, sec. 84.

[5] See *Gas Act*, 1948, Third Schedule, sec. 8; *Electricity Act*, 1947, sec. 57, which incorporates *Electric Lighting (Clauses) Act*, 1899, Schedule, sec. 27; *Water Act*, 1945, sec. 37; *Public Health Act*, 1936, secs. 14-19.

[6] Tax on £6,000 at, say, 8s. in the £ (Schedule A and D) would be £2,400. Against this could be offset £1,200 (tax on the interest payments of 8s. in £ on £3,000)=net tax £1,200.

[7] For this use would be made of the tables for Present Value of £1 per annum, or Present Value of £1, in for example, Parrys *Valuation Tables* (Estates Gazette) or Inward's *Tables of Interest and Mortality* (Technical Press). For an example of the valuation of a building estate which fully introduces the time element see Robinson and Keeble, *Development of Building Estates*, Chap. 38 and Appendix K.

CHAPTER 11

[1] This account relies, in the main, on D. M. Lawrance, *Compulsory Purchase and Compensation* (Estates Gazette, 1952).

[2] *L.G. Act*, 1933, secs. 157-158.

[3] *Lands Clauses Act*, 1845, secs. 49-63.

[4] *Acquisition of Land (Assessment of Compensation) Act*, 1919, sec. 2.

[5] *T.C.P. Act*, 1944, secs. 57-61.

[6] *T.C.P. Act*, 1947, secs. 51-52 and 58-68.

[7] *T.C.P. Act*, 1954, secs. 31, 17, 18.

[8] *M.O.H.L.G. Circular* 34/55, Annexe par. 40-45.

[9] *Acquisition of Land (Assessment of Compensation) Act*, 1919, sec. 2, Rules 1, 3, 4 and 6.

[10] *T.C.P. Act*, 1944, sec. 57; *T.C.P. Act*, 1947, sec. 119 (4); *T.C.P. Act*, 1954, sec. 36.

[11] *Lands Clauses Act*, 1845, sec. 49.

[12] *Lands Clauses Act*, 1845, sec. 92, and, for example, *Acquisition of Land (Authorisation Procedure) Act*, 1946, Second Schedule, par. 4.

[13] *Lands Clauses Act*, 1845, sec. 68.

[14] *T.C.P. Act*, 1944, sec. 30 (1); *H. Act*, 1936, sec. 137, and Eleventh Schedule

[15] *T.C.P. Act*, 1947, sec. 53.

[16] *T.C.P. Act*, 1944, secs. 22 and 24.

[17] *T.C.P. Act*, 1944, secs. 23 and 28.

[18] *T.C.P. Act*, 1944, sec. 30 (3).

[19] See F. E. Price, " Some Aspects of Public Board Finance," *Proceedings of I.M.T.A.*, 1950 (The Institute), p. 120.

[20] *Income Tax Act*, 1952, secs. 169-171. See Frank Mellor, *Guide to Income Tax relating to local authorities* (Shaw & Sons, 1952).

[21] *Final Report of Expert Committee on Compensation and Betterment.* (Uthwatt), Cmd. 6386 (H.M.S.O., 1942), par. 278.

[22] *L.G. Act*, 1933, secs. 163-165.

[23] *M.O.H.L.G. Circular* 34/55, Annexe par. 40-45.

[24] *L.G. Act*, 1933, sec. 198 (2); *Local Authority Loans Act*, 1845, sec. 4.

[25] Our classification of an authority's annual expenditure, into development and operating, is not quite the same as that used by the accountant, who divides it broadly into debt service, the interest and repayment of loans, and running costs, the cost of carrying out services and functions. The accountant will therefore provide debt service for loans on vehicles, furniture and plant; and will include in his running costs the annual costs we have included as annual costs of development.

[26] An investigation into the cost of the principal services of nine county districts of between 50,000 and 70,000 people, chosen to throw light on the financial problems of new towns, showed that about 18·5 per cent of the total expenditure on county district services went on loan charges. See " New Towns," *Local Government Finance*, Vol. 53 (1949), p. 157.

[27] Examples of different units are given in S. Yates and R. E. Herbert, *A Survey of Unit Costing in Local Government* (I.M.T.A., 1953), Appendix 1. Unit cost statistics for the preceding year for, *inter alia*, education, the local health service, welfare services, children's service, police force and fire brigade, are published each year jointly by the I.M.T.A. and S.O.C.T.

[28] *Education Statistics*, 1951-52 (I.M.T.A. and S.C.T.).

[29] These and the following figures of rates levied are taken from *Return of Rates*, 1954-55 (I.M.T.A.). For details of the exchequer equalisation grants and total grants paid to different authorities see *Report of M.O.H.L.G. for the period* 1950/1 *to* 1954, Cmd. 9559 (H.M.S.O., 1955), App. XIV and XV.

[30] *L.G. Act*, 1948, sec. 9.

[31] This was the ironical position in which many of the bomb-damaged towns found themselves with regard to L.G. Act, 1929, block grants. Their loss in population through emigration was greater than the proportionate loss in rateable value through bombing. See N. W. E. Hamm, " Migration and Grants," *Local Government Finance*, Vol. LVI (1952), p. 10; A. R. Thompson, "Neglected Orphans of the Storm," *Local Government Finance*, Vol. LV (1951), p. 233.

[32] There are many definitions of a 1d. rate for various purposes in different statutes. See " When is a Penny Rate not a Penny Rate," *Municipal Journal*, Vol. 59 (1951), p. 567; and J. M. Drummond, *The Finance of Local Government*, p. 198.

CHAPTER 12

[1] *H. Act*, 1936, sec. 1.

[2] *H. Act*, 1936, sec. 71, and *H. Act*, 1949, sec. 1.

[3] *H. Act*, 1936, sec. 89; *Housing (Financial and Miscellaneous Provisions) Act*, 1946, sec. 8; *L.G. Act*, 1948, sec. 126.

[4] *H. Act*, 1936, secs. 72-74.

[5] *H. Act*, 1936, sec. 76.

[6] For clearance area procedure see *H. Act*, 1936, secs. 25-33, and *Housing Repairs and Rents Act*, 1954, sec. 14 and First Schedule.

[7] For re-development area procedure see *H. Act*, 1936, secs. 34-37.

[8] *H. Act*, 1936, sec. 80, and *H. Act*, 1949, sec. 7.

[9] *Interim Report of the New Towns Committee* (Reith), Cmd. 6759 (H.M.S.O., 1946), par. 15.

[10] *H. Act*, 1936, secs. 30 (2) and 79 (3).

[11] *H. Act*, 1936, sec. 79 (2).

[12] *H. Act*, 1936, sec. 79; *H. Act*, 1952, sec. 3.

[13] *M.O.H.L.G. Circular* 64/52.

[14] M.O.H. Central Housing Advisory Committee, *Private Enterprise Housing* (Pole) (H.M.S.O., 1944), par. 4.

[15] *Private Enterprise Housing*, Appendix IV.

[16] M.O.H.L.G., *Housing Return for England and Wales*, 31/12/55, Cmd. 9681 (H.M.S.O.), p. 3. The Return does not give the number of subsidised dwellings; the 1.7 million is the new permanent dwellings provided by local authorities, housing associations and new town development corporations, excluding those provided in the rebuilding of war damage. This is approximately the number of dwellings subsidised.

[17] *Housing (Financial and Miscellaneous Provisions) Act*, 1946, secs. 1-8; *H. Act*, 1949, secs. 37-39; *H. Act*, 1952, sec. 1.

[18] *Housing (Review of Contributions) Order*, 1954, S.I. 1954, No. 1407. See also *Report by Minister of Housing and Local Government*, Session 1953-4, H.C. Paper 200 (H.M.S.O., 1954).

[19] *Housing (Financial and Miscellaneous Provisions) Act*, 1946, sec. 25 (2).

[20] *Housing (Financial Provisions) Act*, 1938, sec. 11.

[21] *Housing (Financial and Miscellaneous Provisions) Act*, 1946, First Schedule, Part I.

[22] The annuity over 60 years at $4\frac{1}{4}$ per cent on £1,000 is £46 2s. per annum; £3 per dwelling at a density of $15 \cdot 5$ equals £46 5s. per annum. The annuity at $3\frac{3}{4}$ per cent on £1,000 is £42 per annum; £2 16s. per dwelling at a density of 15 equals £42 per annum.

[23] The annuity over 60 years at $4\frac{1}{4}$ per cent on £2,000 is £92 8s. per annum; £2 12s. per dwelling at a density of 35 equals £91. The annuity at $3\frac{3}{4}$ per cent on £2,000 is £84; £2 8s. per dwelling at a density of 35 equals £84.

[24] The density of flats for subsidy purposes, in a mixed scheme of houses and flats, is not taken as the actual density in the layout; this would mean establishing the actual acreage occupied by the flats, not always a simple thing to do. The flat density is calculated on a " notional " acreage which is the total housing acreage multiplied by the number of habitable rooms in flats and divided by the number of the habitable rooms in the scheme. In effect this gives the same density as the average habitable room density for the scheme. In the Housing Acts a habitable room is not defined, but for the definition used in land planning see Note 44 below.

[25] *Housing (Financial and Miscellaneous Provisions) Act*, 1946, secs. 3 (1), 5 (4) and 8 (1); *H. Act*, 1952, sec. 1 (1).

[26] *Housing (Financial and Miscellaneous Provisions) Act*, 1946, sec. 7.

[27] *H. Act*, 1949, sec. 39.

[28] H.C. Debate, Vol. 499, col. 230, and H.L. Debate, Vol. 177, col. 1020, for 1946 and 1952 Schemes; H.C. Debate, Vol. 531, col. 1392, for 1955 Scheme.

[29] Housing Committee of Association of Municipal Corporations, " Report No. 3/1949," *Municipal Review*, Vol. 20 (1949), p. 158 of Supplement.

[30] H.C. Debate, Vol. 999, col. 235.

[31] The dwelling rents in Welwyn Garden City and Hatfield vary according to size, design, date of construction, finishes and fittings, inclusion of garage, etc., but averaged as follows in 1954:

Type	Welwyn						Hatfield					
	From			To			From			To		
	£	s.	d.	£	s.	d.	£	s.	d.	£	s.	d.
Houses—monthly												
Four bedrooms ...	9	0	0	13	10	0	10	5	0	13	17	0
Three bedrooms ...	7	0	0	12	10	0						
Two bedrooms ...	6	10	0	7	0	0						
Flats and Maisonettes —monthly												
Three bedrooms ...	10	0	0									
Two bedrooms ...	7	0	0	12	0	0						
One bedroom ...	7	0	0									
Bed-sitting rooms ...	6	0	0									
Houses—weekly												
Four bedrooms ...	2	7	9	2	15	0	2	0	3	2	4	1
Three bedrooms (five persons) ...	1	19	0	2	4	3	1	14	3	2	4	2
Three bedrooms (four persons) ...	1	15	10				1	16	9			
Two bedrooms ...	1	13	4	1	17	10	1	12	3	1	14	3
Flats—weekly												
Two bedrooms ...							2	3	2	2	4	2
One bedroom ...							1	15	2	1	15	8
Bed-sitting rooms ...							1	7	11			

A bed-sitting room here thus earns almost as much as some two-bedroom houses; while a one-bed flat earns as much as some three-bedroom houses. Richard C. Relf, "Progress in New Towns, Welwyn Garden City and Hatfield," *Journal of the R.I.C.S.*, Vol. XXXIII (1954), p. 563. These figures are not necessarily typical of other new towns or of local authority rent policy. For example, in Crawley New Town in 1954 the exclusive weekly subsidised rent for a bed-sitting room flat in a two-storey block was 14s. compared to 22s. 9d. to 30s. for a two-bedroom house; and 18s. to 21s. for a one-bedroom flat compared to 23s. 9d. to 33s. for a three-bedroom house. *Reports of the Development Corporations for the period end 31st March*, 1954, p. 164. But the tendency mentioned in the text applies.

[32] *H. Act*, 1936, sec. 128.

[33] *H. Act*, 1936, sec. 129, and *M.O.H.L.G. Circular* 1/53.

[34] *Housing (Financial and Miscellaneous Provisions) Act*, 1946, sec. 21 (4), and *H. Act*, 1952, sec. 1 (3).

[35] *H. Act*, 1936, Eighth Schedule, sec. 8.

[36] *Housing Statistics*, 1950-51 (I.M.T.A.).

[37] *H. Act*, 1936, sec. 130.

[38] *H. Act*, 1936, sec. 85 (5), and *H. Act*, 1949, First Schedule.

[39] *H. Act*, 1936, sec. 40.

[40] *H. Act*, 1936, sec. 42.

[41] *H. Act*, 1936, Fourth Schedule.

[42] *H. Act*, 1936, secs. 44 and 45. Where unfit houses are included in areas designated in a development plan or are to be acquired under sec. 37 (2) or sec. 38 (2) of the *T.C.P. Act*, 1947, the compensation code for clearance areas can be applied under *T.C.P. Act*, 1944, Fifth Schedule.

[43] *H. Act*, 1936, sec. 46.

[44] A habitable room is defined for density purposes as " a room which is normally used for living or sleeping in. A kitchen should only be regarded as a habitable room when it is also used as a living room." M.O.H.L.G., *Density of Residential Areas*, Appendix 3.

[45] The densities are derived as follows:

Net density	Dwellings		Open space and playing fields in centre	Total acres	" Gross " density pers./acre
200 h.r./acre	5·0	acres	5·0 acres	10·0	100
140 h.r./acre	7·1	acres	5·5 acres	12·6	79
80 h.r./acre	12·5	acres	6·0 acres	11·5	59
60 h.r./acre	16·7	acres	6·0 acres	22·7	44

[46] The 12 acres per 1,000 population would be used as follows: primary schools, 1·5 acres; public open space, 6·0 acres; allotments, 1·5 acres; service industry, 0·5 acre; other buildings and car parks, 2·5 acres. One thousand people at 60 persons per acre would require 16·7 acres for dwellings, and therefore 28·7 acres in all. This gives a gross neighbourhood density of 35 persons per acre.

[47] For these proportions at different densities, which are based on the assumption that the maximum percentage of rooms will be provided in houses, see M.O.H.L.G., *Density of Residential Areas*, Table 4.

[48] The figures for cost of building which are given apply to one locality only and are not typical for the whole country. For advice on them I am indebted to Mr. D. W. Nunn, A.R.I.C.S.

[49] *H. Act*, 1936, sec. 188.

[50] *H. Act*, 1936, secs. 92 and 93.

[51] *H. Act*, 1936, sec. 94.

[52] *Cf.* Reginald Browne, *Housing Societies* (Dent and Sons, 1944), p. 44.

[53] *N.T. Act*, 1946, sec. 9.

[54] *M.O.H.L.G. Circular* 29/53.

[55] *N.T. Act*, 1946, secs. 8 (2) and 12 (2).

[56] *Housing Repairs and Rents Act*, 1954, sec. 33.

CHAPTER 13

[1] *L.G. Act*, 1929, Part III.

[2] *Unemployment* (*Relief Works*) *Act*, 1920, and *Public Works Facilities Act*, 1930. These lapsed in 1936 and 1946 respectively.

[3] *R.R.D. Act*, 1935, sec. 13.

[4] *Trunk Roads Act*, 1936, sec. 4; *Trunk Roads Act*, 1946, sec. 5; *Special Roads Act*, 1949, sec. 14.

[5] *Special Roads Act*, 1949, sec. 10.

[6] *T.C.P. Act*, 1947, secs. 37, 38 and 40.

[7] *T.C.P. Act*, 1947, sec. 44.

[8] E.g. *Highway Act*, 1835, secs. 80 and 82; *Town Improvement Clauses Act*, 1847 sec. 67; *Highway Act*, 1864, secs. 47, 48.

⁹ *M.O.T. Circular* 622, par. 2, and *M.O.T.C.A. Circular* 696, par. 8.

¹⁰ *P.H. Act*, 1925, secs. 33 and 34, where adopted.

¹¹ *P.H. Act*, 1875, sec. 154; *P.H. Act*, 1925, sec. 83.

¹² Made under *P.H. Act*, 1875, sec. 157.

¹³ *P.H. Act*, 1925, secs. 29 and 30, where adopted.

¹⁴ The *P.H. Act*, 1875, contained no powers, in respect of building bye-laws, comparable with those in the *P.H. Act*, 1936, sec. 63, whereby an authority could agree to a lesser width than that referred in the bye-laws. To agree in a particular case an authority can make an amending bye-law by the procedure in *L.G. Act*, 1933, sec. 250; or use the machinery in the *T.C.P. Act*, 1947, sec. 13 (4). By this the Minister of Housing and Local Government can make a development order relaxing the bye-laws in a specific case for the purpose of enabling development to be carried out in accordance with a planning permission, or for the purpose of promoting proper development in accordance with a development plan. Where bye-laws are relaxed, the minimum widths to which streets should be built are suggested in M.O.H.L.G., *Schedule of Minimum Street Widths* (H.M.S.O., 1951). See also *M.O.H.L.G. Circular* 19/51.

¹⁵ *P.H. Act*, 1925, sec. 31, where adopted.

¹⁶ *Public Health Acts (Amendment) Act*, 1907, sec. 17, where adopted.

¹⁷ *P.H. Act*, 1872, secs. 150-152, for urban authorities; *Private Street Works Act*, 1892, for rural authorities, and urban authorities where adopted.

¹⁸ *New Streets Act*, 1951, which applies to urban authorities (not County of London) and can be adopted in rural districts.

¹⁹ *T.C.P. Act*, 1947, sec. 48; and *T.C.P. (Construction and Improvement of Private Streets) Regulations*, 1951, S.I. 1951, (No. 2224.

²⁰ *P.H. Act*, 1875, sec. 154; *P.H. Act*, 1925, sec. 83; *Development and Road Improvement Funds Act*, 1909; *T.C.P. Act*, 1932, sec. 25.

²¹ *R.R.D. Act*, 1935, sec. 13.

²² Ralph Turvey, " Recoupment as an aid in financing 19th century street improvements in London," *Review of Economic Studies* (1953-54), p. 53.

²³ Sir Harry Haward, *The London County Council from Within* (Chapman & Hall, 1932), p. 255.

²⁴ *M.O.T. Circular* 595.

²⁵ *M.O.T.C.A. Circulars* 696 and 697.

²⁶ *M.O.T.C.A. Circular* 696, par. 4.

²⁷ *Cf.* H.L. Debate, Vol. 186, col. 145, and *Local Government Chronicle*, No. 4553 (1954), p. 407. The *Development and Road Improvements Funds Act*, 1909, sec. 13, did authorise borrowing by the Road Board on the security of the Road Improvement Fund provided that the annual loan charges did not exceed £200,000.

²⁸ H.C. Debate, Vol. 521, col. 1811.

²⁹ E.g., *Development and Road Improvement Funds Act*, 1909, Schedule, par. 2; *P.H. Act*, 1925, sec. 33; *R.R.D. Act*, 1935, sec. 13.

³⁰ *Reports on the Administration of the Road Fund.* The figures are given separately for Trunk, Class I, II, III and unclassified roads; and also separately for the roads in the counties, county boroughs and urban county districts in England and Wales; and the counties, large burghs, and small burghs in Scotland.

³¹ H.C. Debate, Vol. 536, col. 1103.

CHAPTER 14

[1] *P.H. Act*, 1925, sec. 68, as amended by *R.R.D. Act*, 1935, sec. 16.

[2] M.O.T., *Parking Places* (H.M.S.O., 1946). D. F. Orchard, " The Problem of Car Parking," *Journal of I.Mun.E.*, Vol. 76 (1949-50), p. 189. R. Nicholas, *City of Manchester Plan* (1945), Appendix C. Pre-war prices are used in this, but they have been scaled up to post-war levels in a letter from R. Nicholas, *Journal of I.Mun.E.*, Vol. 76 (1949-50), p. 379. The post-war figures are used here. M.O.T., *Report of the Working Party on Car Parking in the inner area of London* (H.M.S.O., 1953), par. 90.

[3] *Car Parking in the inner area of London*, Appendix H.

[4] See note 2.

[5] *Car Parking in the inner area of London*, p. 20, recommended for underground car parks the following charges, based on 1952 costs:

	Up to 16 h.p.	17-25 h.p.	Over 25 h.p.
	s. d.	s. d.	s. d.
Up to three hours	1 6	2 0	2 6
Between three and six hours ...	2 0	2 6	3 0
Between six and 12 hours ...	2 6	3 0	3 6

These charges were not visualised as being enough to make the underground car parks self supporting.

[6] It has been argued that the long-term parker at least should pay an economic rent, that is at least the cost to the authority, for this would reduce the demand for car parking space in cities. See Reservation by C. D. Buchanan in *Car Parking in the inner area of London*, and A. C. L. Day and Ralph Turvey, " The Parking Problem in Central London: an economic appraisal," *Journal of I.T.*, Vol. 25 (1954), p. 406.

[7] The land would in fact cost something. If two schemes were designed by a developer for a site, one for a building with a basement car park and one without, the former would involve a higher capital cost for the same or less yield. In other words, for the car park scheme less could be offered for the site. The difference would represent the cost of land in the basement car park scheme.

CHAPTER 15

[1] In 1936 it was stated that almost the whole of the City of London had been re-developed since 1850, and about one quarter since 1905. E. E. Finch and C. Gerald Eve, *Report to the Improvement Committee of Council of the City of London* (Corporation of London, 1936), p. 3.

[2] *Uthwatt Report*, pars. 1 and 135.

[3] *Uthwatt Report*, pars. 144-156.

[4] *T.C.P. Act*, 1944, secs. 1, 7, 9, 10 and 20; *T.C.P. Act*, 1947, sec. 113.

[5] *T.C.P. Act*, 1944, sec. 19.

[6] See *Town and Country Planning*, 1943-51, Appendix IV and V, for progress in acquisitions up till 1951; and for progress in rebuilding till 1954 see D. R. Childs and D. A. C. A. Bayne, *Architects Journal*, Vol. 120 (1954), p. 41.

[7] *T.C.P. Act*, 1947, sec. 5 (3).

[8] *T.C.P. Act*, 1947, sec. 38 (1) and (3).

[9] *T.C.P. Act*, 1947, sec. 38 (1).

[10] *L.G. Act*, 1933, sec. 163 (1) and (3), and *T.C.P. Act*, 1947, sec. 42.

[11] *T.C.P. Act*, 1944, secs. 20 (1) and 19 (3).

[12] For a discussion on the powers under each Act see Ernest S. Collins, " Slum Clearance under Housing and Town Planning Powers," *Journal of Property Law* (1949), p. 624; and Douglas Barlow, " Slum Clearance Under the Planning Acts," *Journal of Property Law* (1955), p. 327.

[13] This account relies on the *Town and Country Planning (Grants) Regulations*, 1950, *Explanatory Memorandum* (H.M.S.O., 1950). The Regulations are S.I. 1950 No. 88, and Amending Regulations S.I. 1954, No. 177.

[14] *T.C.P. Act*, 1947, sec. 93 (1). See also *M.O.T.C.P. Circular* 90.

[15] *T.C.P. Act*, 1947, sec. 95 (1).

[16] *Explanatory Memorandum*, par. 16 and Appendix G.

[17] *Explanatory Memorandum*, par. 7.

[18] See *Explanatory Memorandum*, Appendix A, for details.

[19] See *Explanatory Memorandum*, Appendix B, for details.

[20] *T.C.P. Act*, 1947, sec. 19 (5), and *Town Development Act*, 1952, sec. 18.

[21] See *Explanatory Memorandum*, pars. 19-22 and Appendix F, for details.

[22] Arthur Limon, " Some Financial Aspects of Town Planning," *British Housing and Planning Review*, Vol. 10 (1955), p. 24. This incorporates material published earlier in Arthur Limon, " Costs of Town Development," *Journal of T.P.I.*, Vol. 37 (1950-51), p. 78; and Arthur Limon, " The Cost of Re-development," *Journal of T.P.I.*, Vol. 36 (1949-50), p. 10.

[23] From figures supplied by Mr. Limon.

[24] In accordance with *M.O.H.L.G. Circular* 34/55, Annexe par. 40-45.

[25] In accordance with *Explanatory Memorandum*, Appendix F. Value of land for (a) housing—value of land for residential purposes; (b) highways—actual cost excluding legal or other expenses, disturbance, injurious affection, etc.; (c) open space—one-quarter residential value.

[26] *Housing (Financial and Miscellaneous Provisions) Act*, 1946, First Schedule. The value of the site for subsidy purposes is taken in the condition in which it would be if the expense of making the site suitable were excluded, and to this must be added the cost of works; the Appendix F value for residential purposes is the value of the land in its cleared state for its new use.

[27] T.P.I.: Research Committee, *The Economics of Central Area Re-development* (The Institute, 1952), par. 10.

CHAPTER 16

[1] *H. Act*, 1936, sec. 81. Powers, which have been barely used, also exist in the *T.C.P. Act*, 1947, sec. 38, whereby land can be acquired after its inclusion in an area of comprehensive development for the purpose of relocation of population or industry after re-development.

[2] *Cf.* G. Sutton Brown, " Population Movement from South Lancashire in Theory and Practice," *Journal of the T.P.I.*, Vol. 38 (1951-52), p. 189.

[3] *M.O.H.L.G. Circular* 29/53.

[4] G. Sutton Brown, " Population Movement from South Lancashire," p. 192, and D. W. Riley, " Problems of Overspill Population," *Planning Outlook*, Vol. III (1952), p. 17. County councils have powers and duties in this regard in *L.G. Act*, 1948, sec. 126; *P.H. Act*, 1936, sec. 307; *H. Act*, 1936, sec. 89; *Rural Water Supplies and Sewerage Act*, 1944, sec. 2; *R.R.D. Act*, 1935, sec. 19 (5).

[5] See for an account *Town and Country Planning*, Vol. XXIII (1955), p. 373.

[6] H.C. Debate, Vol. 496, col. 727.

[7] *T.D. Act*, 1952, sec. 1 (1).

[8] The term " exporting authority " is not used in the *T.D. Act*, 1952, but " receiving district " is defined (sec. 1 (2)).

[9] *T.D. Act*, 1952, sec. 7.

[10] *T.D. Act*, 1952, sec. 8 (1).

[11] *T.D. Act*, 1952, sec. 1 (1).

[12] *T.D. Act*, 1952, sec. 12.

[13] *T.D. Act*, 1952, sec. 8 (1), and M.O.H.L.G., *Memorandum on the Town Development Act* (H.M.S.O., 1952), par. 13.

[14] *T.D. Act*, 1952, sec. 6.

[15] *T.D. Act*, 1952, sec. 6 (5), and *T.C.P. Act*, 1947, Eleventh Schedule.

[16] *T.D. Act*, 1952, sec. 17.

[17] M.O.H., *Local Government in England and Wales during the Period of Reconstruction*, Cmd. 6579 (H.M.S.O., 1945), p. 17.

[18] Adapted from the figures given by Lloyd Rodwin, " England's Town Development Act, 1952," *Journal of American Institute of Planners*, Vol. XIX (1953), p. 26. The figures do not include for any income from industrial use. More recent figures are given in U. Aylmer Coates, " Problems of Overspill," *The Surveyor*, Vol. CXIV (1955), p. 1059.

[19] G. Sutton Brown, " Population Movement from South Lancashire," p. 192.

[20] D. W. Riley, " Problems of Overspill Population," p. 22.

[21] Lloyd Rodwin, " England's Town Development Act, 1952," p. 26.

[22] E. H. Doubleday, " Planning Standards for Hertfordshire," *Journal of the T.P.I.*, Vol. 38 (1951-52), p. 42; Hertfordshire County Council, *Budget for Year ended 31st March*, 1952 (The Council), p. 7.

[23] *T.D. Act*, 1952, sec. 4.

[24] *T.D. Act*, 1952, sec. 10 (3).

[25] *M.O.H.L.G. Circular* 29/53. Bristol and other authorities have agreed to pay for 15 years.

[26] *T.D. Act*, 1952, sec. 16.

[27] See note 4 above.

[28] *T.D. Act*, 1952, sec. 2·(1).

[29] *T.D. Act*, 1952, sec. 2 (2).

[30] *Memorandum on the Town Development Act*, par. 18.

[31] *T.D. Act*, 1952, sec. 10 (1).

[32] H.C. Debate, Vol. 540, W.A., col. 43.

[33] *Memorandum on the Town Development Act*, pars. 11 and 15.

CHAPTER 17

[1] *Interim, Second Interim and Final Reports of the New Towns Committee*, Cmd. 6759, 6794 and 6876 (Reith) (H.M.S.O., 1946).

[2] For procedure in establishing new towns see *N.T. Act*, 1946, secs.1 and 2 (1).

[3] *N.T. Act*, 1946, sec. 2 (2).

[4] *N.T. Act*, 1946, sec. 21.

[5] *N.T. Act*, 1946, secs. 4, 3 and 12.

[6] *T.C.P.* (*New Towns Special Development*) *Order*, 1950, S.I. 1950, No. 152, made under *N.T. Act*, 1946, sec. 3 (2).

[7] Under special development orders separately made for the various new towns.

[8] *N.T. Act*, 1946, sec. 11.

[9] *N.T. Act*, 1946, sec. 9, and *Water Act*, 1945, Part II.

[10] *N.T. Act*, 1946, sec. 14.

[11] *N.T. Act*, 1946, sec. 15.

[12] *N.T. Act*, 1946, sec. 4 (1)

[13] *N.T. Act*, 1946, sec. 4 (7).

[14] *N.T. Act*, 1946, sec. 5 (2), which echoes *T.C.P. Act*, 1944, sec. 19 (6).

[15] *N.T. Act*, 1946, sec. 6 (1), which incorporates *T.C.P. Act*, 1944, secs. 22-25 and 28-30.

[16] *N.T. Act*, 1946, sec. 5 (1), and *T.D. Act*, 1952, sec. 18.

[17] Town Planning Committee of the Association of Municipal Corporations, Report No. 3, 1954, *Municipal Review*, Vol. 25 (1954), p. 293 of Supplement.

[18] *N.T. Act*, 1946, sec. 12.

[19] *N.T. Act*, 1946, sec. 12 (2).

[20] *N.T. Act*, 1946, sec. 13.

[21] *N.T. Act*, 1946, sec. 3 (1).

[22] *N.T. Act*, 1946, sec. 12 (7).

[23] *Cf.* the list, compiled by the Crawley New Town Development Corporation, of consultations and approvals required by a Corporation for the execution of plans. *Reports of the Development Corporations for the period ending March, 1949* (H.M.S.O.), p. 58.

[24] In their annual accounts, Corporations include a statement which compares for various classes of development the " gross annual rents excluding rates " where applicable and " cost to date excluding land and site development." The classes are: (1) Land and buildings purchased: houses; flats; commercial; other; open spaces; agricultural. (2) Areas purchased, developed and retained: houses; flats; industrial; other; roads, verges, paths, etc.; open spaces; agricultural. *Report of the Development Corporations*, Statistical Appendix C to Accounts.

[25] Crawley New Town Development Corporation have estimated that administrative and overhead costs amount to 6 per cent of the prime cost of capital works. *Reports of the Development Corporations for year ending March, 1953* (H.M.S.O.), p. 55.

[26] This last method was suggested in *Second Interim Report of New Towns Committee*, Notes to Appendix.

[27] *Cf.* W. O. Hart, " Town Development—Some financial aspects of new towns," *Proceedings of Annual Conference of I.M.T.A.*, 1953 (The Institute), p. 124.

[28] A. V. Williams, " New Towns—Prospect and Progress," *Proceedings of Town and Country Planning Association Annual Conference*, 1954 (The Association).

CHAPTER 18

[1] *M.O.H.L.G. Circular* 65/52, par. 5.

[2] *Cf.* H. W. Wells, " Profit and Loss on Reconstruction," *Proceedings of Town and Country Planning Summer School*, 1945 (T.P.I.), p. 158.

[3] *Cf.* A. C. Pigou, *Economics of Welfare*, 4th Ed. (Macmillan, 1950), p. 134. Professor Pigou is discussing costs in terms of the national dividend, income or product, and so uses the terms " private net product " and " social net product."

CHAPTER 19

[1] For definitions of gross and net output and other terms in farm accounting see the annual reports published since 1945 by M.A.F., *Farm Income in England and Wales* (H.M.S.O.). These reports summarise some of the material in the annual Farm Management Surveys which have been carried out since 1936 by agricultural economists of various universities.

[2] G. P. Wibberley, " The Challenge of Rural Land Losses," *Journal of R.S.A.*, Vol. 102 (1954), p. 658, and G. P. Wibberley, " Rural Land Policies in Urban Britain," *Proceedings of Town and Country Planning Summer School*, 1954 (T.P.I.), pp. 75 and 76.

[3] This point and the fourth column of Table 30 are taken from G. P. Wibberley, " Rural Land Policies in Urban Britain," p. 76.

[4] P. Mackintosh and G. P. Wibberley, " The Use of Gardens for Food Production," *Journal of the T.P.I.*, Vol. 38 (1951-52), p. 54.

[5] R. W. Dale, " The Garden versus Farm Controversy," *Journal of the T.P.I.*, Vol. 40 (1953-54), p. 8.

[6] The results of this survey are unpublished. See for an account *Manchester Guardian*, 13th January, 1955, and Derek Senior, " Gardens and Food Production," *Town and Country Planning*, Vol. XXIII (1955), p. 124.

[7] Unpublished estimates by research staff of M.O.H.L.G. and M.A.F. *Cf. Manchester Guardian*, 31st August, 1953, and 13th January, 1955. See also Colin Clark, " Population Movements into the outer suburbs of large cities," *Proceedings of Town and Country Planning Summer School*, 1953 (T.P.I.), p. 94.

[8] J. Harry Jones, *Road Accident Report* (H.M.S.O., 1946).

[9] The cost of typical accidents is given by R. J. Smeed, " Some statistical aspects of road safety research," *Journal of R.S.S.*, Vol. CXII (1949), p. 12. The use of such figures for savings on particular improvements is in James Drake, *Road Plan for Lancashire* (Lancashire County Council, 1949), p. 141; and C. T. Brunner and James Drake, " The place of a modern road system in the national economy," *Journal of T.P.I.*, Vol. 38 (1951-52), p. 162.

[10] A classification of running costs and fixed (or standing) charges is given in an annual publication, *The Commercial Motor* (Temple Press). This has detailed tables showing calculated operating costs of a great variety of commercial vehicles, buses, coaches and hire cars. The tables are based on the experience of hundreds of operators located in many parts of the country. The classification is as follows: *Running costs:* Fuel, lubricants, tyres, maintenance (routine, repairs, overhaul), depreciation. *Standing charges:* Licences (Road Fund Tax and Levy), wages, rent and rates, motor insurance, interest on capital. The tables give running costs per mile for varying distances run per week; and standing charges per week. To these must be added overheads (supervision, management and office administration) and profit.

[11] Joint Committee of the British Road Federation, Institute of Highway Engineers and the Society of Motor Manufacturers and Traders, *Economics of Motorways* (British Road Federation, 1948). The Committee have the same

classification of running costs and fixed charges as in note 10, except that in the fixed charges are included both depreciation and overhead expenses.

[12] G. Charlesworth, " Research on Town Traffic," *Report of Public Works and Municipal Services Congress*, 1952 (Public Works and Municipal Services Congress and Exhibition Council), p. 447.

[13] To discourage the too precise it should be mentioned that the persistence of lorry drivers in using a congested road through a market town, instead of its by-pass, has been put down to the existence of good pull-ups for drivers on the former and their absence in the latter; and the persistence of lorry drivers in using a ferry rather than the bridge which replaced it, was put down to their not wanting to lose the opportunity for a nap that the ferry crossing gave them.

[14] G. Charlesworth, " Research on Town Traffic," p. 461.

[15] W. H. Glanville, " Road Research and its Bearing on Road Transport," *Journal of the I.T.*, (Vol. 25 (1953), p. 192.

[16] Quoted by E. W. W. Richards, " Why America Builds Better Roads," *Report of Public Works and Municipal Services Congress*, 1952, p. 63.

[17] S. R. Dennison, *Minority Report of Committee on the Utilisation of Land in Rural Areas* (Scott), Cmd. 6378 (H.M.S.O., 1942), p. 104.

[18] G. P. Wibberley, " Challenge of Rural Land Losses," p, 657, and " Rural Land Policies in an Urban Britain," p. 74.

[19] See G. P. Wibberley, " Rural Land Policies in Urban Britain," and Town Planning Institute: Research Committee, *Problems of Land Restoration after Surface Mineral Working* (The Institute, 1954), Appendices B and E.

[20] The calculation is as follows. 20,000 tons of ironstone produces 6,300 tons of steel. If this is sold at, say, £20 per ton but takes £18 per ton to quarry and manufacture, it would be worth £2 per ton to buy the raw material; or £12,600 per acre. W. G. Holford and W. Myles Wright *Corby New Town* (Corby Development Corporation, 1952), p. 54.

[21] *Report of Committee on Air Pollution* (Beaver), Cmd. 9322 (H.M.S.O., 1954).

[22] Under *Mineral Workings Act*, 1951. See M.O.H.L.G., *Explanatory Memorandum on Ironstone Restoration Fund* (H.M.S.O., 1952), and *T.C.P. Act*, 1954, sec. 56.

[23] *Cf.* " Aerodromes and Property Values," *Estates Gazette*, Vol. CLXIII (1954), p. 415; and *Estates Gazette*, Vol. CLXVI (1955), p. 195.

[24] A. C. L. Day and Ralph Turvey, " Car Parking in Central London."

[25] For a discussion, relating to past legislation, see A. C. Pigou, *Economics of Welfare*, Part II, Chap. IX.

[26] *Cf.* Ralph Turvey, " What is the Case for Planning," *Journal of the T.P.I.*, Vol. XII (1954-55), p. 269.

[27] *Cf.* Norman Williams, " Population Problems of New Estates, with special reference to Norris Green," *The Social Survey of Merseyside* (Hodder and Stoughton, 1939).

[28] J. S, Nettlefold, *Practical Town Planning* (St. Catherine Press, 1914), p. 76.

[29] Mabel L. Walker, *Urban Blight and Slums* (Harvard U.P., Cambridge, U.S.A., 1938), Chaps. IV and V.

[30] Quoted by Major H. E. Crawford, *Royal Commission on Transport; Final Report*, Cmd. 3751 (H.M.S.O., 1931), p. 210.

[31] A question raised by Sir Theodore Chambers in the discussion on Thos. Adams, " Regional Planning and Economy," *Transactions of R.I.C.S.*, Vol. LXIV (1932), p. 81.

CHAPTER 20

[1] Select Committee on Estimates, *Report on Schools*, Session 1952-53, H.C. Paper 186 (H.M.S.O.), par. 31. The Committee thought that a programme for at least three years ahead was desirable (par. 33).

[2] James Beattie, " The 1963 Estimates," *Proceedings of Annual Conference of I.M.T.A.*, 1953 (The Institute), p. 72.

[3] M.O.H., *Annual Reports*, 1929-30, p. 131; and 1934-35, p. 193; and also *M.O.H. Circulars* 1311 and 1687.

[4] *M.O.H. Circulars* 1687, 185/45, 9/47; M.O.H., *Annual Report*, 1948 p. 260; *M.O.H.L.G. Circulars* 22/54 and 10/55.

[5] *Board of Education Circulars* 1358/25 and 1431/31; *Education Act*, 1944, sec. 11, and *Ministry of Education Circulars* 28 and 90. The Minister stated that he visualised a programme of 15 years' work, but many authorities planned for longer periods up to 30 years.

[6] *H. Act*, 1930, sec. 25; *M.O.H. Circular* 1331/33; *Housing Repairs and Rents Act*, 1954, sec. 1, and *M.O.H.L.G. Circular* 30/54.

[7] *M.O.T. Circulars* 298/29 and 419/35; H.C. Debate, Vol. 422, col. 590; Vol. 521, col. 1810; Vol. 535, col. 22; Vol. 536, col. 1102.

[8] *M.O.H. Circular* 24/50.

[9] National Coal Board, *Plan for Coal*.

[10] *Ridley Report*, Cmd. 8647.

[11] J. G. Francis, " The British Broadcasting Corporation," *The Place of Finance in Public Administration* (I.M.T.A., 1954), p. 56.

[12] F. E. Price, " Some Aspects of Public Board Finance," *Proceedings of Annual Conference of I.M.T.A.*, 1950 (The Institute), p. 126.

[13] British Transport Commission, *Modernisation and Re-equipment of British Railways* (The Commission, 1955).

[14] *A Programme for Nuclear Power*, Cmd. 9839 (H.M.S.O., 1955).

[15] Iron and Steel Board, *Development of the Iron and Steel Industry*, 1953-58, (H.M.S.O., 1955).

[16] " Acts of will " and " directives to action " are expressions used by Sir Oliver Franks to describe war-time programmes which were not " estimates of need made by the intellect reviewing a situation, nor were they targets of aspiration springing from the heart: . . . they were acts of will." *Central Planning and Control in War and Peace* (Longmans, 1947), p. 31.

[17] H.C. Debate, Vol. 422, col. 592.

[18] M.O.H., *Annual Report*, 1934-35, p. 193.

[19] *Plan for Coal*, par. 175.

CHAPTER 21

[1] *City of Manchester Development Plan* (1952), Written Analysis, p. 125.

[2] Select Committee on Estimates, *Report on Roads*, Session 1952-53, H.C. Paper 163 (H.M.S.O.), par. 17.

[3] H.C. Debate, Vol. 536, col. 1907.

[4] *City of Leicester Development Plan* (1952), Written Analysis, p. 179; *County Borough of Preston Development Plan* (1951), Written Analysis, p. 31 and Appendix II.

[5] *City of Bath Development Plan* (1952), Report and Analysis of Survey, p. 81; *City of Leicester Development Plan* (1951), Written Analysis, p. 179; *City of Nottingham Development Plan* (1952), Report of the Survey, p. 111.

[6] *County of London Development Plan* (1951), Written Analysis, p. 308 and Table 56.

[7] See examples in the following plans: *County of West Sussex Development Plan* (1951), Report of Survey, Southern Section, p. 144; Northern Section, p. 27; *City of Carlisle Development Plan* (1951), Analysis of the Survey, p. 65 and Appendix; *County Borough of Middlesbrough Development Plan* (1951), Report on the Survey, Chap. XXI; *County of Caernarvon Development Plan* (1953), Report of Analysis and Survey, p. 188; *County Borough of Gateshead Development Plan* (1951), Written Analysis, p. 82; *County of Anglesey Development Plan* (1952), Written Analysis, p. 115; *County of Radnor Development Plan* (1951), Analysis of Survey, p. 28.

[8] While this is logical from the accountancy point of view, it would be preferable for development calculations to keep the capital cost to items of development; and to include in operating costs the loan charges on costs such as school furnishings. See note 25 to Chap. 11.

[9] For more details of the method see W. F. B. Lovett, " Strategy of Development," *Journal of T.P.I.*, Vol. 38 (1952), p. 74; Jack Whittle and J. M. Hirsch, " The realisation of a development plan," *Town and Country Planning Textbook*, ed. A.P.R.R. (Architectural Press, 1950), Chap. XXIX; T.P.I.: Research Committee, *Memorandum on Programming and Cost of Development in Urban Areas*.

[10] *M.O.T.C.P. Circular* 97, par. 6 (x).

[11] E. A. G. Robinson, " The Overall Allocation of Resources," *Lessons of the British War Economy*, p. 57.

CHAPTER 22

[1] W. G. Holford, " Design in City Centres," *Design in Town and Village* (H.M.S.O., 1953), p. 71.

[2] See for a general account N. P. Gist and L. A. Halbert, *Urban Society*, Third Ed. (Crowell, New York, 1948), Part II; S. A. Queen and D. B. Carpenter, *The American City* (McGraw-Hill, New York, 1953), Chap. 8; E. R. Dickinson, " Scope and Status of Urban Geography," *Land Economics*, Vol. 24 (1948), p. 221; Homer Hoyt, *The Structure and Growth of American Cities* (Federal Housing Administration, Washington, D.C., 1939). In the same tradition is the generalisation about one detail of town structure by T. Brennan. He suggests from his study of Wolverhampton that local shopping centres will in most cases be found not in the geographical centre of a residential area but on the side of it which is nearest the town centre, since people do not walk away from the centre of the town to their local shopping centre. *Midland City: Wolverhampton, Social and Industrial Survey* (Dennis Dobson, 1948), p. 56.

[3] N. P. Gist and L. A. Halbert, p. 95.

[4] See, for example, Walter Firey, *Land Use in Central Boston* (Harvard U.P., Cambridge, Mass., 1947).

[5] See, for example, E. R. Dickinson, *City, Region and Regionalism* (Kegan Paul & Co., 1947).

[6] See, for example, R. M. Haig, " Major Economic Factors in Metropolitan Growth and Arrangement," *The Regional Survey of New York and its Environs*, Vol. 1 (New York, 1927); and Robert B. Mitchell and Chester Rapkin, *Urban Traffic* (Columbia University Press, New York, 1954), Chap. VII in particular.

[7] Ely and Wehrwein, *Land Economics*, p. v.

[8] Ely and Wehrwein, *Land Economics*, p. 138.

[9] Dorau and Hinman, *Urban Land Economics*, p. 215.

[10] Sir Arnold Plant, " Land Planning and the Economic Functions of Owner-ship," *Journal of the C.A. & E.A.I.*, Vol. 29 (1949), p. 289.

[11] R. U. Ratcliff, *Urban Land Economics*, p. 369.

[12] Central Land Board, *Practice Notes* (H.M.S.O., 1949), p. 18.

[13] *Uthwatt Report*, paras. 23 and 24.

[14] This is not precisely the same as development value in the T.C.P. Act, 1947, sec. 61, since this was the difference between restricted and unrestricted use value.

[15] Economic life of a property has been defined as " that period over which a building has an annual value, and where replacement is not an economic policy." J. F. Q. Switzer, " Land Use and the Life of Buildings," *Transactions of the R.I.C.S.*, Vol. LXXXVI (1954), p. 92.

[16] Homer Hoyt, *The Structure and Growth of American Cities*, p. 56.

[17] T.C.P. Advisory Committee, *Report on the Preservation of the Countryside* (H.M.S.O., 1938), par. 42.

[18] *Uthwatt Report*, pars. 23-26.

[19] *Cf.*, for example, R.I.C.S., *Memorandum on the T.C.P. Act*, 1947 (The In-stitution, 1950), Part III; also T. J. Nardecchia, " Urban Land Values and the Compensation and Betterment Problem," *Estates Gazette*, Vol. 157 (1951), p. 165.

[20] " Population, land values and government," *Regional Survey of New York and its Environs*, Vol. II (1929), p. 132.

[21] In distinction, for example, to the practice in Australia where all trans-actions are noted by the municipality in a register to which there is access by the public. See Ronald Collier, " Real Estate Practice in Australia," *Journal of C.A. & E.A.I.*, Vol. 35 (1955), p. .610

[22] Under *Finance Act*, 1931, sec. 28.

[23] Richard M. Hurd, *Principles of City Land Values,* Third Ed. (Record & Guide, New York, 1911), p. 148.

[24] Homer Hoyt, *One Hundred Years of Land Values in Chicago* (University of Chicago Press, 1933).

[25] Committee of Enquiry, *Report on the Rating of Site Values* (H.M.S.O., 1952), p. 121. Fig. 15 is from F. C. R. Douglas, *Land Value Rating* (Hogarth Press, 1936).

[26] John A. Zangerle, *The Principles of Land and Building Appraisals as scientifically applied in Cuyahoga County* (Board of County Commissioners, Cuyahoga County, Ohio, 1946). For a description of many of these methods and of taxation practice see, for example, Stanley L. McMichael, *McMichael's Appraising Manual*, Fourth Ed. (Prentice-Hall, New York, 1951), Chaps. 35-39.

CHAPTER 23

[1] *Uthwatt Report*, par. 260.

[2] *Uthwatt Report*, par. 32.

[3] *T.C.P. Act*, 1932, sec. 19 (2) (ii).

[4] M.O.H.L.G., *Model Bye-laws:* Series IV—Buildings (H.M.S.O., 1952), Bye-laws 3 and 5; *T.C.P. Act*, 1947, sec. 112 (1).

[5] *T.C.P. Act*, 1932, sec. 19.

[6] *Minutes of Evidence to the Royal Commission on the Distribution of the Industrial Population*, Barlow (1937), pp. 45 and 46.

[7] For comment on the working of this provision see *Uthwatt Report*, pars. 254-255.

[8] *Uthwatt Report*, par. 33.

[9] *Uthwatt Report*, par. 263.

[10] *Uthwatt Report*, par. 264.

[11] *Uthwatt Report*, par. 270. Some other general Acts are the *H. Act*, 1936, Fourth Schedule; *P.H. Act*, 1936, sec. 278.

[12] *Uthwatt Report*, par. 280.

[13] *T.C.P. Act*, 1932, sec. 21.

[14] *Uthwatt Report*, par. 292.

[15] For a statement of the arguments against the proposals see Robert Blake Yardley, *Land Value Taxation and Rating* (W. H. & L. Colingridge, 1929), p. 79; and for the tax see Marshall, *Principles of Economics*, Appendix G.

[16] See for an account Committee of Enquiry, *Report on the Rating of Site Values*, Appendix III.

[17] *The Rating of Site Values*, Chap. II.

[18] *Cf.* Robert Blake Yardley, *Land Value Taxation and Rating*, Section IV and V.

[19] *Barlow Report*, pars. 247-250.

[20] *Cf. Explanatory Memorandum to the T.C.P. Bill*, 1947, par. 21. " To restrict against building 1,000 acres of the London Green Belt would have cost one authority, with a penny rate product of £500, under the 1932 Act provisions, a 2s. rate for half a century or more."

[21] *Control of Land Use*, Cmd. 6537 (H.M.S.O., 1944). See for an account of the close relation between this White Paper and the 1947 Act, Lord Silkin, " Compensation and Betterment," *Proceedings of Town and Country Planning Association National Conference*, 1953 (The Association).

[22] *Amendment of Financial Provisions*, Cmd. 8699 (H.M.S.O., 1952).

[23] *T.C.P. Act*, 1947, secs. 26, 27 and Fourth Schedule.

[24] *T.C.P. Act*, 1947, secs. 27 and 19.

[25] *T.C.P. Act*, 1947, sec. 23.

[26] *T.C.P. Act*, 1947, sec. 20 and Third Schedule, par. 1.

[27] *T.C.P. Act*, 1947, sec. 19, and *T.C.P. Act*, 1954, sec. 70.

[28] *T.C.P. Act*, 1947, sec. 51 (5).

[29] *Uthwatt Report*, pars. 247 and 392.

[30] *T.C.P. Act*, 1947, Third Schedule.

[31] *Cf. T.C.P. Act*, 1947, sec. 51.

[32] *T.C.P. Act*, 1947, sec. 58, and *Explanatory Memorandum to T.C.P. Bill*, 1947, par. 26.

[33] *T.C.P. Act*, 1947, secs. 58-63.

[34] *Uthwatt Report*, par. 49.

[35] *Uthwatt Report*, par. 235.

[36] *Control of Land Use*, par. 17 (f).

[37] *T.C.P. Act*, 1947, sec. 69 (1); *T.C.P.* (*Development Charge Exemption*) *Regulations*, S.I. 1948, No. 1188; *T.C.P. Act*, 1947, secs. 80-85.

[38] *Practice Notes*, par. 35. That the development charge was to be the full difference was stipulated in *T.C.P.* (*Development Charge*) *Regulations*, S.I. 1948, No. 1189.

[39] *Uthwatt Report*, par. 59.

[40] *Uthwatt Report*, par. 311.

[41] *Control of Land Use*, par. 16 (1).

[42] *Amendment of Financial Provisions*, par. 14.

[43] *Amendment of Financial Provisions*, par. 7-25.

[44] H.C. Debate, Vol. 508, col. 1127.

[45] B. J. Collins, " The Impact of Development Plans on Real Estate," *Journal of R.I.C.S.*, Vol. XXXIV (1955), p. 847.

[46] *Uthwatt Report*, par. 254.

[47] *Report on the Rating of Site Values*, pp. 37, 76, 91, 97.

CHAPTER 24

[1] *Cf.* W. A. Leach, *Journal of Property Law* (1950), p. 876.

[2] Michael E. Rowe, " Development Plans: objects and objections," *Journal of the R.I.C.S.*, Vol. XXXIV (1955), p. 671.

[3] *Second Report of Committee on Acquisition and Valuation of Land for Public Purposes* (Scott), Cmd. 9229 (H.M.S.O., 1918), par. 7. For an account of speculation in land bought under the early Housing Acts see W. H. Ashworth, *The Genesis of British Town Planning* (Kegan Paul, 1954), p. 102.

[4] Sir Raymond Unwin, " Land Values in relation to Planning and Housing in the United States," *Land Economics*, Vol. XXVII (1951), p. 6. Reprint of 1941 article with commentary.

[5] Raymond Unwin, *Nothing gained by overcrowding*, Third Ed. (Garden Cities and Town Planning Association, 1918), p. 20.

[6] Mabel L. Walker, *Urban Blight and Slums*, p. 6.

[7] Sir Arnold Plant, " Land Planning and the Economic Functions of Ownership," p. 293.

CHAPTER 25

[1] *M.O.T.C.P. Circular* 97, par. 6 (xi).

[2] " Land Values," *Regional Survey of New York and its Environs*, Vol. II (1929), p. 139.

[3] W. K. Shepherd, " Value as a Factor in Planning," *Transactions of the R.I.C.S.*, Vol. LXXXVII (1955), p. 747.

[4] Improvements and Town Planning Committee of City of London, *Review of Work of the Improvements and Town Planning Committee*, 1947-53 (The Corporation, 1954), Appendix E; and R. Nicholas, " Urban Re-development from the local authority's point of view," *Journal of the T.P.I.*, Vol. XII (1954-55), p. 214.

[5] Sir Patrick Abercrombie, John Owens, H. Anthony Mealand, *A Plan for Bath* (Pitman, 1945), pp. 62-63.

[6] Bryan Anstey, " Value Contour Maps," *Planning Outlook*, Vol. 1 (1948-50), p. 29; and " Isovals: a new system of land value notation for planners," *Journal of the T.P.I.*, Vol. 36 (1949-50), p. 267; and " The Distribution Pattern of Land Values in Urban Areas," *Planning Outlook*, Vol. III (1955), p. 5. Fig. 18 is from this last.

[7] " Population, Land Values and Government," *Regional Survey of New York and its Environs*, Vol. II, plate 6.

APPENDIX III

[1] H.C. Debate, Vol. 546, Col. 1182; and Vol. 545, Col. 378.

[2] H.C. Debate, Vol. 546, Col. 795-798.

[3] These and the following subsidy figures are Budget estimates taken from *Civil Estimates.*

[4] *Private Enterprise Housing,* Appendix IV and *Housing Return* 31st March, 1956, Cmd. 9749 (H.M.S.O., 1956), p. 4.

[5] The notional rent in the subsidy calculations under the Housing Acts, was generally taken as 10 per cent of average earnings. H.C. Debate, Vol. 546, Col. 1386 and 1454.

[6] H.C. Debate, Vol. 546, Col. 798.

[7] H.C. Debate, Vol. 546, Col. 800-1; Vol. 545, Col. 380; Col. 548, Col. 822.

[8] H.C. Debate, Vol. 546, Col. 978 and 2241 and Vol. 548, Col. 782. The redevelopment area procedure had hardly been used and will not, it is thought, be much used in future: H.C. Debate, Vol. 548, Col. 1189 and 1194.

[9] H.C. Debate, Vol. 547, Col. 1312. Vol. 548, Col. 1001.

[10] H.C. Debate, Vol. 548, Col. 2189.

[11] H.C. Debate, Vol. 548, Col. 244, 874 and 935.

[12] H.C. Debate, Vol. 548, Col. 977, 2193.

[13] H.C. Debate, Vol. 546, Col. 802.

APPENDIX IV

[1] *Town and Country Planning (Grants) Regulations,* 1956. S.I. 1956, No. 224; and M.O.H.L.G., *Explanatory Memorandum on the revised system of Exchequer Grants to local authorities under the Town and Country Planning Acts,* 1947 and 1954 (HMSO), 1955.

FURTHER READING

FURTHER READING

NOTE: *The following suggestions for reading are additional to those mentioned in the references to the text. As with those references, they may be also relevant to chapters other than those under which they appear.*

CHAPTER 2

B. J. COLLINS, *Development Plans Explained* (H.M.S.O., 1951).

CENTRAL OFFICE OF INFORMATION, *Town and Country Planning in Britain* (H.M.S.O., 1951).

L. B. KEEBLE, *Principles and Practice of Town and Country Planning* (Estates Gazette, 1952).

F. B. GILLIE and L. P. HUGHES, *Some Principles of Land Planning* (Liverpool U.P., 1950).

M.O.H.L.G., *Town and Country Planning Act, 1947: Report of Survey, Technical Memoranda*, Nos. 1-4 (1955), No. 5 (1956).

W. F. B. LOVETT, "National Land Use Planning," *Proceedings of International Federation for Housing and Town Planning Congress* 1954 (The Federation).

E. G. S. ELLIOT, "The Effect of Development Plans upon the Development of Land," *Journal of C.A. and E.A.I.*, Vol. 33 (1953), p. 527.

"Statistics Relating to the Use of Land in the United Kingdom," *Journal R.S.S.*, Vol. 116 (1953), p. 424.

CHAPTER 3

ROBERT A. WALKER, *The Planning Function of Urban Government*, 2nd Edition (University of Chicago Press, 1952).

LADISLAS SEGOE, *Local Planning Administration* (The International City Managers' Association Chicago, 1941).

CHAPTER 4

W. A. LEWIS, *The Principles of Economic Planning* (Dobson and Allen & Unwin, 1949).

SIR HUBERT HENDERSON, *Uses and Abuses of Economic Planning* (Cambridge U.P., 1947).

BEN W. LEWIS, *British Planning and Nationalization* (Twentieth Century Fund, New York, 1952).

M. P. FOGARTY, *Economic Control* (Routledge and Kegan Paul, 1955).

P. J. D. WILES, "Pre-war and War Time Controls," *The British Economy* 1945-50, Ed. G. D. N. Worswick and P. H. Ady (Oxford, 1950).

G. D. N. WORSWICK, "Direct Controls," *The British Economy 1949-50*

HERBERT MORRISON, *Government and Parliament* (Oxford University Press, 1954).

D. N. CHESTER, "Machinery of Government and Planning," *The British Economy* 1945-50.

M. E. KENDALL, Ed., *The Source and Nature of Statistics in the United Kingdom* (Oliver and Boyd, 1952).

C. F. CARTER and A. D. ROY, *British Economic Statistics* (Cambridge U.P., 1954).

K. S. LOMAX, " Regional Economic Statistics," *Journal R.S.S.,* Vol. 117 (1954), p. 85.

Government Statistical Services (H.M.S.O., 1953).

INTERDEPARTMENTAL COMMITTEE ON SOCIAL AND ECONOMIC RESEARCH, *Guides to Official Sources, No. 3: Local Government Statistics* (H.M.S.O., 1953).

V. J. OXLEY, *Local Government Financial Statistics: A Guide to the published statistical information relating to the finances of local authorities in England and Wales* (Allen and Unwin, 1951).

CHAPTER 5

Various articles on the Nationalised Industries, *The Political Quarterly,* Vol. XXI (1950), p. 109.

D. N. CHESTER, *British Public Utility Services* (Longmans, 1948).

M. PENELOPE HALL, *The Social Services of Modern England* (Routledge & Kegan Paul, 1952).

The Scope for Private Enterprise in Local Government (N.A.L.G.O., 1951).

PEGGY CRANE, *Enterprise in Local Government* (Fabian Society, 1953).

P.E.P., " Business Forecasting," *Planning,* Vol. XXII (1956), p. 38.

U. K. HICKS, *Public Finance* (Nisbet & Co., Cambridge U.P., 1946).

U. K. HICKS, *British Public Finances: Their Structure and Development, 1880-1952* (O.U.P., 1954).

E. N. GLADDEN, *An Introduction to Public Administration* (Staples Press, 1952).

SAMUEL H. BEER, *Treasury Control* (Oxford University Press, 1956).

CHAPTER 6

F. J. GARNER, *The Public Control of Land* (Sweet and Maxwell, 1956).

W. A. LEACH, *Urban Estate Management,* 2nd Ed. (Estates Gazette, 1950).

J. ROOKE CORBETT, " The Economic Theory of Rent," *Transactions of R.I.C.S.,* Vol. XXXIV (1901-2), p. 447.

D. H. BUCHANAN, " The Historical Approach to Rent and Price Theory," *Economica,* Vol. IX (1929), p. 123.

F. W. TAUSSIG, *Principles of Economics,* 4th Ed. (MacMillan Co., New York, 1939), Vol. II.

FREDERIC BENHAM, *Economics,* 5th Ed. (Sir Isaac Pitman, 1955).

JOAN ROBINSON, *Economics of Imperfect Competition* (MacMillan and Co., 1933).

E. H. CHAMBERLAIN, *The Theory of Monopolistic Competition.* (Oxford University Press, 1933).

CHAPTER 7

H. W. ROBINSON, *Economics of Building* (P. S. King, 1939).

G. D. H. COLE, *Building and Planning* (Cassell, 1945).

CHAPTER 8

" Government Control Over the Use of Capital Resources," *Midland Bank Review* (1950).

J. E. MEADE and RICHARD STONE, *National Income and Expenditure* (Bowes and Bowes, 1952).

CHAPTER 9

F. W. Paish, *Business Finance* (Sir Isaac Pitman, 1953).

Report of Committee on Finance and Industry (MacMillan), Cmd. 3897 (H.M.S.O., 1931).

Sources of Capital (The Association of Certified and Corporate Accountants, 1954).

CHAPTER 10

D. M. Lawrance and W. H Rees, *Modern Methods of Valuation*, 4th Ed. (Estates Gazette, 1956).

N. E. Mustoe, H. Brian Eve and Bryan Anstey, *The Complete Valuation Practice*, 4th Ed. (Estates Gazette, 1955).

An Introduction to Engineering Economics for Civil Engineering Students (Institution of Civil Engineers, 1947).

CHAPTER 11

H. W. Singer, "Economics of Planning," *Town and Country Planning Text Book*, Ed. A.P.R.R. (Architectural Press, 1950).

J. R. and U. K. Hicks, *The Incidence of Local Rates in Great Britain* (Cambridge U.P., 1944).

"West Midland Group," *Local Government and Central Control* (Routledge & Kegan Paul, 1956).

CHAPTER 12

Marion Bowley, *Housing and the State, 1919-1944* (Allen and Unwin, 1948).

P.E.P., "Economics of the Council House," *Planning*, Vol. XVI (1949-50), p. 185.

W. L. Abernethy and A. R. Holmes, *Housing Finance and Accounts* (Shaw and Sons, 1953).

H. Ashworth, "Economics and Finance of Twentieth Century Housing," *Proceedings of the Conference of National Housing and Town Planning Council*, 1954 (The Council).

Housing Associations (National Federation of Housing Societies, 1953).

Helen Alford and E. J. Edwards, "The Maintenance and Management of High Density Housing," *Report of the Public Works and Municipal Services Congress and Exhibition* 1954 (The Council).

CHAPTER 13

Rees Jeffreys, *The King's Highway* (Batchworth Press, 1949).

John F. McCarthy, *Highway Financing by the Toll System* (Bureau of Public Administration, University of California, Berkeley, 1954).

John Nolen and H. V. Hubbard, *Parkways and Land Values* (Harvard U.P., Cambridge, U.S.A., 1937).

CHAPTER 14

Traffic and Parking Study (Regional Plan Association, Inc., New York, 1942).

CHAPTER 15

Report of the Central Advisory Committee on Estate Development and Management in War Damaged Areas (H.M.S.O., 1947).

Sir Gwilym Gibbon, *Reconstruction and Town and Country Planning* (Architect and Building News, 1943).

29

H. W. WELLS, "Planning by Lease Control," *Proceedings of Town and Country Planning Summer School*, 1944 (Town Planning Institute).

A. H. MARSHALL, "The Finances of Comprehensive Redevelopment under the Planning Acts," *Journal of T.P.I.*, Vol. 41 (1954-55), p. 206.

R. M. BUCKLEY, "Estate Management in the Work of Local Authorities," *Journal of the National Housing and Town Planning Council*, Vol. 10 (1955), p. 11.

CHAPTER 16

GEOFFREY D. M. BLOCK, *The Spread of Towns* (Conservative Political Centre, 1954).

W. CAIRNS, "Town Expansion Finance," *Local Government Finance*, Vol. LX (1956), p. 10.

SIR HUMFREY GALE, "Some Overspill Problems and the Aims of Decentralisation," *Transactions of R.I.C.S.*, Vol. LXXXVIII (1956), p. 535.

CHAPTER 17

C. B. PURDOM, *The Building of Satellite Towns*, 2nd Ed. (J. M. Dent, 1945).

W. O. HART, "New Towns," *Journal of C.A.E.A.I.*, Vol. 31 (1951), p. 265.

R. L. REISS, "The Finance of New Towns," *Town and Country Planning*, Vol. 21 (1953), p. 13.

BRYAN L. RICHARDS, "Some Practical Aspects of New Town Development," *Journal of R.I.C.S.*, Vol. XXXI (1952), p. 610.

CHAPTER 18

W. H. LUDLOW, "Urban Densities and their Cost," *Urban Redevelopment: Problems and Practices*, Ed. Coleman Woodbury (University of Chicago Press, 1953), Part II.

A. M. MILNE, *The Economics of Inland Transport* (Sir Isaac Pitman, 1955).

CHAPTER 19

E. W. W. RICHARDS, "The Economic Value of Road Improvement," *Roads and Road Construction*, Vol. 31 (1953), pp. 155, etc.; Vol. 32 (1954), pp. 11, etc.

G. J. PONSONBY, "Highway Economics," *Journal of Institution of Highway Engineers*, Vol. 11 (1952).

ARNOLD MARSH, *Smoke* (Faber and Faber, 1947).

Report of the Committee on Air Pollution (Beaver), Cmd. 9322 (H.M.S.O., 1954), Appendix II.

CHAPTER 20

SPENCE GEDDES, *Building and Public Works Administration, Estimating and Costing*, 3rd Ed. (Geo. Newnes, Ltd., 1950).

CHAPTER 22

A. H. HAWLEY, *Human Ecology* (Ronald Press, New York, 1950).

G. S. BROWNLOW, *Site Value of Shops*, 2nd Ed. (Estates Gazette, 1956).

RICHARD U. RATCLIFF, "Efficiency and the Location of Urban Activities," *The Metropolis in Modern Life*, Ed. Robert Moore Fisher (Doubleday & Co., New York, 1955).

P. SARGANT FLORENCE, "Economic Efficiency in the Metropolis," *The Metropolis in Modern Life*.

SIR ARNOLD PLANT, " Land Planning and the Functions of Ownership," *Westminster Bank Review* (1948).

BRYAN ANSTEY, "Land, its Value, Use and Tenure," *Journal T.P.I.*, Vol. 39 (1952-3), pp. 161, 197, 237.

CHAPTER 23

JOSEPH HYDER, *The Case for Land Nationalization* (Simpkin, Marshall, 1913).

FREDERICK VERINDER, *Land and Freedom* (Hogarth Press, 1935).

ERNEST LONG, " The Taxation of Land Values," *Proceedings of Annual Conference of I.M.T.A.*, 1939 (The Institute).

CHAS. HAAR, *Land Planning Law in a Free Society* (Harvard U.P., 1951).

H. R. PARKER, "The Financial Aspects of Town and Country Planning Legislation," *The Economic Journal*, Vol. LXIV (1954), p. 72.

RALPH TURVEY, " Development Charges and the Compensation-Betterment Problem," *The Economic Journal*, Vol. LXIII (1953), p. 299 and Vol. LXIV (1954), p. 358.

D. L. MUNBY, " Development Charges and the Compensation and Betterment Problem," *The Economic Journal*, Vol. LXIV (1954), p. 87.

H. W. WELLS, " The Effect of the Town and Country Planning Bill, 1954, on the Control of the Use of Land," *Proceedings of Town and Country Planning Summer School*, 1954 (Town Planning Institute).

CHAPTER 24

W. A. LEACH, *Planning and Compensation Law* (Estates Gazette, 1955).

F. G. BAXENDALE, "Effect on Values of Town and Country Planning Schemes in their Various Stages," *Transactions of R.I.C.S.*, Vol. LIX (1937), p. 98.

G. LESLIE HEAD, "Town Planning in London," *Transactions of R.I.C.S.*, Vol. LXX (1938), p. 139.

W. F. B. LOVETT, " Planning in Relation to Land Values," *Report of the Town and Country Planning Summer School*, 1938 (Town Planning Institute).

CHAPTER 25

H. W. WELLS, " Planning and Estate Management," *Journal of T.P.I.*, Vol. 36 (1949-50), p. 173.

R. L. REISS, "Land Values and their Relation to Town and Country Planning," *Report of the Town and Country Planning Summer School*, 1934 (Town Planning Institute).

INDEX

INDEX

NOTE: *This index covers Appendices I—V but not the References to the text.*

<h1 style="text-align:center">F</h1>

<h1 style="text-align:center">G</h1>